# Lecture Notes in Computer Science 753

Edited by G. Goos and J. Hartmanis

Advisory Board: W. Brauer   D. Gries   J. Stoer

Leonard J. Bass   Juri Gornostaev
Claus Unger  (Eds.)

# Human-Computer Interaction

Third International Conference, EWHCI '93
Moscow, Russia, August 3-7, 1993
Selected Papers

Springer-Verlag

Berlin Heidelberg New York
London Paris Tokyo
Hong Kong Barcelona
Budapest

Series Editors

Gerhard Goos
Universität Karlsruhe
Postfach 69 80
Vincenz-Priessnitz-Straße 1
D-76131 Karlsruhe, Germany

Juris Hartmanis
Cornell University
Department of Computer Science
4130 Upson Hall
Ithaca, NY 14853, USA

Volume Editors

Leonard J. Bass
Software Engineering Institute, Carnegie-Mellon University
Pittsburgh, PA 15213-3890, USA

Juri Gornostaev
International Centre for Scientific and Technical Information (ICSTI)
21-B, Kusinen Str., 125252 Moscow, Russia

Claus Unger
Praktische Informatik II, FernUniversität Hagen
Postfach 940, D-58048 Hagen, Germany

CR Subject Classification (1991): D.2.2, H.1.2, H.5, I.2.7, I.7, K.3, K.4


ISBN 3-540-57433-6 Springer-Verlag Berlin Heidelberg New York
ISBN 0-387-57433-6 Springer-Verlag New York Berlin Heidelberg

Typesetting: Camera-ready by author
Printing and binding: Druckhaus Beltz, Hemsbach/Bergstr.
45/3140-543210 - Printed on acid-free paper

# Preface

This year's International Conference on Human-Computer Interaction EWHCI '93 was the third conference in a series which started in 1991 in Moscow. Like its predecessors, this conference was occasioned by the long separation of workers in HCI from one another and the new opportunity to learn from one another and start co-operations with each other. EWHCI '93 was indeed international, with papers and attendees from 16 countries around the world.

This publication contains a selection of the best papers presented at the conference; each paper has been reviewed and recommended for this publication by at least three international experts.

We express our appreciation for the work of the two conference co-chairs, Juri Gornostaev (ICSTI Moscow), and Austin Henderson (Xerox Palo Alto Research, USA), as well as for the help of all reviewers: Gilbert Cockton (Univ. of Glasgow, UK), Joëlle Coutaz (IMAG, Grenoble, France), Allen Cypher (Apple Computer, USA), Prasun Dewan (Purdue Univ., USA), Michael Donskoy (Inst. for System Analysis, Moscow, Russia), Alexander Giglavy (Information Technology Lyceum, Moscow, Russia), Christian Gram (Tech. Univ. of Denmark), Jonathan Grudin (Univ. of California at Irvine, USA), Keith Hopper (Univ. of Waikato, New Zealand), Keith Instone (Bowling Green Univ., USA), Victor Kaptelinin (General and Education Psychology Institute, Moscow, Russia), Rick Kazman (Univ. of Waterloo, Canada), Allan MacLean (Rank Xerox EuroPARC, UK), Scott Overmyer (Minot State Univ., USA), Blaine Price (The Open Univ., UK), Marilyn Welles (MITRE Corp., and George Washington Univ., USA).

We further wish to record our appreciation of the co-operation received from Springer-Verlag during the publication of this volume.

Len J. Bass
Juri Gornostaev
Claus Unger

September 1993

# Table of Contents

## Foundations of HCI

## Interface Design: Techniques, Tools and Paradigms

# Multi-Media

# Hypertext

# Customizing Interfaces

# Teaching and Learning

# Applications

# Author Index

# Historical Analysis and Conflicting Perspectives - Contextualizing HCI

## Susanne Bødker

Department of Computer Science
Aarhus University
Ny Munkegade 116
DK-8000 Aarhus C
Denmark
tel. +45-86202711 x5082, fax. +45-86135725, e-mail bodker@daimi.aau.dk

**Abstract.** This paper develops two ways of analyzing the human-computer inter-action of a computer application in use in an organization. The techniques, histor-ical analyses and conflicting perspectives analysis, and the interplay between them, are used in providing the basis for a more detailed analysis.

Historical analyses focus on the historical development of artifacts and their use. Conflicting perspectives analysis reflects on the roles of the artifact in use, as system, tool, or medium. Combined, the two types of analysis allow for a focus in particular on conflicts between the roles of a specific artifact in use.

The techniques are based on human activity theory. They are illustrated by means of a case study of a computer application from a project with the Danish National Labour Inspection Service.

## 1 Introduction

Re-framing human-computer interaction from within the field has been discussed ex-tensively in recent years, driven by a growing concern for practical use of the theory. In particular [7] focuses on this theme, but without much to say about real-life computer applications. Here, I shall present and discuss two techniques to analyze such real-life applications, providing ways to contextualize HCI. Theoretically the techniques are based on a human activity framework as presented in [4,1]. The paper first gives a short introduction of the theoretical basis and vocabulary. Following is a presentation of the case; the analysis of the case based on the two techniques: historical analysis and analy-sis of conflicting perspectives. The case is rather mundane and meant to illustrate the techniques. It does not as such represent an application which is outstanding in any way.

# 2 The Human Activity Framework

In human activity theory, the basic unit of analysis is human (work) activity. Human activity is what a group of people engage in to achieve a certain purpose. This activity is usually mediated by one or more instruments or tools, and it is directed towards a certain object. Tools, as well as the division of work, norms and language can be seen as *artifacts* for the activity: they are created by humans and they mediate the relations among human beings or between people and the object of their activity, the material or product in different stages. They are there for us when we are introduced into a certain activity, but they are also a product of our activity, and as such they are constantly changed through the activity.

The *mediation* is essential when understanding artifacts. That artifacts mediate use means that we are normally not aware of them in use, they are *transparent* to us. Our attention is with the materials and products even though many of our experiences with these are made through the artifact. In many cases of computer-based artifacts, the materials and products worked on have no physical presence outside the artifact [4, see also 12].

In this perspective we cannot study computer applications as *things*, we need to look at how they *mediate use*. Furthermore, artifacts are not just means for individuals, they also carry with them certain ways of *sharing and dividing work*. They are given meaning through their incorporation into social praxis. Human beings always participate in various activities which are collective and structured according to the praxis of the particular society in which they take place.

Artifacts can be seen as *historical devices* which reflect the state of praxis up until the time that they are developed. This praxis in turn is shaped by the artifacts used, and so on. Artifacts can be characterized as *crystallized knowledge* which means that operations which are developed in the use of one generation of technology may later be incorporated into the artifact itself in the next. To learn something about the present shape and use of an artifact, we may apply a *historical analysis of artifacts* [8].

Although *collective*, each activity is conducted through *actions* of individuals. Activity is what gives meaning to our actions, though actions have their own focus. Each action is implemented through a series of *operations*. Each operation is connected to the concrete physical or social conditions for conducting the action, and it is "triggered" by the specific conditions which are present at the time.

Activities are not taking place in isolation but interwoven with other activities, which deal with the same or connected objects, which produce the instruments used in the activity in case, etc. While conducting a specific activity, the object change which may be viewed as a change of activity, or as a change in the purposeful actions, or *clusters* of actions. We can analytically separate the categories of activity, action and operation by the questions: *why* something takes place? *what* takes place? and *how* is it carried out? Actually, we may prefer to look at human-computer interaction as exactly focusing on *how* a certain use of a computer application takes place.

Artifacts may be the instruments of a *web* of activities: In particular computer-based artifacts are often contributing to several activities or clusters of actions conducted by several users.

In literature such metaphors as "system", "media", and "tool" have been discussed extensively as design metaphors to illustrate the role of the computer application in use (See e.g. [9, 10]). In [2,4] they are discussed as analytic perspectives: as different roles for an artifact as seen from the point of view of human activity theory: The systems perspective is the birds-eye, control perspective, viewing human user and computer component as rather equally functioning in exchanging data. The subject is lost in the systems perspective, or removed from the level of those who are conducting actions and operations. In this perspective we may say that overall planning and conception of the activity is detached from the actual conduction of the actions and operations that contribute to the activity. In other words, the people who do the work (the actions and operations) do without knowing why, and those who know why, do not do the work. *A system mediates between the individual contributors of actions and operations, and their object. At the same time the system is the instrument of the acting subject, who is not directly contributing to the production of the outcome.*

The tool perspective emphasizes the human engagement with materials through the computer application. *A tool mediates the relation between the subject and the material object being worked on.* The tool perspective emphasizes production of outcome, and the direct learning taking place by the material "speaking back" to its user.

The media perspective, in a similar way, emphasizes the human engagement with other human beings through the computer application. *A media mediates the relation between the acting subject and the community of practice surrounding the subject and the activity,* thus it is the perspective emphazising communication, and learning through conceptualization and negotiation.

Both of these perspectives may be extended, when at the same time focusing on computer support for cooperative work: Sørgaard's [14] concept of shared material, can be seen as a tool perspective focusing on cooperation, whereas Robinson's [13] concept of common artifact can be seen as an extension of the media perspective.[1]

For both the tool and the media perspective the transparency of the artifact is in focus: it is a quality criteria that computer applications can mediate the normal use activity without "being in the way", i.e. that they can be worked through operations only, not through deliberate actions. Together with this, the perspectives emphasize the human possibilities of planning and controlling the activity.

A brief summary the characteristics of the system, tool and media perspectives with respect to how the view human-computer interaction is given in the following:

|  | *system* | *tool* | *media* |
|---|---|---|---|
| *why* | planning/control | material production | communication |
| *what* | data entry +extraction | shaping material | creating and interpreting signs |
| *how* | "low risk" data entry | transparency good access to material | transparency no disturbance in interpretation |

Analytically these perspectives will be applied by tracing and characterizing the web of different activities that takes place around a computer application and in particular contradictions among the different uses. Relating the various use activities to a historical account of the underlying perspective(s) helps, as we shall see, in understanding the contradictions and problems with use of a particular computer application.

# 3 The NLIS Case

The NLIS project [6] is a research project co-operating with the local branch of the Danish National Labour Inspection Service (NLIS). At NLIS, a centralized computer system (VIRK) is applied to record the interaction of NLIS with companies in the geographical area covered by the local branch. Visits to work sites as well as correspondence with companies are recorded, and various materials can be extracted, ranging from lists of a specific kind of companies within a geographical zone to lists of which recommendations and demands the NLIS has put on a specific company. Also lists of cases under investigation by a single NLIS inspector can be extracted.

VIRK was designed based on a company database shared with other authorities dealing with company inspection and counselling. It is a menu-based system running on terminals. VIRK has been used in the organization for several years. It was developed by a Danish state owned software house, and has **not** been designed in the project.

In our initial investigations we found that people used VIRK in many ways, and that some people actually asked for facilities which existed in the system. Only very few people knew what VIRK really allows for. Thus we sat out to investigate how to help the secretaries and inspectors at NLIS make better use of the system that they had already available. This made an evaluation of the human-computer interaction aspects of VIRK a necessity. To illustrate the techniques, parts of this evaluation will be presented here.

## 3.1 Historical Analysis

Markussen [11] provides a useful historical account of the NLIS as institution and the interwoven development of the work environment laws, the bureaucracy, and the role of the inspectors. This analysis will be used here with more direct emphasis on the implications for the use of VIRK.

Until the mid-1970s NLIS was primarily dealing with the inspection of physical work environment in factories, what was called workers' safety which in particular concerned the set-up of machines etc. The inspectors were engineers, there was little bureaucracy around the activity, and basically each inspector was responsible for selecting and inspecting the factories that he found appropriate. With the work environment act of 1975, the scope was widened to include also non-factory work, and a more holistic approach to work environment. The act prescribed a certain more bureaucratic organization of work, more resources were spread in the organization, and the professional profile of the organization changed: therapists and psychologists were employed, and prevention became a central issue. With the late 80s came further decentralization coupled to client orientation. This also meant a focus on quality assurance and accounting "upwards" in the bureaucracy for what had been achieved locally (i.e. centralization). Furthermore, more and more work was put into cooperative and structured activities, e.g. "the cancer effort" or some other campaign instead of the traditional "random" and individually planned visits to companies.

*This is the setting into which VIRK was created.*

First of all, VIRK was created to help various groups of people, primarily management, get an overview of the many cases and documents that came into play when the organization grew and diversified. Management, furthermore, needed to make sure that all incoming requests were handled according to the law. Historically, VIRK substituted a number of paper based lists, which were kept to maintain an overview of files with material about companies and inspections. With the growing organization these lists had become insufficient. The files are still used, only VIRK has made retrieval easier, and also some overview facilities for statistics have been added. Much of the mechanisms for accounting for, and statistics of the activity were added later, as further decentralization and "upwards" accounting took place. Some of the paper-based lists are still maintained in situations where the support given by VIRK is too poor, e.g. lists of various expiration dates, sorted according to expiration month are still kept, because VIRK offers little support for extracting such lists. Though VIRK was developed rather late in the historical development of work at the Labour Inspection, it has not been designed to reflect this development. In many ways VIRK works to support only a very traditional quantitative perspective, coupled to management planning and control, whereas the more holistic, qualitative perspective underlying the work of contemporary labour inspection is not supported, neither with respect to information and activities regarding a company, that can be accounted for in the system, nor with respect to how the work of the inspectors is viewed. The lacking facilities are typically related to the individual and group case handling, an area that has not been given much attention historically, or with respect to design of the system.

## 3.2 The Roles of the Artifact in Use - a Conflicting Perspectives Analysis

The context of this specific piece of research is hours of interviewing the NLIS employees, of hanging around their offices and of partaking in seminars with them on other aspects of the project [6]. With the specific purpose of understanding VIRK and the HCI problems, three activities, all of which were videotaped, were in focus: A session with two secretaries discussing their daily activities, in particular with respect to documentation and information retrieval in VIRK, a session where a secretary is demonstrating VIRK to the researchers, and finally a similar session with a secretary who is also the "super user" of VIRK. In total we have more than four hours of video-tape of the use of the system.

The initial analysis began by identifying the different activities in which VIRK is applied: who are the users? what are the objects? which are the activities in which VIRK is used (why is a certain activity taking place)? as to identify the role that VIRK plays in use. There are many different use activities going on simultaneously, and VIRK has several roles in this web of activities:

• VIRK is the instrument of management of NLIS to make sure, that the people who contact NLIS get answered in due time (VIRK acts as a **system** with respect to this purpose, because management is not in any direct contact with VIRK - the work is delegated to secretaries, primarily, who enter registration of documents, distribute the documents to the inspectors physically, and follow up on deadlines, using the system, as well as paper based lists). This is the real *raison d'être* of VIRK, and most of the organizational structure as such. The parts of VIRK that have to do with lists of correspondence and with deadlines are important for this activity.

| | |
|---|---|
| *why* | (management) people get answered in due time |
| *what* | (secretaries) enter registration of documents, |
| | distribute documents |
| | follow up on deadlines |
| *how* | (using VIRK) key in document data |
| | extract inspectors deadlines |

• VIRK is used when following up on the work of the inspectors, and more overall of the whole branch office. Various statistics are important output. These statistics are used by management to control and plan the activity. Data entry for this is done by inspectors, in VIRK and in another registration system. Secretaries too do data entry, and extract the statistics, but have little to do with the contents of the statistics or what they are used for, thus VIRK is again a **system** for this purpose.

| | |
|---|---|
| *why* | (management) following up inspectors, and branch office |
| *what* | (management) statistics |
| *how* | (using VIRK) (inspectors and secretaries) key in production data |

• VIRK is used when distributing cases to inspectors. In the current version of VIRK the secretaries and inspectors complain that they lack access to appropriate statistics to see the work distributed to the individual inspectors, and to plan the work. VIRK should act as a **media** with respect to this purpose, but does not.

| | |
|---|---|
| *why* | distributing cases |
| *what* | statistics, |
| *how* | (using VIRK) (mainly secretaries) look up who has case/area, how many cases, etc. |

• Furthermore, VIRK is used by the individual inspector and secretary to handle a certain case. The inspector "takes the travel card", he makes notes, he looks for correspondence of relevance to the present case, etc. The secretary pulls out information about a company for a campaign, she follows up on deadlines, etc. For this purpose VIRK is a **tool,** and in some ways also a **media**, yet, for this purpose as well, the inspectors and secretaries would like more support. In particular the kinds of information that can be written down regarding a visit or a case is very limited, and in most cases very quantitative.

*why*    (inspector) handle case
*what*   (inspector) "takes the travel card", makes notes, looks for correspondence, etc.
*how*    (using VIRK) browse for relevant data, uses search facilities

• Finally, VIRK is used by a secretary every time a document is registered in the system
**(tool)**.

*why*    (secretary) register document
*what*   (secretary) register document
*how*    (using VIRK) key in data using the correspondence form

This analysis brings into focus, that *VIRK is designed as a planning and control system,
which works rather well*: management gets what it wants, both with respect to the delegation of cases, and to monitoring the activity of the individual inspectors and branch offices. Data-entry works rather well too.

VIRK is organized hierarchically, and it is hard to get from one function of the system to another. This is very much in line with the hierarchical way the organization as such is built up, and the division of work, when viewed only from the point of view of planning and control.

With the current organization of work, the inspectors and secretaries try to use VIRK as a *tool* to work on the individual cases, both when registering information about the case, and when retrieving information to get an overview of a case. VIRK is less successful in this respect.

Furthermore VIRK should function as a *media* when distributing cases and working together on or taking over cases, and again there is little support in VIRK for this kind of use.

The needs and wishes of the secretaries and inspectors go in the direction of integration, of media for co-ordination of cases, tools for over-viewing ones own cases, and for registering more informal and qualitative data about the cases. The facilities which are available in the application at present, are not very suitable for these purposes, and there seems to be no easy way of extending VIRK to fulfil these needs even though the data is available in the database. This is because the application is built according to a systems perspective, viewing the human end-user primarily as somebody who provides accurate input to the system, thus input data need to be very well defined, etc.

Generally, the objects that one can work on, in or through VIRK, have to do with recording the state of the overall activity. Descriptions and lists of documents, lists of cases, of deadlines, and various statistics, are the objects *in* VIRK. The contents of the cases, which are the objects dealt with by inspectors and secretaries when handling a case are almost absent in the system. There are some objects of normal daily activity present in VIRK:
• travel cards that the inspectors take (print out and mark in VIRK as "taken") before leaving for an inspection. They contain information about the company, but are also meant to prevent several inspectors from going to the same company, by coincidence, at the same time.

• various lists and overviews, such as companies sorted by street name, and correspondence with respect to individual companies.

• lists and overviews of cases held by the individual inspector.

The latter ones are hard to retrieve in VIRK because they can only be reached through the programming of a report generator. A detailed analysis of the focus shifts during a use situation [5] shows that the artifact is definitely not *transparent* with respect to these lists and overviews. Also the fields available on e.g. the travel cards get in the way of noting what needs to be noted about the case. The user never gets the impression that he or she is working through the artifact. One may say that the few attempts in VIRK to add media or tools features to the system are rather problematic, and that in this case the traditional purpose, the *why*, has caused problems for a good *how* for the new functions, a good user interface. With the activity, or clusters of actions that have to do with planning and control, matters are somewhat different. Since these actions take place remotely from the actual controlling activity, the registration becomes a purpose of its own, handling of the artifact and of the contents, are almost becoming one and the same thing, and the human-computer interaction works rather smoothly. In a way VIRK is a tool for this very limited cluster of actions that have to do with routinized data entry.

### 3.3 Conclusions About the Combined Analysis

In many ways the interaction of VIRK seems to work appropriately with respect to the original core functionality of distributing cases and collecting statistics for "upwards" accounting. The division of work, by which the secretaries are entering data about single documents and cases, and these clusters of actions are rather well supported by VIRK. The additional functionality that is needed to make the branch offices, teams within these, and individual inspectors work with their cases through VIRK is hardly supported at all. These types of work are newer and the pieces of VIRK which support activities related to this are add-ons to the original system, and hard to get to. This despite the fact that VIRK was built after most of these changes of work had been taking place. It is no coincidence that the secretaries and inspectors are the ones who ask for computer support that can be characterized as media or tools, whereas what management has asked for in VIRK is a system. Clashes between these views are seen throughout the use of VIRK.

An open question remains: to what extent does the original systems perspective and purpose restrict possibilities for adding easier and better access to the functions needed by branch offices, teams within these, and individual inspectors? To what extent do the original purpose set limits to a better human-computer interaction?

## 4 Discussion and Prospects for the Approach

Reflecting on use of computer applications as a web of activities with different purposes, in which the computer application plays different roles helps focus on problems and contradictions in the interaction with the computer application. The roles that the computer application plays are appropriately, but in no way exhaustively, described using the perspectives of *systems, tools* and *media*. These are used to characterize important properties of *how* the computer application mediates activities, in particular regarding control of the interaction and transparency of the artifact.

Historical analyses of artifacts and work activities are useful in situating this analysis, bringing focus to the question of *why* use is organized the way it is, why the different roles of the artifact come into play, and in particular in understanding why some of the above contradictions occur. This *why* is reflected in what can be achieved by using the computer application and in how this is done; in the possible actions and operations undertaken by the user in each specific use situation.

My approach provides an alternative to traditional analysis of human-computer interaction which most often has no way of bridging to the specific use context of the artifact. What I have tried to show is that such a bridge can be developed when starting from human activity theory, whereas this paper does not account for a detailed analysis on the human interaction with VIRK in a use situation. In Bødker (in preparation) the actual interaction of users with VIRK is mapped out and studied.

Historical analysis and conflicting perspectives analysis are first steps towards a more contextualized analysis of human-computer interaction. Much more empirical work needs to be done, and more techniques need to be developed. In the end a major challenge may well be to come up with a theoretical framework which is different from but as detailed and operational as the traditional approach in HCI based in cognitive science.

## Acknowledgements

Thanks to Morten Kyng, Markus Stoltse and Kaj Grønbæk for comments on this paper, to Randy Trigg and Liam Bannon for comments on earlier drafts, to Mike Robinson and Ellen Christiansen for recent inspiring discussions about tools, media, etc., to the NLIS project group (Ellen Christiansen, Pelle Ehn, Randi Markussen, Preben Mogensen, and Randy Trigg) and to the folks at NLIS. The work has been supported by the Aarhus University Research Fund.

## References

1. L. Bannon, S. Bødker: Beyond the Interface: Encountering Artifacts in [7] pp. 227-253.
2. O. Bisgaard, P. Mogensen, M. Nørby, M. Thomsen: Systemudvikling som lærevirksomhed, konflikter som basis for organisationel udvikling (DAIMI IR-88). Århus, Aarhus University, 1989.
3. S. Bødker: A Human Activity Approach to User Interfaces. In Human Computer Interaction, T. Moran, (Ed.), Vol. 4, No. 3, 171-196 (1989).

4. S. Bødker: Through the Interface – a Human Activity Approach to User Interface Design, Hillsdale, NJ: Lawrence Erlbaum Associates, 1991.

5. S. Bødker: Understanding computer applications in use - a human activity analysis. In P. Bøgh Andersen, B. Holmquist H. Klein, R. Posner: The semiotics of the workplace, in preparation.

6. S. Bødker, E. Christiansen, P. Ehn, R. Markussen, P. Mogensen, R. Trigg: Computers in Context. Report from the AT-project in Progress. Report of the 1991 NES-SAM conference, Ebeltoft, Denmark, 1991.

7. J. M. Carroll (Ed.): Designing Interaction: Psychology at the Human-Computer Interface, New York: Cambridge University Press, 1991.

8. Y. Engeström: Learning by expanding. Helsinki: Orienta-Konsultit, 1987.

9. J. Kammersgaard: Four different perspectives on human-computer interaction. International Journal of Man-Machine Studies, 28: 343-362 (1988).

10. S. Maass, H. Oberquelle: Perspectives and metaphors for human-computer interaction. In C. Floyd et al. (Eds.): Software development and reality construction., Berlin: Springer Verlag 1992, pp. 233-251.

11. R. Markussen: A historical perspective on work practices and technology. In P. Bøgh Andersen, B.Holmqvist, J. F. Jensen (Eds.): The Computer as a Medium, Cambridge University Press, in press.

12. D. Norman: Cognitive artifacts. In [7] pp. 17-38.

13. M. Robinson: Introduction to "common artefact". COMIC-SF-4-1, 1992.

14. P. Sørgaard: Object Oriented Programming and Computerised Shared Material. In Second European Conference on Object Oriented Programming (ECOOP '88), ed. S. Gjessing, K. Nygaard, 319-334. Heidelberg: Springer Verlag, 1988.

---

[1] In the Esprit EuroCODE project, Ellen Christiansen, Mike Robinson, and I have worked to characterize shared material and common artifact in terms of activity theory.

# Structuring the Field of HCI: An Empirical Study of Experts' Representations

Peter Brusilovsky[†], Ivan Burmistrov[§], Victor Kaptelinin[‡]

[†]International Centre for Scientific and Technical Information
21b Kuusinen Str., 125252 Moscow, Russia
[§]Moscow State University, Faculty of Psychology
18-5 Prospect Marksa, 103009 Moscow, Russia
[‡]Psychological Institute, Russian Academy of Education
9 "V" Mokhovaya Str., 103009 Moscow, Russia

**Abstract.** This paper presents the results of empirical study of mental representations of the field of HCI, obtained by statistical analysis. Eight HCI experts participating in the study were asked to classify the papers presented at the EWHCI'92 Conference. The results show satisfactory agreement between the experts' classifications, as well as high interpretability of the group data. Some conclusions about the implicit "cognitive map" of the HCI field are discussed in the paper.

## 1 Introduction

Probably the most salient feature of Human Computer Interaction (HCI) as a field of research and practice is its interdisciplinary nature. Specialists with very different backgrounds -- psychologists, computer scientists, linguists, etc., work together while solving all kinds of problems related to design, evaluation, and analysis of computer systems. This interdisciplinarity of HCI field is inevitable and is potentially beneficial, since it provides an opportunity to exchange ideas between various paradigms. At the same time, however, it raises the serious problem of creating a common conceptual system which is necessary for any cooperation to be productive. This problem manifests itself in various forms and in various ways.

First, the very status of HCI as a field of study is discussed (see [1, 10]). The major questions of this discussion are: Is HCI a separate discipline? What kind of cooperation between constituent disciplines is possible and desirable? There are different answers to these questions -- from denying the value of any (premature) attempts to reach interdisciplinarity in HCI, through claims to establish separate links between pairs of disciplines, to call for an integrative perspective.

Second, if HCI is a special discipline, then it needs an appropriate theoretical basis. The role of theory in HCI is also under debates. The influential book "Designing Interaction: Psychology at the Human Computer Interface" [3] and the proceedings of the recent conference INTERCHI'93 (see [8]) reflect various points of view on this problem.

Third, the problem of interdisciplinarity is also discussed in studies of cross cultural aspects of HCI. Many specialists emphasize the existence of at least two cultures in HCI community [4]: the technology-oriented and the human-oriented.

In the present paper we also address the problem of an overarching conceptual scheme that could serve as a coherent basis for interdisciplinary studies in the field of HCI. However, we try to approach this problem in an empirical way. The basic assumption underlying the present study is that experts have an implicit representation of the HCI domain which makes it possible for them to coordinate their actual activities while conducting interdisciplinary projects. Our idea was to reveal this representation in a situation which require the "externalization" of the implicit "cognitive map" through structuring various items related to different aspects of HCI.

The last year East-West Conference on Human-Computer Interaction held in St.-Petersburg (EWHCI'92) provided very good opportunity for conducting such a study. First, a lot of world famous experts in the field of HCI attended the conference and it was possible to use some of them as experts in our study. Second, "ecologically valid" tasks for HCI experts were discovered in the process of composing the EWHCI'92 scientific programme. Several members of the scientific programme team came up with different versions of the programme. It seemed that the process of structuring the selected papers into appropriate sections was considered by HCI people as a meaningful kind of activity. At the same time there was a remarkable agreement among those involved on what is the general structure of the field.

Below is a description of an empirical study conducted during the EWHCI'92 conference [6] and aimed at revealing the implicit representation of the field of HCI in a sample of internationally recognized experts.

## 2 Method

**Subjects.** Eight international HCI experts participating in the EWHCI'92 Conference served as subjects in the study. Seven experts were from the West, and one expert was a Ukrainian scientist with experience of working in both Eastern and Western institutions.

**Data collection.** Data was gathered interactively using ExSort, a multiple expert knowledge acquisition tool for classification problems [2]. This program collects data using the free sorting technique [9] and then performs hierarchical cluster analysis of two-way similarity matrix according to Johnson's algorithm [7]. The free sorting procedure consists of dividing a card pack, where each card is labeled by some concept name, into smaller piles that represent similarity classes. The number of these piles and their nature are not predefined, so the expert is free to determine the total number of piles and in choosing principles of classification. This procedure results in a symmetrical matrix $\{a_{ij}\}$, where $a_{ij}=a_{ji}=1$ if the $i$th and $j$th items have been placed into the same pile, and $a_{ij}=a_{ji}=0$ otherwise. After $N$ experts have proposed their different sorts, the measure of proximity between stimuli $i$ and $j$ could then be calculated:

$$\delta_{ij} = \sum_{k=1}^{N} a_{ij} / N$$

The proximity matrix $\{d_{ij}\}$ can undergo cluster analysis to obtain a hierarchical representation of data structure.

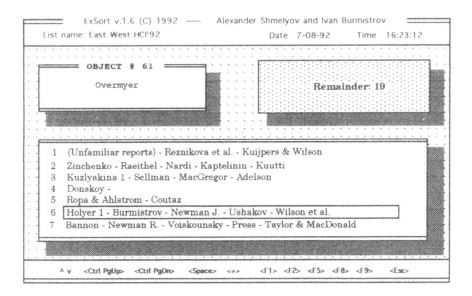

**Fig. 1.** ExSort: data gathering tool.

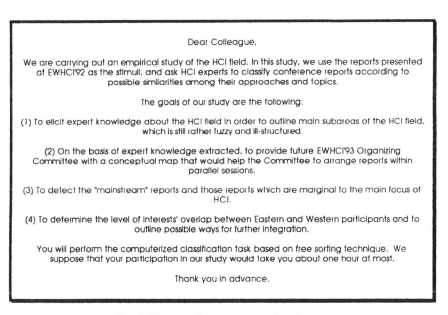

**Fig. 2.** The introductory instruction for experts.

A screen dump for the sorting process is shown in Figure 1. The program makes use simple animation to simulate the sequential extraction of objects from the pack placed at the upper right corner of the screen. Then the current card (item) moves to the upper left corner, and the expert has to place it into one of the existing classes or create a new class if current item cannot be placed into any existing class. Classes are listed at the scrollable window at the bottom half of the screen. The subject uses cursor keys to choose an appropriate class, and as s/he does so, the current card "falls" into the class chosen. Additional ExSort facilities make it possible to return an already classified item back to the pack or disband a whole class of items.

The items presented to experts in our study were names of EWHCI'92 participants accompanied by the titles of their papers. Both verbal presentations and posters were included (79 papers in total).

The subjects were informed of the goals of the study (see Figure 2) and the operational instruction included in the on-line session as the ExSort help screen. Then experts proposed their classifications interacting with the program.

## 3 Results

The hierarchical cluster tree provided by ExSort is shown in Figure 3. The half-split analysis showed satisfactory concordance in experts' classifications.

```
Cluster 1 _____ Cl. 1.1 _____ Cl. 1.1.1
(1) AT ZINCHENKO Activity Theory          (1)          (1)
(2) AT RAEITHEL Activity theory           (2)          (2)
            and cooperative work          (3)          (3)
(3) AT NARDI Approaches to studying context (4)        (4)
(4) AT KAPTELININ Activity theory and HCI (5)          (5)
(5) AT KUUTTI Activity theory and HCI
```

**Fig. 3.** The cluster tree for EWHCI'92 reports (to be continued).
Author names are accompanied with brief topic descriptions. Abbreviations that follow numbers of papers correspond to following sessions within the EWHCI'92 Conference programme:

| | | | |
|---|---|---|---|
| AT | Activity Theory and HCI | KD | Knowledge and Data Based |
| GP | General Principles of HCI | | Systems |
| CW | Computer Mediated | ED | Education |
| | Communication | RE | Requirements and |
| | and Collaborative Work | | Evaluation |
| GI | Graphical Interfaces | CL | Computer Assisted |
| MO | HCI Models | | Learning |
| HM | Hypertext and Hypermedia | ID | User Interface Design |
| DM | Design Methodologies | FU | Future of HCI |
| PS | Psychological Perspectives | P* | Demonstrations and |
| | | | Posters |

**Cluster 2** _____    Cl. 2.1 __ Cl.2.1.1

```
(1) DM UZILEVSKY ea Ergosemiotical approach  |  (2)     |  (2)
(2) GP BARNARD ea Framework for modelling HCI |  (3)     |  (4)
(3) MO USHAKOV Models and standards           |  (4)     |
(4) MO WILSON ea. Modelling perspectives      |         |_ Cl.2.1.2
(5) GP SINGLEY ea. Theory development         |            (3)
                and design evaluation        |_ Cl. 2.2
                                             |   (1)
                                             |_ Cl. 2.3
                                                 (5)
```

**Cluster 3** _____    Cl. 3.1 __ Cl.3.1.1

```
(1) CW BANNON From HCI and CMC to CSCW          (1)    |  (4)
(2) CW NEWMAN R. Collaborative writing          (2)    |  (5)
(3) CW VOISKOUNSKY Speech in CMC                 (3)    |
(4) CW MATSUURA ea. Interactions in virtual      (4)    |_ Cl.3.1.2
                environment                      (5)       (1)
(5) CW BELYAEVA ea. Telecommunication            (6)       (2)
                environment                      (7)       (3)
(6) CW PRESS Participation in CSCW systems                 (6)
(7) PS TAYLOR ea. CMC: group salience and                  (7)
                individual identifiability
```

**Cluster 4** _____    Cl. 5.1 __ Cl.5.1.1

```
(1) HM INSTONE ea. Information retrieval from    (1)    |  (5)
                hypertext                        (2)    |  (8)
(2) HM DOBRINEVSKI HCI in hypertext systems      (3)    |
(3) HM MCKERLIE ea. Hypermedia effect            (4)    |
(4) HM DOBRINEVSKI ea. Integrated hypertext      (5)    |_ Cl.5.1.2
                software                         (6)    |  (1)
(5) HM PEMBERTON ea. Hypertext design tool       (7)    |  (2)
(6) HM LAKAYEV ea. Hypertext structural analysis (8)    |  (3)
(7) HM BERND Graph model of hypertext querying   (9)    |  (4)
(8) P* SIDOROV Hypermedia tool for information          |  (6)
                integration                            |  (7)
(9) P* CRECHMAN ea. Knowledge representation in        |
                hypertext                              |_ Cl.5.1.3
                                                          (9)
```

**Fig. 3.** The cluster tree for EWHCI'92 reports (continued).

```
Cluster 5 _____ Cl. 4.1 __ Cl.4.1.1
(1) GI AVERBUKH ea. Visual programming        |  (1)  |   (1)
            representations                   |  (3)  |
(2) GI GAVRILOVA ea. Cognitive GUI            |  (4)  |_ Cl.4.1.2
(3) GI LIEBERMAN Visual programming by example |       |   (3)
(4) GI BRUSILOVSKY Adaptive visualization in CAL |     |_ Cl.4.1.3
                                              |            (4)
                                              |_ Cl. 4.2
                                                   (2)


Cluster 6 _____ Cl. 6.1 ___ Cl.6.1.1
(1) DM LIM ea. Human factors in system         (1)  |    (1)
        development                             (2)  |    (2)
(2) DM WAGNER Design methodology for HCI        (3)  |    (3)
(3) DM FLOYD ea. Framework for cooperative      (4)  |
        software development                    (5)  |
(4) RE OVERMYER Specifying requirements with         |_ Cl. 6.1.2
        multimedia                                   |    (4)
(5) GP BASS ea. Reference model for system           |
        construction                                 |_ Cl. 6.1.3
                                                          (5)


Cluster 7 _____ Cl. 7.1 __ Cl. 7.1.1
(1) PS MORGAN ea. Gender differences and       (1)  |    (1)
        cognitive style                        (2)  |
(2) PS CONWAY Colour naming models                  |_ Cl. 7.1.1
                                                         (2)


Cluster 8 _____ Cl. 8.1 ___ Cl. 8.1.1
(1) KD SVIRIDENKO Knowledge structuring        |  (1)  |   (1)
        environment                            |  (2)  |   (4)
(2) KD BREZILLON Building explanations          |  (4)  |
(3) KD DOLMATOVA Design of domain models        |       |
(4) KD KUIJPERS ea. Multi-modal interface       |       |_ Cl. 8.1.2
                                                |            (2)
                                                |_ Cl. 8.2
                                                     (3)
```

**Fig. 3.** The cluster tree for EWHCI'92 reports (continued).

```
Cluster 9 _____ Cl.9.1
(1) KD SUN ea. Relational databases           |    (1)
(2) KD POPOV ea. Dynamic query refinement      |_ Cl.9.2
(3) P* MULDERS ea. Document retrieval          |    (2)
                                               |_ Cl.9.3
                                                    (3)


Cluster 10 _____ Cl.10.1 __ Cl.10.1.1
(1) CL KUZLYAKINA System LECAT                 |    (1)   |    (1)
(2) CL SELLMAN System "Gravitas"               |    (2)   |    (2)
(3) CL REZNIKOVA ea. "Japanese writing"        |    (3)   |    (3)
       courseware                              |    (4)   |
(4) CL MACGREGOR Music compositional           |          |_ Cl.10.1.2
       software                                |               (4)
(5) ED COULOURIS ea. Teaching application      |
       design                                  |_ Cl.10.2 ___ Cl.10.2.1
(6) ED GYGLAVY Information technologies         |    (5)   |    (5)
       for teenagers                           |    (6)   |_ Cl.10.2.2
(7) ED ADELSON Scientific inquiry skills       |               (6)
(8) RE DAIBOV ea. Interface educational        |_ Cl.10.3
       component                               |    (7)
(9) P* GRABILINA ea. Training program          |
                   development system          |_ Cl.10.4
                                               |    (8)
                                               |
                                               |_ Cl.10.5
                                                    (9)


Cluster 11 _____ Cl.11.1
(1) ID DONSKOY Object oriented graphic editing |    (1)
(2) ID ROPA ea. Video viewer interface         |_ Cl.11.2
                                                    (2)


Cluster 12 _____ Cl.12.1
(1) ID HOLYER 1 Object-based user interface    |    (1)
(2) PS BURMISTROV Object oriented user interface |_ Cl.12.2
(3) P* BOEVE Edit paradigm for HCI             |    (2)
                                               |_ Cl.12.3
                                                    (3)
```

**Fig. 3.** The cluster tree for EWHCI'92 reports (continued).

```
Cluster 13 _____ Cl.13.1 ___ Cl.13.1.1
(1) PS NEWMAN J. User agent design      |    (2)     |    (2)
(2) FU MOUNTFORD Movie interface        |    (3)     |_ Cl.13.1.2
(3) P* HOWELL ea.1 Multimedia           |    (4)     |    (3)
               information bases        |            |_ Cl.13.1.3
(4) P* HOWELL ea.2 Multimedia           |                 (4)
               property information   |_ Cl.13.2
                                         (1)


Cluster 14 _____ Cl.14.1
(1) P* GAVRILIN ea. Psychoemotional conditions   |   (1)
(2) P* KALINKIN ea. Stimulating exercises.       |_ Cl.14.2
                                                     (2)


Cluster 15 _____ Cl.15.1
(1) P* HOLYER 2  User interface design environment |   (1)
(2) P* ZABOTIN ea. Flowchart based visual          |_ Cl.15.2
                 programming                           (2)

Cluster 16 _____ Cl.16.1
(1) P* TCHEBRAKOV ea. 1 Linear regression    |   (1)
(2) P* TCHEBRAKOV ea. 2 Data analysis        |_ Cl.16.2
                                                 (2)
```

Cluster 17 ID SOYGHIN User interface in computer modelling

Cluster 18 MO SKORODUMOV Fractal approach

Cluster 19 GI PETRE & PRICE Text and graphics in user
                                interfaces

Cluster 20 GI COUTAZ Taxonomy of multimedia and multimodal UI

Cluster 21 ID SCOWN Real-time issues in multi-agent systems

Cluster 22 PS CHEMERIS ea Human factors in ELOIS system

Cluster 23 P* KUZLYAKINA 2 Parametric synthesis

Cluster 24 P* KULIK Algorithm and tool for active dialogue

Cluster 25 P* MIGUNOVA ea. Human factors and programming

Cluster 26 P* MEL'NICHUK ea. Ecological education

**Fig. 3.** The cluster tree for EWHCI'92 reports (continued).

# 4 Conclusions

1. In general, the cluster tree demonstrates a high level of interpretability. Most top level clusters may be given the same names as conference sessions. For example, Cluster 1 in Figure 3 can be interpreted as "Activity Theory Approach to HCI," Clusters 2 and 6 as "General Principles, Design Methodologies and HCI Models," Cluster 3 as "CSCW," Cluster 5 as "Graphical Interfaces," Clusters 6 and 13 as "Hypertext and Hypermedia," Clusters 7 and 14 as "Psychological Aspects," Clusters 8 and 9 as "Knowledge and Data Based Systems," Cluster 10 as "Computer Assisted Learning and Education," Clusters 11 and 12 as "User Interface Design." At the same time, although the overall structure of the cluster tree reproduces the conference sessions, the placement of particular papers into conference sessions often differs from their placement within the cluster tree. In our opinion, in many cases the cluster tree represents better classification of papers than that provided by conference programme. (A good example of such cluster is Cluster 12 that join up papers on object-oriented interface design presented at three quite different sessions.)

2. The poster presentations, which were not structured according the conference sessions, were successfully classified and included into appropriate classes (see, for example, Clusters 4, 9, 10, 12 and 13). This means that our experts had really used their "cognitive maps" for interpretation of items they sometimes were not familiar with.

3. There is general agreement between the representational structure revealed in our study and the actual conference programme. However, the experts had not simply accepted the existing classification of papers. First, most top level clusters are decomposed into smaller ones, i. e. in contrast to the conference programme sessions they have internal structure as well. Second, a number of clusters were composed of papers presented at different conference sessions (see Clusters 2, 6, 10 and 12).

4. It can be hypothesized that the top level clusters reflect the different representational status of different HCI topics. Items related to educational aspects are represented by one cluster (see Cluster 10). At the same time, there are several clusters somewhat related to visualization (Clusters 5, 15, 19 and 20). This probably means that "Visualization in HCI" has a higher representational status as compared to educational aspects, since the latter is represented at the same level as particular subdomains of the former.

5. The Activity Theory approach to the HCI, based on ideas of the Moscow psychological school, remains rather unusual and not quite comprehensible to the Western experts participating in the study. The cluster of Activity Theory related papers (Cluster 1) has no internal structure, in contrast to most other top-level clusters. It might be supposed that experts operated on a "word label" level, simply attributing all Activity Theory related papers to the same class without expressing finer shades of distinction.

6. The analysis of "residua," that is the papers which do not belong to any group and compose one-item isolated clusters (Clusters 16-26), reveals that there are several types of papers which do not fit into the general scheme. These are: (a)papers introducing new approaches (e.g., "fractal approach" or "parametric synthesis"), (b)very specific papers (e.g., "Human Factors in ELOIS System"), and (c)very general ones (e.g., a paper on "human factors, dialogue problems, and programming effect").

## Acknowledgments

We would like to thank International Centre for Scientific and Technical Information (Moscow) for organizing the forum within which this work was undertaken, and Alexander Giglavy for providing the equipment. Special thanks to all the HCI specialists participating in this study: Liam Bannon, Jonathan Grudin, Austin Henderson, Allan MacLean, Scott Overmyer, Larry Press, Blaine Price, and Igor Ushakov.

## References

1. Bannon L. Interdisciplinarity or Interdisciplinary Theory in CSCW? Position paper for the Workshop on Interdisciplinary Theory for CSCW Design. CSCW'92, 1992

2. Burmistrov I. V., Shmeliov A. G. ExSort and DCS: Prototype program shells using a psychosemantic approach to concept acquisition, representation and assessment. In: P. Brusilovsky and V. Stefanjuk (Eds.) Proceedings of the East-West Conference on Emerging Computer Technologies in Education. (April 6-9, 1992. Moscow, Russia). Moscow: ICSTI, 1992, pp. 46-51.

3. Carroll J. (Ed.) Designing Interaction: Psychology at the Human Computer Interface. Cambridge ea.: CUP. 1991, 333 p.

4. Donskoy M. Position paper for Workshop on Cross-cultural Perspectives in HCI. INTERCHI'93, 1993.

5. Draper S. W. Activity Theory: The new direction for HCI? International Journal of Man-Machine Studies 33 (1993)

6. Gornostaev Ju. (Ed.) Proceedings of the East-West International Conference on Human-Computer Interaction EWHCI'93. (St.-Petersburg, Russia, August 4-8, 1992). Moscow: ICSTI 1992, 479 p.

7. Johnson S. C. Hierarchical clustering schemes. Psychometrika 32, 241-254 (1967)

8. Kuutti K., Bannon L. J. Searching for unity among diversity: Exploring the "interface" concept. In: Ashlund S. et al. (Eds.). INTERCHI'93 Conference Proceedings (Amsterdam, The Netherlands, April 24-29, 1993). New York: ACM 1993, pp. 263-268.

9. Miller G. A. A psychological method to investigate verbal concepts. Journal of Mathematical Psychology 6, 161-191 (1969)

10. Rogers Y. More insight or misinterpretation? Interdisciplinary CSCW Research in Context. Position paper for Workshop on Interdisciplinary Theory for CSCW Design. CSCW'92, 1992

# Coupling Interaction Specification with Functionality Description

A. Kameas[1]       S. Papadimitriou[1,2]       G. Pavlides[1,2,3]

[1] Dept. of Computer Engineering and Informatics, Univ. of Patras, Patras 26110, Greece
[2] Computer Technology Institute, 3 Kolokotroni st., Patras 26221, Greece
[3] INTRASOFT SA, 2 Adrianiou st, Athens 12515, Greece

## Abstract

In this paper, the solution used in the context of SEPDS (a Software Development Environment) to the problem of combining interactive behavior specification with functionality description of a distributed interactive application is presented. This solution consists of combining two specification models: IDFG to describe the interactive aspects of applications developed with the system and EDFG to describe their functionality. Both these models are data flow graph based and can be classified as process models. They use "actors" to represent performers of processes and "links" to represent data buffering and exchange, as well as roles and different perspectives. Although the two models have many semantical differences, they also have many common properties, that is why they can be straightforwardly combined in a process that enables designers think in users terms. To this end, action actors are used to represent the functions supported by the application, and context actors to represent the application user interface functions. In addition, links are used to represent the events that take place in the system (these may be user or system actions), the effects that these have on the screen, the context into which these take place and the goals that may be achieved using the application. Furthermore, the reusability and prototyping tools of SEPDS can be used to construct and test the application design.

## 1 Introduction

The need to build increasingly complex software systems has led in the development of SDEs (Software Development Environments) [6, 9], which not only provide assistance in software development, but also guarantee a standard level of quality, as they progressively integrate tools that support more phases of the software development process. With the evolution of technology, the need to build highly interactive applications that address non–computer expert users has recently come up. Despite the attempts, however, there still exists a gap between the designers' and users' model of an interactive application, due mainly to the unsuitability of the traditional application development techniques for the specification of interaction and the construction of user interfaces [11], and to the difficulty of combining an interaction model with an application data model [1].

In this paper, a solution that has been applied in the context of SEPDS, (Software Environment for the Prototyping of Distributed Systems) system [9], which is an engineering framework for the prototyping of distributed systems, is presented. This solution consists of using two distinct specification models: EDFG (Extended Data Flow Graph) for the specification of application functionality, and IDFG (Interactive Data Flow Graph) for the specification of the interactive behavior of this application. Both these models are based on Data Flow Graphs (DFG), and therefore, can be straightforwardly combined. In addition, they are used in much the same way, and as a consequence, designers that use SEPDS do not have to use additional effort to learn two different specification languages, while the prototyping subsystem of SEPDS is able to produce highly–interactive application prototypes.

EDFG and IDFG belong to the class of process models [4]; more specifically, they can be proved equivalent to Petri–Net models. Process models, in general, use the notion of a "process" (which is a set of partially ordered steps called "process elements") to represent an action towards some "goal". In both EDFG and IDFG, actors form the performers of process elements (the notion of agents is generally used in process models), by representing computations of arbitrary complexity. Links are used as a form of role representation (that is, to determine which set of process elements will be executed), as well as for the transportation and buffering of data, and the representation of screen effects that computations may have. Thus, these models represent explicitly the functional (i.e. what process elements are being executed and what flows of information are used by them), behavioral (i.e. conditions for the execution of process elements and how these interact) and organizational (i.e. where and by whom the execution of process elements takes place) perspectives of an application, while they may be used (that is, they include the appropriate constructs) for the representation of informational (i.e. explicit representation of the informational products consumed or produced by a process) perspective as well.

Process models usually distinguish between two enactors of a sequence of processes: users (in this case, the sequence is called a "script") and system (in this case, a "program"). This distinction is also used in this case, by allowing the modeling of both user and system actions as actor execution enablers. In addition, an explicit representation of goal–subgoal decomposition of user actions is used as the means to determine permitted states that may be reached from the current state. In this way, designers are "forced" to create an application that will be functioning close to the way users think when using it.

In SEPDS, EDFG serves as the data model, while IDFG is the event model. In the next two sections, both models are briefly presented, and subsequently the paper focuses on how these models are combined, by presenting their common and distinct properties and a simple example.

## 2 EDFG: The Data Model

The EDFG model [9] is a trade–off between formal models (e.g. [7]) and icon oriented models (e.g. [3]). According to the EDFG approach, a distributed application is described as a set of communicating graphs, with several communication primitives defined to support this communication.

An EDFG is a bipartite graph consisting of a set $L$ of links and a set $A$ of actors. Actors represent the computational components, while links are used for data buffering and transportation. There also exists a set $E$ of directed arcs which connect actors to links and links to actors. A link gives input to an actor if a directed arc exists from the link to that actor; a link receives output from an actor if a directed arc exists from that actor to the link. The links can contain tokens, which are value structures of arbitrary complexity. The number of tokens contained in all links at a given instant may be used to define the state of the EDFG, which is also called "EDFG marking".

An actor $a$ is defined as a 7–tuple consisting of:

- *the set of input links $IFS(a)$*

- *the set of output links $OFS(a)$*

- *a precondition function $PRE(a)$*, which gives the conditions that must hold (that is, which of $IFS$ links must contain tokens) for an actor to be executed

- *a postcondition function $POST(a)$*, which gives the conditions that result from the execution of the actor (that is, which of $OFS$ links will receive tokens)

- *a function $FUN(a)$*, which represents the computation performed by the actor

- *a descriptor $TYPE(a)$*, which describes the level of actor complexity, and

- *a descriptor $\delta(a)$*, which refers to the execution time of the actor

Links are typed: a link type describes a set of actor links that are allowed to contain tokens of the same data type. When the designer constructs an EDFG, all the components of an actor (with the possible exception of $\delta(a)$) must be defined. Then links may be defined, with the system performing consistency and type–matching checks.

An actor is executed ("fires") when a subset of its input links defined by its $PRE$ function contains tokens; all these tokens are then removed from the input links, while tokens are placed in the output links that are specified by the actor $POST$ function. Each actor firing modifies the distribution of tokens on links and thus produces a new EDFG marking (a new state).

## 3 IDFG: The Interaction Specification Model

IDFG combines features from both state–based (e.g. [5]) and user–oriented interaction models (e.g. [2]). It supports the specification of all interactive features of an application in a non–technical way and permits the construction of specialized interactive applications. To achieve this, description of the elements of the screen has been separated from the specification of actions that may be performed with these elements, leading to a more user–centered design.

Each IDFG [8] is also a bipartite graph. Nodes are of two different types: links and actors. Actors represent the actions that the system offers to its users and the goals they may achieve, while links are used to describe conditions. Directed arcs connect actors to links and links to actors. Actor firing and actor marking notions are also used in IDFG as they have been defined (although in the following, an equivalent definition of state will be presented).

Each actor consists of two parts: the behavioural part, which is made up of rules, and the functional part, which contains code segments. For every rule of the behavioural part, there exists a set of left–hand–side conditions that must hold for it to fire (the $PRE$ function of the actor), and a set of right–hand side conditions that result from the firing (its $POST$ function). The set of the left–hand–side conditions of all links make up the $IFS$ of the actor, while the set of the right–hand–side conditions of all links make up its $OFS$ function. The code segments of an actor correspond to the objects that implement the actor's function $FUN$. Two other model properties are inheritance and abstraction. To incorporate inheritance, the component $INHERITS(a)$ of an actor $a$ is used to represent whether an actor inherits the functionality of one or more classes of actors (multiple inheritance), or is a primitive one (used in place of component $TYPE(a)$ of EDFG; component $\delta(a)$ is not yet used in IDFG). Abstraction can be used to improve reusability when the specified user interface will be implemented by the system.

Links are typed (mainly to distinguish between the components of a situation). The types of links currently used by SEPDS are contained in the set { *user action, system action, object condition, goal, incommunication, outcommunication* }. To improve expressibility, more link types can be added to this set. Links are used to describe different actor roles (e.g. "goal" links "assign" actors to user plans) and perspectives with respect to application functionality (e.g. the organizational perspective is represented by "action" and "communication" links).

State transitions take place only as a consequence of an event (that is, a user or system action), and *every actor must have a link of type "user action" or "system action" in its IFS*. In addition, each user action must belong to a goal–leading sequence, that is why, *each actor has also a link of type "goal" in its IFS and OFS* (a "goal" link in the $OFS$ is used to signal successful goal achievement). Therefore, we explicitly represent all the actions (events) that may take place in the system, as well as all the goals that may be achieved using it. In addition, we can use several links of type "object condition" to represent the current state of the screen objects, thus accounting for the screen effects of user and system actions and conforming with the "principle of observability" [11].

To transparently support interaction across distributed contexts, as well as to model user–system communication, we use a special link type, the "communication" type. In effect, there exist "incommunication" and "outcommunication" link types to account for the direction of communication. Actors that contain rules that result in intercontextual communication are called "communication actors". On the other hand, links of type "system action" are used to model system–initiated communication among actors of the same graph.

## 4   Combining the Models

EDFG and IDFG have many common properties that make their combination rather straightforward: they use the same specification methaphor, while based on the same underlying mathematical model. This leads to a uniform treatment by the tools of SEPDS, and consequently facilitates the efficient prototyping and production of distributed interactive applications. In both models, inheritance and abstraction are incorporated using "templates", which are abstractions of the behavior of actors based on the description of their input and output links and firing pre- and postconditions. Templates may be archived and reused based on this description; they may also be combined to form abstractions of complex actor behavior (note that template combination is a different process than actor combination that is described in the following).

However, there also exist differences between the two models, that concern mostly their different semantic interpretation, and their distinct role in application specification. In EDFG, links represent data and consequently, link types represent data types, while actors represent application functions. In IDFG, links represent events and link types represent different perspectives, while actors represent user interface functionality.

Thus, in a complete application graph, actors can be of two kinds: action actors and context actors. With each action offered by the application to its users (that is, with each command that is transferred by the user interface to the underlying application), an action actor is associated. The number of action actors is finite and equal to all the commands supported by the application. Such an actor has a simple behavioural part and fires when the user performs the appropriate action. In order for it to be ready–to–fire, all links in its subset of $IFS$ specified by its $PRE$ function except "user or system action" links must already contain tokens. This means that the user interface must have reached the appropriate state (as represented by the condition links) and the actor must belong in one of the contexts the user is currently working with (as represented by the "goal" link) for the user action to be available. Its functional part contains the code that implements the application command, and produces the appropriate effects (modelled with the production of tokens in the actor's subset of $OFS$ specified by its $POST$ function). This code is represented with an EDFG subgraph.

To model context of operation and to support the goal–based structuring of user actions, context actors are used. These have a behavioural part that contains many rules, while their functional part will in the future be associated with some user interface widget to represent the action on the screen. Their functionality is to correctly interpret user actions in order to appropriately decompose user goals into subgoals, so that eventually the correct action actor will fire. To infer the context of operation, these actors contain rules that fire depending on the user interface action that the user performs. Context actors may be formed by combining action actors or context actors; this process may be applied an adequate number of times so as to represent all user goals and subgoals.

In this way, subgraphs that correspond to user goals can be defined, with the context of user actions encapsulated in their structure. As far as goals and user and system actions are concerned, the following rule holds: *lower level goals are derived from user or system actions and goals of the next higher level*. To achieve such a transformation when a context actor is formed, Primitive Graphs (PGs) [10] are used to specify the type of the context actor.

For example, suppose that one wants to specify interaction with a menu that has four items, the second of which opens to a submenu. Interaction with such a menu is depicted in figure 1. Note that a context actor (MENU) is used to represent the entire menu functionality, while action actors (C1, C3, C4) are used to represent the functions implemented by menu items 1, 3 and 4 respectively[1].

Menu item 2 is represented by another context actor (C2), since when selected, it opens to a second–level menu. Also note how action actors can be straightforwardly analyzed into EDFG actors (the semantics of this decomposition are not explicitly represented due to lack of space).

At any moment, there exists a number of actors (the actor–ready list) each of which contains tokens in the subset of its $IFS$ links specified by its $PRE$ function, except the "action" link. These actors represent the actions that are available to the user. Traditional DFG models interpret the notion of state as the distribution of tokens on the graph links. Our model extends this notion by defining a state as the set of actors in the actor–ready list, or equivalently, the set of user or system actions that the actors in the actor–ready list represent. Since these actions correspond to goals in a lower–level, it may be equivalently

---

[1] in this figure thick and plain circles represent user action and other links, respectively, thick and plain rectangles represent action and context actors, respectively, and dotted rectangles represent EDFG actors

stated that a state is represented with the set of goals that may be achieved as a consequence of user or system actions permitted by the actors in the actor-ready list. State transitions occur as a consequence of an actor firing which causes the output of tokens in the subset of actor's $OFS$ links specified by its $POST$ function, thus modifying the actor-ready list.

Since, however, an actor firing depends on its $IFS$, it is clear that among a set of otherwise identical actors that are ready to fire (the actor-ready list), the one that fires is determined by the link of type "user or system action". This property can be used for the resolution of firing conflicts: all actors that can eventually fire, do so, and the consequences of firing appear in the graph in the form of a new marking.

Referring to the example of figure 1 once more, PG EN creates one token on every "goal" link of the constituent actors when user moves the mouse over the menu. Thus, actors C1 to C4 become ready-to-fire. The one that will eventually fire is determined by the next user action (clicking on one of the menu items), that will create one token on the "user action" link of one of these actors. This actor is subsequently analyzed in the same way. Note that menu closes after one item is selected, as specified by PG OPG, which produces one output token when a token is created on one of its input links.

In an interactive application, there exist several "loci of control", representing the potential for the next user action; these loci are represented in SEPDS by the actor-ready list. Furthermore, the existence of an "external event-handler" (EEH) is assumed, which gets user input and sends it to the IDFGs. EEH does not wait for response to the token it communicates; instead, *it communicates a token each time a user action is recorded and identified.* The task of EEH is not only to capture each user action, but also to assign to it the proper semantics depending on the context. This mechanism, however, is invisible to the user.

## 5   Conclusions

In this paper a solution to the problem of combining an interaction model with an application data model was presented. This solution, which has been adopted in SEPDS, consists of using EDFG for application functionality specification, and IDFG for specification of interaction. These two models are both based on Data Flow Graphs and can be combined straightforwardly.

Designers that use SEPDS may either describe an application in the traditional bottom-up way (by first describing the functionality of the application to be produced using EDFG and then by specifying the interactive features of the application using IDFG) or in a top-down way (first, the interactive features are specified, then the user goals are decomposed and the action paths are defined, and finally, the application functionality is described). In both methods EDFG graphs must be associated with the action actors of IDFG and IDFG actors must be combined to represent user interface functions. Note, however, that in the latter method the applications that will be produced are user-centered in that they directly incorporate the user perspective. Then the prototyping tools of SEPDS may be used to test the appearance and functionality of the application.

The importance of this process lies in that designers do not have to construct the user interface, as is usually the case with other user interface generators. Instead, they specify the flow of interaction between projected end-users and the application to be produced. To do this, designers must specify the actions that will at any moment be available to end-users, the effects that these actions will produce on the screen, as well as the goals that may be achieved using the application. That is why we claim that the presented model enables designers to think in users terms.

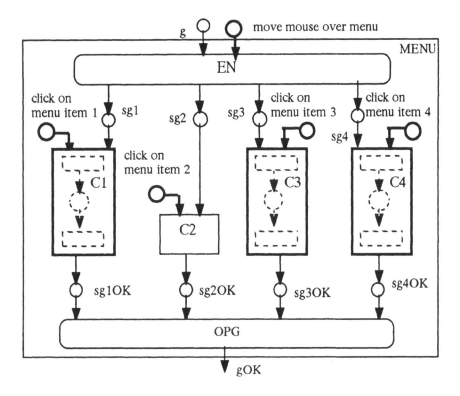

Figure 1: An example of the usage of EDFG and IDFG models

A prototype of SEPDS has been recently completed, but it does not yet support the IDFG model (the model, however, has been independently applied to the descritpion of several interactive systems). We are currently in the process of defining a user interface construction methodology that together with the integration of IDFG, will enable us to test the feasibility of a semi–automated production of user interfaces.

**Acknowledgements**
The authors wish to thank Mr. P. Fitsilis for fruitful discussions on the usability of the approach, and the anonymous reviewers for their constructive comments.

# References

[1] J.D. Foley, D. J. M. J. de Baar and K.E. Mullet, *Coupling application design and user interface design*. Proceedings of the CHI92 Conference: Striking a balance, May 3-7, 1992, Monterey, USA, pp 259-266.

[2] J. Bonar and B. Liffick, *Communicating with high–level plans*. In Intelligent User Interfaces (J. Sullivan and S. Tyler eds), ACM Press, 1991, pp 129-157.

[3] R. Buhr, G. Karam, C. Hayes and C. Woodside, *Software CAD: A revolutionary approach*. IEEE Trans. Softw. Eng., SE-15(3), March 1989.

[4] B. Curtis, M.I. Kellner and J. Over, *Process modeling*. Comm. of the ACM, 35(9), September 1992, pp 75-90.

[5] A. J. Dix and C. Runciman, *Abstract models of interactive systems*. In Proceedings of the British Computer Society Conference on People and Computers: Designing the Interface (P. Johnson and S. Cook eds), Cambridge University Press, 1985, pp 13-22.

[6] P. Henderson, editor, *Proceedings of the second SIGSOFT/SIGPLAN Software Engineering Symposium on Practical Software Development Environments*. ACM SIGPLAN Notices, vol 22, January 1989.

[7] C. Jard, J. Monin and R. Groz, *Development of VEDA, a prototyping tool for distributed algorithms*. IEEE Trans. Softw. Eng., SE-14(3), March 1988.

[8] A. Kameas, S. Papadimitriou, P. Pintelas and G. Pavlides, *IDFG: an interactive applications specification model with phenomenological properties*. Proceedings of the EUROMICRO93 Conference, September 6-9, 1993, Barcelona, Spain.

[9] A. Levy, J. van Katwijk, G. Pavlides and F. Tolsma, *SEPDS: A support environment for prototyping distributed systems*. Proceedings of the 1st International Conference on System Integration, April 1990, New Jersey, USA.

[10] S. Papadimitriou, A. Kameas, P. Fitsilis and G. Pavlides, *A new compression technique for tools that use data-flow graphs to model distributed real-time applications*. Proceedings of the 5th International Conference on Software Engineering and its Applications, December 7-11 1992, Toulouse, France, pp 235-244.

[11] H. Thimbleby, *User Interface Design*. ACM Press, 1990, p 470.

# An Extension to the Human-Computer Interaction Paradigm

R.C.MacGregor

Department of Business Systems, University of Wollongong
Northfields Avenue, Wollongong, Australia 2500

**Abstract.** This paper suggests that the focus of user support has moved from a simple system-user interface to a need to consider a variety of potential interfaces at the work-setting. It argues that the current HCI paradigm still only addresses user support in terms of a technological interface, but that this must be extended to include a number of other alternatives.

## Introduction

An examination of the of the history of Human Computer Interaction (HCI) suggests that it has emerged as a discipline whose primary mandate is the support of the end user in carrying out computer assisted tasks of work. However, there are a number of ways of looking at the history of HCI. Grudin (1990), for example, suggests that the focus of user support was originally found at the hardware-user interface. Thus design, research and solutions to user problems were primarily directed towards the modification of the available hardware. Grudin suggests that over the last decade this focus has shifted through software and the terminal and on towards the work setting. Indeed, this view is supported by Trauth and Cole (1992) who indicate that an obvious trend in information systems is the dynamic growth of end user computing at the work setting. Grudin suggests that despite this change of focus the term 'User Interface' remains one which is technological in its centre. The user interface, he suggests, assumes the computer and then attempts to specify the user. According to Bannon (1990) nowhere is this more apparent than in an examination of the language used to describe HCI. Terms such as 'casual user', 'novice user', and 'expert user' are not used to describe the user's ability with their job or tasks within their job, they are terms which are ascribed to a user depending upon their ability to function with a computing tool. All descriptions of the user have the computer as their referent.

This paper begins by briefly examining the concept of user support. The paper then considers the paradigm upon which HCI research and development is based, in particular its role in user support. It will be suggested that the field of HCI has taken too narrow a stance. It will be argued that this has resulted in the discipline being guilty of technological determinism - the belief that all problems can be solved through technological innovation. This paper will briefly examine current methodologies in the light of this technological determinism, to determine the shortcomings of the current paradigm. Finally, an alternative paradigm for HCI will be described.

## User Support

With the obvious growth in end user computing and the accompanying wide range of characteristics which those end users possess, there is a growing need for support which takes into account both the user and the context of use. In re-examining Grudin's key focal points, while ever the interaction remained with a hardware or software focus, a single task<->user interface could be considered sufficient (see fig. 1). Support for the user involved modification to either the hardware or the software and the effect of such modification was normally predictable. However, if the focus has moved to the work setting, the number of interfaces increases and support through only one interface becomes unpredictable. Indeed, support must be considered in terms of all interfaces.

If, as suggested, the primary mandate of HCI is user support, and if the focus has moved on towards the work setting, it is necessary to consider HCI in terms of all interfaces of support.

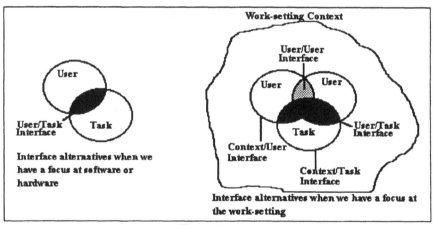

Figure 1

## Human-Computer Interaction

Wixon, Holtzblatt and Knox (1990) suggest that HCI research and development is basically a 'two-pronged' challenge. On the one hand the designer must design interfaces which utilise available technology to produce a unified solution to a problem, this solution being focused at the interface (Constantine 1992). On the other hand the design effort must be timely and cost effective. Freeman (1987) terms this two-pronged challenge 'techno-economic' or 'push-pull', where push-pull is a combination of perceived needs - 'demand pull' (Nelson and Winter 1982) and technological breakthrough - 'technological push' (Elster 1983). Freeman, who considers that computer innovation largely falls into the push-pull category, suggests that an observable outcome of such innovation is that it tends to remain within the techno-economic framework by continuing to look at problems and provide solutions for them from a strictly technical perspective.

An examination of the literature on HCI suggests that not only is it founded upon the push-pull paradigm but, when confronted with the question of support, it continues to seek technical solutions to perceived problems. While it may be argued that HCI has had substantial input from areas such as human factors, psychology, as well as computer science (Lindgaard 1990, Gerlach and Kuo 1991) and has been utilised in Computer Supported Co-operative Work undertakings, ultimately it is concerned with providing ease of use through modifications to hardware and software. The user is always considered to be a generically singular commodity, engaged in formal measurable tasks.

Despite its apparent singularity of focus HCI has provided a substantial contribution to the concept of user support. In particular, HCI has a traditional goal of developing guidelines which can empirically supported. Through the identification of measurable performance criteria and provision for differing cognitive styles HCI has been able to provide mechanisms during system design which will ultimately support the user in carrying out his/her task of work.

However, the singularity of focus has led to a number of perceived weaknesses. Most notable is the inability to provide organisational forms of support (context<->task, context<->user, user<->user). The continual argument that these can only be considered at the point of implementation and thus cannot be planned for has resulted in designs which do not allow for the context or the contextual interfaces. The user is reduced to a generically singular, asocial being, the design becomes potentially unsuitable for the final work situation, and the support is reduced to a question of technological intervention.

## The Effects of this Approach on the Designer and the User

The attempt to find a technical solution to problems is not only proliferated by HCI professionals but it has become the expectation of the user involved with new product interfaces. A recent survey (Constantine 1992) suggests that most users expect little more than to be asked in what order they carry out their tasks and what features will be needed to simplify this process. Indeed, Constantine concluded that the 'Great Law of User Interface Design' appeared to suggest that good interface design involves replacing of one piece of technology with another such that the user does not have to learn anything.

Perhaps epitomising the continued belief in the technological solution was a recent article by Swaine (1992) which called for a paradigm shift in the field of human-computer interaction. While initially this view is appealing Swaine suggests that the last paradigm shift was "the one involving mice and metaphorical desktops"

(Swaine 1992, p119) and that the next is likely to be "in the direction of dynamic media like sound and video" (Swaine 1992, p119).

Kolowich (1992), quoting a Black and Decker Sales Manager's speech to his sales personnel, perhaps best sums up the inappropriateness of continually searching for a technical solution:

"Customers don't want 1/4 inch drills; they want 1/4 inch holes" (Kolowich 1992, p72)

In the same vain, Kolowich suggests that users do not want mice, colour graphics or browsers, they want to be better able and better informed to carry out their work and solve their day-to-day problems.

## An Alternative Approach

If, as suggested by Constantine, the interface is the focus of communication and information exchange, it is valid to consider, as HCI researchers and designers, what is meant by the terms communications and information exchange and how the definitions apply to the various work setting interfaces.

Stamper (1992) considers that there are six levels which must be discussed when considering information exchange or communications. They are:

**Physical** - signal traces, hardware, physical distinctions, component density, speed ....

**Empirical** - patterns, codes, redundancy, channel capacity, noise, efficiency .....

**Syntactical** - formal structures, language, logic, data, fields, files ....

**Semantic** - meanings, signification, denotation, validity ....

**Pragmatic** - intention, negotiation, conversation ....

**Social World** - beliefs, expectations, commitment, culture ....

If we were to reduce HCI to a single user<->task interface, whereby support was synonymous with technical solutions, the final two levels suggested by Stamper would, for the most part be obsolete. Indeed, we could logically deduce that failure at any one of the lower levels (Physical, Empirical, Syntactical, Semantic) would result in interaction not taking place. If, however, we assume that several interfaces exist at the work setting, then discussion of these must be carried out in terms of all six levels provided by Stamper. The following section will assume the adequate functioning of the four lower levels and will concentrate on the final two levels (Pragmatic and Social World), in particular their effect upon all interface types.

### Pragmatic

Stamper suggests that any communication or information exchange must have an intention inputted by the both the creator and the interpreter. Pragmatics examines the relationship between the intention ascribed to the communication or information exchange and the resulting behaviour of the responsible agents in a social context. The context is essential since structures and symbols utilised in the communication or exchange of information can only be interpreted in a social setting. Communication is only considered successful if intention can be passed on and acted upon. The richness of the communication can be a measure of the consequences which stem from an intentional messages. If we consider the context to be a set of shared beliefs and values, then communication and information exchange changes the relationship of those beliefs by either diverting them or reinforcing them.

In the area of human-computer interaction some in-roads have been made in determining the pragmatic level of communication and information exchange, in particular the call for the examination of context of human-computer interaction (Wixon et al 1990, Carroll 1991, Diaper and Hammond 1991). Indeed, Berry and Reeves (1992) call for the introduction of a 'Workplace Model' to extend current thinking in modelling work setting interfaces. Unfortunately, much of the contextual examination has occurred within a defined technical framework and with the exception of Carroll (1991) there has been little voicing of the need to examine beliefs or values. Stamper suggests that if the beliefs and values of communications and information exchange are not examined it becomes impossible to operationalise their input or determine their effect.

## Social Level

This final level of communication and information exchange imparts process, form and reality to the social situation. Stamper suggests that all work is carried out within a 'work community' where the community shares a set of work norms. While at the pragmatic level we are interested in intention, at the social level we are concerned with the actual effects of any communication and information exchange. Stamper suggests that normally at this level the effects are far wider reaching and must be considered in terms of the shared norms of the community. Any change to communication or information exchange, including modification to an interface in the form of support, will effect the work community by altering the shared norms. Thus design must be premised on a firm understanding of the social level of the work community, suggesting due consideration to organisational parameters as well as technical ones.

As suggested, human-computer interaction tends, for the most part, to be focused on a single interface. The interface is described as a combination of software and hardware which act like a set of mirrors and lenses, bringing a hitherto blurred image into focus for the user and allowing the user to communicate with the computer system. With the changing focus of HCI to the work place and the need to include Stamper's pragmatic and social level, this simple mirror and lenses philosophy fails to address the intentions, expectations and beliefs of the workplace community.

# A Change of Paradigm

As suggested, any new approach to HCI must include a recognition of the existence of a variety of interfaces at the work setting and must examine those interfaces in terms of all six levels of information exchange suggested by Stamper. A necessary first step in this approach must be the examination of the methodologies being employed in HCI, not simply with the view to extending them to cover a wider set interface alternatives, but to determine whether they provide support at all levels for the user.

An examination of current methodologies used in HCI would suggest that they clearly delineate between design, testing, implementation and support, focusing squarely on the former two with the belief that the latter two will be covered by 'other experts'. Design is based upon guidelines which have been developed through empirical studies and much of the support provided by HCI is derived from measurable performance criteria and introduced during the design phase. For any methodology to address alternate interfaces it must include support structures for those interfaces in the design phase. Under existing methodologies, support at the user<->task interface is taken into account during design, however, since other forms of support, termed organisational support, cannot be measured or tested until the entire system has been implemented and has been running for some time, they are rarely considered or catered for by HCI professional. A change in methodology must not only embrace organisational forms of support, it must formalise these mechanisms both during the analysis and the design stages and must extend testing beyond implementation.

At the user<->user interface support in the form of peer group assistance needs to be formalised and its effectiveness monitored. Formal peer group support may take the form of regular help sessions, on-the-job training, documentation evaluation, bulletin boards etc. Analysis at this interface must examine methods of information exchange, shared work norms and beliefs and the visible effects of changes to these through communication. Design and subsequent support must reinforce the shared norms and beliefs of the user<->user work group.

At the context<->task, context<->user interfaces support often takes the form of monitoring and feedback, however, under current methodologies these tend to be irregularly fragmented across a number of organisational units. Organisational support at these interfaces require formal regular monitoring of effects to both users and tasks of changes to the work setting. Not only will changes to tasks or changes to user's approaches to tasks affect the work setting, but the HCI professional must become aware of the effect of the work setting context on their own design practices. Analysis at the context interfaces must include the overall organisational objectives, the nature of shared tasks within the organisation, the formal and informal structures utilised within the work setting and the effect of changes to these structures. Design and subsequent support must utilise and reinforce the organisational objectives and structures.

# Conclusion

Research and development in the area of human computer interaction, despite its changing hardware focus (Grudin 1990), has remained, for the most part, technology centred. Despite the growing call in the literature for context, most research and development still is based on technical solutions to technical problems. The contextualist critique needs to be expanded beyond the task requirements and work methods of an asocial user. Likewise the interface must be thought of as two way not as a one way focus.

An alternative paradigm for HCI has been described. It centres on a redefinition of the interface, the user and the methodology of design. By expanding the boundaries of these terms the paradigm provides the designer with a larger set of alternatives from which to design interfaces for specific contexts. While one or more of these inclusions may exist in an organisation, it is only through their collective use that a more viable design is possible.

# References

Bannon L.: From human factors to human actors In: Greenbaum J. and Kyng M. (eds): Design at Work, NJ: Lawrence Erlbaum Associates, (1990)

Berry R.E. and Reeves C.J. : The Evolution of the Common Workplace Model. IBM Systems Journal 31, 3, 414 - 428, (1992)

Carroll J.M.: History and Hysteresis in Theories and Frameworks for HCI In: Diaper D. and Hammond N. (eds): People and Computer VI CHI'91 Proceedings, Edinburgh: 1991, 47 - 56

Constantine L.: Going to the source (how software developers can find out what their customers want. Computer Language, 9, 12, 112 - 115 (1992)

Elster J.: Explaining Technical Change. Cambridge: Cambridge University Press (1983)

Freeman C.: The Case for Technological Determinism In: Finnegan R., Salaman G. and Thompson K. (eds): Information Technology: Social Issues. UK: Hodder and Stoughton (1987)

Gerlach J.H. and Kuo F.Y.: Understanding Human-Computer Interaction for Information Systems Design. MIS Quarterly 15, 4, 527 - 549 (1991)

Grudin J.: The Computer Reaches Out: The Historical Continuity of Interface Design In: Chew J.C. and Whiteside J. (eds): Empowering People CHI'90 Proceedings. Seattle, 261 - 268 (1990)

Kolowich M.: Software developers take heed: your customers are your best critics. PC Computing 5, 2, 72 -73 (1992)

Lindgaard G.: HCI Through the Microscope: Revealing Forests or Trees?. Proceedings of the Second Australian CHISIG Conference. Melbourne. 37 - 44 (1990)

Nelson R.R. and Winter S.G.: An evolutionary theory of economic change. London: Harvard University Press (1982)

Stamper R.A.: Signs, Organisations, Norms and Information Systems In: MacGregor R., Clarke R., Little S., Gould E. and Ang A. (eds): Proceeding of the Third Australian Conference on Information Systems, Wollongong. 21 - 66 (1992)

Swaine M.: User Interface worries. Dr Dobbs Journal, 17, 11, 119 - 121 (1992)

Trauth E.M. and Cole E.: The organisational Interface: A Method for Supporting End User Packaged Software. MIS Quarterly, 35 - 51 (March 1992)

Wixon D., Holtzblatt K. and Knox S.: Contextual Design: An Emergent View of System Design. Proceedings CHI '90. 329 - 336 (April 1990)

# Hierarchical Components of
# Human-Computer Systems

## Mark Sh. Levin

Russia, 113208, Moscow, Sumskoy Proezd 5-1-103,
Tel.: (7-095) 312-57-73
Fax: (7-095) 292-65-11 for"LEVINMARKSH" box 10731

**Abstract.** This paper describes the hierarchical components of human-computer systems (HCS). We will discuss the development and utilization of three packages for the IBM PC: a decision support system (DSS) called 'COMBI' for multicriteria ranking, a hierarchical hypertext system called 'HHS' for multicriteria evaluation, and a DSS for hierarchical design, called 'SED'. The study is based on an analysis of HCS components (information, user, and techniques) and major operations (development, representation, correction, learning and using).

## 1 Introduction

The conventional approach to representing and modeling various components of a human-computer system (HCS) is to use hierarchies [31, 8, 13, 24, 7, etc.]. The movement from elements to a hierarchy of elements is, in our opinion, a major improvement in these systems. Network structures are more complex than hierarchies, and therefore they require significantly more complex operational tools. This point of view is obvious in the fields of combinatorial optimization algorithms [10, etc.]. Complex hierarchies are also used in various information processing systems. General network representation often does not allow for sufficiently simple algorithms and procedures for analysis, design, and transformation. Therefore, the hierarchical approach is the standard one for large scale system and systems engineering [19, 28].

Usually one or two hierarchies are applied. Database hierarchical structures are the usual approach [31]. In this case, many issues of representation, correction and processing are investigated [31, 10, etc.]. Conklin noted that a hierarchical representation of hypertext systems is more natural for users with an engineering background [8]. Saaty used a hierarchical approach for criteria representation and data processing in a well-known analytical hierarchical process [27]. Often, hierarchical structures are applied to planning and problem-solving [32, etc.]. Some papers consider the issues of the design of hierarchical models [2, 12, 34, 33, 14, 25, etc.].

This paper outlines the hierarchical components of HCS. Our consideration is based on the development and utilization of three packages for the IBM PC: DSS 'COMBI' for multicriteria ranking [17], the hierarchical hypertext system 'HHS' which is mainly oriented towards multicriteria evaluation and decision making [15], and the DSS for hierarchical multicriteria morphological design called 'SED' [16]. These DSSs are oriented to standard discrete multicriteria decision making (MCDM) problems: multicriteria selection/ranking and hierarchical design based on ranking and composition.

## 2 Human-computer system components and the use of hierarchies

Fig. 1 and 2 display the following three major components of HCS [31, etc.]:
(i) factual part (information, cognitive data units);
(ii) operational part (techniques, tools, solving schemes);
(iii) human part (user).

In addition, we use the following methodological elements for investigating HCS subsystems:
(a) levels of creativity by Altshuller (fig. 1): (i) usage of initial element, (ii) usage of selected element, (iii) usage of designed new element [3];
   (b) standard functional operations (fig. 2):
   (1) development (design);
   (2) representation;
   (3) correction, analysis, evaluation;
   (4) learning, studying, understanding;
   (5) utilization.

| Part of human-computer system | Levels of creativity (by Altshuler) | | |
|---|---|---|---|
| | Initial components | Selected components | Designed components |
| FACTUAL PART | Initial data (from databases) | Selected data @ | Combinations of data, transformed data |
| OPERATIONAL PART | Initial universal tools | Selected tools oriented to task & user | Designed tools @ |
| HUMAN PART | User | Selected user @ (diagnostics & selection) | Trained user |

@ - example of system

## Fig. 1. Major components of human-computer system and creative levels

Functional operations relate to four stages of user activities which were studied by Norman: (1) forming the intention; (2) selecting the action; (3) executing the action; (4) evaluating the outcome [21]. These actions are based on the well-known decision cycle of Ackoff [1]. In our case functional operations are basic operations for the above-mentioned stages 2, 3 and 4 of user activities. Stage 1 may be executed a priori or as the analysis, evaluation and understanding of the HCS components.

Hierarchical structures provide some features which are oriented to simple execution of the above-mentioned operations. These features involve the following:

(1) clarity and displayability;

(2) facility of analysis and studies;

(3) ease of processing, corrections;

(4) decomposability, including the facility for concurrent execution of operations, distributed processing, for concurrent design by different specialists, etc.

| Components (parts) of HCS | Major Functional Operations | | | | |
|---|---|---|---|---|---|
| | Development (design) | Representation | Correction, Analysis Evaluation | Learning/ studying Understading | Using |
| **I. Information** (factual part) 1. Elements: (a) facts (data collection), (b) connections, (c) logical elements, etc. | Search, Collection, Composition | Text, Image | Adding, Deleting, Transformation | Learning, Analysis | Search, Processing |
| 2. Structures | Design | Text, Graphics | Transformation Approximation Aggregation | Learning, Studying, Analysis | Processing, Adaptation |
| **II. Information processing tools** (operational part) 1. Elements: (a) models, (b) algorithms, (c) procedures, etc. | Selection, Design | Formulas, Description, Graphics | Extension, Modification | Learning, Studying, Analysis, Verification | Implementation, Selection, Adaptation, Composition |
| 2. Solving schemes, solving plans (structures) | Selection, Design | Formulas, Description, Graphics | Extension, Modification | Learning, Studying, Analysis, Verification | Implementation, Selection, Adaptation |
| **III. User** (human part) 1. Elements: (a) Experience (b) Knowledge, (c) Psychophysical features | Selection, Diagnostics, Training | Description, Graphics | Training, Retraining | Learning, Studying as diagnostics | Implementation, Adaptation |
| 2. Creativity | Training | Description, Graphics | Training | Testing | Adaptation |

*Fig. 2. Components of human-computer system and major functional operations*

And it is reasonable to point out the usefulness of working with the composition of elements from different hierarchies. It is important because complex operations based on elements of different HCS parts are coming into practice.

The improvement of creative level is the second major direction for progress in these systems. Thus, we are facing the problems of implementation of functional operations for various HCS components by taking into account an increase in creativity. And these operations have to transform hierarchical elements, including their combinations. An additional important reason is the movement from an off-line mode to an on-line implementation of various functional operations. This requires a higher level implementation of functional operations.

We have acquired a large experience in the design, analysis and transformation of hierarchical models over a period of twenty years. For example, this experience includes the following:

(1) designing hierarchical multilevel models of complex systems [19];
(2) visual representation and understanding of hierarchical graphs [24, 29, etc.];
(3) synthesis of hierarchical structures [33, 2, 36, etc.];
(4) processing tree-like structures [13, 10, etc.];
(5) coordination of hierarchical structures [18, 30]; etc.

The structural modeling tools were studied by Lendaris [14]. In addition it is reasonable to indicate the following three important problems of hierarchy transformation: (i) revealing the hierarchical substructures; (ii) hierarchical approximation; (iii) aggregation of hierarchies.


## 3   Information part

The effective algorithms of tree-like structure processing are well-known (e.g., for binary trees, AVL-tree, etc.). Usually, the operations of search and correction are studied [13, 4, ect.]. We shall consider some issues of design and processing of hierarchical hypertext at the conceptual level, i.e., the issues of development and processing of structures.

Our consideration is based on 'HHS' [15]. The structure of 'HHS' is shown in fig. 3. This system was developed for describing several decision making domains: discrete multicriteria decision making problems, and quality/effectiveness multiattribute evaluation. 'HHS' includes the following sections:

(1) methodology (discrete MCDM-problems, evaluation problems, technological aspects, etc.);
(2) methods, models (selection/ranking alternatives, model design, simulations, clustering, etc.);
(3) application domains as descriptions of various situations (criteria sets, texts, tables for engineering, organizational, economical and ecological tasks);
(4) computer-aided systems (packages descriptions);
(5) description of indices.

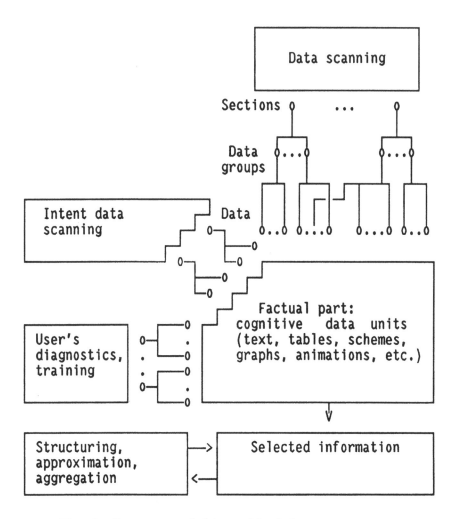

*Fig. 3. Structure of hierarchical hyperetext system*

The main modes of this system are as follows: data collection; modification of data and structure; user's diagnostics and training; search; structuring of information; restructuring of information; approximation of information.

The characteristics of data may be used as special hyper-coordinates. Different sections of the system may be considered as morphological classes and the choice of information in the hypertext system generates the following morpho-analysis operations:

(i) we may reveal several elements in each morpho-class;

(ii) the characteristics of elements may be ordinal/fuzzy;

(iii) it is possible to restructure the selected information.

## 3.1 Some operations of development

The hyper-information system may involve different basic conceptual structural descriptions (universal and/or problem-oriented): technological frames (goal; transforming object; person; tools, etc.); production frame, etc. These standard frames may be useful at the early stages of system development. The process of the HSS development is outlined in fig. 4. It corresponds with the information life cycle [9].

'HSS' was implemented in several additional applications also. Usually the development was based on the following stages:

(a) design of the basic hierarchy (structure, classification, partitioning the problem domain);
(b) collection of data;
(c) adding the other hierarchies and designing the general combined hierarchical structure;
(d) developing the prototype and using it with required modifications.

## 3.2 Representation operations

Representation of hierarchical structures has a large history because it is the traditional approach for data representation [24, etc.].

## 3.3 Correction and transformation operations

These operations are based on selection, composition and approximation. Let us consider the following special operations which are used in 'HHS':

1. Revealing the substructure.
2. Analysis of relations between data or structures.
3. Aggregation of data or structures.
4. Approximating the structure with a similar regular type (tree-like, etc.).

   It is possible to use the following models [15]:

   (a) search of near structure;
   (b) search of structure which has the best features for next operations (representation; correction; analysis; learning; transformation, etc.);
   (c) combination case.

44

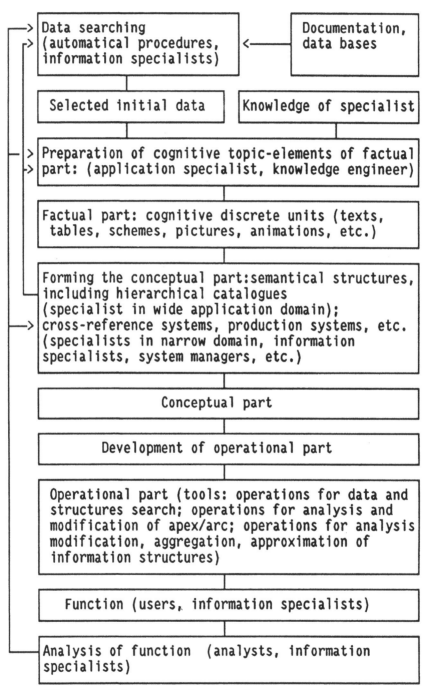

*Fig. 4.   Scheme of hypertext system development*

These models are oriented to the implementation of creative operations such as selection and design (the combination and transformation of structured information). Some of above-mentioned models are studied in the field of preference relation transformation [6, etc.].

### 3.4 Learning and using

We have acquired a great deal of experience in learning and using hierarchical data and hypertext/hypermedia information. This includes experience with hierarchical menus, modes of browsing, etc.

## 4 Human part

Recently, many researchers are oriented to user modeling and evaluating human or team performance in complex systems [26, 5, 7, 35, 37, etc.]. These investigations are executed in cognitive science, management science, knowledge engineering, decision theory, system design, etc.

Our consideration concerns some issues of user's analysis, diagnostics and training which are used in 'HHS' and 'COMBI' [15, 17]. The problem of specialist selection is well-known for various complex engineering systems, but modern computer interactive systems have to implement an on-line mode and it requires the implementation of diagnostics and training of user in this mode also. We consider user knowledge on several technological components of HCS: (i) tasks; (ii) conceptual solving schemes; (iii) algorithms, man-machine procedures; (iv) software; (v) hardware. Many investigations use a similar approach which is related to conceptual modeling [7,26]. Fig. 5 shows a morphoscheme of the user that is based on three levels of user knowledge: (a) preobjective and preoperational; (b) concrete objects and operations; (c) abstract objects and operations [23]. Analogical levels (detailed/specific/concrete - global/general/abstract ones) are applied in some other studies [26, etc.].

Training strategies may be based on the following process: from initial specialist to goal specialist (fig. 5). And the planning of this process is based on the standard training operations [20]: (i) directive indications; (ii) explanations; (iii) observation of examples; (iv) discovery. The elements of the training process based on these operations were partially implemented in 'HHS' and in 'COMBI' (on-line mode).

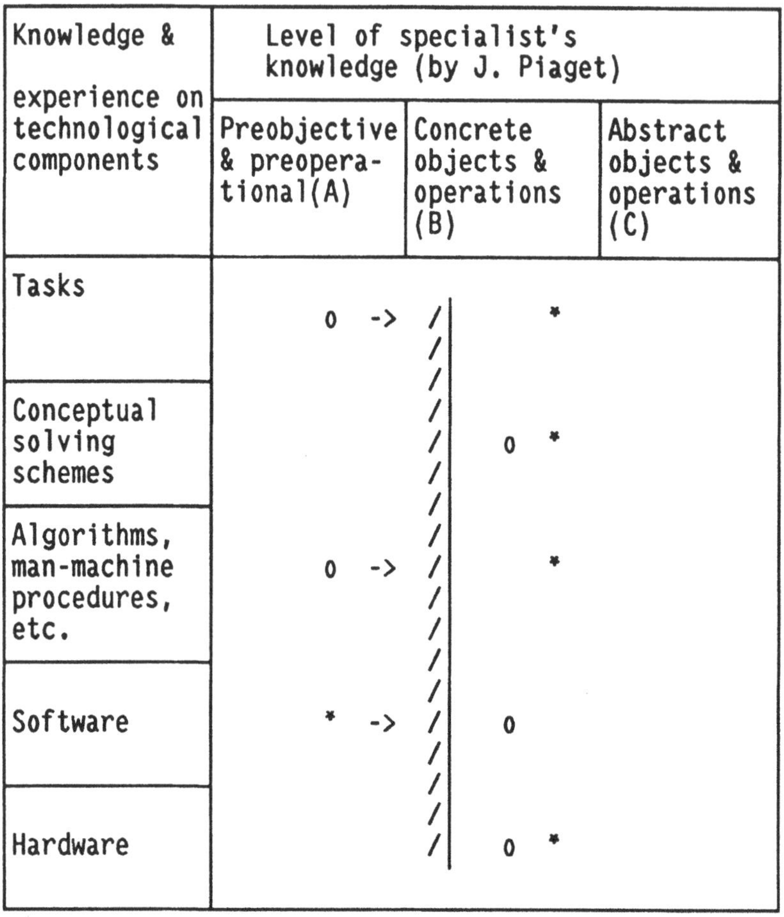

| Knowledge & experience on technological components | Level of specialist's knowledge (by J. Piaget) | | |
|---|---|---|---|
| | Preobjective & preopera-tional(A) | Concrete objects & operations (B) | Abstract objects & operations (C) |
| Tasks | 0 -> / | | * |
| Conceptual solving schemes | / | 0 * | |
| Algorithms, man-machine procedures, etc. | 0 -> / | | * |
| Software | * -> / | 0 | |
| Hardware | / | 0 * | |

*Fig. 5 Morphoscheme of a specialist*

## 5 Hierarchy of the operational part and combined hierarchies

We consider the operational part on the base of the standard MCDM problems: choice or selection, ranking, clustering and their combinations. Fig. 6 shows the morpho-scheme of standard discrete MCDM problems. Thus, the problem-solving process may be represented as a simple sequence of basic actions of standard structural data transformation [6]. It is the more simple representation of user's knowledge [7, p. 5].

| Data type | Notation | Name | Specifying | | | deterministic |
|---|---|---|---|---|---|---|
| | | | complete | incomplete | absent (under development) | |
| initial one | A={1,...,i, ...,n} | Set of objects | o @ | | • | |
| | K={1,...,j, ...,k} | Set of criteria | o | | • | |
| | Z={z,ij} | Estimates | o | | • | |
| intermediate one | G= (A,E) | Preference structure of options | | o | • @ | |
| | Gp=(A,Ep) | Proximity structure of options | | o | • | |
| | Q= (K,V) | Hierarchy of criteria | o | | • | |
| | Qp=(K,Vp) | Proximity structure of criteria | o | | • | |
| resultant one | S | Layer structure (group ranking) | o @ | | | |
| | St | 2-layers structure | | | • | |
| | R | Clustering | | | | |
| | L | Linear ranking | | | | |

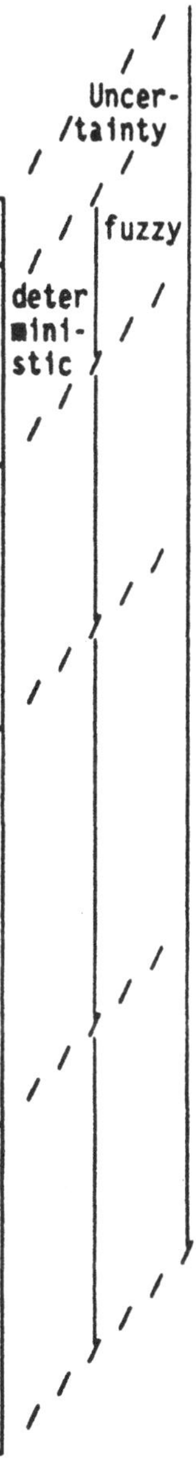

Go, Qo, Gpo, Qpo, Co, So, Sto, Ro - intermediate results
@ - holistic group ranking problem
+ - unique choice problem
o - regular group ranking problem
Main types of problems: clustering -   A=>Z =>Gp=>(Gpo)=>R;
ranking -   A=>Z=>G=>(Go)=>(So,Lo)=>S(St,L).

*Fig. 6. Morphoscheme of discrete MCDM problems.*

Usually, evaluation and selection of technique and the decision-making strategy are investigated in DSSs [22, 38, etc.]. Let us consider the modeling, representation, and on-line design of the operational part. We shall describe the implementation of the following operations: (i) graphical representation; (ii) selection, (iii) design.

Typically, the problem-solving process is based on a hierarchical approach [32, 17]. In the DSS 'COMBI', operational tools are divided into the following hierarchical levels:

(1) algorithm and man-machine interactive procedure for implementation of separate stages of data transformation (basic ones);

(2) strategy, e.g., a hierarchical step-by-step scheme of data transformation, including a parallel-series one;

(3) scenario - iterative process of problem solving based on different strategies with feedback.

The following example illustrates the parallel-series strategy with an aggregation element (Sf is a fuzzy structure):

$$A \dashrightarrow Z \begin{array}{c} \longrightarrow G \rightarrow G_0 \rightarrow S_0 \longrightarrow \\ \longrightarrow G \rightarrow G_0 \rightarrow S_0 \longrightarrow \\ \longrightarrow G \rightarrow G_0 \rightarrow S_0 \longrightarrow \end{array} \longrightarrow Sf$$

Fig. 7 shows a functional graph menu of 'COMBI' which is the network representation of this system. It is the task network model [5]. This network may be called a transition network (GTN) of this system [7, p. 15]. Besides, some vertices of the functional digraph (those are drawn with dotted lines) correspond to data models but others (solid line blocks) represent operations of transformation such as algorithms or man-machine procedures. The technology implemented in DSS 'COMBI' involves the exhaustive strategies of the algorithms and procedures used for the ranking problem. The graphical interface supports the interactive on-line process of problem-solving method design and data transformation. The problem-solving strategy is implemented as step-by-step and parallel-series composition of algorithms and/or man-machine procedures.

Thus, the graph menu of DSS 'COMBI' (fig. 7) implements two hierarchies: operations and data. Another case of combined hierarchies is in the DSS 'SED'. The prototype of this system was developed within the scope of the project which was supported by Israeli Ministry of Trade and Industry (January-September 1992). 'SED' includes a complex of interconnected hierarchies (fig. 8). These hierarchies are represented as a graphical menu on the screen. The hierarchical model of the designed system is the basic one. Other hierarchies are connected with the system model. Finally, the task hierarchy overlaps the system model. The problem-solving process is based on hierarchical concurrent execution of the following task pair: multicriteria ranking of design choices and combining the best design choices of different morphological classes.

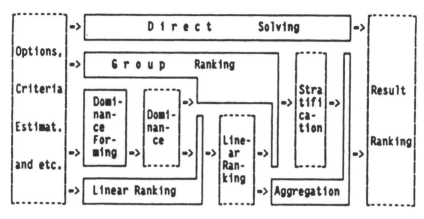

*Fig. 7. Functional graph menu*

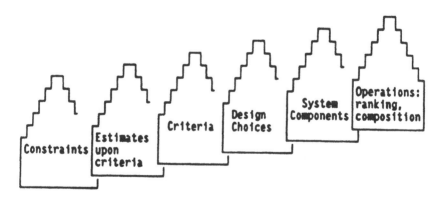

*Fig. 8. Interconnected hierarchies in hierarchical design process*

## 7 Conclusion

Some issues of development, analysis, and transformation of hierarchies and their elements were considered in this paper. It relates to information, techniques, and the user. Recently, many systems include a complex of various components: database, knowledge base, model base, etc. [11, etc.]. As a result, more complicated problems of combining various hierarchies and their elements are important for designing human-computer interaction.

## References

1. R.L. Ackoff: A Concepts of Corporate Planning, New York: A Division of John Wiley & Sons (1966)
2. C. Alexander: Notes on the Synthesis of Form. Cambridge, Mass.: Harvard University Press (1964)
3. G.S. Altshuller: Creativity as Exact Science. The Theory of the Solution of Inventive Problems, Gordon and Breach Science Publishers (1984)
4. A.V. Axo, J.E. Hopcroft, and J.D. Ullman: The Design and Analysis of Computer Algorithms, Addison Wesley (1976)
5. S. Baron, D.S. Kruser, and B.M. Huey (eds.): Quantitative Modeling of Human Performance in Complex, Dynamic Systems. Washington, D.C.: National Academy Press (1990)
6. A.R. Belkin, and M.Sh. Levin: Decision Making: Approximation of Combinatorial Information, Moscow: Nauka Publishing House (1990) (in Russian)
7. J.M. Carrol, and J. Reitman-Olson (eds.): Mental Models in Human-Computer Interaction: Research Issues About What the User of Software Knows. Washington, D.C.: National Academy Press (1987)
8. J. Conklin: Hypertext: An Introduction and Survey. Computer, No 9, 17-41 (1987)
9. A. Dix: Information Processing, Context and Privacy. In: D. Diaper et al. (eds.): Human-Computer Interaction INTERACT'90. New York: Elsevier Publishers B.V., North Holland (1990), pp.15-20
10. M.R. Garey, and D.S. Johnson: Computers and Intractability. The Guide to the theory of NP-Completeness. San Francisco: W.H.Freeman and Company (1979)
11. G.A. Forgionne: Decision Technology System: A Vehicle to Consolidate Decision Making Support. Information Processing & Management, Vol. 27, No. 6, 679-697 (1991)
12. F. Harary, R.Z. Norman, and D. Cartwright: Structural Models: An Introduction to the Theory of Directed Graphs. New York: Wiley (1965)
13. D.E. Knuth: The Art of Computer Programming, Vol. 3. Sorting and Searching, Addison Wesley (1973)
14. G.G. Lendaris: Strtuctural Modeling - A Tutorial Guide. IEEE Transactions on Systems, Man, and Cybernetics, Vol. 10, No. 12, 807-840 (1980)
15. M.Sh. Levin: Hierarchical Hypertext System. Automatic Documentation and Mathematical Linguistics, Ser.2, Vol.23, No.3, 52-59 (1989)

16. M.Sh. Levin: Some Complicated Discrete Multi-Criteria Decision Making Problems. In: Proceedings of Tenth Int. Conf. on Multiple Criteria Decision Making, Taiwan, Vol. 3, 449-458 (1992)
17. M.Sh. Levin, and A.A. Michailov: Fragments of objects set stratification technology. Moscow: Institute for Systems Studies (1988) (in Russian)
18. D. Macko, and Y.Y. Haimes: Overlapping Coordination of Hierarchical Structures. IEEE Transactions on Systems, Man and Cybernetics, Vol. 8, No. 10, 745-751 (1978)
19. M.D. Mesarovic, D. Macko, and Y. Takahara: Theory of Hierarchical Systems. New York: Academic (1970)
20. N.J. Nilsson: Problem Solving Methods in Artificial Intelligence. New York: MacGraw-Hill Book Company (1971)
21. D.A. Norman: Four Stages of User Activity. In: B. Shacket (ed.): Human-Computer Interaction - INTERACT-84. Elsevier Science Publishers B.V. (North Hollands), 507-511 (1985)
22. V.M. Ozernoy: Some Issues in Designing an Expert System for Multiple Criteria Decision Making. Acta Psychologica, Vol.68, 237-253 (1988)
23. J. Piaget: Biology and Knowledge Chicago: The University of Chicago Press (1971)
24. J.S. Reitman-Olson, W.B. Whitten II, T.M. Gruenfelder: A General User Interface for Creating and Displaying Tree-Structures, Hierarchies, Decision Trees, and Nested Menus, Human Factors and Interactive Systems. In: Y. Vassiliou (ed.): Proceedings of the NYU Symposium on User Interfaces, New York, May 26-28, 1982, NJ: Ablex, Norwood, 223-241 (1984)
25. F.E. Roberts: Discrete Mathematical Models. Englewood Cliffs, NJ: Prentice Hall (1976)
26. W.B. Rouse, J.A. Cannon-Bowers, and E. Salas: The Role of Mental Models in Team Performance in Complex Systems. IEEE Transactions on Systems, Man and Cybernetics, Vol. 22, No. 6, 1296-1308 (1992)
27. T.L. Saaty: The Analytical Hierarchical Process, MacGraw-Hill (1988)
28. A.P. Sage: Methodology For Large Scale Systems. New York: McGraw-Hill (1977)
29. K. Sugiama, S. Tagawa, and M. Toda: Method for visual understanding of hierarchical graphs. IEEE Transactions on Systems, Man, and Cybernetics, Vol. SMC-11, 109-125 (1981)
30. K. Tarvainen, and Y.Y. Haimes: Coordination of Hierarchical Multiobjective Systems: Theory and Methodology. IEEE Transactions on Systems, Man and Cybernetics, Vol. 12, No. 6, 751-764 (1982)
31. T.J. Teorey, and J.P. Fry: Design of database structures. Englewood Cliffs, NJ: Prentice-Hall, Inc. (1982)
32. A. Vinze, and A. Sen: Expert Assistance for the Decision Support Process Using Hierarchical Planning. IEEE Transactions "Systems, Man, and Cybernetics", Vol. 21, No. 2, 390-401 (1991)

33. R.J. Waller: The Synthesis of Hierarchical Structures: Techniques and Applications, Decision Sciences, Vol. 7, 659-674 (1976)
34. J.N. Warfield: Toward Interpretation of Complex Structural Models. IEEE Transactions on Systems, Man, and Cybernetics, Vol. 4, 405-417 (1974)
35. M. Wells: Representating the User's Model of Interactive System. In: B. Shackel (ed.): Human-Computer Interaction - INTERACT'84, Elsevier Publishers B.V., North Holland (1985)
36. L. Yelowitz: An Efficient Algorithm for Constructing Hierarchical Graphs. IEEE Transactions on Systems, Man and Cybernetics, Vol. 6, No. 4, 327-329 (1976)
37. R.M. Young, A. Howes, and J. Whittington: A Knowledge Analysis of Interactivity. In: D. Diaper et al. (eds.): Human-Computer Interaction - INTERACT'90. Elsevier Publishers B.V., North Holland, 115-120 (1990)
38. D. Zakay: The role of Personal Tendencies in the Selection of Decision-Making Strategies. The Psychological Record, Vol. 40, 207-213 (1990)

# Synthesis-Oriented Situational Analysis
# in User Interface Design

## Kevin A. Mayo & H. Rex Hartson

Department of Computer Science
Virginia Polytechnic Institute and State University
Blacksburg, VA 24061
(703) 231-4857      (703) 231-6931
*lastname*@cs.vt.edu

**Abstract.** *Analytic evaluation* is a term describing a class of techniques for examining a representation of a user interface design, and discovering design flaws and/or predicting user task performance. In our work with analytic evaluation, we have observed limitations on the effectiveness and efficiency of analytic techniques for formative evaluation supporting the iterative design and re-design cycle. Here we support those observations with arguments based on theoretical limitations of the models underlying these techniques. By way of comparison we discuss desirable characteristics for an alternative approach. In our search for such an alternative, we have developed the Task Mapping Model, a substantively different approach to analysis for supporting the user interface design. We briefly describe the Task Mapping Model and give some examples illustrating its desirable characteristics.

**Keywords:** User Interface Design, User Interface Design Requirements, User Interface Evaluation, Task Description, Task Analysis.

## 1   Introduction

*Analytic evaluation* refers to a class of techniques based on examining a description of a user interface design, often before it is prototyped or implemented, in order to detect usability problems or to predict user task performance. Many of the predictive models associated with these techniques are validated empirically. Analytic evaluation techniques are usually intended as a substitute for early user testing and/or a supplement for later user testing.

One measure of *effectiveness* of a formative evaluation technique is the number of usability problems that can be found in a given design. A related measure, *efficiency*, can be thought of in terms of the number of usability problems identified per unit of designer effort. A measure based on usability problems identified *and solved* per unit of designer effort might be even more useful, since it helps to close the iterative loop by connecting to the redesign process within formative evaluation. These are the kinds of measures we have in mind as we discuss the role of analysis in formative evaluation.

While recently exploring existing analytic evaluation techniques and developing some of our own, we have concluded that most existing models for analytic evaluation are ineffective and inefficient as methods for formative evaluation in an iterative development cycle, for reasons based on the theoretical limitations of the underlying models. We are developing the Task Mapping Model, a model for analyzing usability problem situations highlighted by the empirical formative evaluation process. Knowledge needs that users have for performing tasks are determined, resulting in clear and specific design/redesign requirements for solutions. This papers outlines why we believe that the Task Mapping Model, when used in conjunction with established empirical formative evaluation methods, is inherently more efficient than many commonly known analytic evaluation techniques.

## 2 Background and Related Work

As increasingly intricate computer systems are employed in every area of our society, many people find themselves reluctant computer users. To assist these users in performing computer tasks, human-computer interaction researchers and specialists have devised methodologies and models for aiding the design of complex computer interfaces. These models differ in form and function, including:

*Analysis of user knowledge* (e.g., Action Language [27]; TAG: Task-Action Grammar [26]; TAKD: Task Analysis for Knowledge Descriptions [13]; TKS: Task Knowledge Structures [12]),

*Performance prediction* (e.g., GOMS: Goals, Operators, Methods, and Selection Model [2]; Keystroke Level Model [2]; Cognitive-Complexity Theory [15]), and

*Interface modeling* (e.g., CLG: Command Language Grammar [22]; ETAG: Extended Task-Action Grammar [29]; ETIT [23]).

Most of these involve task descriptions, user mental models, and models of user knowledge for task performance in one way or another. Overviews of these models can be found in [30, 7].

Reisner's Action Language Model [27] is based on a grammatical analysis of a formal grammar description of an interface design. Actions and inputs are viewed as expressions in the language of the user. Complexity measures are applied to grammars of the user's language, revealing inconsistencies, predicting user performance, and identifying design decisions that might cause user errors. The Action Language models computer and user as two cooperating and communicating information processors.

The GOMS model [2] provides a foundation based on psychological theories for purposes of predicting user performance. Complex cognitive tasks are encapsulated within the operators to simplify the modeling. The amount of detail generated in a GOMS interface description allows for a very thorough evaluation at a very low level of detail, but the GOMS description can be an enormous, difficult, and tedious to produce, and typically requires the skills of a trained psychologist.

Using the GOMS model as a basis, Kieras and Polson [14, 15], have built a formal model to describe user knowledge required for the performance of a task and for the use of a device. This model uses computer program-like descriptions, written as sets of production rules of user tasks that are analyzed or run as simulations to predict user performance complexity. Also, Kieras in [16] attempts to relieve the need for psychological training in the NGOMSL model.

The Command Language Grammar approach to user modeling [22] hierarchically decomposes system functions into objects, methods, and operations. The psychological hypothesis underlying the CLG is that ". . . to design the user interface is to design the user's model" [21]. Idealized user knowledge is represented with a somewhat complex grammar having the appearance of a high level programming language. As with GOMS, creating a CLG description is complicated and time-consuming.

The Task Action Grammar [26] is another formal user model—specifically, a cognitive competence model—with a command-language orientation. A meta-language of production rules encodes generative grammars that convert simple tasks into action specifications. As in Reisner's work, a goal of TAG is to capture the notion of consistency. Marking of tokens in production rules with semantic features of the task allows representation of family resemblances, a way of capturing generalities of which the user may be aware [30]. Complexity measures taken on the production rules are predictors of learnability.

Our own perspective in this paper is substantively different from the above approaches, but has several points in common with the work of Carroll and Rosson; we especially recommend their book chapter on usability specification [5]. Like our Task Mapping Model and unlike the predictive models for analytic evaluation, Carroll and Rosson's [3, 4] Task Artifact Framework has a significant empirical flavor. Carroll and Rosson contend that interface designs contain artifacts, user interface objects, that are given meaning by user tasks. The artifacts represent various theories through which properties of the artifacts imply certain psychological consequences with regard to how users will view and use them. The interface designs incorporate certain claims, which are articulated with both positive and negative (Carroll and Rosson's upside and downside) clauses, about how the artifacts support the associated tasks. Later, during evaluation, situated empirical evidence will arise tending to confirm or refute the theory, and redesign, in the context of psychological design rationale, may be necessary as part of the iterative process. The Task Mapping Model also provides a framework in which situations (e.g., critical incidents identifying usability problems associated with tasks) resulting from formative evaluation are analyzed to produce interface design/redesign requirements for supporting user needs.

There is also a class of formative evaluation techniques not based on either formal analysis or empirical user testing. These *review-based* evaluation procedures include cognitive walk-throughs [18], other kinds of walk-throughs [1], heuristic evaluation [24], and other *usability inspection* methods [19]. We believe review-based methods have potential as efficient techniques for formative evaluation; however, the topic is outside the scope of the present paper.

# 3    Theoretical Limitations of Analytic Evaluation Techniques

The limitations in the ability of current analytic evaluation techniques to support the iterative design cycle point directly to desirable characteristics for a more effective approach. The analytic evaluation techniques we are discussing include techniques associated with GOMS, CLG, TAG, TAKD, Kieras and Polson's approach, and Reisner's Action Language Model. In grouping these techniques together, we recognize that they are different techniques and do not all have the same characteristics. However, space does not permit making comparisons one by one, with specific references to the literature. Thus, statements made about limitations apply to the group in general, but each statement does not necessarily apply to every technique.

### 3.1    Analysis vs. Synthesis Orientation

- Current: Most of the analytic evaluation techniques were originally oriented toward analysis, intended to analyze existing interface designs. These methods do not directly support iterative design. To improve an existing interaction design, a developer must create a new design idea, modify the design model, and see if the analysis shows the design to be better.
- Desired: We seek a synthesis orientation, that could be used to capture new interface designs as they occur and to aid the process of creating new designs.

### 3.2    Performance Prediction vs. Design Support

- Current: Many of the analytic evaluation techniques have as a primary goal user performance prediction, and successes have often occurred in special cases where saving a keystroke or two can make a difference. Performance prediction can be used only to compare two designs and, in itself, can suggest nothing to improve a user interface design.
- Desired: We have a goal of more direct design support. In particular, we seek a technique that can produce design/redesign requirements.

### 3.3    Essentially Analytical vs. Essentially Empirical

- Current: The analytic evaluation techniques are based on manipulating design representations and cannot take advantage of empirical data from users.
- Desired: We seek an approach that involves analysis, but is still essentially empirical, able to draw on the strength of empiricism inherent in the iterative design cycle. This distinction is made cogently by Carroll and Rosson [5], as they point out that iterative design itself is essentially empirical.

### 3.4    Error-free Expert Performance vs. Error Handling

- Current: Almost all of the analytic evaluation techniques are based on the assumption of error-free, expert task performance.
- Desired: We seek an approach that considers every task to be a potential error site. As Carroll and Rosson [5] have said, error handling is an essential part of task performance. In fact, error handling itself involves real tasks for interpreting and reacting to feedback, which must also be accounted for in the interface design. The study of error-related situations is essential in designing for usability.

### 3.5 Task Hierarchies Only vs. Temporal Relations

- Current: While most of the analytic approaches produce a hierarchically decomposed task structure, none deal with the temporal relations necessary to provide a complete task-oriented representation of a design.
- Desired: We seek an analytic model in which task descriptions are built upon temporal relations. We need to be able to represent task performance in contiguous time, task interruption, interleaving of tasks in time, and the inter-relationships of concurrent tasks.

### 3.6 Global Modeling vs. Situational Analysis

- Current: The analytic evaluation techniques are global modeling techniques, requiring enormous effort and detail in modeling the entire design before analysis, at any level, can be done.
- Desired: We seek a more *situational* approach that, like the analysis in Carroll and Rosson's task artifact framework, can be applied where it is needed the most—at specific situations or trouble spots identified by formative evaluation—without first having to model the entire system in detail.

### 3.7 Closed-loop vs. Open-loop Interaction

- Current: Most of the analytic evaluation techniques are oriented toward open-loop interaction, where a command is issued and the system executes it.
- Desired: We seek an approach oriented toward closed-loop interaction, which includes direct manipulation and incremental user planning within a tight loop of concurrent action, feedback perception, and adjustment.

### 3.8 Consideration of Different User classes

- Current: Many analytic evaluation techniques cannot take different user class definitions into account.
- Desired: We seek a model for analysis in which user class definitions constitute an explicit separate dimension. The same task situation will yield different design/redesign requirements for different user classes.

### 3.9 Dependency on User Mental Models

- Current: Most of the analytic evaluation techniques are built upon mental models of users. While this facilitates the application of cognitive psychology to the modeling, so far the mental models used have not been powerful enough to provide direct solutions to many of the usability problems encountered in the interface development process. The result is a dependency on mental models, without having sufficient descriptive power of mental processes.
- Desired: We seek an analytic approach that does not depend on user mental models, but that can instead make creative use of empiricism to decide how users view tasks.

## 4 The Task Mapping Model (TMM)

While the TMM can be used for initial design, our discussion here is limited to using the TMM during analysis and re-design of user interface designs.

## 4.1 Supporting the Iterative Interface Design/Re-design Process

Currently we perceive a gap between the formative evaluation phase and re-design phase of user interface design. There is a lack of methodological support for translating formative evaluation findings into new design requirements or solutions. TMM provides methodological support for bridging this gap, as seen in Figure 1. In a nutshell, TMM allows specialists to analyze users' tasks and system interfaces to synthesize new interface design requirements. It is worthwhile to note that TMM analyses produce new interface design requirements and *not* interface design solutions. It is not our intention to tie the hands of the designers, only to aid them in focusing their creativity to meet specific requirements.

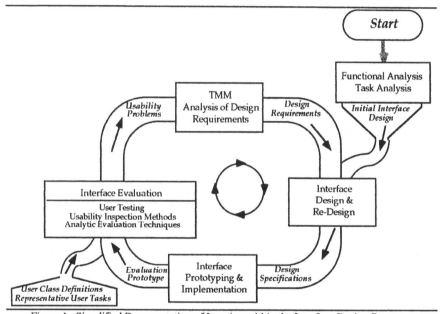

Figure 1. Simplified Representation of Iteration within the Interface Design Process

## 4.2 Task Performance with Computers

It is a basic premise within the Task Mapping Model that the use of computers to perform tasks requires each task to be conceptualized in various domains of abstraction. These domains are viewed as levels (task, semantic, syntactic, and interaction) in CLG [22], which is a model of interaction as well as a model of the interface. Shneiderman, in his model of long term user knowledge [28] calls them the task semantic, computer semantic, and syntactic domains. Since all of the domains contain tasks (just at different levels of abstraction), we prefer to call this first domain the *Problem Domain*. This is the domain in which the user deals with the problem to be solved independently of computer-related considerations.

Figure 2 shows the domains of abstraction that comprise the TMM framework for describing task performance. Each domain contains domain items (actions, objects, and sub-tasks represented in the figure as open circles) associated with its level of abstraction.

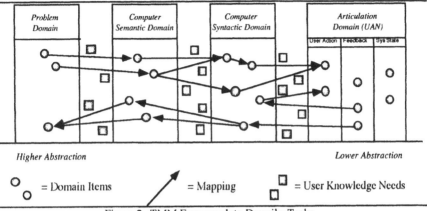

Figure 2. TMM Framework to Describe Tasks

We make three observations about this framework as a model of task performance. Our first observation is that *the user must map* each task to be performed using a computer from one domain to the next, starting from the problem domain, which is known to the user, and going to the computer articulation domain, which contains the necessary physical interactions. Each mappings is shown as arrow in Figure 2, transforming an individual domain item from one domain to the next. The net effect of the mappings between domains is a reconceptualization, by the user, of the task from one domain to the other. The small squares associated with each mapping represent user mapping needs, i.e., knowledge users need to make the mappings. Mappings from higher to lower levels of abstraction correspond to Norman's *execution paths*. [25, 11]

The second observation is that the mappings also exist in the opposite direction—also shown in Figure 2. Originating with the computer feedback in the articulation domain, these mappings represent the abstraction of behavior occurring within interface artifacts back to the problem domain. These mappings from lower to higher levels of abstractions are equivalent to Norman's *evaluations paths*. [25, 11]

The third observation the articulation domain is the site of the User Action Notation (UAN), a task-oriented notation we have developed for behavioral representation of user interface designs [8, 9]. The UAN is based on user actions, system feedback, and interface state changes that occur in the articulation domain.

## 4.3   TMM Task Descriptions

As discussed above, TMM task descriptions are based on a framework within which one can decompose tasks into levels of interaction or abstract domains. This decomposition framework aids well the identification of user knowledge necessary for making the mappings and performing the task, and also provides an indication of

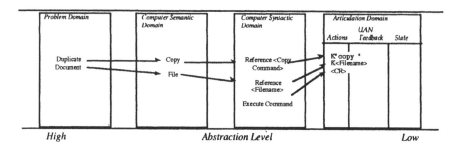

Figure 3:  Example of TMM Domains with Mappings

the level of abstraction corresponding to a given element of this user knowledge.  To elaborate on the four domains that comprise TMM's task description framework:

*Problem Domain*:  Highest level of abstraction that includes items defined within the users' work world, external to the computer system,

*Computer Semantic Domain*:  Highest level of abstraction of computer items involved in a given task being modeled,

*Computer Syntactic Domain*:  Grammatical components of interaction, including commands, computer objects, and associated user actions.  Although more abstract that the specific physical user actions of the articulation domain, these syntactic components are somewhat dependent on interaction style (e.g., action-object order *verses* object-action order, or 'select command' for direction manipulation *verses* 'reference command' for a command line interface).

*Articulation Domain:*  The actual communication sequence between user and computer.  (TMM currently employs the user action notation, UAN [9], as a behavioral notation to describe user action and feedback at the articulation level.)

Figure 3 depicts a command line interface example task (DUPLICATE DOCUMENT) mapped from the problem domain down to the articulation domain.  It should be noted the computer syntactic domain terminology is derived from Lenorovitz's et al. *user-internal* and *user-external* taxonomies. [17]

In order to make the mappings, users have knowledge requirements.  For example, to perform the mapping between DOCUMENT and FILE, the user must know that a DOCUMENT is stored in an abstract computer artifact called a FILE.  Each mapping is potentially associated with a set of knowledge elements—indicating the users' knowledge needs for that mapping.  TMM knowledge elements are not specified within a formal grammar, but in natural language.

The TMM distinguishes different types of knowledge into the following categories:

*Factual Knowledge (FK):*  Specific facts.  E.g., documents are contained in files, files can be grouped into folders.

*Conceptual Knowledge (CK):*  Collections of knowledge that comprises a whole.  E.g., general knowledge about direct manipulation interfaces, pointing devices.

*Procedural Knowledge (PK):* Course of action and outcome knowledge, i.e., knowledge that indicates how to do something necessary for task performance. E.g., double-clicking on a folder shows contents.

The example in figure 4 shows part of a TMM description for the task DISCARD DOCUMENT (problem domain) within the Macintosh environment (computer syntactic domain). Notice that the system feedback starts an evaluation path from the articulation back to the computer syntactic domains, and thus, interaction specialists can incorporate feedback within their analysis. This example also shows various knowledge elements associated with the paths. Of course, this example is only a small piece of the overall description for DISCARD DOCUMENT.

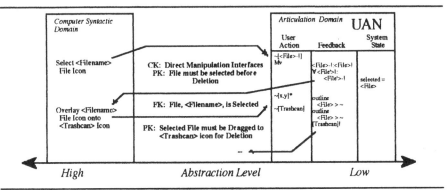

Figure 4: Example Task Description with Knowledge Needs on Mappings

Creating a full TMM task description for a particular task is an iterative process. First a task is chosen, and decomposed as far as possible within the problem domain. (It is possible that only one of its sub-tasks needs to be analyzed.) Next, the task is represented within the computer semantic and syntactic domains, and finally the articulation domain as the user would perceive it. These domains are not foreign to the task analyst, but the notation and mappings among the domains are new. The analyst links related adjacent domain items with mappings and identifies necessary user knowledge for each mapping. This process continues until the analyst is satisfied with the description; satisfaction is attained through task description walkthroughs and peer evaluation.

The *TMM Analysis Guide* [20] further describes notations for knowledge types, variables within task descriptions, and task timing relationships (e.g., sequential, interleaved, concurrent).

## 4.4   TMM Life Cycle

The discussion, thus far, has centered on TMM as a task description technique; however, TMM consists of several methods for describing and analyzing tasks to derive interface re-design requirements. The process begins by focusing on a single situation (thus, we call it *situational analysis*) involving a usability problem identified during formative evaluation. Within the TMM framework, the analysts describe just those user tasks directly related to the usability problem in question, decomposing

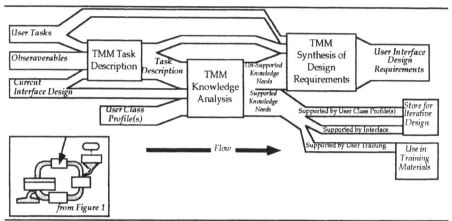

Figure 5. TMM Life Cycle

them over the domains of the model. By analyzing the task description, the designer can determine the total knowledge required by the user to map the task through the domains.

User class profile(s) established for a design, which describe the skills and knowledge users are expected to bring to a task, are used to determine which knowledge requirements can be supported by the user. These are subtracted from the total knowledge needs for the task. Similarly, knowledge already supported in the interface design and knowledge expected to be supported by training can also be subtracted from the total, as shown in the right-hand side of figure 5. The remaining knowledge requirements are unsupported and our experience has been that, by now, these needs are specific enough to be stated almost directly as re-design requirements. Within the broader interface development life cycle these requirement are given to designers who will produce designs, which are passed on to the implementer, and so on back through the iterative cycle of design and evaluation.

TMM provides analyses to derive only interface design requirements and not interface design specifications. This is an important distinction because TMM will not stunt the creativity of the interface designers, only point them to unsupported knowledge needs. This process of task description, analysis for user knowledge needs, and synthesis of interface design requirements represents the TMM life-cycle—depicted in Figure 5.

A complete description of the TMM life cycle, and its component parts, is in [20].

### 4.5 Example

Limited space permits only a brief, simple example to illustrate the TMM life cycle and the production of re-design requirements. Space limitations also preclude the use of forms which have been developed to aid TMM analysts in carrying out this process. Here we can only summarize.

Consider, as part of a broader word processing task, that a user wishes to discard (remove from the system) a specific existing document. In the problem domain, this is an instance of the DISCARD DOCUMENT task that we discussed in section 4.3. In order to make this mapping the user must know that DOCUMENTS on the computer are stored in FILES(factual knowledge, perhaps as part of a body of conceptual knowledge). The user must also know that there is some kind of command (that we are generically calling ERASE here) to remove a FILE within the computer system. So the mapping for this task from problem to computer semantic domain is a mapping of DISCARD DOCUMENT to ERASE FILE. Suppose the user class definition makes it clear that the users we are focusing on should know that documents are stored in files and that files are discarded by erasing, then no re-design requirements are generated.

Next we look at the mapping from the computer semantic to the computer syntactic domain. Since, in the syntactic domain, we are no longer independent of the interaction style of the implementation platform, let us assume we are using an Apple Macintosh computer. The syntax involves a sequence (as seen in Figure 4): SELECT <FILENAME> FILE ICON, followed by OVERLAY <FILENAME> FILE ICON ONTO <TRASHCAN> ICON. A user familiar with the Macintosh will have no problem mapping this to the articulation domain as shown in Figure 4. However, if the user is only a little familiar with desktop-metaphor computers, the knowledge of how to map the ERASE command to the dragging and dropping of the file icon into the trashcan could be missing. In such a case the Macintosh design does not support the users' knowledge needs for this task.

Looking in the user class profile, suppose we determine that, although the user cannot be expected to know the exact command name for erasing, the user will have knowledge the concept of erase (conceptual knowledge). If, however, the profile identifies a general understanding of a WIMP (window, icon, menu, pointer) interface, it is reasonable to assume users in this situation will know how to search for a command name that matches the concept of erase (e.g., by looking at all button labels and through all menus) and, with reasonable command names, will recognize the match when it is found. If the system being used is, say, Microsoft Windows, our analysis leads us to conclude that the user will discover the DELETE command on the FILE menu and the task can be completed. Using the Macintosh, which has no explicit DELETE command for files, the user will not be supported.

This leads directly to the following re-design requirement for this user class and this task: provide an explicit visual cue to aid discovery of the file deletion command. The way in which this requirement is satisfied is the responsibility of the designers and outside the realm of TMM, but it could be something as simple as including a DELETE choice on the FILE menu. To aid learning by the novice user of the drag and drop alternative, the design could also provide animation of the file icon moving over and into the trashcan icon as part of the feedback for the DELETE choice from the FILE menu.

# 5 Conclusions

In our search for an alternative analysis technique for supporting the iterative interface design process [6], we have developed the Task Mapping Model, a substantively different approach. In comparison to the theoretical limitations of most of the established approaches to analytic evaluation, we find the Task Mapping Model more suitable for combining analysis with empirical formative evaluation, as a method for supporting iterative user interface design. Our early experience verifies that this approach possesses most of the desirable characteristics we set as goals for an alternative approach:

- The Task Mapping Model has a synthesis orientation, intended to capture new interface designs as they occur and to aid the process of creating new designs. The Task Mapping Model shares the task orientation of the analytic evaluation models, but is more synthesis-oriented, because the underlying design representation technique (the User Action Notation) was created specifically to communicate interface designs to implementers.
- The Task Mapping Model has a goal of direct design support, rather than user performance prediction, yielding specific design/redesign requirements.
- The Task Mapping Model is essentially empirical in that it is explicitly designed to take advantage of the empirical data generated by formative evaluation and can use empirical observations as models for how users perform tasks.
- Not being limited to error-free, expert task performance, the Task Mapping Model considers every task as potentially an error site. Error handling is described and analyzed just as any other task.
- The Task Mapping Model task descriptions are more complete because they include the temporal relations of the UAN.
- Although the Task Mapping Model can be applied globally to an interface design, a strength of this approach is in situational analysis that can be applied where it is needed the most. Trouble spots identified by formative evaluation can be analyzed without first modeling the entire design.
- The Task Mapping Model is oriented toward closed-loop interaction, which includes direct manipulation and incremental user planning.
- Different user class definitions are an explicit dimension of the Task Mapping Model which uses these definitions to determine very specific user needs.
- The Task Mapping Model does not depend on user mental models (i.e., models of how users store and retrieve information).

TMM fills the gap between formative evaluation and interface design. TMM is a practical task-oriented approach that utilizes situational analysis to derive new user interface design requirements. As a methodology, TMM is still in its infancy and needs empirical validation which is planned as future work.

There are many other avenues of future research for TMM. Task metrics are an obvious extension because of TMM's rich task descriptions. Training is also an area where TMM could be applied. The generated lists of necessary knowledge can provide the bedrock information of user training programs. Moreover, because of TMM's readability, its task descriptions can be used for documentation.

## Acknowledgments

The authors wish to acknowledge the efforts of: Helen Crawford, Sallie Henry, Lucy Nowell, Bill Wake, Robert and Beverly Williges, and the members of the Virginia Tech HCI research group. Ideas expressed in section 3 are also found in [10]. Partial funding of this research was provided by the National Science Foundation, with guidance from John Hestenes. We also wish to extend a special *thank you* to Debby Hix for her insightful comments and continued help with this research.

**CR Categories and Subject Descriptors:** D.2.2 [**Software Engineering**]: Tools and Techniques— *user interfaces*; D.2.1 [**Software Engineering**]: Requirements and Specifications— *methodologies*; H.5.2 [**Information Interfaces and Presentation**]: User Interfaces— *evaluation/methodology, screen design, theory and methods*

## References

1. Bias, R., *Walkthroughs: Efficient Collaborative Testing.* IEEE Software, 1991. **8**(5): pp. 94-95.

2. Card, S. K., T. P. Moran, and A. Newell, *The Psychology of Human-Computer Interaction.* 1983, Hillsdale, New Jersey: Lawrence Erlbaum Associates.

3. Carroll, J. M. *Infinite Detail and Emulation in an Ontologically Minimized HCI,* in *Human Factors in Computing Systems, CHI '90 Conference.* 1990. Seattle, Washington, April 1-5: ACM, pp. 321-327.

4. Carroll, J. M., W. A. Kellogg, and M. B. Rosson, *The Task-Artifact Cycle,* in *Designing Interaction: Psychology at the Human-Computer Interface,* ed. J.M. Carroll. 1991, Cambridge University Press: New York. pp. 74-102.

5. Carroll, J. M. and M. B. Rosson, *Usability Specifications as a Tool in Iterative Development,* in *Advances in Human-Computer Interaction,* ed. H.R. Hartson. 1985, Ablex Publishing Corporation: Norwood, New Jersey. pp. 1-28.

6. Gould, J. D. and C. Lewis. *Designing for Usability—Key Principles and What Designers Think,* in *Human Factors in Computing Systems, CHI '83 Conference.* 1983. Boston, Mass., December 12-15: ACM, pp. 50-53.

7. Haan, G. d., G. C. v. d. Veer, and J. C. v. Vliet, *Formal Modelling Techniques in Human-Computer Interaction.* Acta Psychologica, 1991. **78**: pp. 27-67.

8. Hartson, H. R. and P. D. Gray, *Temporal Aspects of Tasks in the User Action Notation.* Human-Computer Interaction, 1992. **7**: pp. 1-45.

9.  Hartson, H. R., A. C. Siochi, and D. Hix, *The UAN: A User-Oriented Representation for Direct Manipulation Interface Designs*. ACM Trans. on Info. Sys., 1990. **8**(3): pp. 181-203.

10. Hix, D. and H. R. Hartson, *Formative Evaluation: Ensuring Usability in User Interfaces*, in *Trends in Computing: Human-Computer Interaction*, ed. L. Bass and P. Dewan. 1993, John Wiley and Sons: New York.

11. Hutchins, E. L., J. D. Hollan, and D. A. Norman, Direct Manipulation Interfaces, in User Centered System Design, ed. D.A. Norman and S.W. Draper. 1986, Lawrence Erlbaum Associates: Hillsdale, New Jersey. pp. 87-124, Chap. 5.

12. Johnson, H. and P. Johnson, *Task Knowledge Structures: Psychological Basis and Integration into System Design*. Acta Psychologica, 1991. **78**: pp. 3-26.

13. Johnson, P., D. Diaper, and J. B. Long. *Tasks, Skills and Knowledge: Task Analysis for Knowledge Based Descriptions*, in *IFIP Conference on Human-Computer Interaction—Interact '84*. 1984. London, U.K., September 4-7: Elsevier Science Publishers B.V. (North-Holland), pp. 499-503.

14. Kieras, D. and P. G. Polson. *A Generalized Transition Network Representation for Interactive Systems*, in *Human Factors in Computing Systems, CHI '93 Conference*. 1983. Boston, Mass., December 12-15: ACM, pp. 103-106.

15. Kieras, D. and P. G. Polson, *An Approach to the Formal Analysis of User Complexity*. Int. J. Man-Machine Studies, 1985. **22**: pp. 365-394.

16. Kieras, D. E., *Towards a Practical GOMS Model Methodology for User Interface Design*, in *Handbook of Human-Computer Interaction*, ed. M. Helander. 1988, North-Holland: Amsterdam. pp. 135-157, Chap. 7.

17. Lenorovitz, D. R., M. D. Phillips, R. S. Ardrey, and G. V. Kloster, *A Taxonomic Approach to Characterizing Human-Computer Interfaces*, in *Human—Computer Interaction*, ed. G. Salvendy. 1984, Elsevier Science Publishers B. V.: Amsterdam. pp. 111-116.

18. Lewis, C., P. Polson, C. Wharton, and J. Rieman. *Testing a Walkthrough Methodology for Theory-Based Design of Walk-Up-and-Use Interfaces*, in *Human Factors in Computing Systems, CHI '90 Conference*. 1990. Seattle, Washington, April 1-5: ACM, pp. 235-242.

19. Mack, R. and J. Nielsen. *(Workshop) Usability Inspection Methods*, in *Human Factors in Computing Systems, CHI '92 Conference*. 1992. Monterey, California, May 3-7: ACM, pp. 691.

20. Mayo, K. A. *Task Mapping Model Analysis Manual* (TR-93-07). 1993. Department of Computer Science, Virginia Tech (VPI&SU), Blacksburg, Virginia.

21. Moran, T. P., *A Framework for Studying Human-Computer Interaction,* in *Methodology of Interaction,* ed. e.a. Guedj. 1980, North-Holland Publishing Co.: pp. 293-301.

22. Moran, T. P., *The Command Language Grammar: A Representation for the User Interface of Interactive Computer Systems.* Int. J. Man-Machine Studies, 1981. **15**: pp. 3-50.

23. Moran, T. P. *Getting into a System: External-Internal Task Mapping Analysis,* in *Human Factors in Computing Systems, CHI '83 Conference.* 1983. Boston, Mass., December 12-15: ACM, pp. 45-49.

24. Nielsen, J. *Finding Usability Problems Through Heuristic Evaluation,* in *Human Factors in Computing Systems, CHI '92 Conference.* 1992. Monterey, California: ACM, pp. 373-380.

25. Norman, D. A., *Cognitive Engineering,* in *User Centered System Design,* ed. D.A. Norman and S.W. Draper. 1986, Lawrence Erlbaum Associates: Hillsdale, New Jersey. pp. 31-65, Chap. 3.

26. Payne, S. J. and T. R. G. Green, *Task-Action Grammar: The Model and its Developments,* in *Task Analysis for Human-Computer Interaction,* ed. D. Diaper. 1989, Ellis Horwood Limited: Chichester. pp. 75-107.

27. Reisner, P., *Formal Grammar as a Tool for Analyzing Ease of Use: Some Fundamental Concepts,* in *Human Factors in Computer Systems,* ed. J.C. Thomas and M.L. Schneider. 1984, Ablex Publishing: Norwood, New Jersey. pp. 53-78.

28. Shneiderman, B., *Designing the User Interface: Strategies for Effective Human-Computer Interaction.* 1987, Reading, Massachusetts: Addison-Wesley Publishing Company.

29. Tauber, M. J. *ETAG: Extended Task Action Grammar—A Language for the Description of the User's Task Language,* in *IFIP Conference on Human-Computer Interaction—INTERACT'90.* 1990. Cambridge, U.K., August 27-31: Elsevier Science Publishers B.V. (North-Holland), pp. 163-168.

30. Wilson, M. D., P. J. Barnard, T. R. G. Green, and A. Maclean, *Knowledge-Based Task Analysis for Human-Computer Systems,* in *Working with Computers: Theory versus Outcome,* ed. G.C.v.d. Veer, *et al.* 1988, Academic Press: London. pp. 47-87.

# WYSIWYG Editors:

# And What Now?

Eddy Boeve
Lon Barfield
Steven Pemberton

CWI
P.O. Box 4079, 1009 AB Amsterdam, The Netherlands
E-mail: Eddy.Boeve@cwi.nl

**Abstract.** Most editors nowadays are said to be WYSIWYG ('What you see is what you get'). Although this implies that the effects of user actions are made immediately visible to the user, this does not usually include the effects of other causes. This a logical consequence of the fact that the user edits a copy of the document, rather than the document itself. These kind of systems then, can better be classified as 'What you see is what you *will* get' systems.

This report describes an editor model that is a further extension of the WYSIWYG principle: 'Things are exactly as they appear', or TAXATA for short. In these kind of systems, the user carries out every action by editing, and what is more important, by editing the object *directly*. Furthermore, modifications made to objects by the system are made immediately visible to the user.

Amongst other things, the reports describes the underlying model and the necessary editing concepts to construct such a TAXATA editor environment, based on general user-interface principles. Finally the design of one particular edit command has been described, to give an impression of the specific design issues in such an environment.

*1991 CR Categories:* D.2.2 [**Software Engineering**]: Tools and Techniques - *user interfaces*; D.2.3 [**Software Engineering**]: Program coding - *program editors*; D.2.6 [**Software Engineering**]: Programming Environments - *interactive*.

*Keywords:* user-interfaces, syntax directed editors, editor design.

# 1 Introduction

The first interactive user-interfaces used a 'command based' interface: the user (the 'master') gave commands in some arcane command language to the computer (the 'slave'), which then executed the command, or more often, complained about the syntax. Many systems still use command based interfaces. For example command shells such as on UNIX and MS-DOS, and mail programs.

A big step forward were systems based on the WYSIWYG ('What you see is what you get') principle. The term WYSIWYG is usually applied to text formatting systems in which a document being edited appears on the screen as close as possible as it would appear when printed in hard-copy format. In a much broader sense the same principle can be applied to systems in which the effect of a user action is made instantly visible.

The WYSIWYG principle is often bracketed together with *direct manipulation*: a physical action by the user — moving an icon, hitting a key, changing a name — has a direct visible effect in the world of the computer. As with WYSIWYG, the notion of direct manipulation is still used in a narrower sense than warranted: restricted to spatial metaphors such as manipulating icons on a desktop. For instance, many people see selecting an icon and dragging it to the trash can as direct manipulation, while selecting the icon and pressing the delete key as not. A much more common form of user control that can also be viewed as direct manipulation is that of entering text while editing a document: each key hit appears on the screen. Yet another form is that in which modifying the name of a document as it appears in some caption (like a window title) also changes the document name as it is stored in the file system. See [19] for an overview of direct manipulation related aspects.

There is an important drawback to current systems using either the WYSIWYG or the direct manipulation principle: the effects of user actions are made immediately visible to the user, but not the effect of other changes to the file. This is a logical consequence of the fact that the user edits a copy of the document, rather than the document itself. This phenomenon — editing copies instead of the real thing — has not only become a natural habit in editors, but in almost all computer environments. In non-computer work though, besides handing out copies to other people, copies are usually only made in situations when there is a fear of losing some important work. This is comparable with the fear of losing work on computer systems with insufficient facilities of undoing mistakes.

The consequences of these drawbacks for applications modelled on this WYSIWYG principle can be manifold. When editing a document in some text editors, the fact that the user is editing a copy of the document is hidden from the user, but in certain situations this still shows up. For instance, when exiting the editor the document has to be written into a file on disk. If it is the first time the document is written, the user also has to invent a unique name for it. Should the editor crash (due to software or power failure), most of the work done before the accident is lost. Luckily most editors provide some automatic backup facilities in these situations such as 'auto-save' or 'auto-recover'. See Figure 1-A.

On many 'windowing' or 'multi-tasking' systems it is possible to switch tasks while working with the editor. When switching, suddenly two versions of the document exist: the one being edited in memory and the original version on disk. Unexpected things happen when the user accidentally starts editing the original document on disk. In the worst case a lot of editing work is lost, in the best case the user is confused by this phenomenon. See Figure 1-B.

On machines connected together via networks, the same effect can be caused by a colleague on another machine editing the same files the user is currently editing. When examining a listing of editor documents in the user's workspace — for example to decide which document to load into the editor — changes made to this directory from outside the application are normally not made visible to the user. Unexpected things

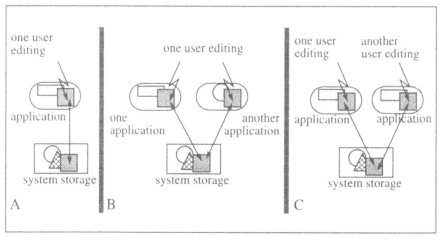

**Fig. 1.** Three WYSIWYG examples.

can happen when the user tries to load a newly deleted document or cannot find a newly created document and starts creating a new one with the same name. See Figure 1-C.

Considering these examples of behaviour of so-called WYSIWYG systems, we can in fact better classify them, as Thimbleby did in [22], as 'What you see is what you *will* get' systems. A further extension of the WYSIWYG principle is where the projection of the data works in both directions. We call this: 'Things are exactly as they appear', or TAXATA for short. The user carries out every action by editing, and what is more important: as far as the user is concerned, by editing the object *directly*. Furthermore, modifications made to objects in the system are made immediately visible to the user.

The authors have already implemented a running prototype, demonstrating some aspects of this editor model: the Views System [17]. Views is an experimental application environment, supplying a framework that new applications can be added to ('open-architecture') and offering a consistent and integrated user-interface across applications. As all communication between the user and the system takes place by means of an inbuilt editor, the design of this editor requires more care even than user interface design does in general.

This report discusses the model underlying such a TAXATA environment.

## 2  Design Principles

Many systems appear to be designed without a proper high-level user-interface model. So before describing our high-level TAXATA model, we will first discuss some high-level design rationales for user-interfaces. Later on we will try to translate these to practical design rules for the TAXATA environment described in this report.

In Human Computer Interaction literature a lot is written about 'design principles'. When we quote some well known authors in the HCI community, we find for instance Norman [16] with '*Make things visible*' to bridge the gulfs of execution and evaluation, *'Design for error'* and *'Exploit the power of constraints'*. In [20] Swinehart presents his *'Principle of least astonishment'*: design a system, or its features, to surprise the user as little as possible. Timbleby lists in [21] the following general design rules: *'Make explanations brief'* (an essential part of designing user interfaces is to explain them, but keep it brief), *'Recoverable'*, *'Mode-free'*, *'Evaluate'* and *'Adopt user experience'*. Finally we quote Nielsen's *'Be consistent'* rule [15].

Although these principles look good at first sight, when applying them to a specific high-level task such as designing an editor, they can be too general or too specific for such a task. For example, Grudin shows in [10] that Nielsen's *'Be consistent'* rule is, when designing a specific application, often too strict. And Barfield argues in [3] that modes are only a problem when there is a lack of mode specific feedback.

Meertens et al. formulated in [14] some basic design rules to guide the design of the structure editor for the ABC programming language and environment [9]:

- *Fair-expectation rule*
  If a concept may be lawfully used in one context, and the same concept is (conceptually) applicable in another context, then it may be lawfully used in that context, with the expected meaning.

- *Economy-of-tools rule*
  The number of concepts is small, but the concepts themselves are powerful and on the appropriate, task-oriented, abstraction level.

It is apparent that these two rules are of a different nature. The application of the first one requires an understanding of the task domain. The way it was used was as follows. For 'candidate' concepts they asked the question: what (higher-level) tasks would they be useful for, and what were the most appropriate *basic* concept(s) for addressing these specific tasks. While it may not be obvious that this helps to keep the set of 'tools' small, it actually does, in particular in combination with the 'economy-of-tools rule', whose application is fairly straightforward. Other design rules that they used, but were not elaborated upon in their report are:

- *Uniformity rule*
  Similar concepts are embodied in a similar way.

- *Logic-error rule*
  The embodiments of the concepts are such that errors cannot arise if this is avoidable by choosing the right embodiment. If this is impossible, then errors are either signalled on concept invocation or signalled before disaster strikes.

- *One-concept-at-a-time rule*
  There are no concepts that mutually depend on each other to fully understand them.

- *semantic-distance rule*
  No two concepts of the system are almost the same.

While these rules were not intended as hard-and-fast design steps to be followed, they did prove to be extremely useful goals when making design decisions. The next section discusses the consequences of these 'Meertens Rules' for the design of a TAXATA editor.

# 3 The TAXATA Editor

The editor described in this report is a *hybrid generic editor*. There is one single editor for all kinds of documents ('generic') and structured and unstructured editing is fully intermixed ('hybrid'); there are no separate editor modes. The editor is fully visible and has therefore no memory of its own. The effect of a command depends only on the state of the document and not on the way that state was reached.

Usually the document visible on the screen is linked to a more structural internal document. Edit operations are interpreted as operations on the internal document, rather than on the unstructured external form. The user cannot edit 'protected' or 'read-only' fields directly (they are added by the function that presents internal objects on the screen), but they can, however, be copied just like other objects.

We discuss the main design issues of the editor, together with the connection with the 'Meertens Rules', in the following subsections.

## 3.1 Every object in the system is editable.

This is a logical consequence of the 'fair-expectation rule'. Users are often surprised by objects that are made visible to the user, but cannot be edited directly by them. For example, on the Atari ST, the system presents documents in the file store by icons labelled with the file name (the well known 'desktop metaphor'). Although these icons can be manipulated directly for edit actions such as copying and deleting, the file name label cannot be edited directly by the user to change the name of the file on disk. The renaming is done by first selecting the icon, then selecting the 'Info' entry under the 'File' menu, changing the name mentioned in the dialogue box after 'Document Name:' and finally pressing the 'OK' button. To novice users of the system this inability to edit the name directly to achieve the renaming comes as a surprise.

## 3.2 Every action is carried out by editing.

This property obeys the 'economy-of-tools rule'. Recent work in user interface design has suggested that editing can be used as a general model of interaction [7, 6]. There are no separate commands for doing specific actions: the user just edits the value with the basic editor commands to obtain the desired value. In the Views System, in general, objects are functionally related with other objects. These relations — called invariants or constraints — are maintained by the system. Performing actions is modelled by changing one or more of the related objects, resulting in updates of other involved objects.

User interaction takes place on the presentation level of the editor, but the system interprets this as interaction with the underlying structured document. Therefore the word 'editing' is used in the broad sense of the word: direct manipulation actions as pressing buttons and moving sliders are handled as edit actions on underlying object structures that implement the functionality of the interaction tool (see [4]).

## 3.3 The object is edited directly.

Since the system is designed to be equally usable for trained computer users as well as users with little or no knowledge of computers, it pays to base the elements of the conceptual model on real-world examples, rather than on computer-science examples.

As we saw before, a good example of such an design aim is the fact that rather than editing a copy of a document in a buffer, that periodically and at the end has to be saved, the user is always editing the document itself.

The editor is 'modeless'; the user is never confronted with different modes of operation. There is instant feed-back on the edit action performed and no notion of 'edit buffers' or 'saving work' in the model. Once an object has been created, it will stay in existence until deliberately deleted by either the user or the system ('garbage collecting'). The same holds for changing the value of an object. Due to the directness of the edit actions, a comprehensive 'undo' facility must be provided to the user (see Section 3.6).

### 3.4 The user edits the presentation of the object.

For the user the presentation is 'all there is' and edit actions have the presentation of the internal document as input parameter. But the system interprets the edit operations as modifications to the internal structured object, rather than to the unstructured external form. For example, the user can copy a slider position to a numeric field whose external presentation is textual. The user can also copy a piece of text to a numerical field, but only if that text represents a number.

### 3.5 There is a general 'selection' concept.

To restrain the number of edit commands ('economy-of-tools rule'), it has proven to be useful to introduce the concept 'edit focus' [11, 12, 13, 14]. The focus is a highlighted area, which generalises the notion of a 'cursor position'. The user can 'focus' on a certain part of the object structure on the screen and commands applied by the user will work on the current contents of the focus. Focus selections and movements work on the object structure presented on the screen. Objects that are focused on are highlighted in some way for the user. The focus is part of a document. A consequence of this is that a record of the last focus is always 'remembered' with each document when it is not being edited. In [1] a set of focus commands on structured documents is given, also suitable for the TAXATA editor presented here.

### 3.6 All edit actions can be undone.

The one real advantage of the 'copy-in-a-buffer' editing model in many systems, is that a user can always abandon the changes and even revert to the original copy. This is offset in the TAXATA editor design by providing a general unlimited undo facility, unlimited in the sense that an arbitrary number of edit operations can be undone. The effects that these operations had on the system state are undone as well. Some actions, like printing a document or sending mail, can in general not be undone. This limitation applies only insofar as physical effects external to the 'metasystem' consisting of user and system are caused by edit operations; otherwise, all operations can be undone. Not only modification operations can be undone by the undo facility, but also navigation operations (e.g. focus movements) can be undone.

Such an undo is not only vital in an environment in which all user actions take immediate effect, it has the added advantage that users are encouraged to try actions out to see their effect; if some action does not exactly what was wanted; it can always be undone.

### 3.7 There is only a small set of basic edit concepts.

Due to the general selection concept, the set of edit concepts can be kept small ('economy-of-tools rule') and they always have the focus as only input parameter. The set of basic commands has been carefully designed with the 'semantic-distance rule' in mind. It is not envisaged that all commands of the full command set will be meaningful for all document kinds. But due to the 'fair-expectation-rule', however, if a specific command is meaningful in a given context, it is also allowed there and has the expected effect.

### 3.8 Results of edit actions are consistent.

As a combination of the 'uniformity' and 'fair-expectation rule', edit actions always have a predictable and consistent result.

## 4 Editing Objects

An object can be for example a text document, the clock, a diagram, or a menu. Objects can be, and almost always will be, structured. To resemble the idea of performing actions by editing these kind of structured objects, we will use the metaphor 'documents' for structured objects in the system. Beside a *structure*, the way the contents of the object is structured, objects have an *interpretation* and a *presentation*. The object's interpretation describes the way the user envisages how the object structure has to be interpreted. The presentation describes how the object has to be presented to the user. These three properties are described in more detail below.

### Structure

As the word already suggests, the object structure defines the way the contents of the object is structured. We distinguish two kinds of structures: the *basic* structures and the *group* structures. Some examples of basic structures are *numeric, character* and *text*. We use these basic structures as building blocks are the group structures:

- ◆ *compound*
  This can be compared with 'records' in other systems and languages. An object of this structure can contain any of the structures mentioned here, including other compounds.

- ◆ *sequence*
  A list of any of the structures mentioned here. Normally the items in a list must be of the same structure, but by using either the 'choice' or 'any' structure (see below), structures can be mixed in a sequence.

Finally we have two structures that do no fit exactly in the basic and group structures. We shall call them *selection* structures:

- ◆ *choice*
  One of the structures mentioned in the declaration of the choice structure.

♦ *any*

Any of the basic, group and selection structures.

When an object has a certain structure, but the contents of that structure has not been set to a value, we will denote the object as being *empty*.

### Interpretation

The interpretation of an object describes the way the user envisages how the object structure has to be interpreted. For instance, depending on the interpretation, an object structure defined as the compound of three numbers can be either seen as the (x, y, z) of a three-dimensional coordinate, or as the day, month and year fields of a date.

### Presentation

The way an object will be displayed to the user is separated from the object's contents. Changing the presentation of an object or changing the contents of an object will adjust the presentation on the screen accordingly. The object structure, interpretation and presentation are closely related. For instance, there could be an interpretation 'clock' in the system, describing a three number compound (hours, minutes and seconds). The graphical presentation belonging to this interpretation will state something like: 'present the time graphically as a circle with two hands on the screen'. Another presentation for this clock interpretation could state: 'present the time textually as three numbers separated by semicolons'. Even if both clock presentations are shown simultaneously on the screen, they still are one and the same underlying clock object (hence the name 'Views' for the system).

### 4.1 Editing objects

In current edit environments the user-interaction is often modelled as in Figure 2. The user applies actions to selected objects on the screen. In fact, these are commands from a master (the user) to a slave (the system). The system in its turn applies the commands to the appropriate data structures in memory. Finally the world (the data storage, special system objects, the presentation on the screen) are changed to fit the changes made by the user.

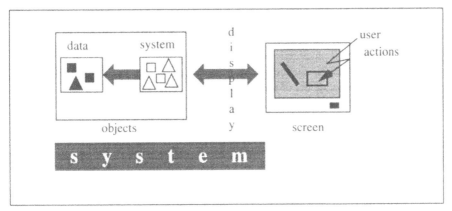

**Fig. 2.** Modelling user-interaction in current edit environments.

In Figure 3 we see the TAXATA user-interaction model. The user applies edit actions on the objects presented on the screen. But there is no master-slave relation in this model: the edit actions are performed on the internal objects directly.

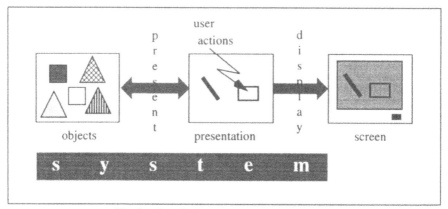

**Fig. 3.** Introducing the presentation level in the model.

Internal objects in the system (the *object level*) are presented on the screen using the presentation description for that object. This presentation is specified using basic graphical and structure descriptions. Such a presentation can still be seen as living within the system. The user performs the edit actions on this level: the *presentation level*. Finally this presentation is brought on the screen as a bitmap (the *bitmap level*). The relation between the presentation level and the object level (the present function) has been drawn in the figure as a two-way arrow, because the user-interactions on the presentation level are modelled with the help of two-way invariants: changing the objects on the presentation level will change the objects on the object level and vice-versa. The relation between the bitmap level and the presentation level (the display function) is modelled as a one-way relation. In [8] a model is described for maintaining presentation invariants under editing.

## 5 Consequences for Designing Commands

Interaction with the (structured) object is done via the presentation on the screen. Often the user will not (or cannot) be aware of the underlying object structure and will build and use her own model of the world she is editing. When, for instance, the user copies a part of the contents of a letter containing a number, and pastes this textual part in a list of numbers in a spread-sheet application, she will probably not be aware of the difference in the underlying object structures (lists of characters versus lists of numbers) and expect that she can normally use the pasted number string as a numeric value in her spread-sheet application.

When the user thinks it should be possible to copy an object from one place and paste it in another place where the system 'expects' different interpretations, conversion should take place to perform these action. For instance, the user can copy a piece of text to a numerical field, but only if that text has a number format. On the other hand, the user can copy a slider position in a graphical scrollbar to a numeric field whose external presentation is textual. The system should take care of the necessary conversions.

To sketch the consequences of the TAXATA model on the semantic behaviour of these commands, we will give the example of designing one basic command, well-known in other traditional applications: the *insert* command.

## 5.1 Insertion

There are a lot of edit commands that use in one format or another the basic 'insert' command: paste, keyboard input, etc. One aspect we will look at in more detail are the conversion aspects belonging to insertion. In general there can be a mismatch on a range of properties of the data inserted and the properties if the location where it is inserted. Properties we will look at are interpretation, structure and presentation and we will regard the situations where they all match, partially match or do not match at all. Although they are not directly part of the objects involved in the action, context information ('where did the action take place?', 'What other objects are closely related to the object copied?', etc.) and other additional information (heuristics, user advise) can also be involved in finding out the right system reaction.

For all clarity: when we say 'the interpretations of these objects match', we implicitly say that also the structures of the objects match, due to the definition of object interpretations. This cannot be reversed: objects with the same structure can (and often will have) different interpretations. In this way we have to investigate the combinations summed in Table 1.

| Structure | Interpre-tation | Presen-tation | For description, see subsection: |
|:---:|:---:|:---:|---|
| + | + | + | *'All properties match'* |
| + | + | - | *'Same interpretation and structure, different presentation'* |
| + | - | + | *'Same structure and presentation, different interpretation'* |
| + | - | - | *'Same structure, different interpretation and presentation'* |
| - | - | + | *'Same presentation, different interpretation and structure'* |
| - | - | - | *'No match at all'* |

**Table 1.** Property match (+) or mismatch (-) when inserting data.

The following subsections will describe these combinations using a familiar insert command: copying information from one position to another.

## All properties match

When we insert an object in a place where the definition of the object structure defines an object of exactly the same interpretation and presentation, we are lucky and can just insert the object there.

In the case of copying an object and pasting it into another place where all properties match, we can have the copy situations as shown in Figure 4. In the first example a copied date object is pasted onto an 'empty' object, an object without a contents. The figure also shows a possible presentation of such an empty object: templates ( **interpretation** ) identifying the interpretations expected there. On the other hand, the selection can also be as in the bottom example of Figure 4: a single insertion point between two other date objects.

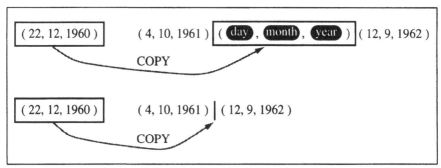

**Fig. 4.** All properties match.

Although the situations look quite different from the outside, the copy command has identical results after applying the command. In the first example, the destination *object* matches the source object. In the latter example the destination *position* where the paste should take place, matches the source object.

### Same interpretation and structure, different presentation

Things become more complex when only a sub-set of properties match. Although interpretations can match, the presentation can be quite different (see Figure 5).

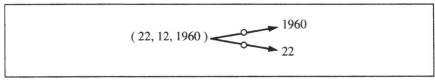

**Fig. 5.** Presentation mismatch.

The date object has been presented twice as an projection of one of the compound fields: first only the year field and finally only the day field. It might be obvious what the user expects to happen if we select one of the projected fields, say the year '1960' field, and paste another date interpretation compound there: the '1960' will be replaced with whatever the year of the copied object was. But what will happen if we have both projection presentations on our screen, we copy the year field, '1960', and paste it onto the selected day field, '22'? There are two obvious system responses possible:

- ◆ *the '22' value changes to '1960'*
  the interpretations of the two presented and selected fields do not match ('year' versus 'day'), but the structures do (both single integer values), so the system copies the year integer value to the day integer position, overwriting the day value.

♦ *nothing changes*

the system knows that both the day as the year field are sub-fields of objects that have identical interpretations (in this case even the same object) and decides to copy the '(22, 12, 1960)' value onto itself, overwriting the value '22' with its own value.

The copy problem sketched above can be stated differently: does the selection mechanism work on the visible presentation of the object or on the underlying object structure? As we stated before, for the user 'the presentation is all there is' and in that light the first system reaction, replacing the '22' with the copied '1960' value, is preferable to the second reaction.

### Same structure and presentation, different interpretation

In Figure 6 we see a copy of the date object from the previous examples to a compound of different interpretation, also containing three fields, but where the field *structures* do match those of the copied object (for instance, a three-dimensional coordinate).

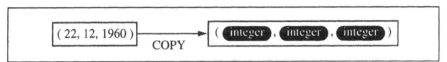

**Fig. 6.**   Interpretation mismatch.

The system has only one reasonable reaction in this case: copy the '22', '12' and '1960' values to the corresponding integer fields.

### Same structure, different interpretation and presentation

In Figure 7 we see the date compound copied to a presentation of a 3D-coordinate compound. For clarity, here we present the interpretation information as a combination of a name and an interpretation ( name: interpretation ) and where *'int'* stands for an arbitrary integer number.

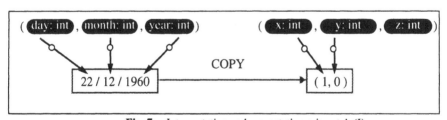

**Fig. 7.**   Interpretation and presentation mismatch (I).

It seems a logical reaction to copy all the three date fields to the coordinate compound, although only two of the coordinates has been presented. The result would be '1' replaced by '22' and '0' replaced by '12'.

But as we saw in *'Same interpretation and structure, different presentation'*, this can have a unpredictable (and perhaps unwanted) result. In Figure 8 we see almost the situation as in Figure 7, but we changed the presentation slightly.

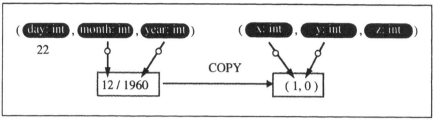

**Fig. 8.** Interpretation and presentation mismatch (II).

When the systems follows the same strategy as in Figure 7, we certainly would not get the result (12, 1960), but the somewhat awkward result '(22, 12)'.

### Same presentation, different interpretation and structure

In Figure 9 we see an example of an often occurring mismatch between interpretations and structures, but where the presentation exactly matches: copying a sequence of characters (all digits) from a text and pasting it into a list of numbers.

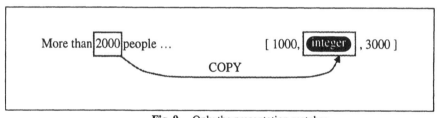

**Fig. 9.** Only the presentation matches.

Obviously the string '2000' should be converted by the system to match the integer specification at the destination location. This system reaction can in general involve much more complex conversions, e.g. the conversion of the string '22 December 1960' to a compound of three numbers: (22, 12, 1960).

### No match at all

Although this seems to be a hopeless case, the user can see reasons to do perform such an action. For instance, in Figure 10 we see the user copying the string '1 plus 4 equals 5' to a compound of two integers.

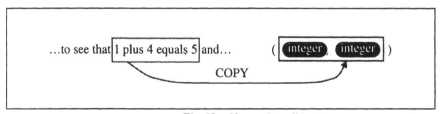

**Fig. 10.** No match at all.

The result can be such that the first two numbers ('1' and '4') of the copied object are placed in the compound object: (1, 4).

# 6 Conclusions

In this report we examined some problems with current WYSIWYG and direct manipulation editors and tried to give a solution for some of them: the TAXATA edit model. We formulated a framework of high-level design rules, appropriate for designing the overall model of the TAXATA editor. We gave one example of designing such operations: the design of the 'insert' command. The example stresses the fact that using these rules for designing edit commands, demands more effort of the designer, but results in powerful edit operations — and what is more important — that operates the way the user expects. Although the design of other general edit operations in the model works identically, still some research has to be put in finding a 'basic' set of operations, suitable for all kind of data types.

As stated before, the basic aspects of the model described in this report have already been implemented by the authors in the Views System. The next step in the project is the development of specific Views applications (see [5] and [18] for two examples of recent applications). Since the set of basic commands depends heavily upon the kind of applications being developed, the tuning of existing editor commands and the design of new ones will go on in parallel with the design and evaluation of new applications.

# 7 References

1. Barfield, Lon. *Editing Tree Structures.* Report CS-R9264. CWI, Amsterdam, 1992.

2. Barfield, Lon. *Graphics in the Views System.* Report CS-R9260, CWI, Amsterdam, 1992.

3. Barfield, Lon. *The User Interface. Concepts & Design.* ISBN 0-201-54441-5, Addison-Wesley Ltd., 1993.

4. Boeve, Eddy. *Modelling Interaction Tools in the Views Architecture.* Report CS-R9261, CWI, Amsterdam, 1992.

5. Bordegoni, M. *Multimedia in Views,* Report CS-R9263, CWI, Amsterdam, 1992.

6. Dewan, Prasun and Solomon, Marvin. An Approach to Support Automatic Generation of User Interfaces. In *ACM Transactions on Programming languages and Systems,* **12** (4), pp. 566—609, October 1990.

7. Fraser, C.W. A Generalized Text Editor. In *Communications of the ACM,* **23** (3), pp. 154—158, March 1980.

8. Ganzevoort. J. *Maintaining presentation invariants in the Views system.* Report CS-R9262, CWI, Amsterdam, 1992.

9. Geurts, L.J.M., Meertens, L.G.L.T. and Pemberton, S., *The ABC Programmer's Handbook.* ISBN 0-13-000027-2, Prentice-Hall, 1989.

10. Grudin, J. The Case Against User Interface Consistency. In *Communications of the ACM,* 1989. **32** (10), pp. 1164—1173.

11. Huls, C. and Dijkstra, A. Structured Design of Word Processing Functionality, In *Proceedings of the HCI '92 Conference,* pp. 291—306, September 1992.

12. Koorn, J.W.C. Connecting Semantic Tools to a Syntax-Directed User-Interface, Report P9222, University of Amsterdam, December 1992.

13. Logger, M.H. *An Integrated text and syntax-directed editor.* Report CS-R8820, CWI, Amsterdam, 1988.

14. Meertens, L.G.L.T., Pemberton, S. and Rossum, G. van. *The ABC structure editor — Structure-based editing for the ABC programming environment.* Report CS-R9256, CWI, Amsterdam, 1992.

15. Nielsen, Jakob. *Coordinating User Interfaces For Consistency.* Academic Press, 1989.

16. Norman, Donald. A. *The Psychology of Everyday Things.* ISBN 0-465-06709-3, Basic Books, Inc., New York, 1988.

17. Pemberton, S. *The Views Application Environment.* Report CS-R9257, CWI, Amsterdam, 1992.

18. Pemberton, S. and Barfield, Lon. The MUSA design methodology. Report CS-R9262, CWI, Amsterdam, 1992.

19. Shneiderman, B. Direct Manipulation: A Step Beyond Programming Languages. In *IEEE Transactions on Computers,* **16** (8), pp. 57—69, August 1983.

20. Swinehart, D.C, Zellweger, P.T., Beach, R.J. and Hagmann, R.B. A Structural View of the Cedar Programming Environment. In *ACM Transactions on Programming Languages and Systems,* pp. 419—490, **8** (4), October 1986.

21. Thimbleby, Harold. Basic User Engineering Principles for Display Editors. In *Pathways to the Information Society. Proceedings of the Sixth Informational Conference on Computer Communications*, pp. 537—541, M.B. Williams (Ed.), September 1982, London. North Holland Publ. Co. Amsterdam, 1982.

22. Thimbleby, Harold. User Interface Design. ACM Press (Addison-Wesley Publishing Company), pp. 247-249, ISBN 0-201-41618-2, New York, 1990.

# Architecture Elements for Highly-Interactive Business-Oriented Applications

François Bodart, Anne-Marie Hennebert, Jean-Marie Leheureux,
Isabelle Sacré, Jean Vanderdonckt

Facultés Universitaires Notre-Dame de la Paix, Institut d'Informatique
Rue Grandgagnage, 21, B-5000 Namur (Belgium)
Tel : + 32- (0)81- 72 50 06 - Fax : + 32- (0)81- 72 49 67 - Telex : 59.222 Fac. Nam.B
E-mail : fbodart@info.fundp.ac.be

**Abstract.** It is now widely recognized that powerful architecture elements are
needed for implementing highly-interactive business-oriented applications during at least two stages of the whole lifecycle, namely the specification and the
design. In this paper, we deal with the architecture model of the TRIDENT
project, which introduces three components : the semantic core component, the
dialog component and the presentation component. This is a hierarchical object-oriented architecture relying on the use of three kinds of objects : application objects, dialog objects, and interaction objects. Specification and rule
languages are given for developing the dialog component. An abstract data
model is used for characterizing the application objects. Selection rules are
given for choosing appropriate interaction objects for the presentation component according to the abstract data model and to the user level.

## 1 Introduction

It is highly desirable to have a stable methodology addresing the whole development
process of interactive applications. The results of using such a methodology should
be such that the programming efforts required from software designers and programmers are reduced. In particular, they should be spared from learning about low-level
details of the underlying physical toolkits. Nowadays, any methodology should provide a complete *process* to follow, be founded on *models*, and be supported by
computer *tools*. The main goal of the TRIDENT project (Tools foR an Interactive
Development EnvironmeNT) is to extend the IDA (Interactive Design Approach) [3]
methodology for business-oriented applications in order to encompass highly-interactive applications as well. Before extending such a methodology, it is necessary to
build an architecture model of the interactive application which shows benefits [2].
This paper only reports the architecture model of the TRIDENT project involved in
the models part of the methodology. It will not tackle the questions raised by the process and tools aspects. Several goals to be considered are stated in TRIDENT :

- The context of this work concerns highly-interactive business oriented applications. We consequently assume that
  - application processing basically consists of manipulating data managed by a
    database management system (DBMS);

- the implementation of the human-computer interface relies upon either a traditional character-oriented user-interface manager (e.g. DECforms) or a bitmap-oriented manager more suited to modern windowing technologies (e.g. X-Windows, Microsoft Windows [8,9], OSF/Motif [16], Open Look).
- The architecture model should include a *dialog model* supporting a **first** obvious autonomy (or separation) between the semantic core of application domain functions and the human-computer dialog (fig. 1) in order to guarantee seven advantages : the ease of specification, the ease of design and automatic generation, the concentration of the dialog, the high modifiability and maintainability, the reusability, the multi-interfacing ability, the parallel design and the distribution of competences among the development team.

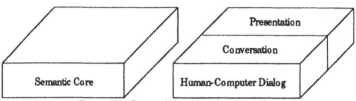

**Fig. 1** The first and the second autonomies

- The dialog model should be divided into two parts allowing a **second** autonomy (fig. 1) : the *conversation*, which is responsible for managing high- and mid-level interactions between the application and the user, and the *presentation*, which is responsible for the input/display application data in a convenient way. This second autonomy separates the dynamic content of the dialog, contained in the conversation, of the static part of the dialogue, contained in the presentation.
- The second autonomy should also encourage the explicit use of software ergonomics, that is, the common human-computer principles and guidelines as described in [7,8,9,11,16,20,21,22,23]. The aim behind this idea is to get a computer-aided software engineering tool that helps the designer to define the presentation according to these guidelines, and independently of the conversation [26].
- The architecture model should take into account asynchronous and multi-threaded dialogs [2].
- The task analysis should play a vital role in specifying the key elements of the resulting interface. IDA already supported functional requirements, whereas TRIDENT is intended to support task-oriented descriptions and user stereotypes.
- A Computer-Aided Sofware Engineering (CASE) environment with interactive tools should support the methodology to enable the creation of an user-interface as automatically as possible.

The rest of this paper is structured as follows. In section 2, the TRIDENT architecture model of highly-interactive business-oriented applications is described in details : its main components are identified and compared with respect to a metamodel in subsection 2.1, and the objects composing the architecture model are explained in subsection 2.2. The components identified in subsection 2.1, the Semantic Core Component, the Presentation Component and the Dialog Component are defined respectively in subsections 2.3, 2.4 and 2.5. The specification of the Dialog

Component and the development of the Presentation Component are addressed in sections 3 and 4. Conclusions are presented in section 5.

## 2 Architecture Model

### 2.1 Identifying Architecture Elements.

The Arch metamodel [25] is recognized as the most generic and comprehensive interactive application architecture metamodel up to date. It highlights five components depicted in fig. 2, and detailed below. This architecture metamodel has been proved successful for varying application model such as PAC [5] and UIDE [19].

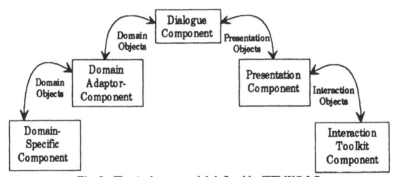

**Fig. 2.** The Arch metamodel defined by IFIP WG 2.7

The five components are :
1. Domain-Specific Component - controls, manipulates and retrieves domain data and performs other domain-related functions.
2. Interaction Toolkit Component - implements the physical interaction with the end-user.
3. Dialogue Component - has responsibility for task-level sequencing, both for the user and for the portion of the application domain sequencing that depends on the user.
4. Presentation Component - a mediation component between the Dialogue Component and the Interaction Toolkit Component that provides a set of toolkit-independent interaction objects for use by the Dialogue Component
5. Domain-Adaptor Component - a mediation component between the Dialogue Component and the Domain-Specific Component.

The architecture model of TRIDENT also fits this generic architecture (fig. 3). It identifies three components : the Semantic Core Component, the Dialog Component and the Presentation Component. The *Semantic Core Component* comprises the set of all *semantic functions* whose aim is to retrieve data from and update the database. These functions are elementary and do not involve interaction with the user. They form a semantic server and preserve database integrity [3]. Four types of semantic functions can be found :

1. semantic validation functions (e.g. to validate the identification number of a customer);
2. database retrieve functions (e.g. to list all customers in a given region);
3. database update functions (e.g. to insert, delete or modify customer data);
4. computation functions (e.g. to perform statistical analysis on the customer population).

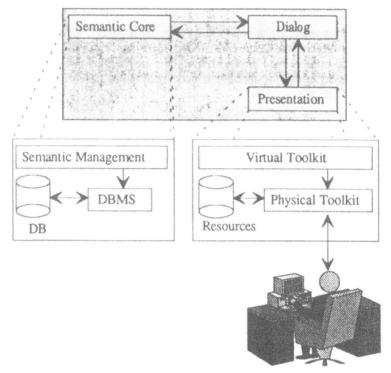

**Fig. 3.** The TRIDENT architecture model

The *Presentation Component* manages the communication between the user and the Dialog Component. This communication is carried out through interaction objects (e.g. controls, buttons, edit fields, radio boxes, windows) contained in the user-interface development toolkit, to which we refer to as the *Physical Toolkit*. The Presentation Component is also responsible for performing syntactic controls such as the verification of the type, format and image of the data input by the user. The *Virtual Toolkit* is introduced to ensure independence of any particular target environment, which traditionally is limited to a Physical Toolkit.

The *Dialog Component* is responsible for the good execution of the interactive application in order to achieve the goal assigned to the interaction application. This component integrates the following functionalities : the triggering of semantic functions, the dialog management, and the management of consistency between the data stored in the database and the data displayed.

## 2.2 Architecture Model

The Dialog Component plays a central role in the architecture : it is responsible for the good sequencing of semantic functions and dialog functions. The difficulty to implement this component resides in the diversity of alternative course of actions to accomplish a user task when multi-threaded dialogs are supported. Therefore, we propose to structure this component as hierarchy of *dialog objects*. Each dialog object is responsible for a partial goal of the task, and cooperates with other dialog objects during the execution of the application.

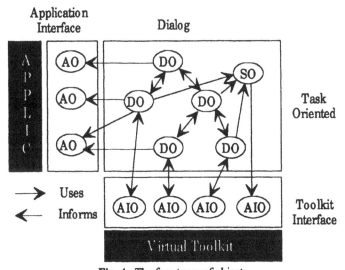

Fig. 4. The four types of objects

Each component of the architecture model is characterized by a particular type of object (fig. 4). The Semantic Core Component is composed of *application objects* (AO). The Presentation Component is characterized by *interaction objects*, of which two types exist, namely *concrete interaction objects* (CIO) and *abstract interaction objects* (AIO). These belong to the Physical Toolkit and the Virtual Toolkit, respectively. The Dialog Component is characterized by *dialog objects* (DO), of which the *supervisory object* (SO) is a special kind.

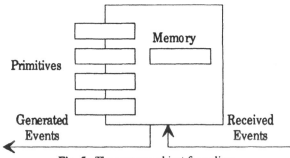

Fig. 5. The common object formalism

A uniform representation formalism is adopted for describing objects, regardless their respective type. Each object provides in its interface two kinds of services : the *primitives* and the *events*. The purpose of the primitives (fig. 5) is to consult the memory of the object or to modify its content according to the evolution of the dialog. The events are raised due to significant state changes resulting either of the execution of some primitive or of events received from other objects.

## 2.3 Semantic Core Component

As already mentioned, the Semantic Core Component shelters a set of semantic functions translating any elementary task goal into minimal consistent actions performed on the memory of application objects. If the object-oriented paradigm is followed for programming these functions, then they are the methods provided by each application object. If a traditional procedural paradigm is followed, then the semantic functions are encapsulated in the Semantic Core Component. Each data exchange, either between two semantic functions or between a semantic function and a dialog function, cannot be decomposed [3]. Therefore, the semantic functions must be performed without any user intervention. However, some interaction will take place before triggering the semantic function in order to obtain required data, and after terminating the semantic function in order to display the results. Other *utility functions* can also be added when they have different purposes : for example, to retrieve information from the database in order to improve the quality of the interface (e.g. to display an alphabetical list of customers sorted by region, zip code), to provide some semantic feedback (e.g. to automatically retrieve the zip code for any city or vice versa).

## 2.4 Presentation Component

The Presentation Component is the visible part of the application and results from a process called *Development of Presentation Component* described in section 4.

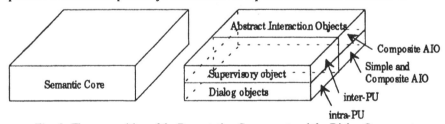

**Fig. 6.** The composition of the Presentation Component and the Dialog Component

Each concrete interaction object designates a dialog entity visible and manipulable by the user. It is the only communication channel between the application and the user. Interaction objects (concrete or abstract) can be either *simple* (e.g. check box, push button) or *composite* (e.g. dialog box, panel, window, group of radio buttons). The latter contains two or more interaction objects, either simple or composite . The concrete interaction objects related to the application data are aggregated into *presentation units* (fig. 6) respecting some ergonomic criteria such as consistency, work load, visual density [20].

## 2.5 Dialog Component

The Dialog Component manages dialog objects. Each dialog object represents an abstract dialog entity invisible to the user and whose aim is to manage a consistent set of abstract interaction objects and/or other dialog objects. This management is related to a precise goal or sub-goal assigned to the user task. Each dialog object has to manage some part of the global conversation. To reach this goal, one can refine the main goal of a dialog object into decomposed sub-goals related to other *child dialog objects* created for this purpose. Hence, each dialog object encapsulates the behaviour of just one part of the overall dialog, representing a user task. From these successive refinements results a hierarchy of dialog objects. The hierarchy highlights "uses" relationships among dialog objects. The Dialog Component becomes a hierarchy of autonomous objects communicating asynchronously with each other. Every dialog object calls (fig. 4)

- semantic functions provided by none to many application objects wherever they are located,
- services provided by none to many child dialog objects,
- services provided by none to many interaction objects.

The Dialog Component employs one special type of dialog object: the *supervisory object*. Its role consists in fixing the *inter-presentation units* conversation (or inter-PU for short, see fig. 6), that is the global sequencing of presentation units such as dialog boxes, primary or secundary windows. Concentrating this sequencing in a single object allows the easy modification of the global behaviour of the conversation. But this approach still needs basic interaction between the supervisory object and dialog objects, that are responsible for *intra-presentation units* conversation (or intra-PU for short, see fig. 6). The supervisory object can display, remove, enable, disable, iconize, restore any presentation unit. It is the only object knowing global conversation information about the presentation units. Except for the supervisory object, dialog objects do not know anything about the presentation units themselves, but they manage the concrete interaction objects constituting the presentation units.

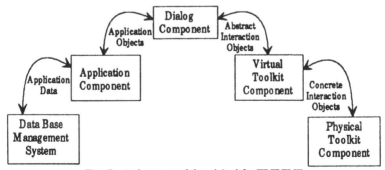

**Fig. 7.** Arch metamodel revisited for TRIDENT

Having discussed in detail the three general components of the TRIDENT architecture model and their respective subcomponents, we can now show how it fits in the

Architecture Metamodel (fig. 7). Recall that the Dialog Component is characterized by dialog objects nd supervisory objects, not depicted in the picture. Dialog objects and Supervisory objects are contained in the Dialog Component.

# 3 The Specification of the Dialog Component

## 3.1 The rule language

The behaviour of any dialog object results from its reaction to the triggering of the primitives it provides and from its reaction to the events received from child dialog objects. The reaction of any dialog object to events coming from children dialog objects is decribed by a rule language [17], where each rule has the general form of :

IF **triggering condition** THEN **actions**

The *triggering condition* of each rule can be expressed by :

$$(e_1 \vee e_2 \vee ... \vee e_i) \wedge (exp_1 \vee exp_2 \vee ... \vee exp_j)$$

where $e_i$    = received event

$exp_j$ = any boolean expression testing the current state of the object

$\vee$    = OR boolean operator

$\wedge$    = AND boolean operator

One dialog object can receive any event either coming directly from concrete interaction objects which were manipulated by the user or generated by a child dialog object. Events coming from a father object to any child object are not allowed. Possible actions are :

- the triggering of any primitive in a child dialog object or concrete interaction object;
- the triggering of own primitives of the dialog object on its memory, i.e. to access or update;
- the generation of events from one child dialog object to any father dialog object;
- the triggering of semantic functions;
- the sequencing of actions (e.g. condition, iteration, duplication).

## 3.2 State Transition Diagrams

Our experience showed that it remains difficult to build "If **triggering condition** Then **actions**" rules without guidance and to validate the behaviour of the dialog object described using this formalism. We consequently propose a graphical formalism allowing the definition of the behaviour of any dialog object. Behaviour rules for deriving states as systematically as possible have been established. The behaviour of each dialog object is defined with the help of a state transition diagram where :

- each state transition diagram depicts the local behaviour of a single dialog object;
- each node of the diagram related to a particular dialog object represents a state of this object. As a matter of fact, each dialog object is characterized at any given moment by a state belonging to a finite set of possible states. Each possible state is defined with respect to the child dialog objects and to the concrete interaction objects;
- each arc is related to the events that the dialog object can receive from its child dialog objects and the primitives to be performed when receiving events. All raised events are reported. But each event related to the concerned dialog object is considered significant for this dialog object. This significance is allowed by examining each diagram arc on which events are written.

Therefore, the diagram graphically shows how the dialog object can go from one state (the source of the considered arc) to another (the target of the considered arc). Events related to at least one action appear on the state transition diagram. This graphical representation is compatible with the object-oriented paradigm where all objects all autonomous and where the current state of the user-interface results from the states of the different dialog objects.

## 3.3 Specifying the Behaviour of a Dialog Object : an Example

Let us illustrate the rule language and the state transition diagram. The dialog object DO_Validate_Customer is specified. This dialog object lets the user retrieve an existing customer from a database either by his/her identification number (Customer_id) or by a pair (firstname, lastname).

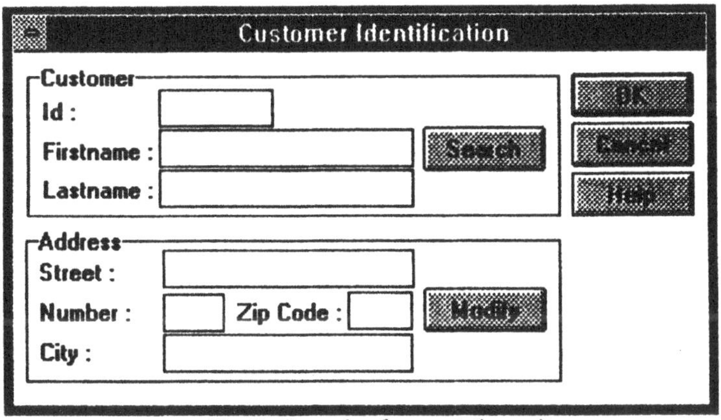

Fig. 8. Example of presentation unit

An example of presentation unit related to this dialog object is depicted in fig. 8.

The state transition diagram of the dialog object is drawn in fig. 9. The circle in the uper-left orner denotes the initial state prior to state 1. Each ellipse denotes a particlar state of the dialog object. Each transition is graphically represented as an arc branching from source state to any target state.

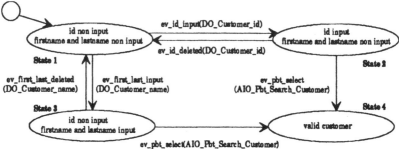

**Fig. 9.** State transition diagram of the DO_Validate_Customer dialog object

The behaviour rules for this dialog object can be expressed using the rule language introduced in section 3.1 The abbreviations are : ev stands for event, pr stands for primitive, Pbt stands for pushbutton.

State 1 : IF ev_id_input (DO_Customer_id)
        THEN pr_activate (AIO_Pbt_Search_Customer)
           State = 2
        IF ev_first_last_input (DO_Customer_name)
        THEN pr_activate (AIO_Pbt_Search_Customer)
           State = 3
State 2 : IF ev_id_deleted (DO_Customer-id)
        THEN pr_activate (AIO_Pbt_Search_Customer)
           State = 1
        IF ev_pbt_select (AIO_Pbt_Search_Customer)
        THEN current_id = pr_get_id (DO_Customer_id)
           IF Validate_Cust_id (current_id) = TRUE
           THEN State = 4
                Generate (ev_Valid_Customer)
           ELSE Display_message ("Invalid Customer Identification")
State 3: IF ev_first_last_deleted (DO_Customer_name)
        THEN pr_desactivate (AIO_Pbt_Search_Customer)
           State = 1
        IF ev_pbt_select (AIO_Pbt_Search_Customer)
        THEN current_firstname = pr_get_firstname (DO_Customer_name)
           current_lastname = pr_get_lastname (DO_Customer_name)
           IF Validate_Cust_fl(current_firstname,current_lastname)= TRUE
           THEN State = 4
                Generate (ev_Valid_Customer)
           ELSE Display_message
                ("Invalid Customer firstname and lastname")

The behaviour of State 4 is obvious since it only sends the event ev_Va-
lid_Customer to any father dialog object. The resulting partial dialog object
hierarchy is depicted in fig. 10.

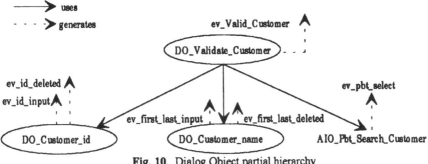

**Fig. 10.** Dialog Object partial hierarchy

The dialog object DO_Validate_Customer uses two child dialog objects, i.e.
DO_Customer_id and DO_Customer_name, and one interaction object, i.e.
AIO_Pbt_Search_Button. For instance, DO_Customer_id manages the
user input of the identification number. It generates the event ev_id_input to
DO_Validate_Customer if the user inputs something in the id edit box
(fig.8). It generates the event ev_id_deleted to DO_Validate_Customer
if the user deletes the content of the id edit box.

## 4  The Development of the Presentation Component

Developing the Presentation Component involves at least the specification and the
design of a user interface whose interaction objects must be appropriate to the user's
task. Three general approaches can be followed to develop interaction objects [12] :

1. *Build from scratch* : select and code manually the interaction objects according to
   the task analysis;
2. *Modify existing objects* : select, modify and adapt the interaction objects from any
   existing physical toolkit;
3. *Use a design tool* : specify the application data with a high-level specification
   language in order to automatically generate the user interface.

While the first two approaches can be restrictive, complex, time and resource consuming, the last one has gained today much acceptance and overspreading. Analogous-
ly to the development of software, one has experimented the validity of the third
approach with respect to the first two approaches. Numerous examples of design
tools and User Interface Management Systems (UIMS) belonging to the third
approach are found in the literature [1,2,25,27]. Generating the user interface resting
on the previous object-oriented paradigm implies two activities :
1. select appropriate interaction objects according to a data model defining some
   application sementics (selection activity),

2. lay out these objects into presentation units with a visual and logical arrangement (placement activity).

An example of automatic placement activity appears in [10]. We concentrate on the selection activity because it seems to be more than an ongoing research problem, but also a very frequent question asked by the designer and/or the software ergonomics specialist. The selection technique [27] should :

- automatic and explicit [12],
- driven by the application semantic [2],
- present interaction objects according to the application data structure and not to the presentation [27];
- based on a dialog model [1],
- based on a user model [1,4],
- able to group interaction objects [1],
- able to consider screen space [7],
- be environment independent.

### 4.1 Abstract and Concrete Interaction Objects

*Concrete interaction objects* (CIO) are those graphical objects for inputing and displaying data related to the user interactive task and belonging to the Physical Toolkit (fig. 5). Concrete interaction objects are sometimes called widgets (window gadgets), controls or physical interactors. They comprise two major aspects :

1. the graphical appearance univocally determined by both presentation tool (e.g. OSF/Motif) and graphical tool (e.g. X-Windows);
2. the behaviour and constraints to be respected when manipulated by the user.

When one looks at different Physical Toolkits (e.g. Apple Toolkit, Microsoft Windows, Presentation Manager), one can find again the same concrete interaction object, but with different presentations depending on the graphical appearance. This observation led us to redefine interaction objects independently of their presentation, but not independently of their behaviour. The *abstract interaction object* (AIO), or logical interactor, belongs to the Virtual Toolkit Component (fig. 4) and provides an abstract view of the CIO that disappears physical characteristics. The concept of AIO presents several benefits :

- when the most adequate object for input/display application data has to be chosen, the designer can decide upon a clear matching between the semantic properties of the application data and the behaviour of AIOs;
- the presentation of any CIO in specific Physical Toolkit can be changed without affecting its behaviour. For example, a bounded value can be displayed as a scale, a thermometer, a scroll bar, a dial or a simple edit box;
- the concept of AIO allows to work with a multi-platform interactive application or when porting some application in a character-based environment to a multi-windowing system.

After examining different Physical Toolkits have been examined, we defined a comprehensive object-oriented AIO typology divided in 6 groups sorted according to interactive properties (table 1).

| AIO sets | AIO elements (some) |
|---|---|
| action objects | menu, menu item, menu bar, drop-down menu, cascade menu,... |
| scrolling objects | scroll arrow, scroll cursor, scroll bar, frame |
| static objects | label, separator, group box, prompt, icon |
| control objects | edit box, scale, dial, check box, switch, radio box, spin button, push button, list box, drop-down list box, scrollable list box, combination box, table,... |
| dialog objects | window, help window, dialog box, expandable dialog box, radio dialog box, panel,... |
| feedback objects | message, progression indicator, contextual cursor |

**Table 1.** Table of abstract interaction objects

Each AIO is identified by a unique generic name (e.g. `list box`), general and particular abstract attributes (e.g. `height`, `width`, `color`, `number of visible items`, `position of current selected item`, `states`), abstract events (e.g. `value selection`, `mouse click`), and primitive (e.g. `Pr-ListBoxItemSelected`). By definition, an AIO has no graphical appearance, but instead it can be connected to 0, 1 or many CIO belonging to different environments, and which have different names and/or presentations.

**Fig. 11.** (a) List box (left) ; (b) Drop-down list box (right)

AIO objects are linked together in their definition by aggregation and inheritance relations. For example, a list box consists of a frame containing the different items and a scroll bar, which in turn consists of two scrolling arrows and a scroll cursor (fig. 11a). Tus, the list box inherits some abstract attributes, events and primitives coming from its inherited objects either directly or by redefinition. The list box can become a drop-down list box (fig. 11b) by adding a pointing-down scrolling arrow on which the user must click to visualize the items of the list box.

An edit box can be combined with each of these list boxes to make the list expandable with type-in capabilities : these are the combination box (fig. 12a) and the drop-down combination box (fig. 12b). List or combination boxes, either drop-down or not, can become scrollable if double-arrow buttons are fitted at the two extremities of the scroll bar (Fig. 13a,b).

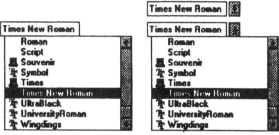

**Fig. 12. (a)** Combination box (left) ; **(b)** Drop-down combination box (right)

Whilst list and combination boxes are useful to select an item among a list of items, scrollable list box (fig. 13a) and scrollable drop-down combination box (fig. 13b) are better suited for item selection in a large pool of items.

**Fig. 13. (a)** Scrollable List box (left) ; **(b)** Scrollable Drop-down Combination box (right)

Whereas static objects are just graphical embellishment objects, action and control objects have a reactive behaviour. Scrolling, feedback and control objects are by nature simple, whereas dialog objects are typically composite : users may input, modify and/or select the values buffered within the composite objects before to be propagated to the application.

## 4.2 Selection of Abstract Interaction Objects

Selection rules generally contain four information sources: data from the application model, information on these data (e.g. *metadata* in UIDE [1]), others parameters, and user preferences. Four information sources are required :

1. every application data $d$ is specified by a quadruplet *(V, dt, Nvc, dv)*, where $V$ is the domain of all possible values of $d$ (if known); $dt$ belongs to one of the implemented data types (hour, date, logical, graphical, integer, numeric, real, alphabetic, alphanumeric); $Nvc$ is the number of values to choose (1 for simple choice, N for multiple choice); $dv \in V$ is the default value of $d$ (if known). $V$ is partitioned as $V = PV \cup SV$, where $PV$ is the set of principal values and $SV$ is the set of secondary values. This characterization allows a presentation of most frequently used values first, minimizing input and scrolling. The number of principal values and secondary values are given by $Npo = \# PV$ and $Nsv = \# SV$, respectively. Maximum data length is given by $l = max(length\ (v_i))\ \forall\ v_i \in V$.

2. application data can be further refined by the following parameters, if relevant : *Precision*- whether the data precision is low, moderate or high; *Orientation*- whether the data should be presented horizontally, vertically, circularly or it is undefined; *Known values*- whether $V$ is well defined; *Ordered list*- whether the values of $V$ are sorted according to a particular order (numerical, alphabetical, logical, temporal, physical, by frequence); *El= expandable list*- whether the user can add new values to $V$ and/or modify $V$; *Cr=continous range*- whether the values are contained in a continuous range or interval. If there is some order in the values of $V$, then an appropriate AIO is selected (e.g. a spin button for chronological data).

3. one parameter specifies *constrained display space*- whether the selection must consider screen density to avoid too large AIO. The more constrained is the screen space, the smallest is the AIO selected (e.g. a drop-down list box in place of a complete list box).

| Level | User experience |
|-------|-----------------|
| 3 | beginner |
| 4 | novice |
| 5 | intermediate |
| 6 | expert |
| 7 | master |

**Table 2.** User experience level

4. a common user model is clarified by a *user experience level* provided by Card *et al.* [4] (table 2) where a number is assigned to each user experience, and by a *user selection preference* (low or high)- whether the user is more skilled to select one value among a list of values or to enter it with the keyboard. The less is the user experience level, the more guidance is brought by the object.

**4.3 Selection Rules**

We now present selection rules for choosing interaction objects to input/display, but we limited to hour data (tables 3 to 5), logical data (table 6) : other rules can be found in [3]. Selecting the appropriate AIO depends on the four information sources defined in section 4.2. Each table is a decision table stating all alternatives for one specific type of information (hour, calendar,...). The boundary Tm=50 is defined as the maximal number of items in a list [24]. Each row defines one possible selection.

| Npo | AIO |
|-----|-----|
| [2,3] | radio button with Nvc items + single edit box |
| [4,7] | radio button with Nvc items + single edit box + group box |
| [8,Tm] | drop-down combination box |
| [Tm+1,2Tm] | scrollable combination box |
| > 2Tm | drop-down and scrollable combination box |

**Table 3.** Rules for a hour data with mixed domain

Table 3 for instance can be interpreted as :

- first row : if the user must input a hour data among a set of 2 to 3 possible values (Nvc ∈ [2,3]) with ability to input an alternative one, then the suggested AIO is a radio button with Nvc items (to display the possible values) with a single edit box (to let the user input an unforeseen value);
- second row : if the user must input a hour data among a set of 4 to 7 possible values with ability to input an other one, then the suggested AIO is a radiobutton with Nvc items, with a single edit box and a surrounding group box (fig. 14a);
- third row : if the user must input a hour data among a set of 8 to Tm=50 possible values with ability to input an other one, then the suggested AIO is a drop-down combination box (fig. 14b);
- fourth and fifth rows : by analogy.

| Nsv | El | Npo | AIO |
|---|---|---|---|
| = 0 | no | [2,3] | Nvc check boxes |
| | | [4,7] | Nvc check boxes + group box |
| | | [8,Tm] | list box |
| | | [Tm+1,2Tm] | scrollable list box |
| | | > 2Tm | drop-down and scrollable list box |
| =0 | yes | | combination box |
| > 0 | | | list box |

Table 4. Rules for a hour data with known domain and multiple choice (Nvc>1)

Table 4 can be interpreted as :

- first row : if the user must input with multiple choice (Nvc>1) a hour data whose domain is known and if there is not any secundary values (Nsv=0) and if the domain is not expandable (El=no) and if the number of possible values is from 2 to 3 (Nvc ∈ [2,3]), then the suggested AIO is a set of Nvc check boxes (fig. 14c);
- sixth row : if the user must input with multiple choice (Nvc>1) a hour data whose domain is known and if there is not any secundary values (Nsv=0) and if the domain is expandable (El=yes), then the suggested AIO is a combination box;
- seventh row : if the user must input with multiple choice (Nvc>1) a hour data whose domain is known and if there is some secundary values (Nsv>0), then the suggested AIO is a list box (fig. 14d).

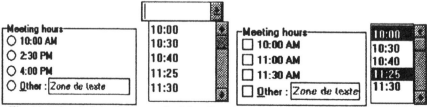

Fig. 14. (a,b,c,d) Selection examples taken from table 3 (rows 2, 3) and table 4 (rows 5, 7)

Table 5 shows rules for a hour data with known domain and simple choice :

- row 14 : if the user must input with simple choice (Nvc=1) a hour data whose domain is known and if there is not any secundary values (Nsv=0) and if the domain is not expandable (El=no) and if the domain is continuous (Cr=yes) and if the number of possible values is greater than Tm=50 (Nvp>Tm) and if the precision is high, then the suggested AIO is a spin button (fig. 15a);
- row 17 : if the user must input with simple choice (Nvc=1) a hour data whose domain is known and if there is not any secundary values (Nsv=0) and if the domain is not expandable (El=no) and if the domain is continuous (Cr=yes) and if the number of possible values is greater than Tm=50 (Nvp>Tm) and if the precision is low, then the suggested AIO is a clock (fig. 15b).

| Nsv | El | Cr | Npo | Precision | Orientation | AIO |
|-----|-----|-----|-----|-----------|-------------|-----|
| > 0 | | | | | | list box |
| = 0 | yes | | | | | combination box |
| | no | no | [2,3] | | | radio button with Nvc items |
| | | | [4,7] | | | radio button with Nvp items + single edit box + group box |
| | | | [8,Tm] | | | list box |
| | | | [Tm+1,2Tm] | | | scrollable list box |
| | | | > 2Tm | | | drop-down and scrollable list box |
| | | yes | [1,10] | | vertical | scroll bar |
| | | | | | horizontal | scale |
| | | | | | circular | clock |
| | | | | | undefined | scale |
| | | | [11,Tm] | high | | spin button |
| | | | | low | | scale |
| | | | > Tm | high | | spin button |
| | | | | low | vertical | scroll bar |
| | | | | | horizontal | scale |
| | | | | | circular | clock |
| | | | | | undefined | scale |

**Table 5.** Rules for a hour data with known domain and simple choice (Nvc=1)

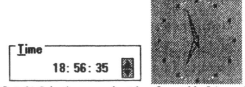

Fig. 15. (a,b) Selection examples taken from table 5 (rows 14, 17)

| Domain | Antagonist values | Orientation | AIO |
|---|---|---|---|
| known | yes | vertical | vertical switch |
| | | horizontal | horizontal switch |
| | | circular | two-value dial |
| | | undefined | horizontal switch |
| | no | | check box |
| unknown | | | check box |

**Table 6.** Rules for a logical data

Table 6 shows rules for a logical data with known domain and simple choice :

- row 1 : if the user must input a logical data whose domain is known and if the values are antagonist and if the orientation is vertical, then the suggested AIO is a vertical switch (fig. 16a);
- row 3 : if the user must input a logical data whose domain is known and if the values are antagonist and if the orientation is circular, then the suggested AIO is a dial (fig. 16b);
- row 5 : if the user must input a logical data whose domain is known and if the values are not antagonist, that is purely boolean, then the suggested AIO is a check box (fig. 16c).

**Fig. 16. (a,b,c)** Selection examples taken from table 6 (rows 1, 3, 5)

The complete references on which selection rules are based are the following :
- general algorithms : [1], p. 261-263; [10], p. 16; [12], p. 281-290; [27]
- interval from [2,3], [4,7] elements : [2] ; [12], p. 87, p. 281 ; [13]
- maximal length for an alphanumeric item : Lm=40 : [20], p. 81
- maximal item number in a list : Tm=50 : [24]
- visually distinctible group : [20], p. 83
- number of items : [4]; [13]
- calendar, profiled edit box for hours and dates : [6]
- scroll bar : [8], p. 59-60; [11], p. 118; [12], p. 86, p. 281; [16], p. 5*10-5*12
- group box : [8], p. 74; [20], p. 92
- single-line edit box : [8], p. 66; [11], p. 136; [12], p. 91, p. 281; [16], p. 5*6
- multiple-line edit box : [8], p. 66-67; [11], p. 130; [16], p. 5*6.
- check box : [8], p. 64; [16], p. 5*3; [23]
- options box : [11], p. 115-117; [12], p. 87, p. 281
- radio button : [8], p. 63-64; [9], p. 65; [11], p. 85-86; [16], p. 5*2-5*3; p. 281; [21]
- switch : [11], p. 84-85, p. 281
- scale : [11], p. 94; [12], p. 86, p. 281; [16], p. 5*9
- list box: [8], p. 65; [9], p. 65; [11], p. 85-86; [16], p. 5*4-5*5
- unitary list box : [8], p. 70; [11], p. 73 ; [16], p. 5*13.
- graphical list box : [15]
- drop-down list box : [8], p. 68-69; [9], p. 28-29.

- combination box: [8], p. 68; [20], p. 81
- drop-down combination box : [8], p. 68; [20], p. 81
- normal table: [22], rule 1.5*1
- extended table : [22], rules 2.3*1, 2.3*6
- set of values : [7], p. 239; [12], p. 89
- circular menu : [14], p. 424
- list numbering : [24], p. 272

## 4.4 Rules Management and Graphical Selection

Rules must be organized in a proper way which is modifiable and visible. UIDE's [1] and DON [10] selection rules are organized as *if...then* rules contained in a file that can be edited by the designer. This approach induces communication problems for the designer because his responsibility is to choose the right AIO at the right place in a simple and efficient way. Drawing a flowchart benefits to the designer: this organization seems natural (assimilating rules is easier), concise (the organization is intrinsically kept short and non-redundant) and visualy more rapid to understand (following a path is fast). Nevertheless, the flowchart fails to show the entire space of possible values covered by each parameter.

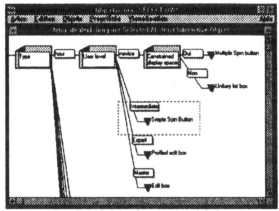

**Fig. 17.** AIO Selection tree (partial view)

We adopted a decision tree technique [27] showing at each node the possible values space as a partition (fig. 17). A *decision tree* depicts the decision tables graphically, using arcs and nodes. Each node consists of a current AIO selected and a set of nodes. Each node states a simple logical condition (e.g. is Level=5?); all arcs leaving a node cover the space of possible values (e.g. Level<5, Level=5, Level>5 in fig. 4; *nvc*=1 for a simple choice, *nvc*>1 for a multiple choice). The arcs leaving the root node concern the choices about the different data types (hour, date, boolean,...). Therefore, the selection becomes either a fully automatic process if the designer does not want to participate in the selection, or a computer-aided process, if the desiner wants to revise the selectec AIOs.

In this section, we showed ergonomical rules only for selecting interaction objects, but the TRIDENT methodology will encompass other rules such as :

- rules for choosing appropriate dialog attributes (e.g. locaus of control, dialog sequencing) from the task analysis and user profiles;
- rules allowing the computer-aided derivation of an interaction style (e.g. menu selection, direct manipulation) according to the dialog attributes and user preferences;
- rules selected by ergonomical criteria to be included as a checklist in the programming steps;
- rules for proposing presentation units to each interactive task according to the dialog model;
- rules for laying out contrete interaction objects to obtain a consistent and understandable screen format.

# 5 Conclusion

In this paper, we presented the complete TRIDENT architecture model for a business-oriented highly-interactive application supporting goals stated in the introduction. The goals for the identified components are reached : the separation between the Semantic Core Component and the Presentation Component guarantees the autonomy between the application semantics and the application user-interface ; the Semantic Core Component includes a Semantic Management to favour independence with physical DBMS ; the Presentation Component comprises the Virtual Toolkit (with abstract interaction objects) and the Physical Toolkit (with the concrete interaction objects) to assume independence between conversation and presentation. Selection rules have been introduced to build up the Presentation Component of the User Interface for multiple data types. These rules mainly work in terms of abstract rather than concrete interaction objects to extract the behaviour from the presentation. Therefore, the cornerstone for a future methodology with computer-aided tools seems to be faced.

## Acknowledgments

The authors gratefully acknowledge Benoît Sacré, of METSI, for his participation in the TRIDENT project, Joëlle Coutaz for suggesting us to use the IFIP WG2.7 meta-model and the EWHCI'93 anonymous referees for helpful comments on a previous version of this manuscript. This work was supported by the "Informatique du Futur" project of "Service de la Politique et de la Programmation Scientifique" under contract N°IT/IF/1. Any opinions, findings, conclusions or recommendations expressed in this paper are those of the authors, and do not necessarily reflect the view of the Belgian Authorities. Copyright © 1993 TRIDENT Project.

## References

1. D. de Baar, J.D., Foley, K.E. Mullet: Coupling Application Design and User Interface Design. In P. Bauersfled, J. Bennett, G. Lynch (eds.): Proceedings of CHI'92 (Monterey, May 1992). Reading: Addison-Wesley 1992, pp. 259-266
2. L. Bass, J. Coutaz: Developing Software for the User Interface. Series in Software Engineering. Reading: Addison-Wesley 1991

3.  F. Bodart, J. Vanderdonckt: Expressing Guidelines into an Ergonomical Style-Guide for Highly Interactive Applications. In S. Ashlund, K. Mullet, A. Henderson, E. Hollnagel, T. White (eds.): Adjunct Proceedings of InterCHI'93 (Amsterdam, 24-29 April 1993), New York: ACM Press 1993, pp. 35-36

4.  S.K. Card, T.P. Moran, A. Newell: The Psychology of Human-Computer Interaction. Hillsdale: Lawrence Erlbaum Assoc., 1985

5.  J. Coutaz: PAC: an Implementation Model for Dialog Design. In H.-J. Bullinger, B. Shakel (eds.): Proceedings of Interact'87 (Stuttgart, Sept. 1987). Amsterdam: North Holland 1987, pp. 431-436

6.  I. Greif: The User Interface of a Personal Calendar Program. In Y. Vassiliou (ed.): Human Factors and Interactive Computer Systems, NYU Symposium on User Interfaces Proceedings (New York, 26-28 May 1982). Series in Human/-Computer Interaction. Norwood, Ablex Publishing Corp. 1984, pp. 207-222

7.  W.K. Horton: Designing & Writing On line Documentation - Help files to Hypertext. Chichester: John Wiley & Sons 1991

8.  IBM Systems Application Architecture, Common User Access: Advanced Interface Design Guide. Document SC26-4582-0. Boca Raton: International Business Machines (June 1989)

9.  IBM Systems Application Architecture: Basic Interface Design Guide. Document SC26-4583-0. Cary: International Business Machines (December 1989)

10. W. Kim, J.D. Foley: DON: User Interface Presentation Design Assistant. In Proceedings of the UIST'90 Conference (Snowbird, October 1990). New York: ACM press 1990, pp. 10-20

11. S. Kobara, Visual Design with OSF/Motif. Hewlett-Packard Press Series. Reading: Addison-Wesley 1991

12. J. A. Larson: Interactive Software - Tools for Building Interactive User Interfaces. Yourdon Press Computing Series. Englewood Cliffs: Prentice Hall, 1992

13. G.A. Miller: The Magical Number Seven, Plus or Minus Two: Some Limits on Our Capacity for Processing Information. Psychological Science 63, 81-97 (1956)

14. Z. Mills, M. Prime: Are All Menus the Same? - An Empirical Study. In D. Diaper, D. Gilmore, G. Cockton, B. Shackel (eds.): Proceedings of Interact'90 (Cambridge, 27-31 August 1990). Amsterdam: Elsevier Science Publishers 1990, pp. 423-427

15. P. Muter, C. Mayson: The Role of Graphics in Item Selection from Menus. Behaviour and Information Technology 5, 89-95 (1986)

16. Open Software Foundation. OSF/Motif™ Style Guide, rev 1.0. Englewood Cliffs: Prentice Hall, 1990

17. B. Sacré, I. Provot: Vers une approche orientée objet de la modélisation du dialogue d'une application de gestion hautement interactive [Towards an object-oriented approach for modelizing dialog in business-oriented highly interactive application]. Fac. Univ. N.-D. de la Paix, Institute of Computer Science. Internal report (October 1990)

18. B. Sacré, I. Provot: Proposition d'un langage de spécification de l'interface homme-machine d'une application de gestion hautement interactive [A Proposition for specification language dedicated to the man-machine interface of

business-oriented highly interactive application]. Fac. Univ. N.-D. de la Paix, Institute of Computer Science. Internal report (December 1991)

19. P. Sukaviriya, J.D. Foley, T. Griffith: A Second Generation User Interface Design Environment: The Model and The Runtime Architecture. In: S. Ashlund, K. Mullet, A. Henderson, E. Hollnagel, T. White (eds.): Proceedings of the Conference on Human Factors in Computing Systems InterCHI'93 "Bridges Between Worlds" (Amsterdam, 24-29 April 1993). New York: ACM Press 1993, pp. 375-382

20. D.L. Scapin: Guidelines for User Interface Design : Knowledge Collection and Organization. Report ITHACA.INRIA.89.D12.03. Rocquencourt: Institut National de Recherche en Informatique et en Automatique, 30 December 1989

21. B. Shneiderman: Designing the user interface: strategies for effective human-computer interaction. Reading: Addison-Wesley 1987

22. S.L. Smith, J.N. Mosier: Design guidelines for the user interface software. Technical Report ESD-TR-86-278 (NTIS No. AD A177198). Hanscom Air Force Base: U.S. Air Force Electronic Systems Division 1986

23. B. Tognazzini: The Apple // Human interface guidelines. Cupertino: Apple Computer 1985

24. T.S. Tullis: Designing a Menu-Based Interface to an Operating System. In L. Borman, B. Curtis (eds.): Proceedings of CHI'85 (San Francisco, 14-18 April 1985). New York: ACM Press 1985, pp. 79-84

25. The UIMS Workshop Tool Developers: A Metamodel for the Runtime Architecture of An Interactive System. SIGCHI Bulletin, 24, 1, 32-37 (January 1992)

26. J. Vanderdonckt: Prise en compte des facteurs ergonomiques dans la conception des interfaces homme-machine. In M. Adiba, F. Bodart, M. Léonard, Y. Pigneur (eds.): Actes des journées de travail de Beaune '91 (Beaune, 5-7 March 1991). Genève: Les Editions Systèmes et Information 1991

27. J. Vanderdonckt, F. Bodart: Encapsulating Knowledge for Intelligent Automatic Interaction Objects Selection. In: S. Ashlund, K. Mullet, A. Henderson, E. Hollnagel, T. White (eds.): Proceedings of the Conference on Human Factors in Computing Systems InterCHI'93 "Bridges Between Worlds" (Amsterdam, 24-29 April 1993). New York: ACM Press 1993, pp. 424-429

# Designing Multimedia Interfaces

Alistair Sutcliffe and Peter Faraday

Center for HCI Design,
School of Informatics, City University,
Northampton Square, London EC1 0HB, UK
sf328@uk.ac.city
+44 - 71 - 477 - 8411

**Abstract.** Multimedia interfaces are currently created by intuition. Development of a method for analysis and design of multimedia presentation interfaces is described. The study investigates task based information analysis, persistence of information, selection attention and concurrency in presentation. The method gives an agenda of issues, diagrams and techniques for specification, and guidelines for media selection and presentation scripting. Use of the method is illustrated with a case study of shipboard emergency management.

## 1 Introduction

Multimedia (MM) interfaces are now an established part of the HCI repertoire, however, little is known about how to design such interfaces. Some studies have reported approaches to planning output with different media (eg [2],[7]), however, no systematic approach to MM interface design has emerged and most systems are created from inspired intuition. Given the complexity of MM interaction it is unlikely that craft style approaches [11] will produce effective interfaces. The paper reports the first stage of the investigation - development of a method and guide-lines for multimedia interface design. The method is illustrated with a case study application of shipboard hazard management.

## 2 Method Requirements

The problem is how to design multimedia interfaces to support users' tasks. Information relevant to the task resides on different databases in a variety of media. As a first step we conducted a case study to develop a method for designing MM interfaces which can be refined into rule sets capable of automation.

Some pragmatic guide-lines are known from previous reports [1,2,7] and experimental studies [16] although these have not proposed a systematic means of assigning media to information requirements within a task. Guidelines are required to cover selection of media resources for representing different types of information and presentation design. In addition, we argue that the prime issues in MM interfaces are selective attention, persistence of information, concurrency and limited cognitive resources such as working memory.

Our study concerns design for task support interfaces. The agenda of issues which the method must address were, first creation of a task model with specification of information requirements, followed by a resources model describing the available media, a process of selecting appropriate media for the task context, and then scripting a coherent dialogue which combines information in different media. Other parts of the method are sketched in outline. A sample application of a shipboard hazard management is used to illustrate the method.

## 3 Systematic Multimedia Interface Design

### 3.1 Task Analysis

The method starts with a standard task analysis using Task Knowledge Structures (TKS) [10] as the basis for the task model. A small fragment of the overall task model, the procedure for dealing with fire hazards in shipboard cargo, is illustrated in figure 1. TKS does not explicitly state what information is required for each task step, although this is implicit in the object descriptions. Accordingly, the task model is annotated with a description of the information necessary to achieve the task. The information types are similar to those found in many task or data models (e.g. actions, objects, procedures) although these categories have been refined by addition of more types to describe the information content.

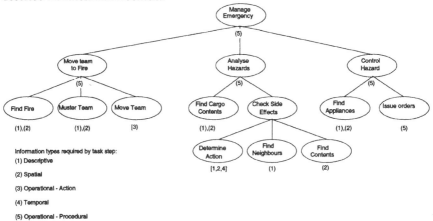

Figure 1 Task Model for Case Study Example

### 3.2 Resource Analysis

The second method component is resource analysis. This describes the media resources available to the system and their access procedures. Each resource is annotated with its type (Animation, Still Image, Language based), the information type(s) it contains (Spatial, Descriptive, Temporal, Operational) and the type of application data it embodies (eg 'Fire_Location'). The table below gives an example of the resources available for the example task :

| Application data | Information type | Media Resource type |
|---|---|---|
| Fire location | Spatial, Descriptive, Temporal, Operational | Animation |
| | Spatial, Descriptive | Language |
| Team location | Spatial, Descriptive Temporal, Operational | Animation |
| | Spatial, Descriptive | Language |
| Appliance locations | Spatial, Descriptive | Still Image, Language |
| Cargo contents | Descriptive | Language |
| Cargo locations | Spatial | Text, Still Image |
| Hazard descriptions | Descriptive | Language |
| Hazard Procedure | Operational, Descriptive Spatial, Temporal | Language, Still Image, Animation |

# 4 Planning the Presentation

## 4.1 Presentation Scripting

The task information model is elaborated by attaching dialogue acts to specify the desired communicative effect for each task step. Dialogue acts owe their heritage to speech act theory [19] and have been widely used in explanation systems (eg [13]). Our dialogue acts are based on Rhetorical Structure Theory (RST) [12]. The acts are divided between those which specify the content of the presentation (Subject acts : specify the content of the media resource instance to be presented) and those which control the reading of the presentation (Presentation Acts : directing the viewers attention). A selection of dialogue acts used in the Case Study are :

Subject based acts

Enable: communicate actions to achieve a task step
Result: give information about the outcome of an action
Cause: give information concerning the causality of a task step
Summary: provide overview of task procedure
Inform : display information as-is

Presentation based acts

Background: give general context information.
Locate: draw user attention to a particular information type
Emphasise: make a particular information type prominent

The dialogue acts are intended for task steps where system explanation or selective attention is necessary. Subject based acts involve giving further information to help the user accomplish the task (Cause, Result acts) or actual knowledge about how to carry out the task itself (Enable acts). Presentation based acts are used to draw the users attention to particular information within a Subject act, such as the Descriptive object state given by a Cause act. The dialogue acts are linked to the task model by a simple 'walk-through' technique of asking 'what information or explanation is required at this step ?'.

## 4.2 Media Selection

Having specified the desired communicative effect for each task step, the method now gives advice on the choice of media for presentation. We distinguish between guidelines which give more targeted advice about selecting media for information types and dialogue acts, high level advice about media combinations to use (general heuristics) and situations to avoid (validating heuristics). Some of our guidelines are as follows (with the source reference if appropriate) :

### Selection guidelines

These advise on choice of presentation media for specific information types.

(i) spatial object relationships - prefer visual media [5]

(ii) physical object composition - prefer visual media [5]

(iii) physical situation/content information - prefer visual media [5]

(iv) complex, abstract object relationships - prefer visual media [3]

(v) procedures, operating instructions - use language, prefer text for persistence [6]

(vi) abstract object properties, values - use language, prefer text for persistence

(vii) event sequence, history of action - use animation or sequence of still images if information has to be extracted from each image [18]

(viii) warning messages - use speech or sound to draw attention, back up by visual attribute for attention (redundant signal effect [14])

(ix) summary acts -use visual media if information relates to object relationships [3]

(x) locate acts- use visual media with attention marker

(xi) emphasise act- prefer visual media with highlighting

(xii) result act- prefer visual media of post condition state physical

(xiii) cause- prefer animation if physical event sequence available

### General Heuristics

(i) present same material on two channels if available- encoding redundancy [20]

(ii) use text and still images for key messages - display persistence

(iii) use text for instructions - display persistence [6]

(iv) use sound for warning

**Validating Heuristics**

These are used to check the combination of media to ensure attention and human information processing are not overloaded

(i) do not present different subject matter on separate channels - interference effect (auditory-visual dissonance [8], semantic interference [15])
(ii) do not present a large amount of information on non persistent media- limited retention visual working memory [9]
(iii) present only one animated sequence at a time - poor information retention from images, selective attention (dichotic viewing task [4])
(iv) use only visual-verbal channels concurrently (multiple resource theory [20])
(v) beware visual media tend to dominate over verbal- place important messages in visual channel in concurrent visual/verbal presentations [17]

As with many guidelines, some are merely stating common sense while others offer no guarantee of good design. Abstracting rules for psychological models is always open to problems of interpretation, for instance, it is not entirely clear what constitutes different subject matter - Validating Hueristic (i). To test out these ideas we used them in the case study to associate the appropriate media resources with the required information and dialogue act. While the method does not directly specify the process of generating the information displays, it does indicate the requirements for information retrieval which can then be developed in SQL or programming languages.

**4.3 Case Study Example**

In the case study scenario a fire breaks out in the ship's cargo hold. The ship's master requires information about the location and type of problem. This requires information about where the problem is (Locate act) in the context of the ships compartments (Background). The next step is to alert fire fighting teams ('Muster teams') and tell them where to go ('Move teams'). Information needs for these steps are the available teams and their location. Selection Guideline (i) indicates that spatial information should be given in an image and a diagram showing the ship's architecture highlighting the problem compartment is used. The fire location is in one of the cargo holds, so 'Find Contents' requires linguistic based information about the type of cargo, hence a text display is used  : Selection Guideline (vi). The resulting screen design is shown in figure 2.

The next sub-goal ('Analyse Hazard') requires procedural information which is available as text based instructions, picture sequences illustrating what to do for certain hazard classes, and video for some operations. General Heuristic (i) suggests that redundant presentation should be used where possible, so both pictures and text based descriptions of hazard control procedures are chosen. Selection Guideline (vii) prefers animation over still images when action is being presented, hence video with spoken commentary may be used for the Enable function. However in real operation time constraints may be critical so there may be no time to view a video sequence; hence text instructions are displayed with a short spoken summary, and use of other media is reserved as an option.

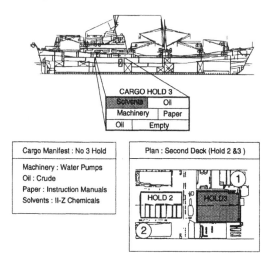

Figure 2. Screen Design for 'Move Teams' task step

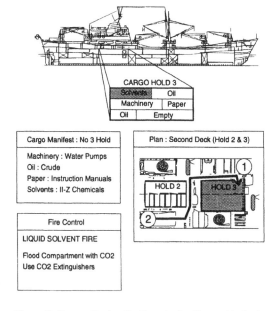

Figure 3. Screen Design for 'Locate Appliances' task step

'Check Side Effects' involves looking at cargo in the vicinity of the hazard to ensure there are no 'knock on' effects. The last actions are to locate the appliances and safety equipment to deal with the hazard and issue instructions to the emergency teams. Further Locate and Emphasise acts are required to show access routes and fire extinguishers in relation to the problem compartment while instructions for hazard control come from the previous task step (see figure 3).

## 5 Presentation Scripting

At this stage the media choice has been made but the sequence and duration of presentation needs to be scripted as information items have to persist for varying duration's. A bar chart illustrates the time-line of presentation (see figure 4). This allows the presentation sequence to be specified and synchronised with task actions.

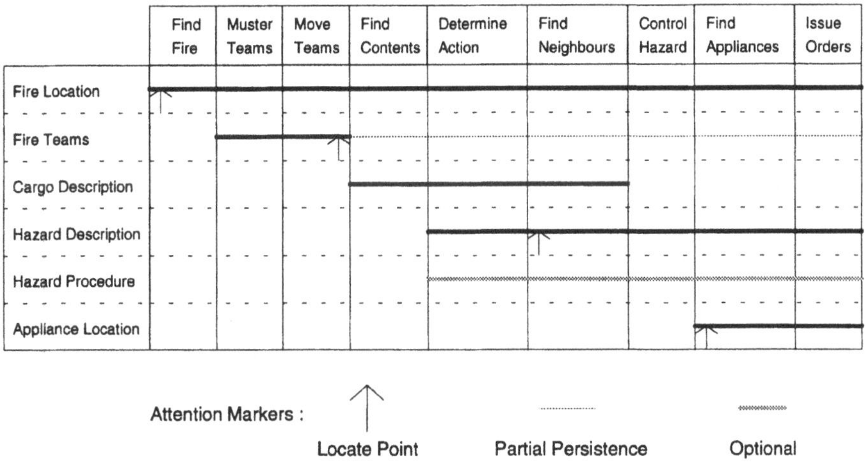

| | Find Fire | Muster Teams | Move Teams | Find Contents | Determine Action | Find Neighbours | Control Hazard | Find Appliances | Issue Orders |
|---|---|---|---|---|---|---|---|---|---|
| Fire Location | | | | | | | | | |
| Fire Teams | | | | | | | | | |
| Cargo Description | | | | | | | | | |
| Hazard Description | | | | | | | | | |
| Hazard Procedure | | | | | | | | | |
| Appliance Location | | | | | | | | | |

Attention Markers :  ↑ Locate Point  ⋯⋯ Partial Persistence  Optional

Figure 4 Presentation time line

## 5.1 Presentation act effects

Presentation markers are added for locate and emphasise acts to draw the user's attention to the specific information necessary for the task :

(i) Point information.- Locate : use arrow to designate location
(ii) Object location - Locate : highlight, show as icon
(iii) Object Id - Emphasise : highlight object
(iv) Object relations - Emphasise: highlight connection and associated objects, use animation to illustrate directionality (source, link destination)
(v) Actions / Event -Emphasise : use animation with freeze frame for important event

### 5.2 Case Study Example

The guidelines result in a number of attention markers being used : highlighting emphasises (guideline 5.1 (iii)) the position of the problem compartment, while icons (guideline 5.1 (ii)) denote the location of fire extinguishers and show the approximate location of fire fighting teams, arrows are used to show access points to the hold compartment (guideline 5.1 (i)). The resulting display following the 'Locate Appliances' step is shown in figure 3. Presentation boxes have been added giving information about dealing with the hazard and this is visually cross referenced to the cargo list. The captain now has all the information required to issue fire fighting instructions : where the teams are, appliances and their locations and access to the compartment.

## 6 Conclusions

So far the method has proved useful as a means of exploring the issues involved in multimedia design. The diagrams provide tools for thought about presentation issues concerning what information is required and when. Our investigations have however focused on well structured tasks, in other domains a deterministic scripting approach may not be so appropriate and the method may be used to describe a range of presentation options. Our method and guidelines give an agenda of design issues, planning persistence of messages, selective attention, and avoiding information overload, which we believe has not been explicit in previous work ([2], [7], [13]]). Whereas redundancy by concurrent presentation may help learning in multimedia computer based training systems, multi channel presentation can be disadvantageous in a task context if the message is lost in too much information. More focus is required on the message within the media and this study has made some modest progress in that direction. However, methods may be criticised for being over-elaborate for economic use. We intend to progress in two directions, one is to produce a cut down method for rapid specification and secondly to formalise the method steps and guide-lines into rules for development of a multimedia presentation planner. We expect to develop further guide-lines as our experience progresses. Although the guidelines proposed so far are based on survey of the relevant psychological literature, there is no guarantee of their effectiveness. To evaluate their effectiveness Wizard of Oz techniques will be employed to test usability problems with the proposed design. The method so far, while making no claim to have solved the problem of multimedia interface design, has explored the issues which must be addressed in MM interfaces and made some progress towards providing sound design advice.

## Acknowledgements

The work outlined here was undertaken as part of INTUITIVE (P6593) : a project partially funded by the Commission of the European Communities Esprit programme.

The help of Lloyds Register, UK is gratefully acknowledged. Thanks in particular to Clive Bright, John Hobday and Derek Rhoden of Lloyds.

# References

1.  J. Alty & C.D.C. McCartney : Design of a Multi-media Presentation System for a Process Control Enviroment. Eurographics Multimedia workshop : Stockholm (1991)

2.  E. Andre & T. Rist : Generating Illustrated Documents : A plan based approach. InfoJapan 90, Vol 2, 163 - 170 (1990)

3.  D.J. Bartram: Comprehending spatial information : The relative efficiency of different methods of presenting information about bus routes. Journal of Applied Psychology, 65, 103 - 110 (1980)

4.  R. Becklem & D. Cervone: Selective looking and the noticing of unexpected events. Memory & Cognition, 11(6), 601 - 608 (1983)

5.  G.R. Bieger & M.D. Glock: The Information Content of Picture-Text Instructions. Journal of Experimental Education, 53, 68-76 (1984)

6.  H.R. Booher: Relative Comprehensibility of Pictorial Information and Printed word in Proceduralized Instructions. Human Factors, 17(3), 266 - 277 (1975)

7.  S. Fiener & K.R. McKeown: Generating Co-ordinated Multimedia Explanations. In 6th IEEE Conference on Artificial Intelligence Applications (Santa Barbara CA) (Pg 290 - 296) (1990)

8.  T. Grimes: Mild Auditory-Visual dissonance in TV News may exceed viewer attention. Human Communication Research 18(2) 268 - 298 (1991)

9.  G.J. Hitch: Working memory. In B. Christie & M. Gardiner (eds.): Applying cognitive psychology to user interface design. London: J. Wiley (1987)

10. P. Johnson, H. Johnson, R. Waddington, & A. Shouls: Task-Related Knowledge Structures : Analysis. Modelling and Application. In D.M. Jones, R. Winder (eds.): People and Computers IV. Cambridge University Press. (1988)

11. J.B. Long & J. Dowell: Conceptions of the Discipline of HCI : Craft, Applied Science and Engineering. In A.G. Sutcliffe, L. Macaulay (eds.): People and Computers V., Cambridge University Press. (1989)

12. W.C. Mann & S.A Thompson: Rhetorical Structure Theory - Toward a functional theory of text organisation. Text, 8(3), 243 - 281 (1988)

13. M. Maybury: Planning Multimedia Explanations Using Communicative Acts. In Proceedings of 9th National Conference on Artificial Intelligence (Pg 61 - 66) (1991)

14. J. Miller: Timecourse of coactivation in bimodal divided attention. Perception & Psychophysics, 40(5), 331-343 (1986)

15. D. Navon & J. Miller: Role of Outcome Conflict in Dual Task Interference. Journal of Experimental Psychology : Human Perception and Performance, 13(3), 435 - 448 (1987)

16. M. Petre & T.R.G. Green: Is graphical notation really superior to text, or just different ? Some claims by logic designers about graphics in notation. In Fifth European Conference on Cognitive Ergonomics (Urbino, Italy) (1990)

17. M. Posner: Visual Dominance: An Information Processing account of its origins and significance. Psychological Review, 83, 157 - 171 (1976)

18. L.P. Rieber: Animation in Computer Based Instruction. Educational Technology Research & Development, 38, 77 - 86 (1990)

19. J.R Searle: Speech Acts : An essay in the philosophy of language. Cambridge University Press (1969)

20. C.D. Wickens: Processing Resources in Attention. In R. Pararsuraman & D. Davies (eds.): Varieties of Attention (Pg 63-102). New York : Academic Press (1983)

# Iconic Signs and Languages
# in User Interface Development

## Gennady Uzilevsky*, Vladimir Andreev**

* Head of HCI laboratory of joint-stock company "Techn&com",
Schenogina 4a, 123007, Moscow, Russia, fax (095) 182-7568
** President  of joint-stock company "Techn&com"

Abstract. Various aspects of the complex problem of icon construction
for user interface design are considered, ergosemiotic requirements for icon
design are presented, and features and functions of iconic languages are
defined.

Uzilevsky et al [24] presents an analysis of five periods in the
evolution of the means of communication: prevocal; vocal and written
language; vocal, written language and book printing; vocal, written
language, book printing, video, TV and personal computer. Comparing
the first and the fifth periods, we note that they both have iconic
languages. Indeed, iconic signs and iconic languages play an important
role in the design of new information technologies, especially
multimedia, scientific visualisation and computer-aided design.

In this paper we define and consider various problems of iconic
signs and iconic languages (IL). Let us begin with icons. Various
investigations carried out during the past 25 years in a number of
countries provide a systematic approach, leading to a new scientific
specialization "iconics" (on its directions see [45] that deals with the
study of nonverbal communications with the help of untraditional
means (TV, computers, video).

Icons denote functions of computer systems, the system objects,
various types of system status and represent commands, cursors,
menu, items, windows, screen selection buttons, utilities, processes,
programs and the like. They are a defining component of WIMP and
SILK technologies.

First, consider icon classification. The sign was interpreted by the
semiotician Ch. Peirce. as "something which stands to somebody for
something in some respect or capacity" [17, p. 135]. This definition
differs from other definitions in that a human being is at its center.

Signs were divided by Peirce into three groups: icons, indexes and
symbols. Signs were related to objects by resembling them ("icons"),
being causally connected to them ("indexes") or being conventionally

tied to them ("symbols"). Icons were classified into images, diagrams and metaphors.

Current researchers have somewhat different approaches to icon classification. K.N.Lodding, for instance, provides an icon taxonomy based on their design (representational, abstract, arbitrary) and function (picture, symbol, sign). The design style classifies the visual representation of the image; function classifies the use of the image [12].

Lodding defines a context as a selection criterion which places an icon into one of these three categories. A sign classification differing from Ch. Peirce's is proposed by A.Marcus who offers the following sign groups: representational, abstract and semi-abstract [13].

The analysis of these classifications leads to the conclusion that they are artificial. Therefore, it is useful to work out a system-semiotical classification of icons. The elaboration of such a classification is one of the important facets of the icon design problem.

The analyzed classifications favour the acceptance of the term "icon". In this connection, the term "iconic interface" is broader than both "visual" or "graphic interface".

P.Kolers proposed a general structure of icons consisting of two components: elements and compounds [10]. An element is a graphical image whose decomposition would result in uninterpretable parts. Examples might be pictographic images, geometric shapes, marks. A compound is a combination of elements.

A specific approach to this general structure is the icon system design of S.-K.Chang [5] which dominates computer graphics and related domains. (On S.K.Chang and his school in Russian scientific literature, see [30]).

When designing and developing icons, it is important to take into account certain restrictions that are laid on the process by the nature of icons, hardware and software, and the specific character of the perception and processing of visual information by the end user. Therefore to create a systemic approach to icon perception, understanding and design, it is necessary to collect and generalize different knowledge and data from many specializations, including engineering psychology [42], ergonomics [37], psychosemiotics [32], visual semiotics [23], psycholinguistics [33], psychology [39]

In this connection, we consider ergosemiotic aspects of icon design. (On ergosemiotics, see [25; 44]. One of the aims of this specialization is the creation of effective and comfortable visual sign systems and their elements - iconic signs. The usage of the icons on such workstations as "Star" and "Lisa" showed that they were good for creating user interfaces. The investigations that were carried out in the eighties lead specialists to the conclusion that HCI using icons could be successful.

One of the reasons for such success lies in the fact that icons rely on human ability to perceive natural form and shape quickly [9]. In addition, icons can represent a great deal of information in a small amount of space. It was found out that the users spot, recognize and process icons faster than they do with words [20]. A.Marcus came to the conclusion that icons were selected from iconic menus faster than from word- or phrase-based menus [13], 1984). Woodgate showed that icons were recognized quicker than equivalent sets of character, and that pointing was faster than selecting using a keyboard [27].

Obviously, this could be explained by the fact that in using icons there is no need to compress information in the way that takes place when decoding messages expressed in a natural language.

A non-verbal form of language used by human intelligence seems to have a positive influence on icon processing. N.Zhinkin's investigations showed that this language was an object-representational or object-schematic code because there was no material evidence of natural language words and designated objects were used as signs [35, p. 51].

Since icons and iconic languages have no verbal language barriers, they are attractive as vehicles of international information exchange. However, we should consider the phenomenon very cautiously since every natural language has its own iconic base [38].

At the same time other investigations indicated that things are not so simple in the iconic kingdom. For example, Schulman et al show that although verbal and iconic signs which denote text editors commands have equal learning and retention rates, a preference was given to the verbal form of commands [21].

G.Rohr found that users showed no preference for a verbal or a pictorial representation if a notion appeared as a referent object [19]. It was stated that commands which initiate a process without control operations are best represented in a pictorial form. In contrast, commands which initiate a process with manipulative control actions are best described by abstract visual symbols.

Drawbacks with icons that follow from their advantages are ambiguity and polysemanticity. Lodding showed that a triangle appears as either a picture, an abstract, or an arbitrary sign according to the context [12].

Obviously, the revealing of ergosemiotic requirements is of scientific and practical use. The analysis of the scientific literature that we carried out produced the following requirements:

- icons should be easy to detect, understand and memorize, unwarranted loading on cognitive structures of a user's intelligence should be avoided [8]

- icons should be mostly designed to resemble objects and operations, but not by analogy [8]). Icons that were created in the form of concrete pictograms and abstract symbols ([18] were most effective. Rogers also showed that the adding of a concrete analogy element to a concrete metaphoric icon and an abstract symbol results in great difficulties in the process of recognizing such a complex sign. The icons that were designed by analogy appeared to be the least effective. It was found out that functions with a high level of abstraction do not always yield to the pictorial depiction;
- the specificity of various types of icons is to be taken into consideration. In this connection the paper [22] is interesting. The users' perception of abstract symbols and concrete metaphoric icons that represent the same functions of the workstation UI was studied. The experiments showed that concrete icons were better detected than abstract symbols and with fewer errors. After five trials the scores were equal. The users' perception of concrete icons gave similar results. It could be said that concrete icons are characterized by complexity, but abstract symbols representing common visual forms are perceptually much simpler. The two groups of signs are very different in cognitive terms. According to the comments of subjects that were questioned after the experiments, when understanding abstract symbols an attempt is being made to learn the matching of the latter to functions. As to concrete icons, it is necessary to reveal the meaning of the elements and to generalize the received knowledge for the function definition;
- in order to create comfortable and effective icons, self-organization of the iconic language should be realized. Self-organization lies in first producing the simplest signs (elements), and then constructing the higher level icons out of them. This will favour the processes of icon creation, detection, recognition and association formation. This approach was followed when designing a language for computer graphics users the basis of which was a language of geometric configurations [31].

In the case when icons consist of two or three elements, whenever possible the elements should be placed according to N.Tarabukin's law of painting composition, on the diagonal axis from lower left to upper right [41]. Such positioning will impart action and tension to the user's work with tablet menus [2] and screen menus [1].

When creating complex icons, one could use such modes as combining, transforming and inheriting [3]. It is also possible to use the following ways of creating complex icons: overlapping, interpenetration, addition, and insertion [34] in the design of CAD user interface [31].

How to use icons and verbal signs together is not yet well understood. Let us consider it from various positions. Recent investigations [46] convincingly showed that the specificity of right and left hemispheres contribution to the cognition is determined not by verbal or non-verbal information but by the mode of information usage.

A distinctive peculiarity of the strategy of the left hemisphere is that it uses "strong" connections when organizing monosemantical context. Not only words but also other signs including icons could be used. The strategy of the right hemisphere, based on other principles, creates polysemantical contexts. The two cognitive strategies sometimes function simultaneously and cooperatively in processing information; sometimes they not only interfere but also suppress each other. This results in three "states of mind": logical, intuitive and cooperative [15].

Taking the above into account, we turn our attention to HCI. Uzilevsky outlined the following types of UI functions: communicative, learning, illustrative, cognitive, creative, feedback and professional activity [25; 43]. By their nature, communicative and feedback functions possess only one meaning; other functions are typically polysemantic.

It follows from this that a person interacting with a user interface deals only with "pure" meanings, but interacting with a program operates with "pure" senses that results in getting a non-trivial conclusion. The use of icons could favour this [36]. In other words, an iconic interface seems to promote a cooperative state of mind. Proceeding from the functional brain asymmetry research [46], conception of dual coding (verbal or non-verbal) [16], from the cognitive theory of parallel information processing [11], from experimental investigations of verbal and iconic signs [7], one could come to the conclusion that the mutual usage of both information processing strategies in the creation of complex icons will promote not only their exact, but also their quick, detection and learning.

The investigation showed that in icon evaluation and selection it was necessary to use two criteria: learning and preference that gave the possibility of choosing the most appropriate signs with fewer errors [4].

We have considered some facets of the problem of icon perception, understanding and design. Now let us consider the connection of icon design with gestaltpsychology. Yesterby made an attempt to connect the problem with semiotics and gestaltpsychology [28]. He revealed five features that define "good" icon quality: closure, continuity, symmetry, simplicity and unity.

According to D.Deutsch, the signs can be grouped with the help of such simple criteria as proximity, similarity, continuity [6].

We suspect that it would be possible to develop a tool aimed at ascertaining the set of icons belonging to the same system.

We have discussed various inner features of icons. Now it is useful to note the characteristics of icons which make them suitable for HCI. Webb et al formulated and examined five such characteristics: detectability, legibility, interpretability and preference [26].

Naturally we can not consider all facets of the problem, but nevertheless various revealed aspects testify to the formation of systemic, complex approach to its solution. An example is the investigation carried out by Hewlett Packard company aimed at the creation of empirical methods of icon evaluation. The methods used by researchers were: psychophysics, scaling, recognition/memory testing, statistical modeling/analysis [26].

Now let us turn our attention to iconic languages (IL). Research and design of ILs is a very complex problem. We have space here only to discuss features and functions of ILs.

In the beginning of world cultural development, people used iconic signs and languages not only for communication but also for the fixation of the ideas about external world, world of humans and animals [29]. After the appearance of written language, iconic sign systems began to be developed in three directions:

- towards the greater correspondence of vocal and written series in natural languages;
- towards the achievement of equivalence of sign and notion; this was realized by the development of mathematics;
- towards the achievement of an iconic likeness principle of sign and designatum used in constructing diagrams, draughts, graphs etc. [40].

The development of iconic signs and languages from the representation of external spatial forms to the transmission of the structure and functions of objects testifies to the existence of a similarity feature for these semiotic formations. This feature is implemented in concrete iconic systems through the realisation of a simulation function.

The second feature of IL consists in the substitution and representation of simulated objects. Substitution is implemented by forming communicative and illustrative functions of the UI.

The third feature of IL is iconic information compression and realised through the representation, description and simulation of iconic signs and designated objects. For example, we see compression in such presentations as charts and draughts. These three features of ILs lead to the appearance of a peculiar function of ILs: the formalisation (mathematical simulation) of icons, iconic systems and represented objects.

The fourth feature of ILs is polysemanticity of information of the designated object and is realized through a cognitive and creative function (see, for instance, [36]).

The fifth feature of ILs is self-organisation and is realized through the usage of elementary signs in construction and realisation of complex signs. The feature is used not only to reveal the structures of the languages of engineering and computer graphics, but also to construct the language of computer graphics users and to form communication languages (e.g., tablet-and screen menu) [31]. The features and functions of ILs are shown in table 1.

*Table 1*

| Features and functions of iconic languages ||
|---|---|
| Features | Functions |
| similarity | simulation |
| substitution and representation | illustrative communicative |
| iconic information compression | formalisation and iconic simulation |
| polysemanticity of information | cognitive creative |
| selforganisation | communicative and of activity |

The formal approach to icons and iconic systems (including ILs) is useful not only for giving formalized descriptions of the set of iconic signs [5], but also as a mathematical tool for the simulation of various objects in science and engineering.

Space does not permit us to reveal and discuss other aspects of the research, design and implementation of iconic languages. We think that the creation of a complex scientific program aimed at the investigation, design and testing of iconic signs and iconic languages could yield not only new scientific results but also the formulation of concrete recommendations that will aid user interface designers to competently and easily create iconic langauges that effectively incorporate color, music codes and other sign systems.

*The authors express their sincere gratitude to A.Henderson for his valuable remarks concerning content and style of the article.*

## References.

1. V.N. Andreef, T.P. Zinchenko: Psychosemantic metrics of the VDT screen. In: I-st Moscow International Workshop Proc. Moscow, 1991, pp.304-307.
2. V.O. Andreev, G.Ja. Uzilevsky: On the requirements to the tablet menus creation and estimation. In: 1-st Moscow International HCI'91 Workshop Proc. Moscow, 1991, pp.86-93.
3. M.H. Blattner, D.A. Sumikava: Greenberg, R.M. Earcons and icons: their structure and common design principles Human-computer interaction (4), 1, 11-44 (1989)
4. D.J. Brems, W.B. Whitten: Learning and preference for icon-based interface. In: Proc. on the Human Factors Soc. 31th Annual Meeting. N.-Y., 1987, v.1, pp. 125-129.
5. S.K. Chang: Icon semantics - a formal approach to icon system design. Intern. J. of pattern recognition and artificial intelligence, (1), 1, 103-120 (1987)
6. D. Deutsch: Grouping mechanism in music. In: The psychology of music. N.-Y., 1982, pp. 99-134.
7. S.J. Guastello, M. Traut: Verbal versus pictorial representations of objects in a human-computer interface. Intern. J. Man- Mach. St., (31), 1, 99-120 (1989)
8. K. Hemenway: Psychological issues in the use of icons in command menus *In:*. Proc. of the CHI'82 Conference on Human Factors in Computer Systems. Gaithersberg, 1982, pp. 20-25.
9. W.H. Huggins, D.R. Entwisle: Icon communication: An annotated bibliography. Baltimore & London: The J.Hopkins Univ. Press, 1974, 167 p.
10. P. Kolers: Some formal characteristics of pictograms. American Scientist, (57), 3, 348-363 (1984)
11. R. Lachman, J.L. Lachman, E.C. Butterfield: Cognitive psychology and information processing: an introduction. Hillsdale & N.-Y.: Lawrence Erlbaum, 1979
12. Lodding, K.N. Iconics - a visual man-machine interface. In: Proc. of National Computer Graphics Assoc. Conference. Vol. 1. Arnheim, 1982, pp. 221-233.
13. A. Marcus: Corporate identity for iconic interface design: the graphic design perspective. Computer graphics and applications, (4), 12, 24-32 (1984)
14. C. Niemitz: Visuelle Zeichen, Sprache und Gehirn in der Evolution des Menschen - Eine Entgegnung auf McFarland. Zt. fur Semiotik, (12), 4, 323-336 (1990)
15. M. Patterson: Design considerations for a graphical human/computer interface. In: Computer Graphics: Proc. of the Intern. Conference. Pinner, 1983, pp.73-83.
16. A. Pavio: Mental representations: a dual coding approach. N.Y.: Oxford Univ. Press, 1986, 323 p.
17. Ch.S. Peirce: Collected papers. Vol.1-2. Cambridge., Mass., 1960
18. Y. Rogers: Evaluating the meaningfulness of icon sets to represent command operations. In: People and Computers.- Cambridge, 1986, pp. 586-603.
19. G. Rohr: Understanding visual symbols. In: IEEE Computer Workshop on Visual Languages. Hiroshima, 1984, pp.184-191.
20. B. Shneiderman: Designing user interface: Strategies for effective human-computer interaction. Reading, M.A.: Addison Wesley, 1987, 448 p.

21. H.G. Shulman, S. Shute, O. Weissman: Icons versus names as command designators in text editing. In: Proc. of the Intern. Conference on Cybernetics and Society.-N.-Y., 1985, pp. 268-272.

22. R. B. Stammers, D.A. George, M.S. Garey: An evaluation of abstract and concrete icons for a CAD package.In: Contemporary Ergonomics. London, 1986, pp.416-421.

23. The semiotics of visual  Amsterdam: Mouton, 1984

24. G. Uzilevsky, V. Andreev: View on the information technologies from the positions of information environment evolution. Information technologies and people: In.: Proc. of Intern. Conference. Moscow, 1993.

25. G.Ja. Uzilevsky, V.P. Zinchenko: User interface research: an ergosemiotical approach. In: East-West International Conference on Human-Computer Interaction Proc. St. Petersburg, p. 2., 1992, pp. 303-313.

26. J.M. Webb, P.F. Sorensen, N.C. Lyons: An empirical approach to the evaluation of icons. SIGCHI Bull., I, 87-90 (1989)

27. H.S. Woodgate: The use of graphical symbolic commands (icons) in aplication programms. In: Eurographics' 85. Amsterdam, 1985, pp.25-36.

28. R.S. Yesterby: The perception of symbols for machine displays. Ergonomics. (13), 1, 149-158 (1970)

29. З.А. Абрамова: Древнейшие формы изобразительного творчества (археологический анализ палеотического искусства).In: Ранние формы искусства. М., 1982, pp. 9-29.

30. В.Л. Авербух: Изобразительные средства визуального программирования. Пользовательский интерфейс: исследование, проектирование, реализация. Вып. 2. М., 1992, pp. 51-57.

31. В.О. Андреев, Г.Я. Узилевский: Язык геометрических изображений как основа формирования языка пользователей машинной графики для общего машиностроения. Пользовательский интерфейс: исследование, проектирование, реализация. Вып. 2. М., 1992, pp.58-71.

32. М.В. Гамезо, В.Ф. Рубахин: Психологическая семиотика: методология, проблемы, результаты исследований. Психологический журнал, 6, 22-34 (1982)

33. Л.В. Головина: Взаимовлияние иконических и вербальных знаков при смысловом восприятии текста: Автореф. на соиск. учен. степ. канд. филол. н. М., 1986, 20 с.

34. Л.Э. Городжий: Графические совмещения неязыковых знаков. In: Дизайн знаковых систем. М., 1984, pp.57-77.

35. Н.И. Жинкин: Речь как проводник информации. М.: Наука, 1982, 159 с.

36. А.А. Зенкин: Когнитивная компьютерная графика. М.: Наука, 1991, 192 с.

37. И.И. Литвак: Системы отображения информации. М.: МИЭМ, 1980, 74 с.

38. Г.П. Мельников: Иконическая основа естественных языков. In: Российская научно-техническая конференция "Исследование, проектирование и реализация пользовательского интерфейса в САПР. Орел, 1992.

39. С.С. Педько: Психологические особенности смыслового содержания графических знаков: Автореф. на соиск. учен. степ. канд. псих. н. Тбилиси, 1986, 24 с.

40. М.В. Попович: Философские вопросы семантики. Киев: Наукова думка, 1975, 299 с.

41. Н. Тарабукин: Смысловое значение диагональных композиций в живописи. In: Учен. записки Тарт. гос. ун-та. Вып. 308., 1973, pp.471-481.

42. М.К. Тутушкина: Психологические основы кодирования зрительной информации для человека-оператора: Автореф. на соиск. учен. степ. д. психол. н. Л., 1982, 35 с.

43. Г.Я. Узилевский: Выбор цвета при создании пользовательского интерфейса: предпосылки и рекомендации. Орел: НПП "ГрафОр",1992,162 с. (электронная книга).

44. Г.Я. Узилевский: Об эргосемиотическом подходе к созданию визуальных знаковых систем. In: Графические знаки: проблемы исследования, разработки, стандартизации. Киев, 1988, pp.13-15.

45. Г.Я. Узилевский, А.А. Зенкин: Иконика: современное состояние и перспективы развития. Пользовательский интерфейс: исследование, проектирование, реализация. Вып. 2. М., 1992, pp. 7-18

46. С.И. Чесноков, В.С. Ротенберг: Два способа организации контекста и проблема взаимопонимания. In: Учен. записки Тарт. гос. ун-та. Вып. 793, 1988, с.149-165.

# E$^3$: Towards the Metrication of Graphical Presentation Techniques for Large Data Sets

Ying K. Leung

Centre for Systems Methodologies
Department of Computer Science
Swinburne University of Technology
Victoria 3122
Australia

Mark D. Apperley

School of Mathematical and
Information Sciences
Massey University
Palmerston North
New Zealand

**Abstract.** Rapid advances in communications and computer technologies in recent years have provided users with greater access to large volumes of data from computer-based information systems. Whilst researchers have developed many novel techniques to overcome the problems associated with the presentation and navigation of large data sets on a limited display surface, the choice of a technique in a particular application remains very subjective. This paper proposes an evaluation framework E$^3$ which aims to provide a basis for the comparison of different presentation techniques, given the nature and characteristics of the data to be presented, and the interpretation required. E$^3$ focuses on three aspects of graphical data presentation: expressiveness, efficiency, and effectiveness. This framework lays the foundation for the development of a set of metrics to facilitate an objective assessment of presentation techniques.

## 1. Introduction

Graphics has long been exploited to represent abstract quantitative data, since William Playfair published his *Commercial and Political Atlas* nearly two hundred years ago. Graphical charts and plots are now standard tools in presenting statistical data; they are superior to tables of numerical values by being more compact and aesthetically pleasing, and by their ability to attract viewers' attention and convey the underlying information quickly. There is research evidence in experimental psychology and cognitive science to suggest that well designed graphics aid comprehension, decision making and recall [13]. Conversely, poorly prepared graphics misrepresent the inherent data and mislead the viewer. Considerable skills and experience are required to design effective graphics to achieve optimal visual communication. Fortunately, well established guidelines are available for designers to exploit the potential of this powerful medium to the fullest [2,6,9,21,26,27].

With the advent of video display units, the use of computer generated graphics to present information has grown at a phenomenal pace since Ivan Sutherland embarked on his SKETCHPAD project [25] three decades ago. The enormous computational power of personal computers available these days has made them ideal vehicles for presenting graphical information, not only statically, but also dynamically. Sophisticated user interfaces have been developed relying principally on the use of computer graphics. Nowadays, a typical graphical user interface enables the user to manipulate directly any object or item of interest on the display screen. The high resolution of the graphics monitor coupled with a near instantaneous system response time provides the user with a feel of realism and complete control.

At the same time advances in communications and computer technologies over the past decade have provided users with greater access to large volumes of data from computer-based information systems. This trend is set to continue as ever improving networking facilities and transmission rates enable greater connectivity to an expanding range of remote databases. This increasing facility for information access has the potential to improve operational efficiency and provide high productivity in a business environment. However, these advantages will only materialise if users of these computer-based systems can operate and manage this information explosion effectively.

The issue addressed in this paper relates to the problem of accessing large data sets via relatively limited display surfaces. Whilst researchers [23,10,14,4,18,20] have developed a variety of novel techniques to overcome these problems, the choice of a technique for a particular application remains very subjective. This is partly attributable to the fact that current evaluation methodologies for these techniques, particularly those pertaining to spatial data and/or involving geometric transformations, are inadequate. Furthermore, there are many system-specific parameters related to these techniques making generalisation of experimental results very difficult, if not impossible. This paper proposes a framework $E^3$ which aims to provide a basis for the comparison of different presentation techniques, given the nature and characteristics of the data to be presented, and the interpretation required. $E^3$ focuses on three aspects of graphical data presentation: *expressiveness*, *efficiency*, and *effectiveness*. (Throughout this paper, the use of any of these three words in the context of $E^3$ is italicised.) It is suggested that this framework could lead to the development of a set of metrics to facilitate an objective assessment of presentation techniques, and the choice of an appropriate technique for a given circumstance.

## 2. Presentation of Large Data Sets

The front end of a user interface is what the user sees on the computer screen. In designing interfaces for large data sets, much effort has been placed in perfecting the presentation of the data for optimal visual communication. However, this can be achieved only if the designer has a thorough knowledge of the capabilities and limitations of the hardware at hand, a good understanding of the nature of the data to be presented, and an insight into the potential mental operations that the user performs on the data. The following subsections describe in detail the three key areas of consideration in the course of designing and implementing graphical user interfaces for large data sets - classification, representation and presentation.

### 2.1   Classification of Data Types

Whilst digital computers represent and store information in binary form, where each piece of data is encoded in a string of 1s and 0s, data can be classified in a variety of ways depending on the perspective to be taken. Stevens provided a useful classification of data in the context of measurement [24]; the four measurement scales of data proposed are nominal, ordinal, interval and ratio. In the context of presentation, data can be broadly classified according to whether it is inherently graphical in nature, with implicit spatial relationships, or whether it is non-graphical. In many cases, however, data of the latter type can be represented in an abstract graphical form. This classification is illustrated in Figure 1.

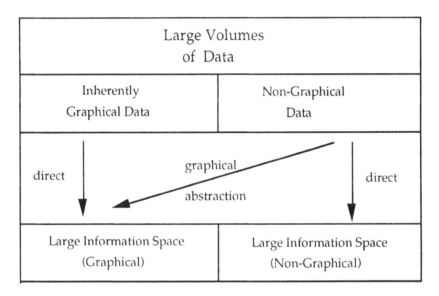

**Figure 1.** Classification of Graphical and non-Graphical Data Spaces

The way in which a piece of data is stored in a computer is similar to that in which a folder is put away in a personal filing system. An orderly, and often hierarchical, structure must be in place to allow speedy data deposits and retrievals. In the case of a collection of unstructured data, it may be ordered arbitrarily; for example, the data set may be sequenced by an alphabetical index or by the data's physical size. Data sets with an inherent linear structure may be organised as link lists. Pieces of data are often conveniently grouped together to form a single unit of information or a record; for example, a student has a name, an ID number, an address and a list of enrolled subjects, etc. These units of information may in turn be grouped together to form a hierarchical tree structure with multiple levels depending on the size and complexity of the data set. It is interesting to note that an orderly data structure not only allows speedy system access but also enables the viewer to establish and maintain a conceptual model of the data set; the latter advantage is particularly beneficial for large data sets. To facilitate the process of constructing such a model, various levels of abstraction may also be applied to represent the underlying data in the hierarchical structure.

## 2.2     Representation of Data

A set of data may be represented graphically in a number of ways. Students' performances in a class test may be presented by a standard bar chart with the x axis showing the grades and the y axis the number of students; the length of bar represents the number of students achieving a particular grade. Similarly, a pie chart could have been used with sections of the pie chart representing the number of students in each of the grades. The choice of a particular representation method usually depends on the information intended to be conveyed, and the mental operations the viewer is likely to perform on the information presented. In the previous example, if the user wishes to extract proportion information relating to the population quickly, a pie chart will be more appropriate. On the other hand, if the user is more interested in comparing two exemplars, a bar chart will be superior. Much experimental work has been carried out to study the perceptual properties of a wide range of representation techniques, and there are well established guidelines available to designers [2,6,9,21,26,8,27]. These guidelines enable the designer to match the specific perceptual tasks carried out by the viewer, with the most appropriate representation method. Furthermore, many novel representation techniques, for example using cartoon faces [7], stars [11], glyphs [1], trees and castles [12], have been invented to represent multi-dimensional data.

It should be pointed out that the encoding process involved in data representation often reduces the precision of the underlying data. Precision, however, is not always desirable; although a table of numbers contains highly precise numerical data, it requires much mental effort for the viewer to extract useful information from it. In many applications, viewers do not require data accuracy to the level of numerical values, and they would willingly trade such accuracy for reduced cognitive load in locating and interpreting the data.

In a large hierarchical data set, abstraction serves as a useful means for information hiding, enabling the viewer to visualise the global structure of the data set. Such data sets are represented in an abstract form primarily to save space as the display surface is limited in size. In a multi-level hierarchical data structure, different degrees of abstraction may be applied at each level, and due design consideration must be given to ensure consistency in representation.

## 2.3     Presentation of Data

Despite the large variety of computer-based information systems and their wide span of application domains, there are fundamentally three functions which a user performs when interacting with such a system: (i) locating an item of interest in the data set, (ii) interpreting the data, and (iii) relating an item to other data in the set. Over the years, user interface designers have expended much effort in producing 'easy-to-learn' and 'easy-to-use' human-computer interfaces for large data sets, to enable the user to carry out these three operations. Although experimental psychologists and cognitive scientists have made much progress in the understanding of the human visual system, presentation of data, especially large data sets, remains the most challenging aspect of an interface design.

A major problem associated with the presentation of large data sets is the relative small window through which an information space can be viewed. A consequence of this 'keyhole' effect is that the user is unable to relate the current view on the display surface with the overall context of the data structure, thus giving rise to the 'where am I?' problem. This undesirable effect may be ameliorated or eradicated by using special presentation techniques.

Whilst presentation techniques can be broadly be classified as non-distortion- and distortion-oriented [16], there are generally two approaches in presenting information from large data sets, as shown in Figure 2. The first approach (Figure 2a) is to reduce systematically the size of the data set to the extent where the desired data can be adequately displayed on the computer screen. In a typical implementation of this approach, the user is prompted by the system either through a query language or a menu selection process, to specify the subset of the large data set which is of interest. For example, in a financial database application, the system might ask the user a series of questions relating to the particular year, division and department required before presenting the information specified. By restricting the amount of data to be presented, the subset of data can be entirely accommodated on a limited display surface. Hence, presentation no longer remains an issue, and the problem reduces itself to one of data representation.

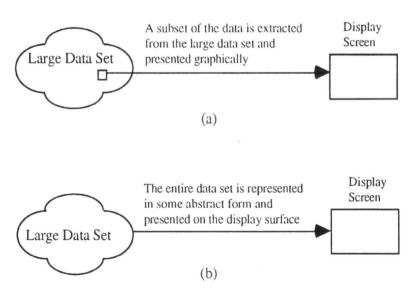

(a)

(b)

**Figure 2.** Two common approaches in presenting large data sets

This approach is very popular in many PC-based applications because of its simplicity in implementation. In recent years, intelligent and sophisticated systems enabling automatic presentation of small data sets which can fit well in a single window have been developed [17,5,19]. When applied to a section of a large data set, this approach can be described as a non-distortion oriented technique, and is most suited to applications where the user has well-defined goals and a good understanding of the internal structure of the data.

The second approach for presenting a large data set, and one which is particularly suitable for spatial data applications, is to represent the entire data set through an abstraction or geometric transformation process (thus reducing its size) and then to display the transformed image of the data set on the computer screen (Figure 2b). This approach can be described as a distortion-oriented presentation technique; the user is provided with a complete, but distorted, view of the data set. Commonly this will combine an overview of the structure of the large data set and at the same time, the user is able to examine a small section of data in detail. Figure 3 gives a summary of the implementation strategies for distortion- and non-distortion-oriented presentation techniques for different types of data.

Depending on the complexity and the size of the data set, special navigation techniques may have to be devised and implemented to provide adequate global context. This presentation approach is most suitable for browsing where the user may not have a well-defined goal and has very little familiarity or pre-conceived idea of the internal structure of the large data set. When interacting with a new computer-based information system, novice users generally spend much of their time in exploration - casually and often aimlessly moving from one section of the large data set to another. As the user gains experience and becomes familiar interacting with the system, a refined conceptual model of the system is gradually developed.

| Data \ Techniques | Large Information Space (Graphical) | Large Information Space (Non-Graphical) |
|---|---|---|
| Non-Distorted View | zooming windowing | paging clipping |
| Distorted View | encoding spatial transformation (geometric) | data suppression (abstraction and thresholding) |

Figure 3.   Presentation techniques for large information space

## 2.4   Presentation Evaluation

In recent years, there has been a growing interest in the development of novel techniques focusing on distortion-oriented presentation approaches as larger databases are becoming more accessible to users. Evaluation of these techniques has tended to be subjective in nature because objective evaluations pose a practical problem that an element of luck may affect the task completion times. This problem, however, may be overcome by conducting an extensive evaluation involving a great number of subjects. However, because of the time and effort constraints, an exhaustive evaluation is often not possible. Even if an exhaustive objective evaluation is made to compare user performance with these interfaces, there is an additional problem of generalisation of results. Distortion-oriented presentation techniques have various system-specific parameters which are different from technique to technique, making a comparison of like-with-like impossible. An evaluation of these techniques using conventional methodologies would, at best, conclude that one interface was better than the other under the test conditions with the system parameters used. Further generalisation than this runs into the danger of conjecture. A multi-dimensional approach [3] to interface evaluation consisting of critical, subjective and objective evaluations, is often desirable as it provides the designer a richer overall picture of the strengths and weaknesses of an interface. Critical evaluation involves the comparison of the user interface design with established, or generally accepted, design principles. The proposed framework $E^3$ complements this approach to enable more objective critical evaluation of interfaces.

## 3. $E^3$ : the Framework

Mackinlay proposed A Presentation Tool (APT), which was primarily intended for small data sets, to automate the design of graphical presentations of relational information [17]. He identified two graphic design criteria: expressiveness and effectiveness; the former criterion is associated with graphical languages that express the desired information while the latter is concerned with the most effective graphical language to exploit the capabilities of the output medium and the human visual system. In his framework, graphical presentations are sentences of graphical languages that have precise syntatic and semantic definitions. If a graphical sentence is able to (i) encode all the facts in the set and (ii) encode only the facts in the set, the set of facts is said to be expressible. Effectiveness relates to the ranking of a presentation based on accuracy and perceptual tasks. Whilst Mackinlay's framework is appropriate for his APT system, which is concerned with static presentation of small sets of graphical data, a more generalised framework for a wider application domain covering large data sets is desirable.

$E^3$ focuses on three aspects of graphical data presentation: *expressiveness* ($E_1$), *efficiency* ($E_2$) and *effectiveness* ($E_3$). Various components of the framework are illustrated in Figure 4, showing the notations used, their relationships and the stages involved in designing a presentation system for large data sets. It should be pointed out that because of the differences in the approach adopted in developing $E^3$, the interpretation of the terms *expressiveness* and *effectiveness* used is different to that of Mackinlay [17]. In $E^3$ the original data set S is transformed to a representation $S_1$ through an abstraction process selected from a set of representation techniques R. The represented data set $S_1$ in turn is transformed to $S_2$, the data set to be presented on the screen; a set of presentation techniques P is available to support this transformation. Consider the flow of information from one point to another in the framework. The amount of information contained in the sets S, $S_1$, and $S_2$ are I, $I_1$, and $I_2$ respectively. The information flow from $I$ to $I_1$ is closely related to *expressiveness* and that from $I_1$ to $I_2$ *efficiency*. $I_1$ and $I_2$ can be given by the functions,

$$I_1 = F_1(E_1, I, R)$$
$$I_2 = F_2(E_2, I_1, P)$$

*Effectiveness*, however, deals with the overall information flow from the original data set to the viewer. Whilst information is invariably lost in these transformation processes, $E^3$ helps to identify and relate the cause to a particular aspect of the presentation. The following subsections provide a detailed explanation of the mathematical framework showing the relationship of the key $E^3$ components.

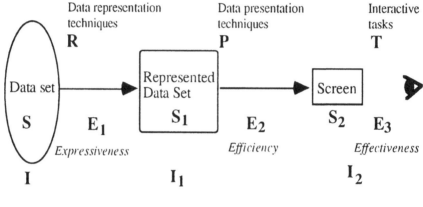

Legend

I  information content in S
$I_1$  information content in $S_1$
$I_2$  information content in $S_2$

P  set of presentation techniques
R  set of representation techniques
S  set of original data
$S_1$  set of the abstracted data
$S_2$  set of the data presented
T  set of interactive tasks

**Figure 4.** Stages involved in designing a presentation system for large data sets

## 3.1  Expressiveness

*Expressiveness* ($E_1$) in the $E^3$ framework is defined as the ability of a representation technique to encode the underlying data accurately and consistently. It can be given by the function,

$$E_1 = F_R(S, R)$$

There are two aspects of *expressiveness*. The first aspect relates to Tufte's concept of a Lie Factor [26] which is defined as,

$$\text{Lie Factor} = \frac{\text{Size of effect shown in graphic}}{\text{Size of effect in data}}$$

The Lie Factor (LF) provides a quantitative measurement of graphic misrepresentation; the graphic representation is perfect with a Lie Factor of 1. The logarithm of the Lie Factor can be used as a means to compare overstating (log LF > 0) with understating (log LF < 0) errors. In print media, graphic exaggerations are sometimes used on purpose to attract the attention of the reader. Such misrepresentation can be easily eliminated by proper encoding of the data.

The second aspect of *expressiveness* relates to the human visio-perceptual capability. Cleveland and McGill's research on graph perception [8] provided an accuracy ranking order of ten encoding techniques for quantitative data which Mackinlay later [17] extended to include ordinal and nominal data. These rankings help to identify the degree of information loss resulted from the representation technique selected.

### 3.2 Efficiency

*Efficiency* ($E_2$) is defined as a ratio of the amount of information presented data on the display surface ($I_2$) to that in the represented data set ($I_1$),

$$E_2 = F_p(I_1, I_2) = \frac{I_2}{I_1}$$

The concept of presentation efficiency bears a philosophical semblance to Tufte's data-ink ratio (Tufte 1983 p.93). One of Tufte's principal graphic design guidelines is that the share of data-ink should be maximised (other relevant matters being equal). The data-ink ratio is given by the following expression,

$$\text{Data - ink ratio} = \frac{\text{data - ink}}{\text{total ink used to print the graphic}}$$

$$= 1.0 \text{ - proportion of a graphic that can be erased}$$
$$\text{without loss of data-information}$$

In $E^3$, *efficiency* will normally be 100% for small data sets where the entire $S_1$ can be adequately accommodated on the display screen. In the case of large data sets, this is often not the case. The proportion of $S_1$ presented on the display screen is therefore presentation *efficiency*.

### 3.3 Effectiveness

*Effectiveness* ($E_3$), which is an overall measure of how effective a presentation is, is dependant on the other two criteria, *expressiveness* and *efficiency*, and the set of interactive tasks performed by the user. It can be given by the function,

$$E_3 = F_E(E_1, E_2, T)$$

*Expressiveness* and *efficiency* affect the overall *effectiveness* of a presentation as these two presentation criteria directly determine the information flow from the original data set to the user. *Effectiveness* is task-oriented; the nature of the tasks performed by the user affect significantly a system's *effectiveness*. Further, the selection of representation and presentation techniques for a particular application is primarily made with due consideration of the three fundamental user tasks: locating, interpreting, and relating.

## 4. Discussion

In the following subsections, two applications of $E^3$ are examined to illustrate how the framework may be applied to practical situations. In the first example, the presentation of a spatial information system, the London Underground Map, is considered using two different presentation techniques (Figure 5), simple windowing and the Bifocal Display [23,14]. In this case, the original data is in graphical form. For the simple windowed display (Figure 5a), only a rectangular sub-section of the map is seen. However, with the Bifocal Display (Figure 5b), the entire map is shown, albeit with some areas distorted. In the second example (Figure 6), the presentation of data from a spreadsheet using two representation methods, one based on position and the other on length, is investigated. The spreadsheet, which consists of sales data of four products over a ten year period, is taken from experimental work on the appropriateness of alternative forms of graphical data presentation [22]. The original data is in numeric form (Figure 6a), and is represented as either a stacked bar chart (Figure 6b) or a multiple line graph (Figure 6c). In either case, the graphical form is not large, and may be readily displayed on the screen in its entirety.

### 4.1 Expressiveness

As defined in $E^3$ (Figure 4), *expressiveness* is ($E_1$) a measure based on the nature of the data and its representation. Because of the graphical nature of the data inherent in the spatial information system (Figure 5), direct representation is involved and no additional data encoding takes place in either the Bifocal Display or the simple windowing presentation. *Expressiveness* ($E_1$) is maximum for both techniques as $S_1$ is the same as $S$.

In the spreadsheet example (Figure 6), the *expressiveness* of the two representation techniques may be compared according to the accuracy of the encoding methods used, based on human visio-perceptual capabilities. According to Cleveland and McGill's relative ratings [8], the position representation (line graph) of this quantitative data set is one rank higher than the length representation (bar chart) in terms of *expressiveness*. It is interesting to note that the superiority of position encoding is more prominent in ordinal and nominal data according to Mackinlay [17].

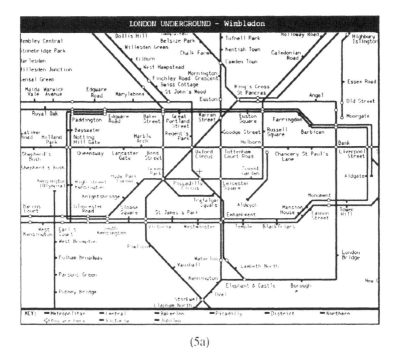

(5a)

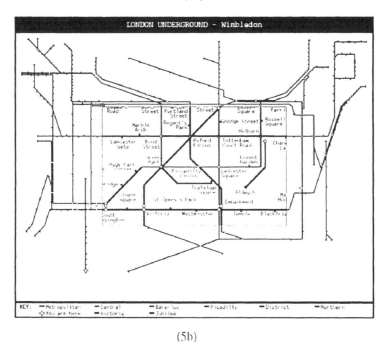

(5b)

**Figure 5.** Two Presentation Techniques (a) Simple Windowing (b) Bifocal Display

## 4.2    Efficiency

*Efficiency* (E$_2$) is defined as the proportion of the represented data set which may be presented on the display screen at one time.  In the spatial data example, the *efficiency* of the Bifocal Display for the London Underground map is 100% as the entire representation is displayed (although distorted); S$_1$ is the same as S$_2$ (Figure 4).  With the simple window presentation technique for the same map, however, the *efficiency* is calculated as follows:

$$\textit{Efficiency}\ (E_1)_{\text{windowing}} = 0.4\ \text{(width)}\ x\ 0.5\ \text{(height)}\ x\ 100\% = 20\%$$

In the spreadsheet example (Figure 6) all of the data is displayed, and because S$_1$ is the same as S$_2$, the *efficiency* is 100%.

## 4.3    Effectiveness

As mentioned previously, in E$^3$ *expressiveness* is data dependent while *effectiveness* is task dependent.  Assessment of the relative *effectiveness* should therefore be based on the underlying tasks performed by the user.  In the context of the London Underground map, the user may wish to search for a station and plan a route using station-related information as search keys; the search keys may be in the form of station name, general position in the map, proximity to a landmark station, the colour of the railway line or the intersection of two lines.  A critical evaluation of these tasks [15] suggests that the Bifocal Display is superior to simple windowing for a search key with station name and proximity information, while the reverse is true for a search key with  information about the intersection of two lines.

Six types of information have been identified by Sparrow [22] as most commonly required by users of spreadsheets.  They are information about specifics, limits, conjunction, accumulation, trends and proportion.  Two of the tasks investigated in Sparrow's experiment are considered here.  One is concerned with identifying the year when a product's sales was the highest or lowest (information about limits), and the other involves determining the year when one product sold less than another (information about conjunction).  In the spreadsheet example, Sparrow found that overall, the stacked bar chart was more effective for assessing limits (about twice as good based on error rate).  However, the multiple line graph was superior for conjunction and trends assessments.

## 4.4    General Comments

The analysis of the two examples is summarised in Figure 7.  It should be pointed out that screen resolution influences the *effectiveness* and not the *efficiency* of a presentation as defined in E$^3$.  Further, it is possible that a system may have high *expressiveness* and *efficiency* ratings, but due to implementation inadequacies such as poor screen resolution, a low *effectiveness* rating results.

The two examples above show how E$^3$ may be applied in the comparison of graphical interfaces for two typical information systems.  It is apparent that the three

| Sales figures | | | | | |
|---|---|---|---|---|---|
| | | | | | |
| Year | Product 1 | Product 2 | Product 3 | Product 4 | Total |
| | | | | | |
| Year 1977 | 75 | 130 | 10 | 120 | 335 |
| Year 1978 | 75 | 120 | 20 | 110 | 325 |
| Year 1979 | 80 | 110 | 30 | 120 | 340 |
| Year 1980 | 90 | 105 | 40 | 125 | 360 |
| Year 1981 | 105 | 97 | 50 | 115 | 367 |
| Year 1982 | 110 | 95 | 60 | 120 | 385 |
| Year 1983 | 100 | 90 | 70 | 110 | 370 |
| Year 1984 | 90 | 80 | 80 | 115 | 365 |
| Year 1985 | 80 | 70 | 90 | 115 | 355 |
| Year 1986 | 70 | 60 | 100 | 120 | 350 |
| | | | | | |
| Total | 875 | 957 | 550 | 1170 | 3552 |

(6a)

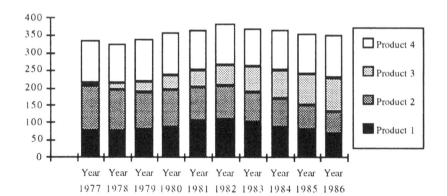

(6b)

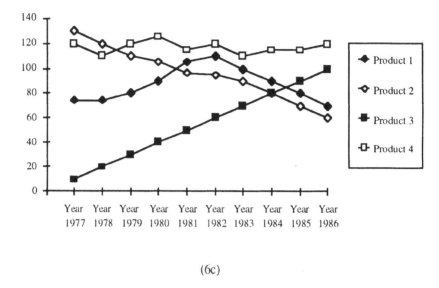

(6c)

**Figure 6.** Example diagrams as used by Sparrow [22]. (a) The spreadsheet of the
original sales data used in Sparrow's illustrations; (b) representation of the
data set based on length in a stacked bar chart; and (c) representation of the
same data set based on position in a multi-line graph.

| | Spatial Data Example | | Numerical Data Example | | |
|---|---|---|---|---|---|
| | Window | Bifocal | Bar Chart | Line Graph | |
| $E_1$ | 1 | 1 | x | y | $(1 > y > x)$ |
| $E_2$ | 0.2 | 1 | 1 | 1 | |
| $E_3$ specific | a $<$ b | | limits e $>$ f | | |
| intersection | c $>$ d | | conjunction g $<$ h | | |

**Figure 7.** A summary of analysis of the two examples

graphic criteria, *expressiveness*, *efficiency* and *effectiveness* impinge on each other. It is often not possible for a design to yield maximum ratings in all three criteria, as these criteria generally place competing demands on the limited system resource. A good interface design would, therefore, be the one which compromises these criteria to yield the optimal result in achieving the desired goals. It should be emphasised that whilst $E^3$ provides the designer with a better understanding of an interface and may also serve as a useful design guide, $E^3$ does not offer a recipe for how these criteria should be compromised.

## 5. Concluding Remarks

This paper proposes an analytical framework $E^3$ for evaluating presentation techniques for large data sets. $E^3$ also serves as a useful guide for the designer to focus attention on the three graphic criteria when designing these types of interfaces. However, one area which the current framework does not address is the dynamic interaction aspect of the interface with implications on system response time and input device characteristics.

It will be of great value to the interface designer if a set of metrics for presentation techniques is available for an objective evaluation of interfaces in different applications. Whilst $E^3$ has provided the necessary groundwork for metrication, further work is required to extend the current framework to achieve this goal.

## References

1.  E. Anderson: A semi-graphical method for the analysis of complex problems, Technometrics, 2, pp. 287-292 (1960)
2.  J. Bertin: Semiology of Graphics, translated by W.J. Berg, Milwaukee: University of Wisconson Press (1983)
3.  S.V. Burger and M.D. Apperley: A multi-dimensional approach to interface evaluation. Proceedings of the IFIP Conference on Human Jobs and Computer Interface - WG 9.1, pp. 205-222 (1991)
4.  S.K. Card, G.G. Robertson and J.D. Mackinlay: The information visualiszer, and information workspace. Proceedings of CHI '91, pp. 181-188
5.  S. Casner: A task-analytic approach to the automated design of graphic presentations. ACM Transactions of Graphics, 10, 2, pp. 111-151 (1991)
6.  J.M. Chambers, W.S. Cleveland, B. Kleiner and P.A. Tukey: Graphical Methods for Data Analysis. Belmont: Wadsworth (1983)
7.  H. Chernoff: The use of faces to represent points in k-dimensional space graphically. Journal of the American Statistical Association, 68, 342, pp. 361-368 (1973)
8.  W.S. Cleveland and R. McGill: Graphical perception: theory, experimentation, and application to the development of graphical methods. Journal of the American Statistical Association, 79, 387, pp. 531-554 (1984)
9.  H.T. Fisher: Mapping Information, Cambridge, Mass.: Abt books (1982)
10. G.W. Furnas: Generalized fisheye views. Proceedings of CHI '86, pp. 16-23 (1986)

11. R.M. Goldwyn, H.P. Friedman and T.H. Siegel: Iteration and interaction in computed data bank analysis. Case study in Physiological classification and assessment of the critically ill. Computers in Biomedical Research, 4, pp. 607-622 (1971)

12. B. Kleiner and J.A. Hartigan: Representing points in many dimensions by trees and castles. Journal of the American Statistical Association, 76, 374, pp. 260-276 (1981)

13. J. Larkin and H. Simon: Why a diagram is (sometimes) worth 10,000 words. Cognitive Science, 11, pp. 65-99 (1987)

14. Y.K. Leung: Human-computer interface techniques for map-based diagrams. In Designing and using Human-Computer Interfaces and Knowledge Based Systems, (Eds. Salvendy, G. and Smith, M.). Amsterdam: Elsevier pp. 361-368 (1989)

15. Y.K. Leung: A comparative study of graphical user interfaces for topological maps, Massey University School of Mathematical & Information Sciences Report Series A No. 92/1 (1992)

16. Y.K. Leung and M.D. Apperley: A taxonomy of distortion-oriented techniques for graphical data presentation. Proceedings of 5th International Conference on Human Computer Interaction, Orlando, Florida (1993)

17. J.D. Mackinlay: Automating the design of graphical presentations of relational information. ACM Transactions on Graphics, 5, 2, pp. 110-141 (1987)

18. J.D. Mackinlay, G.G. Robertson and S.K. Card: The Perspective Wall: detail and context smoothly integrated. Proceedings of CHI'91, pp.173-179 (1991)

19. S.F. Roth and J.A. Mattis: Automating the presentation of information. Proceedings of the Conference on Artificial Intelligence Applications, IEEE Press, pp. 90-97 (1991)

20. M. Sarkar and M.H. Brown: Graphical fisheye view of graphs. Proceedings of CHI'92, p83-91 (1992)

21. C.F. Schmid: Statistical Graphics. New York: John Wiley (1983)

22. J.A. Sparrow: Graphical displays in information systems: some data properties influencing the effectiveness of alternative forms. Behaviour & Information Technology, 8, 1, pp. 43-56 (1989)

23. R. Spence and M.D. Apperley: Data base navigation: an office environment for the professional. Behaviour and Information Technology, 1, 1, pp. 43-54 (1982)

24. S.S. Stevens: On theory of scales of measurement. Science, 103, 2684, pp. 677-680 (1946)

25. I.E. Sutherland: SKETCHPAD: A man-machine graphical communications system. AFIPS Spring Joint Computer Conference, pp.329-346 (1963)

26. E.R. Tufte: The Visual Display of Quantitative Information. Cheshire, Connecticut: Graphics Press (1983)

27. E.R. Tufte: Envisioning Information. Cheshire, Connecticut: Graphics Press (1990)

# Navigating in a Process Landscape

Haakon Tolsby

Dept. of Computer Science, Ostfold Regional College,
Os alle 9, 1757 Halden, Norway
E-mail: hakont@dhhalden.no

**Abstract**: User interfaces in process control systems are often organised as landscapes - usually a process chart - where the display is a window into the landscape. The window can move over the landscape and view different segments of the process. Normally there is no overlap between the views - they are discretely organised. Operators often claim they get lost in such interfaces. I suggest that the problem is a matter of how the operator moves in the landscape how one changes ones view of the process. Two different interactive methods of movement - discrete vs. continuous - are tested. The results of the experiments are discussed.

## 1 Introduction

Just a few decades ago the process operator could be standing in attendance by the machines watching the process. The control and maintenance was direct and information was transmitted through sensory contact with the machine (feeling, smelling, watching and listening).

Today, process control is performed from remote centres. Information is transmitted from sensors in the process to indicators in the control room, normally in a one-to-one relation.

In conventional control rooms analog and mainly mechanical indicators are placed on large wall panels. Although these panels are expensive to build, almost impossible to change and strictly limited by the available wall area, the process operators get a good and fairly imediate impression of the state of the process by scanning the panel.

**Fig. 1**. A process operator inspecting the quality of the cellulose mass in a paper-mill. He takes the cellulose in his hand, feels and smells it. The picture was taken around 1950.

The introduction of computer displays in the control room has changed this situation. Information which earlier was displayed over large, clear areas is scaled onto relatively small displays. Normally, operators have a few 20" colour monitors, and they can view only segments of the process at a time. In order to view the whole process they would need several hundred displays. Instead the operators use each display as a window to the process information, and they move the window around to view different segments of the process. The large number of different views often confuse the navigation process, and the operators complain that they get lost in the information. In addition there are segments of the process they seldom view and therefore are not familar with (even though they have routines where they view all the segments during a workshift).

## 2 What is Navigation?

It may be said that navigation is the process of knowing:

- where one came from
- where one is
- where one is going

Navigation demands interpretable information in the landscape - it demands structure and variation. Landscapes without structure and variation (for example featureless exposures of snow or ocean) are hard to navigate in. In addition, different types of informational aids such as maps, compass, signs and even computerised agents may be used to assist in navigation.

Another important factor of navigation is how one move. There are two fundamental different methods - one can either move continuously or discretely.
The chosen method has influence on the possibility of interpreting the landscape. Normally, we move continuously and we may continuously interpret the surroundings. All the time we know where we came from, and we use the information for navigating. Moving discretely is totally different. Imagine that you take the underground in a city you seldom visit. When you get up to the surface you are quite confused. You can't tell the difference between north and south. You haven't seen the continuous path from where you came, and you don't know where you are.

Based on the factors mentioned above, one would choose a navigation strategy to reach the goal. Several strategies come to mind:

**Searching** is a navigation strategy where you know what you are looking for, but you don't know how to find it. E. g., you want to borrow a book, but you don't know its name. You know the cover is red with a yellow flower. In order to find the book, you have to search through all the books in the library or you need the help of an assistent/agent.

**Analogy** navigation is a strategy where you believe there are certain analogies or consistencies between different environments. You use the knowledge about one environment to navigate in another one. For example using a window application one expects to find a file menu in the upper left corner because that is where it is found in other applications.

**Top - down** navigation is a strategy where you always try to get an overview of the landscape before you start navigating. To get an overview you can use a map, climb a hill, go to the main menu in a menu driven computer system etc.

**Landmark** navigation is a strategy where you use landmarks (like a church) or connections between landmarks (like a boulevard). When you don't know the environment you have very few landmarks to navigate from. The number increases as you learn to know the landscape better.

## 3 Navigating in a Real vs. a Virtual Landscape

A normal method for structuring information on a display is to use what I will call a landscape or map model. Information is ordered into a relevant structure. In process control it is normal to use a process chart as the context. The chart gives the operator a spatial description of the process, and the positions of the indicators tell where the sensors are placed in the process.

There are several arguments in favour of using a landscape model as the context for information. We may assume that one finds it «natural» to navigate in a landscape because humans have knowledge about this kind of navigation. We can find our way in landscapes that are complex and detailed, quite effortlessly and almost unconsciously using a combination of the strategies mentioned above.

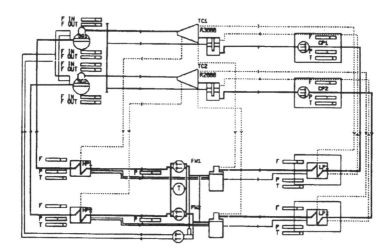

**Fig. 2**. An example of a process chart, showing the secondary loop in a nuclear reactor. The chart is the one used in the experiment.

I have observed different control systems in various industries (oil, energy distribution and a nuclear reactor), and the interfaces seem to be organised in a similar manner: Process charts are being used as landscape models to help in navigation. In order to move around in the process chart, the operators use the display as a window. The window can move over the process chart and view different segments of the process. Normally there is no overlap between the views, they are discretely organised, and the operators can't choose explicitly what they want to see. What they see is restricted by the number of possible views of the process chart.

I have interviewed the operators at a nuclear reactor, and they complained that it was hard to navigate on the process chart, especially when they were navigating in parts of the process they seldom monitored, and when they were under strain. In particular, they found it complicated to see how different subsystems of the process were connected.

I suspected the discrete motion of the window to be the problem. It didn't stimulate the operator's real life experience of navigation which is based on continuous motion. Like the example with the underground, the operators using the systems couldn't see the path they were coming from when they moved discretely on the process chart. They couldn't follow tubes that connected subsystems, and they couldn't see how different segments were related.

Giving the operators an extended degree of freedom would perhaps improve the navigation. If the operators could pan continuously on the process chart, they could also follow tubes between subsystems, they could see the path from where they were coming, making it easier to navigate. Also, if the operators could zoom in and out continuously, they could view whatever area of the process at whatever level of detail, making it possible to view different parts of the process simultaneously.

I expected that letting the operators move continuously on the process chart would improve the navigation, and I made a hypothesis that:

*Navigation is faster and safer, when you move continuously in the process chart and not discretely.*

## 4 The Test Application

In order to test the two methods of navigation - continuous and discrete - I had to build a mock-up application. It was implemented using C and X-windows on a HP workstation with a 21" colour screen.

The application used a process chart of the secondary loop in a nuclear reactor as the navigation landscape. The user could zoom in and out on the process chart, and view it at different levels of detail. At the largest magnification there were 2400 discrete displays (Giving large distances to navigate.)

The mouse was chosen as input device for the application, and I let the display be a window from which the user could view different parts of the process chart. An input technique[1] was implemented for the continuous method where the user clicked in the direction he/she wanted to pan. For example, a click at the right side of the centre, moved the window continuously to the right. Depending on where the screen was clicked, the user could move in any angel. The distance from the centre of the screen to the cursor determined the speed. This method allowed the user to follow the path of tubes between different subsystems (like driving a car on a road between different towns).

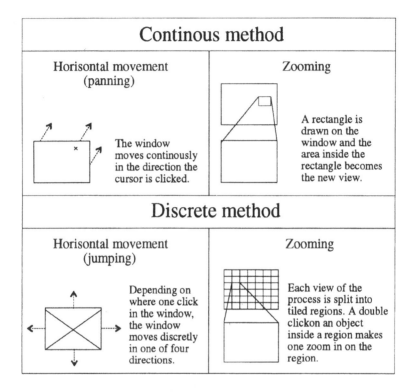

**Fig. 3.** The two different interaction techniques.

I chose a zoom-in method were the user drew a rectangle on the window, and the process segment inside the rectangle became the new view. This input action was not continous itself, but it worked on a continous landscape, making it possible to view whatever area of the process chart at different levels of detail. Using this method one could view different subsystems of the process simultaneously. The zoom-out was accomplished by dragging the rectangle «outside» the window and the view would start shrinking. In addition there was a button on top of the display, letting the operator go to the top level which gave an overview of the whole process.

The input technique for the discrete method was similar. When the user clicked to

---

[1] *Several different input techniques where implemented before we ended up with the techniques mentioned above. However, most of them were unfit for the purpose. They were either too fast, slow or imprecise.*

the right of the screen centre, the window moved one discrete position to the right. The new view was tiled with the previous one (no overlap). One click above the centre moved the window one position up etc. The movements were restricted to left, right, up and down. A double click on an object zoomed in one level viewing another discrete picture of the process chart. This made it impossible to view different segments of the process simultaneously if they did not happen to appear on the same discrete picture. The zoom-out function was implemented by two buttons on top of the display. One zoomed out one level, and the other let the user go straight to the top level, viewing a display of the whole process.

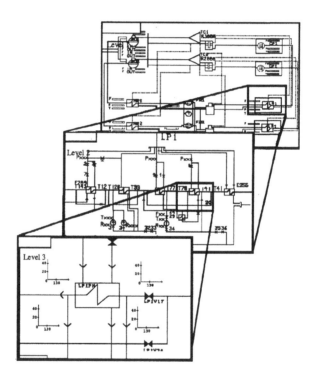

**Fig. 4.** The user could zoom in and out on the process chart, and view it at different levels of details. There were totally three levels of details: Level 1 gave an overview of the process, level 2 showed the different subsytems, and level 3 gave detailed information about the process elements.

## 5 The Experiment

The two methods were tested on thirty computer science students in their first semester. The test subjects were divided into two groups one for each method. The groups were balanced with regard on experience, age and gender. Everybody had experience in using a mouse as input device.

The students were familiarized with the process. This was done in groups of fifteen students and took 60 minutes. After the course they had a brief test, making sure that they all had adequate knowledge of the process.

Each student participated in the experiment within a week after the course, and they were tested individually. Before the experiment started they were asked to explain the process for the experimenter.

Then the students were given one hour to learn one of the interaction methods (continuous or discrete). First they were given a short demonstration by the experimenter, 15 minutes. Then the students had 30 minutes to get familiar with the system. During the last 15 minutes they were given a few examples of the type of tasks they were going go accomplish during the experiment.

After the learning period, the students were given a set of 25 tasks. The time they spent on each task and navigation errors (Ex. locating wrong subsystem) was logged. In addition, I tried to capture what strategy of navigation they used.

The students were tested in different types of tasks during the experiment. The tasks were of three categories:

**1. Locating**     Find a specific part of the process.
Example:     Locate preheater LP1PH4. Note the temperature of the flow into the preheater.
**2. Tracking**     Follow links between subsystems.
Example:     The preheater LP1PH4, uses steam to heat water. Where does the steam come from?
**3. Comparing**     Look at indicators in different subsystems.
Example:     Compare the temperature in the feedwater tanks FW1TA1 and FW2TA1. Which has the highest temperature?

After the first test, a 30 minutes break with refreshments was given. Then the experiment was repeated using the second method. I wanted to see to what extent the result would differ when they were familar with the process chart. I expected the discrete method to improve considerably during the second round of the experiment.

## 6 Discussion

The results of the experiment was analysed according to the three task categories. However, there were no indications in the result from the first round of the experiments that could confirm my hypothesis. As a matter of fact, the subjects (the students) seemed to use the same amount of time and do the same number of errors independent of the method. See table 1.

The first task category was *locating,* where the test subjects should find a specific process element. These tasks were solved using the same strategy by almost all the subjects. First they went to the top-level to get an overview of the process. Then they zoomed in the appropriate segment of the process. This is similar to the top-down strategy described earlier. Using the same strategy may explain why the result was independent of the interaction technique. In addition, nobody seemed to prefer moving horizontally which I thought that the subjects using the continuous method would do (even though the navigation distance was short they prefered to go to the top-level to get an overview of the process).

| | Result - 1. Round | | | | | |
|---|---|---|---|---|---|---|
| **Task Type** | Locating | | Tracking | | Comparing | |
| **Method** | Continous | Discrete | Continous | Discrete | Continous | Discrete |
| **Time Used (sec.)** | 345 | 325 | 406 | 321 | 370 | 418 |
| **Errors** | 6 | 7 | 11 | 7 | 6 | 7 |

**Table 1.** The results from the first testing round

The second task category was *tracking* where the subjects should follow a link between two subsystems, for instance a tube. I expected this to be easier to do continuously (and that may be true), but panning continuously is time consuming vs. moving in discrete steps (it's like crawling vs. walking). In addition, if one pan too rapidly using the continuous method one will soon loose track of where one is. It is impossible to interpret the information in the landscape when the speed gets too high. Therefore, it didn't seem to matter that the persons using the discrete method did some navigation errors, and that they had to make some extra navigation steps. After all, they didn't spend more time accomplishing the same task.

The third task category was *comparing* where the subjects should compare parameters of different subsystems. Using the continuous method the subjects could draw a rectangle around the necessary subsystems and compare them in the same view. They didn't have to switch between different views to do the comparison as was the case using the discrete method. However, the problem was that the view they got using the continuous method was seldom optimal. If they were unlucky, they could get a view where the indicators were to small to read, or one indicator happened to be just outside the view so they couldn't do the comparison. In order to get an adequate view, the subjects had to do additional pan and zoom actions. Therefore, the number of operations used in both methods were more or less the same.

| | Result - 2. Round | | | | | |
|---|---|---|---|---|---|---|
| **Task Type** | Locating | | Tracking | | Comparing | |
| **Method** | Continous | Discrete | Continous | Discrete | Continous | Discrete |
| **Time Used (sec.)** | 257 | 188 | 281 | 184 | 278 | 221 |
| **Errors** | 10 | 8 | 4 | 8 | 1 | 5 |

**Table 2.** The results from the second testing round

During the second round of the experiment, I assumed that the discrete method would be the fastest, and that appeared to be true. The result was statistically significant (Wilcoxon rank-sum-test, $p < 0.05$). At this state in the experiment, the test subjects were familar with the process chart. They knew were to go, and could do it directly using the discrete method. However, the number of errors was still independent of the method used.

## 7 Conclusion

The result of the experiment showed that the continuous method didn't improve the navigability of the process chart. On the contrary the discrete method seemed to be a better choice, especially when the user had good knowledge of the process chart (the result of the second round of the test).

Nevertheless, I still find that the continuous method may have its advantages. The method lets the user follow links in the landscape, and it lets him/her view the landscape at different levels of details. However, it didn't seem to be the right choice for the tasks I was testing.

An interesting aspect of the experiment is that the choice of navigation strategy seemed to be more important than whether the test subjects moved continuously or discretely. I counted the number of pan[1] and zoom operations performed by the users, and the figures where almost the same for both methods (The subjects used 2.5 pan operations and 3.5 zoom operations per task in average). The top-down strategy was the mostly used strategy, and it was independent of the input technique. It was used in more than 50% of the solutions in the tasks where the goal was to locate a process element.

I didn't have any professional process operators participating in the experiment, but I let some of them try the input techniques afterwards. Their response was also positive when I showed them the continuous method. «This is what we have been asking for», one expressed. But when they went through the test tasks themselves, they all did best using the discrete method.

Another conclusion may therefore be that we can't be critical enough when we choose interaction techniques. What seems like an improvement doesn't have to be one. What seems to be the correct and intuitive solution may show to be the opposite.

## 8 Future Work

I have tried to find improvements to the navigation problems in process control, but my proposals didn't seem to solve the problem. Therefore it is interesting to look at the problem from another point of view.

As mentioned earlier, a few decades ago the operator was not sitting in a remote control room. He was monitoring the process directly, and he could sense the state of the process directly. Today's operator have to look at a vast amount of indicators to get

---

[2]*A continuous pan operation may be very long, we therefore defined it to be the distance of one display, the same as a discrete pan operation*

the same information. A suggestion for improvement would be to provide the operators with a display that gives them an immediate understanding of the state of the process and not indirectly through a lot of indicators. This would reduce the need of navigation in the control system. Fig. 4 shows an approach in that direction. This display has the goal to show the state of a nuclear process, not through a large set of indicators, but through simple graphical symbols. The question is whether the information is adequate or not?

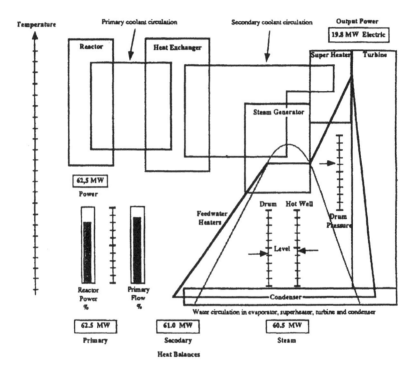

**Fig. 5**. The display is designed by Jens Rasmussen at RISØ research centre i Denmark. The two rectangles in the upper half of the picture are graphs showing the teperatures in the primary an the secondary coolant circulation in a nuclear reactor. When they have a rectangular shape, the process is stable.

Another interesting question is what new technology will bring to the control room. For example wallsized computer displays will have other demand and constraints, and the navigation will be different.

# 9 Acknowledgements

Acknowledgements to: Tord Akerbaek who was collaborating on the experiment, Jon Lovstad who did the layout and Borre Stenseth and Conny Holmstroem who guided the project.

# References

1. Card S., Moran T. & Newvell A., «The Psychology of human-computer interaction». Hillsdale NJ: Erlbaum Ass. 1983.

2. Gibson J.J., The theory of affordances. In R.E. Shaw & J. Bransford (Eds.), «Perceiving, acting and knowing». Hillsdale NJ: Erlbaum Ass, 1977

3. Gibson J.J., «The ecologiocal approach to visual perception». Boston: Houghton, 1979.

4. Hollnagel E., «A survey of man-machine system evaluation methods» Halden, Norway: OECD Halde Reactor Project, 1985.

5. Norman D.A., «Some observations on mental models», In: Centner D., Stevens A.L., Mental Models. Hillsdale N.J: Erlbaum Ass., 1983.

6. Norman D.A., «The psycholgy of everyday things», Basic Books 1988.

7. Rasmussen J. & Vicente K.J., «A theoretical framework for ecological interface design». Risø National lab., Denmark, 1988.

8. Schneiderman B., «Designing the userinterface: Strategies for effective human-computer interaction». MA: Addison-Wesley, 1987.

# Visualisation of Complex Information

## Matthew Chalmers

Rank Xerox EuroPARC, 61 Regent St., Cambridge CB2 1AB. U.K.
*chalmers@europarc.xerox.com*

**Abstract.** In information retrieval, sets of documents are stored and categorised in order to allow for search and retrieval. The complexity of the basic information is high, with representations involving thousands of dimensions. Traditional interaction techniques for such complex information therefore hide much of its complexity and structure, and offer access to it by means of isolated queries and word searches. Bead is a system which takes a complementary approach, as it builds and displays an approximate model of the document corpus in the form of a map or landscape constructed from the patterns of similarity and dissimilarity of the documents making up the corpus. In this paper, emphasis is given to the influences on and principles behind the design of the landscape model and the abandonment of a 'point cloud' model used in an earlier version of the system, rather than the more mathematical aspects of model construction.

## 1 Introduction

Bead is a prototype system for the graphically-based exploration of information. The underlying notion of the system is one of our most familiar metaphors: spatial proximity to represent similarity in some more abstract interpretive framework [7]. We represent the relationships between articles in a bibliography by their relative spatial positions. We attempt to place similar articles close to one another and dissimilar ones further apart. The emergent structure is a model of the corpus: a landscape or map of the information within the document set.

This 3D scene can be used to visualise patterns in the high–dimensional information space. The aim is to make interaction with a database of information more graphically-oriented, and to move away from interaction styles requiring knowledge of query languages and the database material itself. This allows people to move from cognitive problem–solving to more natural sensorimotor strategies, and to support more exploratory and cumulative modes of use.

The modelling techniques involved were the main focus of a description of an earlier version of Bead, published as [3]. That paper describes the kind of numerical techniques used and their combination with text analysis techniques to make 3D 'point clouds' of graphical data. An example point cloud is shown in Figure 1. This type of graphical structure is common in statistical graphics [4]. The raw material was a small

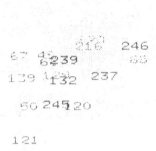

**Figure 1.** A point cloud constructed from articles in an human-computer interaction conference, CHI91. A search on the words 'information retrieval' leads to some of the document numbers being highlighted. Documents mostly lie in a central cluster, but documents matching the search are mixed throughout the corpus. This is more apparent in an animated display but occlusion and overall scene complexity still inhibit corpus comprehension.

bibliography of articles on HCI. Since then, the interface style has progressed to the use of a more accessible graphical structure, and the issues underlying this progress are the subject of this paper.

Low dimensionality is in accord with our everyday experience. We are used to a space of three physical dimensions wherein we perceive individual characteristics of objects and also their patterns and interrelationships. Given our lives on the surface of the earth, our experience is of a world with greater extent in the horizontal thean the vertical: one might even call our everyday world '2.1-dimensional'. Physical spaces of high dimensionality are unfamiliar to most of us, and it is generally more difficult to present, perceive and remember patterns and structures within them. If our activities depend on judgements based on both the individual characteristics of documents and their relative properties then we will gain by employing a representation which shows both in a space of familiar dimensionality.

In initial experimentation within EuroPARC this was found to be a problem of the 'point cloud' representation which, even with only three dimensions, did not easily afford overview of the entire set of documents. Occlusion of distant information, the lack of a fundamental ground plane and weakness with regard to other bases of everyday perception meant that it was difficult to become familiar with a significantly-sized corpus. The features that make graphical display most effective were not being brought to bear in making the information design effective and useful. Users found it difficult to orient themselves and navigate within the space, and consequently did not build up a useful mental model of the corpus. Instead they found occasional items of interesting data but had difficulty in assessing their relevance or significance in the wider context of the corpus. This seemed to echo a point forcefully put in [1]:

> Items of data do not supply the information necessary for decision-making. What must be seen are the relationships which emerge from consideration of the entire set of data. *In decision-making the useful information is drawn from the overall relationships of the entire set.* [Author's italics]

A goal of Bead is to represent a corpus of documents in a way which helps with tasks which rely on the relationships of the entire set of documents as much as the properties of individual members. A document must therefore play a dual role: it must act as an autonomous unit and it must also play a role as a component within a higher-level structure. We wish the corpus to have a layout which represents the more abstract patterns within it. The model of a corpus used in Bead emphasises patterns of thematic similarity as estimated by similarities in word usage. Individual documents take their places in these patterns by dint of the words used within them, but they also have important characteristics not used in constructing the overall layout. Labelling Bead as an information retrieval system is to take a narrow view. In a wider, more general sense, it is a system intended to aid in tasks which rely on consideration of the overall relationships of the themes and words active in a corpus, as well as the individual elements.

There is a point of view which holds that most information retrieval tasks are better performed if the overall relationships within a corpus are presented. As this view has spread, a more general model of the use of information systems than that traditionally used in Information Retrieval has arisen. The word 'retrieval' suggests an action by some agent to find and bring back information to a somehow detached or uninvolved user. The agent is given a specification of what is wanted, and the user waits for the results to be returned. However, it is becoming more accepted that people may not be able to express what they want to access in a corpus in a query language or even a natural language, for that matter, because they may not know exactly what they are looking for. Instead, they may be able to do what they want to do if they can begin by finding out roughly what is available in the corpus and, in an exploratory manner, refine and adapt their inquiries.

An individual document may initially appear 'relevant' but later be discarded if other documents better serve the interests of the user. There may be a great number of relevant documents, or there may be none: both are fair and on occasion appropriate results. There may be documents that are relevant in different ways, and this may lead to a continuation and adaptation of work as these different associations are assessed. Initially known documents may be dispersed among other unknown but potentially relevant ones. These examples stress the relative judgements that drive an adaptive and exploratory style of use that contrasts with and complements the less interactive 'retrieval' approach. This approach has been labelled information *access*, and to some extent reflects the increasing awareness of the importance of exploration and dynamism in perception and model construction [6, 12]. These ideas have also been influential upon the designers of other information interfaces e.g. the work of the User Interface Research and Intelligent Information Access groups at PARC [2, 9, 10, 11]. The following section goes slightly further into these and other areas of work that have been influential in attempts to make the design of Bead better suited to information access.

## 2 Background, Influences and Comparisons

In this section, some of the issues, techniques and concepts behind the Bead system are presented and discussed. From the basic infrastructure of information retrieval techniques to influential examples and metaphors, a wide range of areas of study have had their effect on the choice of information displayed and the structure of the display: collectively, the *information design*.

As in most Information Retrieval systems[1], a document is essentially represented as a list of the words which occur within it, and some numeric measure of the relative frequency of each occurring word. The most simple measure is a one for a word occurring in a document, and a zero for non–occurrence. For reasons which include efficiency, not every word is actually used: common 'noise words' such as 'the' and 'or' are discarded.

This representation has a geometric interpretation. It is as though each document is a point in space. The large number of words means a large number of dimensions to this space: each unique word in a corpus of documents defines one dimension, and the frequency of occurrence for each word is a coordinate for that dimension. Word frequencies can be further weighted to take account of extra information. 'Noise words' are effectively given zero weight. In the case of the bibliographic data used in Bead, words in the 'keywords' and 'title' sections of a bibliography entry are given more weight than those from the abstract. Documents are close in this type of high-dimensional space if they have roughly the same words occurring with roughly the same weights. The assumption — generic and fundamental to all of Information Retrieval — is that if this is so then the documents are most likely to be similar in themes and topics i.e. spatial distance corresponds to some degree with thematic similarity.

Since the number of words in a corpus of documents can easily run into thousands, the number of dimensions is too large to display directly. We can get some information about what documents are close to each other by the more traditional means of information retrieval: in effect we get a list of the documents near to one or more documents

---

1. [13] is one introduction to the basics of Information Retrieval techniques and systems.

known *a priori*. The system can then find the nearest (most relevant) documents and return them to the user, usually in order of spatial distance (relevance ranking). A simple view of a query to an information retrieval system is that we make a fake, temporary document with just the keywords we give and with chosen (presumably high) weights, find where that document is placed in the high–dimensional space, and then return a list of nearby documents. Again, we get an idea about documents close to the item of information we placed into the space, but we obtain little global information. We find out about the locality near to the query, but we gain no idea about documents further away (involving different words) and how they relate to each other.

Note that we have to start off with some clear, *a priori* knowledge of what we want to find out. Unfortunately this is not so often the case, for example when we want to explore and browse our way towards whatever it is we come to decide is of interest or relevance. We can only do this by many repeated samples of localised regions, and in ourselves building up some sort of cognitive model of what there is in the corpus and how they fit together. Defining such samples means either having many well–understood documents in the corpus from which one can work outwards, or knowing how to put the words together in a query (i.e. how to use a query language) to sample in the region you want to know more about. It would be better for those who do such sampling less often (or who know less about the corpus or the query language) if some of the cognitive load could be taken on by the representation of the corpus.

Another approach using the same underlying representation is to partition the space into some number of regions which share roughly the same words and weights. We can then show representative members or the highly weighted words which typify each region. We therefore obtain a concise but more approximate representation which we can show in a list. We now get some idea of the overall range of the documents in the corpus, but our accuracy is limited because we can only write so much about each one on a screen or page. We could then choose one or two of these selected regions to look at more closely, perhaps by gathering in the members of the regions and then trying to spread them out again into another list of regions to select from, scatter out again and so on with ever more refined choices of documents. This is a rough description of the Scatter/Gather technique described in [5].

This approach is better for someone browsing the corpus because at each stage they get some idea of the overall contents of the corpus presented to them, and they need not know a query language. They choose one or more relevant members of a list, and in so doing move themselves closer to their goal. By reducing dependence on initial knowledge of keywords and query languages, Scatter/Gather is intended to favour information access more than information retrieval.

The model of the document corpus in Bead is similar to Scatter/Gather in its focus on the perception of the global structures and relationships of documents rather than the techniques associated with a hidden, high–dimensional representation. The model of the individual document is one which creates these larger–scale aggregate structures. In

Bead, each individual document has as the dominant factor in its behaviour the resolution of the similarities and differences with all other documents. By making visible the setting of each document within the larger-scale structure of the corpus, browsing and exploration is aided. For this to work, the layout must impart to the user relationships and structures which 'make sense' and yet it must also let users orient themselves, navigate and examine the corpus. In other words, Bead should make the corpus 'imageable'.

This term is drawn from a work on the theory of a certain type of complex spatial structure of varied use and interpretation, namely the city. In *The Image of the City* [8], Lynch described properties of cities which led to people being able to orient themselves and navigate within the city so as to carry out tasks related to the spatial structure e.g. finding the way to some location or sketching out a rough city map. Lynch carried out surveys of people performing such tasks, and collected and analysed the results to come up with some ideas about the characteristics needed for imageability. These included: landmarks visible from most of the region, which allow for orientation; a delineated border (and perhaps borders of subregions) which serve as reference points; viewpoints, so that parts of the city region can be overviewed before travelling into the more local neighbourhoods; a skeleton of routes into and through the region which one can use to go to particular local areas and from which one's knowledge of local detail can grow and be fleshed out; and consistency of local texture (e.g. building styles) so that one can determine from a street's local detail information about the subregion one is in.

In the studies of perception, there is a significant body of work that explores the dynamism that is an essential and everyday characteristic of our behaviour [6]. Gibson argues that direct perception, memory and interpretation act together as we explore our environment, build up our mental models, and plan uses and actions within that environment. We resolve visual ambiguities, direct our attentional focus, add areas of the environment to our memory, and perceive shapes and uses all in relation to our body and its movement.

When we look at one area close up, the detail there has as its context the neighbouring regions which extend on out to the boundary or horizon. Continuity of movement over a landscape, coupled with perspective viewing, allows one to incrementally refine one's attentional focus down to more local areas, while smoothly adding more information to the context or periphery of view. We select areas to examine in detail by moving closer, while distant areas are seen in a less detailed (or more abstract) way. There is continuity between the close and detailed, and the far and abstract. Reference is continually made to the ground plane of the landscape, as perceived by the variations in size and texture of objects as well as larger-scale features such as the horizon and directionality of light. Although areas of the environment become hidden as we move, we are experienced in maintaining a mental model which lets us return to or otherwise use such areas.

Note that in the case of point clouds and other 'strongly 3D' structure, the environment is more complexly structured with many occlusions and obstructions of view. Without references such as a horizon and a consistent ground plane, information gained by overview and exploration is more difficult to come by. Our skills in perception mental model–making, as honed on our everyday '2.1D' world, become more difficult to employ.

In this section the fundamental data to be accessed has been described, along with the basic notion of using a landscape metaphor for data representation, and some issues relevant to the design and perception of such landscapes have been presented. The next section describes some ways in which these different threads have been, or are being, woven together to improve the information design.

## 3   Improving the Information Design

In coming to advance the design of Bead's information display, the collective effect of the issues pointed out in the preceding section suggested a move away from strongly 3D structures and towards map-like (2D) or landscape-like ('2.1D') structures. The decision was made to sacrifice the greater exactitude of relative distances that can be gained in full 3D, and the modelling process of Bead was changed accordingly. An attempt is under way to use the greater accessibility and familiarity of a landscape metaphor to display a corpus of documents.

In the type of visualisation system common to 3D graphics, viewpoints are easily available since one can place one's eye arbitrarily in space so as to get an oveview of any region of interest. Similarly, one need not really have 'routes' in or through the corpus, as one is free to move above the landscape. In trying to introduce other useful characteristics, though, the structure and appearance of the modelled data must serve to provide such features as landmarks and borders, and the positions of documents must be done so that it is apparent that there is local consistency of themes and topics. Individual documents are shown as coloured markers placed within the setting of the landscape and they consequently produce collective patterns of density and locality.

The open landscape affords an overview of the patterns and structures of the corpus. Perspective viewing heightens the visual effect, emphasising nearer documents but also fitting in with our everyday framework of vision and perception. The lack of more literal (and constraining) 'ways in' such as routes or other surface features, however, suggests that more abstract and flexible means should be provided. This also means that one should be aware of some of the variety of means by which people initially approach such bodies of information.

In the absence of a genuine task or 'way into' the information, general features such as physical features such as dense clusters, exceptionally close pairs and the overall centre of the layout were initially examined. Other initial activities included the location of

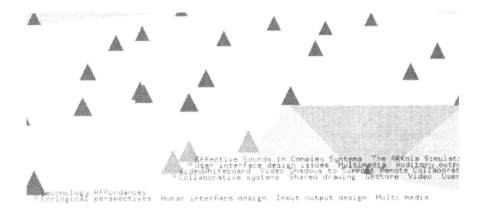

**Figure 2.** After a search for the word 'collaborative', some documents near to a 'valley' region at the centre of the corpus have been highlighted. Browsing with the mouse reveals the title of a nonmatching document (Technology Affordances) that is near to one of the matching papers (Effective Sounds in Complex Systems) and may be of interest as the two papers have more general issues in common as well as an author, Bill Gaver.

familiar or relevant articles and scanning for consistency of documents in randomly-chosen subareas of the layout.

Apart from physical features such as patterns of local density, word searching provides perhaps the most significant 'way in' to the landscape of documents, affording access to its basic patterns and themes, and providing the initial experiences which support later browsing and exploration. When a search for a keyword is made in the animated Bead interface, matching documents have their colour changed. The resulting patterns of colour show the distribution of matching documents in the corpus of documents. The patterns show how discriminating the search is and how matching documents are distributed throughout the corpus. The latter point tends to show the areas where there are different uses or aspects of the words searched for.

The landscape model means that one can immediately obtain an overview of the entire set which is the basis for such judgements. More information such as the title and key-word list are shown when an individual document (matching or non-matching) is selected with the mouse. Figure 2 shows an example.

From such initial searches and selections, one gains basic knowledge which one can use to browse and explore other nearby documents. These might be close to those previously inspected but may not have matched one's initial search. One can find documents which are relevant but do not contain familar keywords, and one can move beyond one's initial search by using interesting words found as one explores. One can shift smoothly from browsing to searching and back again, all the while maintaining continuity and context by reference to the static landscape framework

Movement, viewing and selection, along with simple searches for word occurrences, make up the means of access to the model. This small set seems straightforward to use; the limitations on use are pushed over more towards the model itself. Given a good corpus model, it should not be necessary to be an expert in query languages or on the database itself — the ideal is that this load should be taken on by the system.

The modelling process of Bead sometimes leads to peaks and valleys, and there is always a surrounding contour or 'shore'. These serve as natural reference points (or, more literally, landmarks) and are important in orientation and navigation. Slopes are shaded in accordance with their gradient, so that steep slopes are darker then gentler slopes and flat areas. The peaks and valleys also show areas where the 'fit' of the documents is rough. This may mean that the system could not find a good layout in 2D, although such a layout may exist. Alternatively, it could be that there is an inherent conflict in the set of desired mutual distances of documents, and therefore no planar layout can be found. In either case, the roughness of fit is an important property which should be conveyed to the user. This type of metalevel information is not often shown in an information display, although it does convey an extra dimension of the modelled information which could be influential in judgements based on proximity and implied similarity of documents.

The shore delimits the corpus and is usually made up of documents which are less strongly associated with any central theme (or themes) of the corpus. In the modelling process, such documents are pushed out to the physical periphery, which adds to the consonance of the model. Lastly, areas of density show clusters of strongly related documents, serve as landmarks and reference points, and offer bases for initial exploration of the corpus model.

Although more realistic shading and texturing could make the landscape more 'naturalistic', such colours and textures might be better put towards informational content rather than the 'framework' of the landscaping. Indeed, there is a danger that adding such detail might produce distracting visual clutter, obscuring information content. In all information design, one must choose which dimensions of the display should be used for information content (e.g. the position and colour of individual documents), which for a framework which conveys the basic style of interpretation of the information (e.g the shading of the slopes of the hills and valleys) and which should be unused so as to avoid clutter. Adding more information to the landscape design in this way is one of the topics of current work discussed in the next section.

# 4 Conclusion

The system described attempts to give access to a body of complex, high–dimensional information by using a model or metaphor of a landscape. The display design is directed towards a more exploratory and dynamic style of use than that of most traditional information retrieval systems, and it tries to take advantage of our natural sensorimotor skills by presenting a corpus as a mostly open landscape. This model supports overview and browsing, as well as searches for keywords represented by the colouring of individual documents. It is intended that the dynamics of movement, selection and searching can be combined in a way which favours information access rather than information retrieval.

Current work focuses on the modelling algorithms which construct the landscape, and how low-level issues such as word weighting affect the accessibility and quality of the resulting model. Apart from pairwise properties such as relative distance of documents, the emergent properties of the layout such as patterns of density and overall 'texture' are significant features in the perception and use of the modelled corpus. A related topic is the extension of the construction techniques to more robustly and efficently handle larger–sized corpora. Other lines of interest are directed towards the enrichment of the information content of the display while avoiding excessive and counter–productive visual clutter, making the 'information space' able to be shared by people working on different workstations, and improving the tools for movement and navigation within the space.

Ideally, the modelled information space should reflect the documents and document–related activities of the people using the system. It should help to guide and should be guided by their work with other systems and in other media. In this way, Bead might offer new possibilities for computer–based support of both individual and collaborative work in a semantically rich virtual environment, and might take a useful place amongst the more general environment of everyday work.

# 5 Acknowledgements

Thanks are due to my fellow researchers at EuroPARC and PARC for discussion and comment, in particular Bob Anderson, Victoria Bellotti, Bill Gaver, Gifford Louie, Diane McKerlie, Tom Moran, Abi Sellen and Andreas Weigend.

# 6 References

1. J. Bertin: Graphics and Graphic Information Processing, Walter de Gruyter, Berlin, 1981.
2. S.K. Card, G.G. Robertson & J.D. MacKinlay: The Information Visualizer, an Information Workspace. Proc. CHI'91 (New Orleans, Louisiana, 28 April – 2 May, 1991), ACM, New York, pp. 181–188.
3. M. Chalmers & P. Chitson, Bead: Explorations in Information Visualisation. In: Proc. SIGIR'92, published as a special issue of SIGIR Forum, ACM Press, pp. 330–337, June 1992.

4.  W.S. Cleveland & M.E. McGill (eds.): Dynamic Graphics for Statistics, Wadsworth & Brooks/Cole statistics/probability series, Belmont, CA, 1988.

5.  D.R. Cutting, J.O. Pedersen, D. Karger & J.W. Tukey: Scatter/Gather: A Cluster–Based Approach to Browsing Large Document Collections. Proc. SIGIR'91, published as a special issue of SIGIR Forum, ACM Press, pp. 318–329.

6.  J.J. Gibson: The Ecological Approach to Visual Perception, Lawrence Erlbaum, 1979.

7.  G. Lakoff & M. Johnson: Metaphors We Live By, University of Chicago Press, 1980.

8.  K. Lynch: The Image of the City, MIT Press, 1960.

9.  J.D. MacKinlay, G.G. Robertson & S.K. Card: The Perspective Wall: Detail and Context Smoothly Integrated. Proc. CHI'91 (New Orleans, Louisiana, 28 April – 2 May, 1991), ACM, New York, pp. 173–180.

10. R. Rao, S.K. Card, H.D. Jellinek, J.D. MacKinlay & G. Robertson: The Information Grid: A Framework for Information Retrieval and Retrieval–Centred Applications. Proc. UIST'92 (Monterey, California, November 1992), ACM, New York, pp. 23–32.

11. G.G. Robertson, J.D. MacKinlay & S.K. Card: Cone Trees: Animated 3D Visualizations of Hierarchical Information. Proc. CHI'91 (New Orleans, Louisiana, 28 April – 2 May, 1991), ACM, New York, pp. 189–194.

12. D.M. Russell, M.J. Stefik, P. Pirolli & S.K. Card: The Cost Structure of Sensemaking. Proc. InterCHI'93 (Amsterdam, April 93), ACM, New York, pp. 269–276.

13. G. Salton: Automatic Text Processing, Addison–Wesley 1989.

# Three-Dimensional Visualisation of Knowledge Structures: Prototyping for Design Evaluation

U. K. Patel, A.G. Sutcliffe

Centre for HCI Design, School of Informatics, City University,
Northampton Square, London, EC1V OHB, UK.

**Abstract.** A conceptual framework for specification of 3D visualisations is introduced, and a task knowledge modelling approach to designing 3D visualisations of knowledge structures is described. Using this approach, a three-dimensional interactive graphical user interface to a medical diagnosis knowledge based system has been designed and specified. The design has been implemented as a prototype and evaluated. We found that there are individual differences in the way users explore three dimensional visualisations, and that usability is dependent on both the morphology (visualisation) and manipulations (interface functionality). Implications of these findings for the design of 3D visualisations are discussed.

## 1 Introduction

For some time Three-Dimensional (3D) graphics have been used to display complex information structures [17, 29]. Recently the addition of interactivity to components of the display has resulted in a new computing paradigm [21]. The 3D Interactive Graphical User Interface [GUI] is characterised by:

- Display. The x, y, and z spatial dimensions are used to display large, complex and abstract information structures [18].
- Navigation. The visual representation of the information structure can be navigated [7, 9].
- Interaction. The user can interact with the underlying information structure by manipulation of image components [4].

The advantages of 2D graphics over text based representations are well documented [20, 22, 26]. Interactive 2D graphics have been used in the human-computer interface of a number of KBSs [33], and knowledge engineering environments [18, 28]. Unfortunately 2D visualisation is limited when complex information structures with considerable connectivity need to be represented. When large diagrams are reduced in scale there is a reduction in the size of detail. Zooming to enlarge details causes loss of contextual information. The representational power of the third dimension can offer significant gains in terms of, summarisation, and complexity reduction.

A number of projects have experimented with 3D Interactive Graphics as part of an integrated system concept (see figure 1). The Information Visualiser project developed 3D representations of hierarchical structures based on an investigation of tasks which involve large information spaces [2]. In the domain of engineering interface in the CoCo project (Control and Observation of Circuit Optimisation) [4]. In the SemNet system perceptual cues such as size, colour, and orientation were applied to displays of 3D network structures with nodes positioned in clusters [12]. Unfortunately, apart from a few notable exceptions [18, 30], there has been little evaluation of design or usability of the artifacts, and very little is known about how people interact with the 3D GUIs.

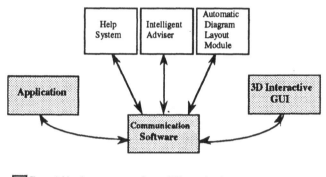

▓ Essential basic components for usability evaluation

**Fig. 1.** Integrated System Concept for 3D Interactive Visualisation

The evaluation gap is not surprising given the problem of building a sufficiently complete prototype to evaluate. In a real system the 3D Interactive GUI is one component of the integrated system shown in figure 1. Evaluation is difficult if: 1) the system is an intelligent UI without an application, 2) a diagram editing tool, 3) if the components are largely prototypes or 4) if the application itself is novel and it is not understood how the system will be used. All the projects cited above, fall into one of these categories. Colgan et al [4] has identified the wide gap between early evaluation of design ideas via story boarding, and evaluation of a prototype with real tasks and users. At present there is no technological solution only an obvious need for 3D prototyping tools. We adopt an inventive use of existing technology for developing an evaluation prototype and investigating the process of user interaction with 3D GUI artifacts.

This paper is organised as follows. The first section describes a conceptual framework for specification of 3D diagrams. The rational for the design of a 3D visual interface to a medical KBS is outlined and the vocabulary of the conceptual framework is used to describe the evaluation prototype. This is followed by a summary account of the evaluation process. Findings are then reported in terms of usability claims which contribute to a feedback cycle [6]. The paper concludes with a discussion on the significance of prototyping and evaluation for the design of 3D Interactive GUIs.

## 2 Conceptual Framework

To realise the power of visual expression, images have to encode knowledge in a comprehensible format. Our hypothesis assumes that usability and learnability will be enhanced by a close correspondence between spatial features of the visualisation and the logical structure of task related knowledge. This implies that the design of the 3D visual interfaces should be based on domain and task modelling, and suggests the need for a modelling language to specify the design.

Development of a conceptual framework has been motivated by the need to place such design on a logical footing. The conceptual framework consists of a modelling language for 3D diagram interfaces . We distinguish the morphology or appearance of the image from interactive manipulations. A combination of morphology and manipulations results in a diagram paradigm, hence a diagram paradigm is a logical specification of form and interaction which may then be realised in one or more user interfaces.

## 2.1 Building a Morphology

Diagrams are made up of *primitive components* taken from an arbitrary set of atomic shape symbols which are declared as having meaning. In most diagrams, the primitives shapes will be nodes and links, although other primitives such as planes, contours, bubbles, and icons may be used.

Primitive components may be assigned *visual attributes* such as border, size, colour (hue, and saturation), shading, texture, and brightness. The visual attributes determine their appearance. Some visual attributes of a primitive may be reserved for coding the logical components of the KBS while others may be used to create visual depth in 3D e.g. shading.

Combination of primitives into meaningful representations are referred to as *composites*, e.g. hierarchies, networks, monocyclic graphs. These are higher order structures recognised to be meaningful within a diagram.

A *Diagram morphology* is a scheme for arranging components of a diagram in 2 or 3 dimensional space. Diagram morphologies are graphical representation of the logical components in an application domain, based on some explicit design rational. The morphology consists of primitive components and composites. The morphology may be assigned visual attributes which determine how the diagram as a whole will appear to the user, e.g. illumination from a fixed light source, and shadows.

## 2.2 Manipulations

To navigate around the visual representation, access text details and interact with the underlying information structure, diagram morphologies can be manipulated in three ways.

First, by *View Point changes*. The user's viewpoint is altered by changing the origin of the user's line of vision and/or the distance between the user and the diagram. e.g. include: compress, zoom (see figure 5), pan, view (angle), animation of rocking motion, and rotation of the diagram around the x, y, and z axis. Figure 2C is an example of view(angle). In addition viewpoint changes can be effected by dynamic simulation of virtual reality type flight through the diagram. For example in the SemNet system the user navigates the information space by flying through the display in a metaphoric helicopter [12].

Second, by *filtering* . The system utilises routines in the application to select the diagram elements to be displayed to the user. One example of filtering is fish eye viewing which may be expressed as a morphology of folding in a perspective wall

[23]. Another example is Aide Memoire type browsing where the filtering is driven by the underlying application functionality [31].

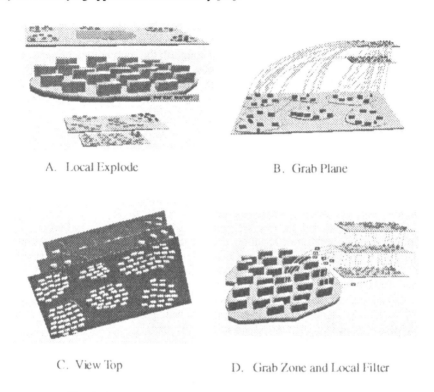

A. Local Explode                     B. Grab Plane

C. View Top                D. Grab Zone and Local Filter

**Fig. 2**. IM1 Diagram Manipulations [Cut From Screen Dumps].

Third, *interactive changes*. These are triggered by interaction with diagram components where the end state is a shape change in the morphology rather than in the user's orientation to the visualisation. Interactive changes are characterised by actions on diagram components e.g. pull(zone), open(node), and enter(viewport). Six examples of diagram manipulations are described below:

* Local Explode. The purpose of this manipulation is to enable easier inspection of small groups of nodes. It differs from Zoom operations in that it not only magnifies a diagram area but also leaves the surrounding area unchanged (whereas zoom applies throughout the display). Local explode approximates to a fisheye view if the exploded part of the image corresponds to semantic category relevant to the application. Figure 2A is an example of local explode, in this case the zone category is part of the design. The exploded zone maintains its' relative structural position but links are switched off. On the other hand the exploded area may be arbitrarily selected by the user in a bounding wire box. In both cases the selected area is magnified while maintaining the context e.g. relative structural position and links to the surrounding diagram.

- Local Implode. Local complexity is 'collapsed' while context is maintained in links to the surrounding diagram. Local complexity is reduced in two ways. First the number of diagram elements on display are reduced. Second, screen real estate is released for enlarging the visibility of surrounding context details.
- Grab. This operation gives the user more direct control over diagram elements which are recognised as primitives or composites. Selected parts of the diagram (e.g. planes, zones, active node/link), can be pulled out from the original plane. The new display state is consistent with the diagram morphology and reversible by a 'tidy' operation. Figure 2B is an example of grab plane where the links have followed the plane. Figure 2D is an example of grab zone with a local filter so only links connected to two nodes are visible.
- Enter Viewport. This operation involves the user selecting nodes which act as expansion ports into another diagram space.
- Access. Operation for inspecting and editing text details associated with diagram components.
- Edit. Operations for editing diagram components e.g. add(node), delete(node), and replace(node).

## 3   Visual Representation of Knowledge

The term representation is used in two senses. Firstly for visual coding of graphical elements (and attributes) to represent components of knowledge in the KB. Second, to recognise the semantic binding between the user's task and knowledge model (embedded in the KBS) and the diagram morphology. Ultimately strength of semantic binding can only be assessed by usability evaluation.

Our model based approach to design is well supported by generic knowledge modelling schemes [3], and knowledge modelling methodologies.[34] The first stage of the process is to identify the underlying *logical components of* KBSs. The term *logical components* is used to emphasise that there is a specifiable isomorphism between the form, structure, and functionality of the KBS, and the visual coding, diagram layout and interactively of the visualisation. The design of the morphology and the manipulations is essentially a creative act, however our approach is to analyse task and domain knowledge as input for identifying *requirements for representation.*

The purpose for specifying *requirements for representations* is to ensure close correspondence between the spatial features of the visualisation, and the *logical properties* of the knowledge in the KB. For example in a medical KBS, information on patient history is a set., which visually requires an enclosed boundary, so all primitives shapes representing patient history (e.g. age, sex) can be located on a zone, enclosed in bubble, or surrounded by a net. Another example is the use of colour to represent salience. If the degree of salience is a set range, and slight variations in values are not important, then colour may be an appropriate coding dimension, as in the case of a medical KBS, e.g. *red alert see your doctor now you are describing dangerous symptoms*, and, *orange alert this could be serious see your doctor in the next few days.* On the other hand, colour cannot be used as a coding dimension for representing a real number accurate to four decimal places, because the maximum number of colours that humans can perceive is an order of magnitude smaller than four digits.

## 3.1 The KBS

The application component (Figure 1) is a prototype expert diagnosis system called IM1 [11]. IM1 is rule based with backward chaining, to output diagnostic advice, and forward chaining to output a list of queries with *question worthiness* scores. The purpose of the query list is to suggest observation data required by the system to refine the advice. The system is mixed initiative so the user can input observation data as it becomes available, then the system displays an updated query list, and current system hypothesis.

The original prototype IM1 KB was designed to be used by General Medical Practitioners and Knowledge Engineers. With advice from domain experts, the KB was modified and extended to make it more appropriate for non-experts seeking general gynaecological information and advice [11, 13, 23, 33, 37].

## 3.2 Knowledge Model

The design for the 3D diagram paradigm was based on a task knowledge model drawn from literature, and analysis of medical text, manuals and journals [14]. Since we began with an existing KBS the task knowledge model was also used to reverse engineer and modify the IM1 KB.

Medical knowledge is classified according to the steps used in problem solving. The goal of the diagnostic task is to gather quantifiable data (signs, symptoms, tests), to build a picture of the patient and arrive at an interpretation of the case which accounts for all the salient findings, [See Appendix A1 for an extract from the task analysis]. The importance of the diagnosis goal will vary depending on, amongst other things, the urgency to begin treatment.

So, for example, the first stage in solving a medical problem is to gather data e.g. difficulty in breathing, legs weak, blue skin. The next step is to abstract this in terms of a pathophysiological process and identify circulatory distress caused by gas poisoning. Further diagnosis is delayed because the condition is critical, and instead, the goal to determine the type of immediate treatment is instantiated.

In the IM1 morphology design knowledge is organised in goal related clusters positioned in layers which reflect the task sequence.

## 3.3 Task Model

Consultations traces from IM1 were examined to identify typical tasks. These tasks were then translated into actions requiring 3D graphical interaction. In this way it was possible to anticipate manipulation requirements based on task modelling.

For example, in a task involving investigation of gynaecological problems, the user may sort through a list of medical particulars to find a unit of knowledge called *pregnancy* and then request more detailed information about *pregnancy* to find its current certainty value. In terms of the 3D visualisation this task would require the user to search for a node with the text label *pregnancy* and access the text details. This in turn suggests that the task can be supported with zoom, local explode, and open node manipulations.

# 4 The Prototype

## 4.1 Prototyping Environment.

A standalone prototype interface for IM1 has been created using Macromind Director™ an animation and prototyping tool supported by a high level programming language called Lingo [25]. In order to maintain proper perspective and movement constraints the visualisation ideas were created as models using Swivel 3D™ Professional [15]. A series of stills were exported to Macromind Director and stored in a library for animation sequences. Animation of specified manipulations could then be interactively triggered by user actions via the mouse button and keyboard. The technique supports dragging and stretching of elements in the morphology to create the impression that diagram elements are being pulled. In this way 3D manipulation is simulated while avoiding the problem of burdening the user with the additional cognitive load of precise positioning in 3D [16, 19, 34].

## 4.2 IM1 Morphology

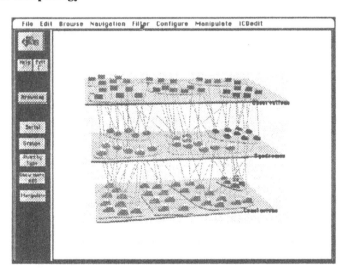

**Fig. 3**. Screen Dumps of IM1 Prototype Interface. The Planar Node/Link Network Morphology

The task model of medical diagnosis influenced the specification of the IM1 KBS visualisation, since three planes have been used to correspond to three phases of the medical diagnosis task :
- Observation Plane: corresponds to the phase of gathering quantifiable data
- Syndrome Plane: to the phase of inferring abstractions from the observations
- Conclusion Plane: corresponds to the action phase which may include diagnosis, treatment or referral.

(See figure 3)

Primitive units of knowledge in IM1 (medical particular) are represented by nodes. Nodes on different planes are represented using different shapes. Within each plane facts are spatially clustered according to semantic relatedness, so for instance all facts related to *Patient Case History* are clustered together, while details of possible tests are clustered in a zone called *Investigations*. Nodes have attributes which represent properties of the knowledge e.g. an orange border represents importance, while the icon " ? " represents question worthiness.

Links between planes are used to represent rules showing the causal connections between observation, syndrome and conclusion states. The IM1 reasoning model classifies rules into different types e.g. "suggests", "treated_by", "is-caused-by". These are colour coded. Depth cueing takes the form of subtle variations in shading

In response to the evaluation by Jones [18], $x$, $y$, and $z$ dimensions have not been used to represent information, and size coding has been avoided because of reported confusion with the use of perspective.

In the initial view, 95 nodes are displayed dispersed over 14 clusters, and 152 links. At this level of detail it was possible to optimise the arrangement of nodes so that all nodes are visible and can be selected.

### 4.3   IM1 Manipulations

Visualisation of the KBS is supported by navigation and interaction techniques for accessing information. Basic user tasks such as open node/rule (see Figure 4), edit node/rule or value of node/rule, search, and browse are supported by a combination of filtering and zoom diagram manipulations.

The filtering function controls the proportion of the KB presented on the screen. The selection of presented elements is determined by parameters derived from the system's reasoning model. Generalised filtering is also used to give the user control over the volume and type of connectivity displayed, e.g. show all "treated_by" rules hides other rule types. In addition, local filtering functionality is available when the object of interest is a node e.g. show all "caused_by" rules with target *pregnancy* (node) , or all rules which reference *pregnancy*.

A pilot study of three planes visualised in a scroll window suggested that the spaghetti effect of 2D representations and the conceptual disorientation in Hypertext interfaces [5] is transferred to 3D visualisations when the only way of navigating the diagram is by scrolling. In the IM1 prototype a combination of filtering and navigation techniques have made it possible to avoid using scroll window.

Our approach to 3D visualisation is characterised by the organisational metaphor embodied in the diagram, and this is used as a reference point for maintaining context and orientation during manipulations. The IM1 prototype navigation functionality includes the following.

View Top:         for viewing the top of the structure.
Local Explode:  for obtaining a detailed view of part of the KB while reducing the size of the surrounding parts of the diagram.
Grab Plane:      for pulling the plane forward along the z axis while pushing the other planes into the background.
Grab Zone:       for pulling a zone forward while pushing the rest of the diagram into the background.

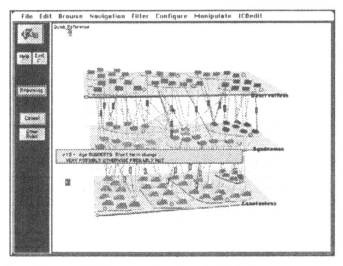

**Fig. 4.** Screen Dumps of IM1 Prototype Interface. A Rule Link is Opened to Show Text Details

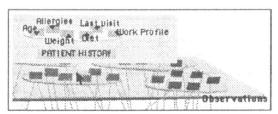

**Fig. 5.** Screen Dumps of IM1 Prototype Interface. A Zoom View Showing Text Details

The simulations are intended to convey the impression that these functions are invoked by direct manipulation of the diagram. To assist visual tracking, animation with smooth movement has been used for all diagram manipulation transformations except View Top.

## 5  Evaluation

We investigated a broad range of factors affecting the usability of the IM1 3D diagram paradigm, and gathered data on individually different patterns of interaction with the prototype interface. Usability objectives were defined in terms of effectiveness, efficiency and satisfaction [1]. The evaluation approach combined the collaboration philosophy in the York Manual approach [35], with the taxonomic approach to observing patterns of interaction, and model based analysis of usability in the task context [30].

The IM1 prototype interface was evaluated by fourteen subjects with extensive computing experience, graduate level education and an interest in health information. Incomplete data from four subjects was used to debug the prototype and design the study. Data from the remaining ten subjects (four female, six male) is the basis for the results discussed in this paper.

## 5. 1 Procedure

Each evaluation session took an average of two hours five minutes. Subjects were encouraged to ask questions, and provide verbal protocol [10]. The sessions were tape recorded. Errors and problems with the interaction were recorded by the investigator during the session. (See table 1 for a summary of the types of data collected)

| TABLE 1 Data collected during the evaluation | |
|---|---|
| Data collected: | Comment on data collection means |
| Verbal protocol: | Taped |
| Patterns of interaction: | Recorded by the investigator at fixed points. See Figure 6. |
| Pace of interaction: | Elapsed time between ten random mouse clicks. |
| Task Completion times: | Task: *'Search Guided by Inference'*. Completed by subjects without intervention from the investigator. |
| UI functionality used and error data: | With reference to a task model [28]. See Appendix A2 for generic task and interaction model. |
| Orientation test: | Subjects asked to locate diagram elements after various manipulations |
| Spatial memory test: | The number of mouse click(s) required to locate the correct node/zone were recorded |
| User's perceptions and satisfaction score: | Structured questions, questionnaire, informal discussion. |

The basic form of the evaluation task, was *Search Guided by Inference*. The objective of these tasks was to locate the diagram element traceable from other semantic clues, e.g. "Find 'Age' in 'Patient History' on the 'Observation Plane' ". Some versions of the task required the subject to read a rule text to find the certainty factor attached to that rule. Other more complex forms of the task also required the subject to compare certainty values between rules.

# 6   Results

A detailed analysis of the results is reported elsewhere [31]. Table 2 shows a summary of the activity pattern observations and task performance data. All subjects completed the core search tasks, however, there was considerable variation in total task completion times ranging from six minutes to nineteen minutes. This variation was due to two main problems:

- Ineffective or limited use of diagram manipulation functionality (s2, s4, s5, s9). All the subjects with an above average task performance time made optimum (s1, s3, s8, s10), or nearly optimum (s7), use of the manipulation functionality.
- Inaccurate or Incomplete User Model. Five subjects (s2, s4, s5, s7, s9), failed to make accurate inferences about relationships between components in the KB. All users were able to identify the subgoal target for the core tasks (see Appendix A2 for details), but problems arose when the subjects failed to reduce the search space effectively.

| TABLE 2 Activity pattern observations and performance Indicators | | | | | | | | | |
|---|---|---|---|---|---|---|---|---|---|
| | P1 | P2 | P3 | P4 | P5 | P6 | Pace | U of M | P I 1 | P I 2 |
| s1 | | | | | ••• | ••• | V | 1 | 6 | 13 |
| s2 | | •• | | ••• | | • | S | 3 | 16 | 17 |
| s3 | | | | | •••• | •• | V | 1 | 6 | 24 |
| s4 | | •• | | •••• | | | S | 4 | 17 | 11 |
| s5 | | | •• | •••• | | | S | 3 | 14 | 8 |
| s6 | | | ••••• | | • | | V | 1 | 10 | 30 |
| s7 | | | •• | | • | ••• | V | 2 | 11 | 36 |
| s8 | ••••• | | | • | | | F | 1 | 9 | 27 |
| s9 | | ••• | | ••• | | | S | 3 | 19 | 13 |
| s10 | ••••• | | | • | | | F | 1 | 8 | 41 |
| Average Pace of Interaction [PI 1] & Spatial Memory Score [PI 2] | | | | | | | | | 11.6 | 17.9 |
| Range Pace of Interaction [PI 1] & Spatial Memory Score [PI 2] | | | | | | | | | 6-16 | 11 - 41 |

**KEY**

| Observed Patterns of exploration (See Figure 6 for illustration ) | Pace of Interaction: |
|---|---|
| P1--Serial | F-Fast: average less then 6 second time lapse between mouse clicks |
| P2-Whole Group Sampling | |
| P3-Cluster Sampling | S-Slow: average more than 10 second time lapse between mouse clicks |
| P5-Horizontal Connectivity Explored | |
| P6-Vertical Connectivity Explored | V-Varied: range between less then 4 seconds and more than 15 seconds time lapse between mouse clicks. |
| • - Predominant pattern of interaction at predefined observation point (total 6). | |

Use of Manipulations: (U of M)
1- Optimum where optimum sequence of manipulations were used throughout the task as defined by an expert,
2- Nearly Optimum where subjects used the more complex UI functionality
3- Inefficient where subjects erratically shifted between different UI functionality and less powerful functions
4- Limited where subjects used only the less powerful functions.

| Performance Indicator 1 (PI 1) | Performance Indicator 2 (PI 2) |
|---|---|
| Total core task completion times in minutes | Spatial memory scores measured as total number of mouse click(s) to target node/zone. |

Figure 6 illustrates the patterns of exploration observed by the investigator. A slower pace of interaction was associated with *Localised Exploration*, *Whole Group Sampling*, and *Cluster Sampling* (s2, s4, s5, and s9), while *Serial* type of exploration was combined with a fast pace of interaction (s8 and s10).

For subjects with the shortest task completion times two exploration activity patterns were predominant. First exploration cued by *Connectivity Horizontal* and

*Vertical* (s1 and s3) and second, *Serial* search approach which seemed largely to ignore the morphology structuring cues (s8 and s10).

The predominant activity patterns for the subjects with the longer performance times (s4 and s9) and above average memory score were cued by the morphology (*Cluster Sampling*).

Some subjects experienced difficulty with the View Top function (which had not been animated), and with other viewpoint changes where the structuring cues (clusters and planes) were not visibly salient in the new views (e.g. zoom).

In retrospective interviews, subjects reported that the Grab and Local Explode functions conformed with their expectations, and also that locating diagram elements after a diagram manipulation was fairly easy rating average 5.7 on a scale of 1 to 7, (1= hard - 7 = easy). Morphology was judged to be easy to remember with a rating average of 6.2. In addition six subjects said that the most useful feature of the design was the morphology.

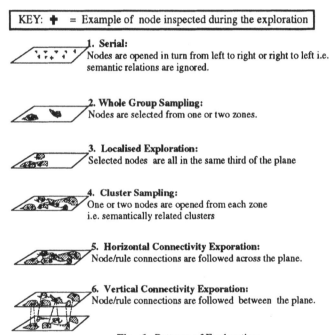

KEY: ✚ = Example of node inspected during the exploration

**1. Serial:**
Nodes are opened in turn from left to right or right to left i.e. semantic relations are ignored.

**2. Whole Group Sampling:**
Nodes are selected from one or two zones.

**3. Localised Exploration:**
Selected nodes are all in the same third of the plane

**4. Cluster Sampling:**
One or two nodes are opened from each zone i.e. semantically related clusters

**5. Horizontal Connectivity Exporation:**
Node/rule connections are followed across the plane.

**6. Vertical Connectivity Exporation:**
Node/rule connections are followed between the plane.

**Fig. 6.** Patterns of Exploration

Interacting with the diagram to access detailed information was also favourably received (average score 6.1, range from 5-7). However rule connections were hard to see (average score 2.2). In particular eight subjects said that it was difficult to work with nodes accessed by more then three rules.

## 7 Discussion

3D Interactive Visualisation shows much promise for managing the complexity of interacting with large or complex information structures. However, there is little evidence that the diagram paradigms employed to date are usable or effective in supporting the user's understanding, although one exception to this may be the design of a knowledge browser interface [30]. From problems encountered in this study and elsewhere [18], high connectivity, complexity, and disorientation during viewpoint changes, appear to be the principle 3D diagram design problems.

Design of the diagram morphology based on User Modelling (UM) is important in structuring task related information. Our findings suggest that a close correspondence between the UM and the diagram morphology can enable users to understand information structure more easily, and in that sense 3D representation can reduce complexity. Automatic layout algorithms as used in the SemNet Project [12] which have no structural template based on a UM may therefore not produce comprehensible displays. We suggest that a strong organisation metaphor is vital for the success of 3D visualisations and argue that this should be based on modelling the user's domain knowledge.

However the 3D Visualisations are only usable if supported by a suitable set of manipulations facilitating diagram-wide navigation and interaction with diagram components. The manipulations in turn are a source of additional intrinsic complexity of interacting with 3D graphics. For the IM1 Visualisation this had been addressed by evaluating the disorientation effect of various DM diagram manipulations. Manipulations clearly linked to structural elements of the image contribute to the effectiveness of interaction. Our evaluation process will be continued for iterative refinement of manipulations.

Three main styles of interaction were identified in this study. The subjects who explored the connectivity in the visualisation also demonstrated an effective grasp of manipulation functionality and showed general comprehension of the overall visualisation but poor recall of detail. Another group of subjects showed poor spatial memory results, and adopted a serial pattern of exploration but achieved good task performance results by effective and rapid use of manipulations. The third style of interaction was systematic and focused on the categorial aspects of the visualisation. These subjects demonstrated good spatial memory, however they did not use the manipulations effectively and their task performance times were longest. There are two tentative conclusions from this. First that spatial memory does not seem to be important for effective use of the manipulation functionality. This conclusion is in agreement with the finding reported by Mayes et al [27], that visual memory for DM interfaces was poor but posed no barrier to successful interaction. Second, the rapid serial search mechanistic style of interaction may not scale up to tasks which are more complex since the user is ignoring the information structuring in the morphology. This suggests that different interactive styles should be supported so long as they are effective, and that users may need to be trained to use the manipulations effectively.

We found that the problem of high connectivity can be addressed by additional view point and filter manipulations, and that integration of text and image is an important concern. Users need to move from manipulating components of the diagram to inputting and inspecting text details. The design solutions of opening diagram elements rules and nodes need to be refined.

The study has also contributed to our understanding of how people interact with complex 3D images, while uncovering usability errors in the M1 design, through artifact analysis. These findings will need to be refined with a full prototype to evaluate if the users' tasks will impose constraints which require other types of interaction support.

## Acknowledgements

The work reported in this paper has been funded by the Science and Engineering Research Council as part of the Cooperative KBS Browsing Project, (Grant number GR/G 56478) City University.

## References

1. J. Brooke, N. Bevan, F. Brigham, S. Harker, D. Youmans: Usability Statement and Standardisation-Work in Progress at ISO. In: INTERACT Human-Computer Interaction, D. Diper, D. Gilmore, G. Cockton, B. Shackel (eds.). Cambridge: UK. Elsevier Science North-Holland, 357-361, (1991)

2  S. K. Card, G. G. Robertson, J. D. Mackinlay: The Information Visualiser, an Information Workspace. In: Proc. CHI'91 Human Factors in Computing Systems, S. P. Robertson, G. M. Olson (eds.), ACM Press, 181-188, New Orleans, 28 April- 2 May, (1991)

3. B. Chandrasekaran, T. R. Johnson, J. W. Smith: Task-Structure Analysis for Knowledge Modelling. In :Comm. of the ACM, September, 35, 9, 124-136 (1993)

4. L. Colgan, P. Randin, R. Spence: Steering automated design. In: Artificial Intelligence in Design, J. Gero (ed.). Butterworth Heinmann, 211- 230, (1991)

5. J. Conklin: Hypertext: An Introduction and Survey. In: IEEE Computer, September (1987)

6. J. M. Carroll, W. A. Kellogg, M. B. Rosson: The Task-Artifact Cycle. In: Designing Interaction: Psychology at the Human Computer Interface, J. M. Carroll (ed.). Cambridge University Press (1991)

7. D. D. Dodson: Interaction with Knowledge Systems through Connection Diagrams: Where Next. In: Expert Systems: Human Issues, D. Berry, A. Hart (eds.). Chapman and Hall (1990)

8. D. D. Dodson, A. L. Rector: Importance Driven Distributed Control of Diagnostic Inference. In: Research and Development in Expert Systems, M. Bramer (ed.). Cambridge University Press (1984).

9. D. D. Dodson, A. G. Sutcliffe: Case for Support: Cooperative KBS Browsing. Application for SERC Project Grant, (1990)

10. A. Ericsson, H. Simon: Verbal Reports as Data. Psychological Review, 87, 3, (1980)

11. A. Evans, V. L. Patel (eds.): Cognitive Science in Medicine: Biomedical Modelling. MIT Press (1989)

12. M. F. Fairchild, S. E. Poltrock, G. W. Furnas: SemNet: Three Dimensional Graphic Representations of Large Knowledge Bases. In: Cognitive Science and its Applications for Human Computer Interaction, R. Guindon (ed.), Hillsdale N J: Lawrence Erlbaum Associates (1988)

13. E. H. I. Friedman, R. E. Moshy: Medicine the Bare Bones: a Comprehensive Systematic Approach. Wiley J. (1986).

14. M. M. Glykas, U. Patel, A. G. Sutcliffe, D. C. Dodson, T. Hackett: Towards Interactive Explanation by 3D Visualisation. In: Proc. Workshop on Task Based Explanation. Research Laboratory of Samos, University of the Aegean, (1992)

15. Y. Harvill: Swivel 3D Professional version 2.0, VPL Research, (1991)

16. S. Houde: Iterative Design of an Interface for Easy 3-D Direct Manipulation. In: Proc. CHI'92 Human Factors in Computing Machinery. ACM Press, 135-142, Monterey, May 3-7, (1992)

17. M. Jarrett, S. Feiner, G. Robertson: Information Visualisation with Interactive 3D Representations. Tutorial notes INTERCHI, Amsterdam, Netherlands (1993)

18. S. Jones: Graphical Interface for Knowledge Engineering. Knowledge Engineering Review, 3, 3, 221- 246 (1989)

19. S. Jones: Three-Dimensional Interaction Connection Diagrams for Knowledge Engineering. PhD thesis [submitted], Computer Science Department, City University, UK. (1993)

20. S. M. Kosslyn: Image and Mind. Harvard University Press (1980)

21. L. Lewis: Situated Visualisation: Building Interfaces from the Mind Up. Multimedia Review, Winter/Spring, 23- 40, (1991/92)

22. R. MacAleese: The Graphical Representation of Knowledge as an Interface to Knowledge Based systems. In: Proc. INTERACT '87, H. J. Bullinger, B. Shackel (eds.). IFIP/North Holland pp. 1089-1093, (1987)

23. F. J. Macarthney: Logic in Medicine. In; Journal of the British Medical Association, 295, (1987)

24. J. D. Mackinlay, G. G. Robertson, s. K. Card: The Perspective Wall: Details and Context Smoothly Integrated. In: Proc. CHI'91 Human Factors in Computing

Systems. S. P. Robertson, G. M. Olson (eds.), ACM Press, 173 - 179, New Orleans, 28 April- 2 May, (1991)

25. Macromind, Inc: Interactivity Manual, Macromind Director version 3.0, (1991)

26. C. Marshall, C. Nelson, M. M. Gardiner: Design Guidelines. In: Applying Cognitive Psychology to User Interface Design, M. M. Gardiner, B. Christie (eds.). Wiley J. (1987)

27. J. T Mayes, S. W. Draper, A. M. McGregor, K. Oatley: Information Flow in a User Interface: the Effects of Experience and Context on the Recall of Mac Write Screens. In: People & Computers IV, D. M. Jones, R. Winder (eds.). Cambridge University Press , Proceeding of HCI'88, Manchester, September, 275-289. (1988)

28. B. S. Murray: Visualising and Representing Knowledge for the End User: a Review. In: International Journal of Man-Machine Studies, 38, 23-49 (1993)

29. G. G. Robertson, S. K. Card, J. D. Mackinlay: Information Visualisation using 3D Interactive Animation. In: Communications of the ACM, April, 36, 4, 57-71 (1993)

30. A. G. Sutcliffe, R. Kral: Knowledge Browser: A Novel Human Computer Interface for Knowledge Based Systems. Research Report, Department of Computing, UMIST, Manchester, (1988)

31. A. G. Sutcliffe , U. K. Patel ,:The Three-Dimensional Graphical User Interface: Evaluation for Design Evolution. In: Proc. HCI '93, UK (forthcoming) September (1993)

32. A. G. Sutcliffe, M. V. Springett: From User's Problems to Design Errors. In: People and Computers V II, A. Monk, D. Diaper, M. Harrison (eds.). Cambridge University Press, Proceedings of HCI'92, York, September, 117-131.(1992)

33. P. Szolovits (ed.): Artificial Intelligence in Medicine. Westview Press, (1982)

34. L. R. Wanger, J. A. Ferwerda, D. P. Greenberg: Perceiving Spatial Relationships in Computer-Generated Images. In: IEEE Computer Graphics and Applications, 12, 3, 44-58, May, (1992)

35. B. Wielinga, J Breuker, M. van Someren: KADS: A Modelling Approach to Knowledge Engineering". Knowledge Acquisition, 36, (1992)

36. P. Wright, A. F.Monk: Evaluation for Design. In: People and Computers, A. G. Sutcliffe, L. Macaulay (eds.). Cambridge University Press (1989)

37. H. R. Wulff: Rational Diagnosis and Treatment: An Introduction to Clinical Decision Making. Blackwell (1981)

# Appendix A

## A1    Fragment From a Task Model of Medical Diagnosis

**Begin:**

1    Initial collection of data.

    **Goal:**  details of the case sorted in expected order

1.1   Gather information about the nature of the complaint, and     chronological account of
    the illness,
    Seek  numeric values for quantities [e.g. time, duration, size],
    Estimate 'truth' [e.g. allow for exaggeration, underplay, poor memory ]
1.2   Collect information about patient's background and history,
    Ask questions, and seek clarification,
    Inspect  patient records,

2.    Developing and supporting diagnostic hypothesis.

    **Goal:**  identify a valid hypothesis  OR active hypothesis ranked in order of plausibility.

2.1   Formulate initial hypothesis about possible causes(s)
2.2   Cross examine patient to gather data for hypotheses testing.
               provoke symptom reporting
               listen for volunteered symptoms
               quantify symptom and attach truth value,
2.3   Evaluate new data to refine hypothesis, eliminate hypothesis,  or confirm hypothesis,
2.3   Perform physical examination.
2.4   Evaluate and quantify signs to refine hypothesis, confirm hypothesis, or eliminate
    hypothesis.

3.    Select a course  of action

    **Goal:**    maximise utility and minimise risk (and cost?)

3.1   Evaluate interpretation of the case in relation to current salient        findings.
3.2   Take action
    Options: begin treatment
    *OR*  wait and see because additional evidence will emerge as  a
    hypothesised disease  develops.
    *OR*  gather more information by testing.

**End.**

## A2    Generic Task and Interaction Model for *Search Guided by Inference*.

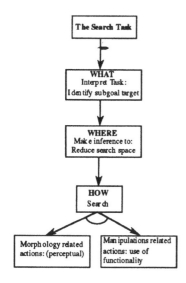

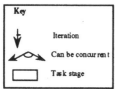

**EXAMPLE TASK :** What *Conclusion* medical particular is DEFINITELY 'suggested_by' "Excessive Weight Loss" ?

[WHAT] Define Subgoal: "Excessive Weight Loss"

[WHERE] Infer: A medical particular on the *Conclusion Plane* is the main goal therefore "Excessive Weight Loss" is an antecedent. If the conclusion particular is on the *Conclusion Plane* then the antecedent particular (i.e. "Excessive Weight Loss"), will be on the *Syndrome Plane*.

[HOW] Search for a node with the text label "Excessive Weight Loss".

[REPEAT]

[WHAT] Define Next Subgoal: A rule, with the certainty value DEFINITELY, with antecedent "Excessive Weight Loss" and a goal medical particular on the *Conclusion Plane* .

[WHERE] Infer: The (suggested_by) rule is represented as an orange link connected to a the node labelled "Excessive Weight Loss" and situated between the *Syndrome Plane* and the *Conclusion Plane* .

[HOW] Search links between the *Conclusion Plane* and *Syndrome Plane*.

[REPEAT] Define next Subgoal and continue..........

# Visual Programming in R-technology: Concepts, Systems and Perspectives

Igor Ushakov[1] and Igor Velbitskiy[2]

[1]Human Cognition Research Laboratory, The Open University
Walton Hall, Milton Keynes, MK7 6AA, UK

[2]International Software Technology Research Center -TECHNOSOFT
44 Academician Glushkov Avenue, Kiev 252207, Ukraine

**Abstract.** This paper describes an efficient framework for software development environments based on R-charts and gives main concepts and aims of a project to the develop a visual user interface for the C++ programming language. R-charts are structured graphs which are used for visual specifications of algorithms, visual programming and debugging. They have been applied to different languages and have adopted by ISO as an alternative charting notation for the program constructs in ISO/IEC 8631. The user interface for C++ described in this paper incorporates the R-charts, OO diagrams and other visualization methods for visual specifications, data browsing and control flow visualization.

## 1 Introduction

The object-oriented approach has spread widely and led to a large number of programmers who use C++ for software development. However few C++ software development environments (SDEs) possess a good visual interface and can support the OO paradigm in adequate and valuable way [1]. There exist some SDEs which support project and data browsing by indicating classes, member functions and data members in different windows [1, 2, 12], but they support a basically textual representation with icons or some graphical elements for indicating objects to browse. They show, for example, direct inheritance like the class browser of ObjectCenter does, displaying any class as a base class and indicating all derived classes for it [12]. Such focus class methods permit searching and can correct local dependencies but does not provide an opportunity to show a large scale view on hierarchy of browsing objects.

There is also a lack of SDEs for C++ in UNIX with visual support of the main software development processes. Some SDEs can support the separate processes of the software development life cycle [13, 14] and there are systems which do it by using well known and well tested design methodologies (Teamwork, Software through Pictures, Spreadbuilder, PDF). Nevertheless, there is great need for integrated tools to support design, implementation and maintenance of the software systems by using coordinated visual facility and better program understanding.

This paper represents an efficient framework for a software development environment based on a graphical notation known as R-charts and gives short description of a project designed to develop an integrated visual user interface for a C++ programming environment in UNIX. R-charts are structured graphs which are used for visual specifications of algorithms, visual programming and debugging [5-9]. They are also used for program documentation and have applied to different languages. R-charts have been adopted by the ISO as an alternative charting notation for program constructs in ISO/IEC 8631 [11]. The user interface for C++ described in this paper incorporates R-charts and other visualization methods for visual specifications, data browsing and control flow visualization.

A brief description of the visual notation for C++ control statements based on R-charts is given in section 2. It introduces the reader to a syntax-oriented graphical editor and contains examples of a C++ function written by means of R-charts. The visual design approach, design unit, operational diagrams and design browser are described in section 3. Project and class browsing with visual manipulation abilities are discussed in section 4 of this paper. Section 5 describes the overall structure of the integrated visual interface for C++ and discusses further directions of research and implementation. In section 6 the results of the empirical studies and comparative analyses are given. The conclusion summarizes the short basic features and benefits of the integrated user interface which we have described in this paper.

## 2　Visual Interface for Development Processes

There is a wide variety of charts and diagrams for control flow representation [3, 8, 11]. Some recent systems provide automatic derivation of a graphical representation from source code and compute control flow metrics [4]. The International standard proposes several kinds of charting notation for program control flow constructs [11]. One of them is R-charts which have been widely used in the former USSR since the beginning of 1980s and was adopted as USSR State standard in 1985 and as ISO standard in 1989. The visual paradigm of R-charts consists of a simple graphical metaphors for representing selective and iterative program constructs. It has been implemented as a visual programming interface for C/C++, Pascal, Modula-2, Assembler, Fortran for IBM PC [8, 9].

### 2.1　R-charts Visual Paradigm

The main idea consists of weighting the arrowed line (the arc of a control flow graph) with text or graphics. This line designates the transition from one program state to another. The weight above the line is always a condition and the weight under the line is an action which can be executed if the condition becomes true. The program states are indicated by cycles and each graphical construct of R-charts has one starting node (entry) and one final node (exit). This graphical notation is very flexible for adaptation to different languages and keeps the same rules of construct interpretation.

All selective constructs are regarded from the top arrowed line to the bottom one when the corresponding condition is true. In the case of truth, the block of statements placed underneath the line is executed and exit from the current construct through the final node is performed. If the condition is false the next arrowed line from top to bottom is chosen to test the condition. If no line contains successful condition then the construct is regarded as unexecutable. The absence of the condition is treated as truth.

An iterative construct may be of two types: one with top double line to indicate **while** and **for** control structures, and another one with the top line arrowed to right and the bottom one arrowed to left to represent **do-while** control structure. The iteration is running if the condition is true. Any two graphical constructs may be connected sequentially or be embedded in one another. These rules of connection permit a variety of different composite constructs to describe the complex control flow in real programs.

## 2.2 Graphical Notation for C++ Control Flow Statements

Table 1 shows the graphical notation for C++ control flow statements represented by means of R-charts. All statements have a rigorous visual representation and can be easily combined to construct the control flow structure of a program.

The R-chart representation is rigorous and can be fully automated [5, 8]. A graph-grammar for R-chart generation and parsing has been developed [7] and a number of automated methods for measuring the program complexity have been proposed [22]. The graphical editor for R-charts has a special menu to input, edit and manipulate graphical constructs directly (see Figure 2). By clicking the mouse button one can choose any R-chart fragment consisting of one or more lines or one or more constructs including a whole R-chart for the conventional manipulations: copying, deleting, moving, etc. Our previous experience with R-chart usage suggests that this charting notation usefully differs from many other notations used for control flow representations. The R-charts are very compact, easy to understand and learn, and permit automatic transformations and syntax-oriented editing. The graphical editor constructs only correct control flow statements and eliminates a number of errors bound with the keywords and semicolons. This notation is language independent and that is why it was adopted as an ISO Standard [11]. The R-charts can support the different software development processes: system and detailed design, coding, testing and debugging, documenting and maintenance [5, 6, 8, 9].

For comparison we present below the text representation (Figure 1) and the graphical representation (Figure 2) of the same C++ function *insert* which creates a one-node tree if the tree is initially empty. R-charts may be placed one after the other as shown in Figure 2. One may also put text lines between R-charts and R-charts between text fragments going after each other from top to bottom. The graphical editor has a left/right scrolling and the function *insert* may be represented by single R-chart containing all three graphical fragments connected sequentially.

The current R-chart element is indicated by cursor position. The arrowed line is a minimum graphical element, which means the transition from one node to another and may be added to or deleted from any construct: deleting the single arrowed line in the construct means deletion of this construct. The small pop-up menu in Figure 2 helps users to choose where they want to add a new construct (after, before the current one or insert into the current line of the current construct). The menu commands *after* and *before* create a sequential connection the command *insert* creates an embedded one. For the arrowed lines commands *before* and *after* can only add a new line before or after the current one.

**Table 1.** Graphical notation for C++ statements

| C++ statement | R-chart |
|---|---|
| 1. label-identifier : statement | l-i ——————→<br>   statement |
| 2. **case** const-expr : statement | const-expr ————→<br>statement |
| 3. **default** : statement | ——————————→<br>statement |
| 4. **if** (expr) statement ‹**else** statement› | |
| 5. **if** (expr) statement<br>    **else if** (expr) statement<br>        **else** statement | |
| 6. **switch** (sw-expr)<br>    **case** const-expr-i : statement-i<br>    **default** : statement | |
| 7. **while** (expr) statement | |

**Table 1.** Continued

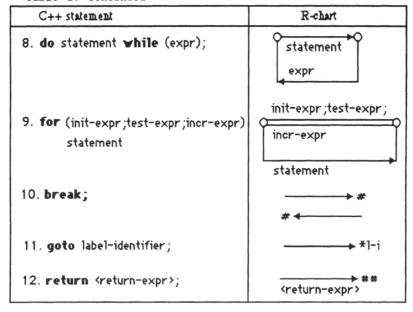

| C++ statement | R-chart |
|---|---|
| 8. **do** statement **while** (expr); | |
| 9. **for** (init-expr;test-expr;incr-expr) statement | |
| 10. **break;** | |
| 11. **goto** label-identifier; | |
| 12. **return** <return-expr>; | |

```
void bstree::insert(p_gen d)
{
    bnode* temp = root
    bnode* old;
void bstree::insert(p_gen d)
{
    bnode* temp = root
    bnode* old;
    if (root ==0)  {
        root = new bnode(d, 0, 0);
        return;
    }
    while (temp != 0)  {
        old = temp;
        if (comp(temp -> data, d) == 0)  {
        (temp -> count)++;
        return;
        }
        if (comp(temp -> data, d)
        temp = temp -> left;
        else
        temp = temp -> right;
    }
    if (comp(old -> data, d) > 0)
        old -> left = new bnode(d, 0, 0);
    else
        old -> right = new bnode(d, 0, 0);
}
```

**Fig. 1.** Text representation of the function *insert*

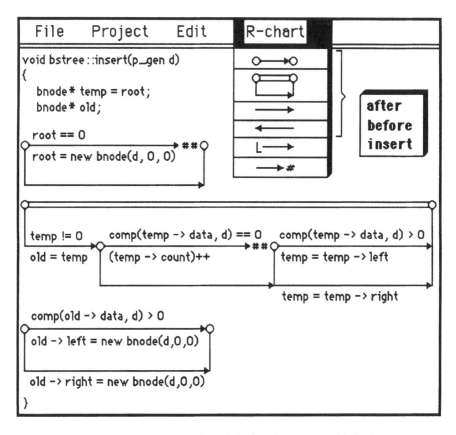

**Fig. 2.** Graphical representation of the function *insert*  with R-charts

## 3  Design Interface

The system supports structured design with visual design specifications and advanced browsing facilities. The basic concept of a visual design approach is a *design unit* (Figures 3 and 4). It is a logical idea which means the module, function or class at any level of abstraction. The design unit (as a module) contains four types of definitions for *unit specifications, internal data definitions, algorithm definition* and *definitions of abstractions*. The specifications contain descriptions of the input and output data, unit name, application domain, information on process of software development and representation method. The internal definitions describe the internal data of the unit and may be represented in different forms: textual, tabular or graphical. The algorithm definitions present the procedural part of the unit in textual or graphical form with an informal or formal description of what this unit will do. The definitions of abstractions allow a developer to refer to another unit or to write an equivalent fragment using C++. The design window (Figure 5) shows the design tree and the current design unit which may be indicated by inverse video or a rectangle. A developer can easily navigate through the design tree by using the mouse and manipulate the unit definitions

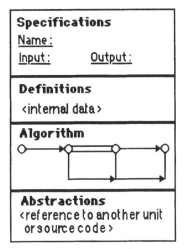

**Fig. 3.** Design unit

choosing different commands in the design menu. Most commands are applicable to the unit as a whole and any unit components. The system provides specific windows for operations such as editing or browsing correspondent unit definitions. The design browser provides a pop-up menu for manipulating unit components and interunit links. One can trace certain refinements for module or object definitions. The command *fullrefr* builds the full project tree with all references on and calls of any modules so that you can find repeated subtrees (like subtree *Operations* shown in Figure 5). An additional window shows, for any current unit (module, function) or unit component, all of the units which are referred to by it and all the units which have a reference to it.

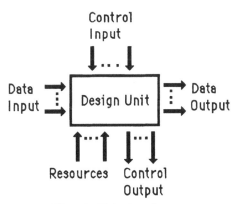

**Fig. 4.** Unit interface

The design unit interface is shown in Figure 4. There are three input points and two output points, namely: *Data Input, Control Input* and *Resources Input, Data Output* and *Control Output*. A unit can have many points of each types. The system provides a special view of the design tree indicating all interface links in the *Operational Diagram*, as shown in Figure 6.

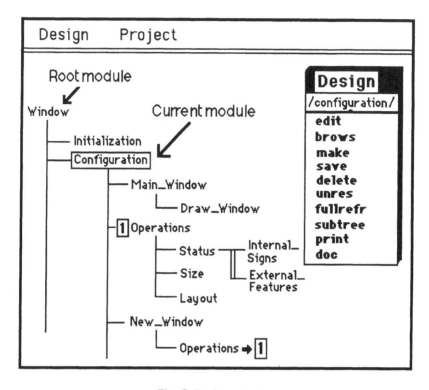

**Fig. 5.** Design window

The design process has two control structures for choice: "one unit of several" and "all units in sequence". The first operation is similar to a logical OR, and the second one is a logical AND. The OR-like control structure is represented on the design tree and operational diagram by single line branches. The AND-like control structure is drawn by means of double vertical (for design tree) or double horizontal (for operational diagram) lines and connects the units which are executed sequentially and transfer data from one to another. An output of the unit "Internal_Signs" serves as an input for the unit "External_Features". The subtree "Operations" (Figure 5) contains both these control structures and is shown by the operational diagram in Figure 6.

The system will support several design processes. It is applicable to the "system design" and "detailed design" which are components of a "structured design". The definition of an algorithm contains Data Flow Diagrams and R-charts for system design and R-charts for detailed design. The source code of the program will be automatically generated from the detailed design specifications which can be regarded as system documentation. The system documentation is generated automatically and is based on the standardized R-chart graphical representation [6, 8, 11]. Both types of design specifications may be verified for consistency and correctness automatically. A user may check, for example, the input/output balance in the system under design. The concept of a Design Unit may be also applied to the requirements analysis so that the system requirements may be represented graphically as a set of design units. In this case the units may not contain definitions (like the definition of algorithm) but rather describe correspondent information.

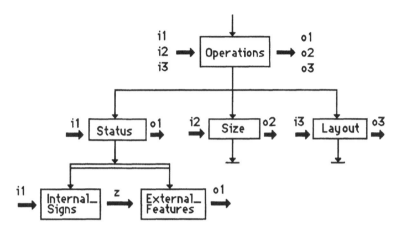

**Fig. 6.** The operational diagram

# 4 Project and Classes Browsing and Visualization.

The system will provide advanced facilities for project and classes browsing and uses tree-like graphical representation for visualization. The *Browsing window* for projects or classes contains special menus and correspondent pop-up menus for manipulating functions and classes. By means of moving and clicking the mouse one can easily navigate through the tree and choose any browsing unit (function or class) to open it in an additional pop-up window for searching and editing. This window may also be opened automatically if the debugger finds an error in some function and the graphical editor would be loaded automatically. There will be several such loops for error detection and correction in accordance with the error type after which a user can return to the C++ source code, detailed specification or system specification. The last option is hard to perform automatically in all cases and therefore can be done manually. These three loops are shown in Figure 9, where the functional overview of the system is presented. They are achieved by closed integration of the visual debugger and the browser. The project tree presents all dependencies of the functions in the style of operational diagrams. It shows static information obtained from the design specifications.

## 4.1 Object-Oriented Interface

There are many different charting notations for Object-Oriented software development [31]. Some of them are well known [23, 24], whereas other graphical representations are rather new and designed to be a unified charting notation for the whole OO systems life cycle [25, 26]. Various OO approaches have been analyzed [14, 28] and some recommendations on the application of OO diagrams have been made [25, 28] to represent the advantages of the OO paradigm in a better charting notation. But much more should be done to suggest a standardized form of the OO representation. An international standardization project [31] is surveying numerous charting notations in the area of OO programming. It is linked conceptually with two projects: "Basic symbols and Diagrams for Software Development" [29] and "A Description of Data for Software Development" [30], which are the main projects in Subcommittee 7 on graphical representation of information for software engineering [27]. The project, 7.19.02.06 [31], is also aimed at achieving better quality of OO systems through facilitating the metrics measurements, software reuse, and project and configuration management. Some of the ideas on OO diagram unification have been used in this research. At the first stage of the system implementation, we are proposing a charting notation for the basic OO concepts. We only use a static view of the classes and their structure. The system suggests a simple graphical representation that is derived partly from our survey of OO diagrams [31]. C++ classes are represented by the design unit which has, in this case, three components for *class name*, *member data*, and *member functions* as shown in Figure 7.

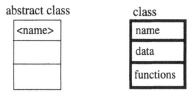

**Fig. 7.** Class icons

Abstract classes are represented by an icon drawn with a thin line. The name of an abstract class is put in angle brackets (see Figures 7 and 8). By clicking on the data or functions component of the class icon one can have detailed description of the component. Descriptions of the functions may be represented by R-charts. Data components are represented by text. To show the class structure, the system uses a tree-like graph that represents the class hierarchy (Figure 8).

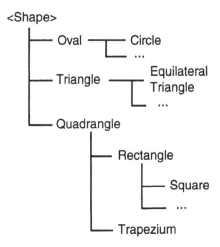

**Fig. 8.** Class hierarchy

All "parent" or base classes (including multiple inheritance) and derived classes can be shown for any current class. The system allows the user to move along the tree, choose any class as current and show its components in detail.

This inheritance tree represents the "kind-of" relationships among classes. The "part-of" construct is not available and it will be introduced later. For this purpose, the direct line that represents class relationship will be drawn with some modifications. The dynamic representations that occur when the program is run and functions are called will be also developed and incorporated into the system in a future version. That will require modifying the debugger and introducing the "state-transition" concepts in the OO interface. Another issue that should be developed is a function invocation graph. It is a special kind of behavioral view of the sequence of functions that are invoked as a program runs. An invocation trace will allow the user to depict the nested structure of the function calls.

## 5   System Structure and Tools Integration

This system combines several tools in an integrated environment which can support a visual user interface. The structure of the system, software development processes supported and graphical user interface used are shown in Figure 9. At the first place in tool hierarchy of the system structure is the *Designer* which can construct a design tree. The design window contains the Designer menu shown in Figure 5. By using the option *save* one can save the *Specification* of the project. To generate a *Project* consisting of source code files it is necessary to use option *make* which calls the *Transformer* (the second tool of the system) with different parameters in an additional pop-up menu provided by user. The option *doc* allows the user to generate the *Documentation* of the *Specification* and *Project* in various configurations and fragments by means of the pop-up menu *doc*. The *Preprocessor* may represent separate processes in software development by converting the Project from R-chart notation to the textual C++ source code and checking some syntax errors. It can also be used automatically in the *make* option of the Design menu together with the C++ compiler. These three integrated tools are included in the system prototype which is now under development and will provide the following software development processes: system requirements analysis, system design, detailed design, coding, specification and project browsing and documenting. (The C++ compiler shown in Figure 9 is not a part of the system).

Like other SDEs [14, 21], the system will use different graphical interfaces for software development processes. As shown in Figure 9, *Trees, DFD, R-chart* and *Operational diagrams* are used in the user interface. Some new graphical notation for an alternative representation of the software development information or for more complete coverage this information by using a visual metaphor will be introduced in the system after the prototype is developed.

The design specifications are typically very useful for preparing the project documentation and helping with maintenance of the software systems and their modifications. This system will automatically perform various documentation task for the system under development and provide a facility for source code generating. The prototype will support structured design with manual transition from the informal specifications to the programming language during detailed design phase. Later versions of the system will include a formal specification for the object-oriented design methodology [20, 21].

The future version of the system will also use a visual *Debugger* and new version of the *Browser*. These tools will be closely integrated with each other and the Graphical Editor to support program tracing, data value checking and changing, incremental execution and local source code correction after the errors. Programs with the R-chart control flow representation are easier to debug and their logical structure is easier to understand and modify. The Debugger has been designed as a tool with a testing facility. The test principle of complete control paths coverage has a visual representation due to the R-charts [22]. The test specifications are designed to be automatically generated from the formal specifications which provide test data. The control trace is often more interesting in this approach as all possible control paths are shown on the screen directly and can be easily checked. Another positive feature of the R-charts is their suitability to the program complexity metrics, which are based on the estimating the topological complexity of the program control flow graph [22]. All of these tools are aimed at improving program quality and increase programmer productivity.

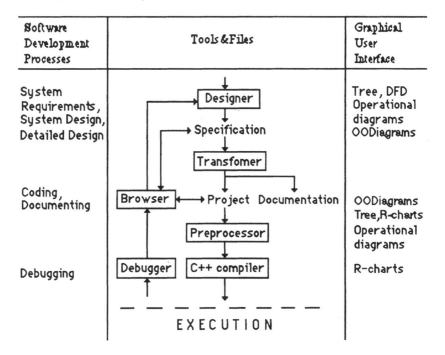

**Fig. 9.** Functional overview of the system

Using the C++ programming language, a programmer have to manage memory allocation and release. Research shows that a great number of bugs are linked with incorrect memory management. For the projects with large number of library and user classes and members, the necessity of memory management and an adequate visual metaphor during testing and debugging is crucially increased. That is why the Debugger will support the visual monitoring for dynamic memory allocation by using the visualization approach developed in [17-19]. We adopt the "story-telling" metaphor for representing program execution as series of history events happening [17]. The history events are performed by players: arbitrary parts of the program. For visualization of the objects and memory allocation we intend to choose a set of object-oriented ideas (class, member function, data member etc.) and memory management statements as a players set.

## 6  Empirical Studies and Comparative Analyses

The software development environments based on R-charts for IBM PC, PDP-11-like and micro-VAX-11-like computers have been widely used during several last years in the former USSR [8]. These environments have been used by many different kinds of users: students have studied this approach as a special programming course, novice programmers have learned it as a first programming environment, and skilled programmers have mastered it for real programs. Most of the experience is with C and Pascal, and less with Fortran and Assembler. There was an empirical study at Technosoft [8] to compare software development by each categories of users which were organized into two groups: those who used R-charts and those who used textual form of programming language (C and Pascal). The graphical paradigm of R-charts was more easily accepted by the students and the novice programmers then the skilled programmers. It can be explained by the absence of any other paradigm and more flexible acceptance in this sorts of learners. After some time, the skilled programmers became more skilled with the new approach and were able to use the graphical notation successfully. This study has shown that the graphical programming environments based on R-charts help the students and novice programmers achieve better understanding of programming, shorten software development time due to easier testing and debugging. We expect our system could improve teaching and learning of programming.

Another topic of empirical studies and comparative analyses is qualitative and quantitative characteristics of the programs using R-charts. Because of special graphical notation, this approach is more compact and more understandable then many other graphical representations for control flow structure (such as the different charting notations of the standard ISO 8631-1989). The experience of usage of the software developments environments based on R-charts at Technosoft and other organizations in the former USSR shows that the united graphical notation for the different software development processes allows users to write more reliable and more understandable code. The number of errors should be lower because the same notation is used on the different software development processes: detailed design, coding, documenting, testing and debugging. The source code of the programs also have a more efficient space layout on the screen and in a hard copy [16].

## 7  Conclusion

Being language independent, R-charts promote reuse and multipurpose design specifications at different levels of detailed design. They also support space efficient integration of graphical and textual representations, and our experience suggests that visual debugging and testing will be beneficial.

The prototype of the system will support several software development processes, and the visual debugger will be developed and integrated with the other tools in the system. The main contribution of the system will be its visual user interface and tool integration that permits more easier understanding and manipulation of program control and data structures.

Further attention will be paid to incorporating a unified graphical representation for Object-Oriented techniques (which is currently under consideration in Subcommittee 7 of the JTC1 ISO/IEC [31]). The system will be implemented on a Sun SPARCStation platform using C++ and X11 with ObjectWindows or OSF/Motif environments. The C++ target environment will be ObjectCenter.

## Acknowledgments

This research was supported by The Human Cognition Research Laboratory at The Open University. The first author wishes to thank Professor Marc Eisenstadt for useful discussions and comments which helped in the realization of this research.

## References

1.Grass, J.E.: ParcPlace fills C++ tools gap for some projects. IEEE Software, Jan. 1992, pp.107-110.
2. Boker, H.-D., Herczeg, J.: Browsing Through Program Execution. In Proceed. of the Conference INTERACT'90, pp.991-996.
3. Tripp, L.L.: A Survey of Graphical Notations for Program Design: An Update. ACM SIGSOFT Software Engineering Notes, Vol.13, No4, 1988, pp.39-44.
4. Robillard, P.N., Simoneau, M.: A New Control Flow Representation. Proceedings of the 15th Annual Intern. Computer Conf. on Software&Applications, Tokyo, Japan, Sept. 11-13, 1991, pp.225-230.
5. Velbitskiy, I.: Software Engineering (in Russian). Tekhnika, Kiev, 1984.
6. Velbitskiy, I., Ushakov, I.: Graphical Form for Writing Algorithms and Programs (in Russian). Journal "Upravlyayushchiye Sistemy i Machiny", No.6, 1984, pp.51-56.
7. Ushakov, I.B.: Graph Grammar Approach to Description of R-charts (in Russian). In Proceedings of the Glushkov Institute of Cybernetics "The Problems of Development and Putting into Effect the Software of Computers and Systems", Kiev, 1988, pp.97-103.
8. Ushakov, I.B.: Research and Standardization of graphical Form of Writing Algorithms and Programs as R-charts (in Russian). Thesis of Ph.D. (Computer Software Science), Glushkov Institute of Cybernetics Publishing, Institute of Cybernetics Publishing, Kiev, 1990, 160 p.
9. McHenry, W.K.: R-Technology: A Soviet Visual Programming Environment. Journal of Visual Languages and Computing, 1(1), March 1990.
10. Ushakov, I.: Models and Standards for Human-Computer Interfaces. East-West International Conf. on Human-Computer Interaction EWHCI'92, Sankt Petersburg, Russia, August 4-8, 1992, pp.197-209.
11. ISO/IEC 8631-1989 "Information technology - Program constructs and conventions for their representation". Second edition, ISO/IEC, 1989.
12. The C++ programming environment ObjectCenter. CenterLine Software, Inc. Cambridge, MA, 1991.
13. Bass, A., Boyle, M., and Ratcliff, B.: PRESTIGE: A CASE Workbench For The JSD Implementor. Proceedings of 13th Intern. Conf. on Software Engineering, May 13-16,1991, Austin, Texas, pp.198-207.

14. Korson, T. and Vaishnavi, V.K. Analysis and Modelling in Software Development. Comm. of ACM, Vol. 35, No. 9 (Sept. 1992), 32-47.

15. Parnas, D.L.: "On the criteria to be used in decomposing software into modules". IEEE Trans. on Software Engineering, Dec. 1972.

16. Haarslev, V., Moller, R.: Visualization and Graphical Layout in Object-oriented Systems. Journal of Visual Languages and Computing, 1992, 3, pp.1-23.

17. Domingue, J., Price, B.A., and Eisenstadt, M.: A Framework for Describing and Implementing Software Visualization Systems. Proceedings of Graphics Interface'92, Vancouver, Canada, pp.53-60.

18. Eisenstadt, M., Brayshaw, M.: The Transparent Prolog Machine (TPM): An Execution Model and Graphical Debugger for Logic Programming. Journal of Logic Programming, 5(4), pp.277-342, 1988.

19. Eisenstadt, M., Domingue, J., Rajan, T., and Motta, E.: Visual Knowledge Engineering. IEEE Transaction on Software Engineering, Vol. 16, NO. 10, October 1990, pp.1164-1177.

20. Ellis, R.: Data Abstraction and program Design. Pitman, 1991, 254p.

21. Kramer, J., Finkelstein, A.: A Configurable Framework for Method and Tool Integration. Proceedings of the European Symposium on Software Development Environments and CASE Technology (A.Endresand H.Weber, Eds.), June 1991, pp.233-257.

22. Ryapolov, S.I., Ushakov, I.B.: Software Quality Assessment in R-technology. Proceedings of the Third European Conference on Software Quality, Madrid, Nov. 4-6, 1992.

23. Booch, G.: Object-Oriented Design with Applications. Benjamin/Cummings, 1991.

24. Coard, P., and Yourdon, E.: Object-Oriented Design. Prentice Hall, Englewood Cliffs, N.J., 1991.

25. Edwards, J.M., and Henderson-Sellers, B.: A graphical notation for object-oriented analysis and design. J. Object-Oriented Program. (Feb. 1993), 53-74.

26. Ackroyd, M., and Daum, D.: Graphical notation for object-oriented design and programming. J.Object-Oriented Program 3, 5 (Jan. 1991), 18-28.

27. Ushakov, I.B., Werling, R., Nagano, H., et al.: Graphical Representation of Information in Software Engineering: ISO-IEC JTC1/SC7 Framework, Concepts and Standards Activity. Proceeding of the Software Engineering Standards Symposium, August 30-September 3, 1993, Brighton, England.

28. Monarchi, D.E. and Puhr, G.I. A Research Typology for Object-Oriented Analysis and Design. Commun. ACM, Vol. 35, No. 9 (Sept. 1992), 35-47.

29. ISO/IEC JTC1/SC7/WG1 "Basic Symbols and Diagrams for Software Development", 1993.

30. ISO/IEC JTC1/SC7/WG11 "A Description of Data for Software Development", 1993.

31. Ushakov, I.B.: Survey of Diagrams on Charting Techniques in the Area Of Inference-Based Systems and Object-Oriented Programming", personal contribution to JTC1/SC7 Project 7.19.02.06 "Representations of Object-Oriented Techniques", Tokyo, June 1993.

# Interface Semantics and Procedural Knowledge: A Study of Novice Understanding of MacDraw

M.V. Springett, A.S. Grant and A.G. Sutcliffe

Centre for H.C.I. Design
Dept. of Business Computing
City University, Northampton Square,
London EC1V 0HB

**Abstract.** This paper presents an analysis of issues affecting the choice of usability evaluation strategies for highly interactive Direct Manipulation interfaces. It reports memory tests on novice users of MacDraw I which investigate the degree of reliance on the interface for cueing, and the sources of information, both within the interface and outside, that may be utilized. A study of the novice subjects' (verbalised) reasoning during experimental task-performance on MacDraw is then reported. Examples of subjects reasoning are used to illustrate the nature of Direct Manipulation evaluation. Issues affecting the selection and development of evaluation methods are then discussed.

## 1  Introduction

Recent research into interface design and evaluation addresses the problem of applying established approaches to more advanced interfaces [9,17]. Direct Manipulation (DM) interfaces provide a particular problem in this respect. Recent reports have recognised that highly interactive DM interfaces present evaluation problems that may be beyond current approaches, or at least demand considerable attention. Wharton et al [17] studied the applicability of 'Cognitive Walkthrough' style evaluation for complex interfaces. They found that the suitability of the method (in its present form) was diminished by its focus on low-level issues. Conversely, evaluation studies of DM [10,15] emphasise the danger of ignoring low-level issues such as feature presentation. Sutcliffe and Springett [16] report a range of usability issues varying from high-level metaphor design to the level of individual features. This paper investigates some of the reasons why DM usability evaluation may require a modified approach to provide coverage of key usability issues.

Our approach in this paper is to use empirical evidence to characterise both the range of ways in which novice DM users perform tasks at the interface, and the range of roles that interface components play. This approach emphasises the widely recognised need to study of environmental factors in user performance [2,12]. The relevance of this approach to HCI centres around display-based dialogues and DM interfaces. Both theoretical and empirical work on such systems [5,8,11,12] suggest that an understanding of how the display affects users' behaviour is the essence of understanding DM interaction. The studies of Mayes et al [8] describe how users across a range of experience levels could not recall much of the task relevant information that they were successfully employing in performance. These tests also showed that users had much better recall of procedures than for actual features of the interface. Studies on representing concepts at the interface [1] and the cognitive presentation of task concepts [4,14] also demonstrate a range of issues pertinent to presentational aspects of the display.

Our studies are intended to illustrate the way in which novice users comprehend and interact with functionally rich displays. Our first study investigates the memory retention of subjects seven days after their first interactive session on MacDraw I, a DM drawing package. It analyses novice users' reliance on the interface for prompting, and the range of ways in which the interface may provide such prompts.

Our second study presents examples of users' verbalised reasoning during experimental task-action. These explore possible explanations for the success (or otherwise) of the interface in its prompting role. The study shows the ways in which interface items and concepts may influence the specification of action by users, and the range of evaluation problems that this presents.

## 2    Studies of MacDraw Recall and Recognition

### 2.1    Overview of Study

Eight novice subjects were studied using the Protocol Analysis technique [3] performing a drawing task on MacDraw I. They were given basic training in selecting, drawing, and operating on objects, and a brief demonstration of menu and palette options. They were then filmed constructing a data flow diagram. The subjects were asked to verbalise their reasoning. Their verbal accounts of the session were recorded and checked with them for accuracy after the session.

Seven of the subjects were invited back seven days later and tested on their recall of features and basic procedures. They were then presented with the system image and asked to repeat the exercise. These test results are presented and analysed in detail below.

### 2.2    Memory Tests

**Unseen Recall Tests.** Each subject was asked to describe the features on the MacDraw palette, in the order that they appear on the screen. The same was asked for all the MacDraw menus with the exception of the 'Apple utilities' and 'File' menus. All subjects had had experience of an interactive session plus the brief training described above. The results of this test are shown in Figure 1.

| | Palette (10) | Edit (11) | Style (9) | Font (2) | Layout (11) | Arrange (12) | Fill (1) | Lines (2) | Pen (1) |
|---|---|---|---|---|---|---|---|---|---|
| Subject A | 9 | 2 | 0 | 2 | 0 | 0 | 1 | 2 | 1 |
| Subject B | 4 | 3 | 0 | 2 | 1 | 0 | 1 | 2 | 0 |
| Subject C | 9 | 2 | 0 | 2 | 2 | 4 | 1 | 2 | 1 |
| Subject D | 6 | 1 | 1 | 0 | 2 | 0 | 1 | 2 | 0 |
| Subject E | 0 | 0 | 0 | 0 | 0 | 0 | 0 | 0 | 0 |
| Subject F | 7 | 1 | 1 | 1 | 0 | 5 | 1 | 1 | 0 |
| Subject G | 10 | 2 | 1 | 2 | 1 | 1 | 1 | 2 | 0 |

**Figure 1.** Subjects' performance on feature recall seven days after protocol sessions. Unaided recall of features i.e. no screen available to view

As was expected, given the findings of [8], the subjects' feature recall was generally poor. In particular, subjects' recall for some of the more detailed menus was very poor indeed. No subject was able to remember more than three features on the Edit menu, three subjects could not remember the Layout menu, and four could not remember the Arrange menu. Palette feature recall was better, with only one subject failing to recall the options available. Performance was also better for the Font and Lines menus. In the latter case the explanation may be that all subjects had occasion to use this menu during the sessions. In the case of the Font menu only one subject had used this facility. The good recall scores may be explained by the strong semantic connection between the header and the relatively uncomplicated set of facilities contained in the menu.

Along with feature recall, subjects were asked to describe four procedures using MacDraw. Four questions on straightforward operations were presented to the subjects. These are described in Appendix A. They show stronger recall for a range of basic operations than was apparent in their performance on feature recall. All the subjects remembered procedures better than actual features.

**Seen Tests.** The brief for subjects in the second test was slightly different. The seven subjects were asked to indicate how features could be operated, as well as simply noting their presence in various screen locations. They were only scored correct if they demonstrated that they would be able to select and use the feature successfully. Subjects were presented with the same features to identify, but had the MacDraw screen to consult. They were allowed to observe the screen and pull down the relevant menus into view. Subjects were also asked to guess the utility of features if they were unsure. Figure 2 shows the subjects' performance in these tests. We now describe each menu in turn.

| | Palette (10) | Edit (11) | Style (9) | Font (2) | Layout (11) | Arrange (12) | Fill (1) | Lines (2) | Pen (1) |
|---|---|---|---|---|---|---|---|---|---|
| Subject A | 10 | 5 | 4 | 2 | 4 | 8 | 1 | 2 | 1 |
| Subject B | 8 | 7 | 4 | 2 | 3 | 6 | 1 | 2 | 0 |
| Subject C | 10 | 8 | 4 | 2 | 7 | 7 | 1 | 2 | 1 |
| Subject D | 9 | 5 | 4 | 2 | 6 | 4 | 1 | 2 | 0 |
| Subject E | 7 | 1 | 3 | 2 | 3 | 1 | 1 | 2 | 0 |
| Subject F | 9 | 9 | 4 | 1 | 7 | 6 | 1 | 2 | 0 |
| Subject G | 8 | 8 | 4 | 2 | 8 | 5 | 1 | 2 | 0 |

**Figure 2.** Subjects' performance on feature identification seven days after protocol sessions, with the interface avaliable to view. Successful guesses are included in the statistics.

On the *File Menu*, only the 'Round Corners' feature was successfully explained by all subjects. The 'Undo' facility was mistaken by three subjects for a delete facility (i.e. where the user specifies the object to be removed). Three of the four subjects who failed to identify the 'Copy' facility were unable to explain how it differed from the 'Cut' facility. Two subjects thought the 'Clear' facility removed all the objects from the draw space. All except one subject gave incorrect explanations of how the 'Reshape' facility operated.

On the *Style Menu*, all subjects were able to explain the procedures for the options, with the exception of one subject who admitted to not knowing the meaning of 'justify' in this context. This is despite the fact that no subjects had used these features during the sessions. The likely explanation for this is that subjects were familiar with the concept through using word-processing packages.

On the *Font Menu*, with one exception, the subjects achieved maximum score.

The *Layout Menu* shows a number of features which are denoted by two- or three-word descriptions. The only two single word features 'Reduce' and 'Enlarge' produced the best scores from the subjects. Suprisingly, most of those who succesfully identified these items were unable to explain 'Reduce to Fit' which is located directly above them. The 'Turn Grid Off' feature caused most confusion with six subjects making erroneous references to the visible ruler lines on the draw space. The 'Hide Ruler Lines' facility prompted two subjects to refer to measuring facilities. The 'Show Size' facility was mistaken for the 'Drawing Size' function by two subjects.

On the *Arrange Menu*, five subjects who had identified the paste facility were unable to identify 'Paste in Front' and 'Paste in Back'. Most subjects were unable to offer an explanation of the 'Flip' functions. The same applied to the 'Group' and 'Lock' facilities. Five subjects mistook the 'Align to Grid' function to mean align to the on-screen ruler lines.

The *Fill* and *Lines Menus* were faultlessly identified by all subjects.

The *Pen Menu* was not explained well by most subjects. The failure of all but two subjects to identify this menu provided an interesting contrast with the 'Fill' menu. The only visible difference between the two is the menu name.

**Discussion.** The unseen tests suggest that basic procedural knowledge is internalised, but very few feature specifics are. This may be explained simply: minimal training and use produces swift grasping of techniques which are of general use and not bound to specific features. This supports the suggestion of [8] that features themselves are less likely to be memorised, simply because the user does not need them and can rely on the display to provide information. Further to this, it suggests that the interface has a role in prompting the selection of the correct procedures for task-action.

The seen tests showed some indication of how the display can serve (or fail to serve) in helping the user to select procedures. Despite the fact that all subjects had been shown demonstrations of the features seven days before the test, the evidence suggested that, in most cases, they were attempting a best estimate of the likely functionality through semantic information from the cue. Features which proved difficult tended either to have failed to provide sufficient information for guesswork, or had cued subjects in an ambiguous manner. In former case, examples such as the 'Pen' menu failed to support any reasoning about functionality. By contrast, the 'Fill' menu (with an identical set of options) is denoted by a verb which can straightforwardly map to a task-action, namely the selection of patterns to fill shapes on-screen. This tends to suggest that 'Pen' failed as a cue due to the fact that it refers neither to action (i.e. the actions that the menu options support) nor the object of an action.

A more common obstacle to understanding seemed to be feature representaions that mislead subjects. For example, 'Clear', a verb which corresponds to clearing an item from the screen, may also be taken to mean clearing the whole screen. Similarly, the feature 'Turn Grid Off' and 'Align to Grid' depends on knowledge of what the 'grid' is in order to be identified. The subjects clearly did not have such knowledge and scanned the screen for the object most likely to fit that description. The evidence suggests that the effectiveness of feature representations depended on the clarity of the reference to relevant task-action. This could either be verbs such as 'fill' (i.e. what to do with a selection of patterns offered), or object representations such as the palette options.

The evidence suggests that users rely on feature representation for what a feature will do (e.g. 'Clear'), the focus of its utility (e.g. 'Align Objects') or other supplementary information. Hence we may suggest that usability evaluation should consider these information-supplying functions. However, the variance observed in the nature of representations is significant. The examples in this section show a diversity of approaches to representing individual features, and also groups and group headers. Indeed the 'Palette' has no header and is merely represented by a panel of shape icons. Naturally, some of the differences in representation are explained by the differing functions represented. However, there is also evidence suggesting that differences can be seen in the context of the wider interface. For example, minimal representations of shape and line options are deemed sufficient by the MacDraw I designers. The subjects performance suggested that this design worked effectively. The reseblance of the palette concept, and its accompanying operations, to a central element of MacDraw's pen and paper drawing metaphor seems to allow such minimalism in feature design. However, other concepts (such as the 'grid', or operations on the dimensions of the drawing space) seem to demand more explanation from the feature representation itself. The role of the feature cue seems to be considerably changed in this case. This presents an evaluation problem in that examination of the feature level without reference to higher level metaphor and task contexts seems insufficient. Reference to the influence of the system image as a whole is necessary in assessing the adequacy of feature representations.

# 3 Study of Verbalised Reasoning During Task Performance

## 3.1 Outline of Study

The aim of the second study was to provide a sample of the range of ways in which novices use both internalised (in the head) knowledge and information from varying parts of the display in deciding how to perform tasks.
The study analysed the influence of the display on users' reasoning within the context of actual task performance. Seven days prior to the memory tests the subjects were asked to perform a drawing task, providing a continuous commentary as their sessions unfolded. They each attempted to construct a data-flow diagram in a thirty-minute session. Their verbalisations were then studied for examples of reasoning in novel situations.

We gathered a sample of 40 verbalisations from our subjects. These were then categorised to glean what knowledge was being employed, and the way in which interface items were being interpreted. We categorised users' utterances by describing the 'storyline' of their explanations of why they selected certain features and procedures in particular cases (see Appendix B). These were then compared for similarities and grouped according to how different knowledge sources were used by the subjects. The four categories described in Appendix B illustrate the varying ways in which users may reason using DM interface prompts. Examples from the four categories illustrate two basic roles of the display. These roles are: prompting the user to select the correct procedure; and informing the user about the identity and utility of features. These roles are now discussed in turn.

## 3.2   Analysis of Interface's Influence on Procedure Selection

**Reapplying Known Device Procedures.** The Type 4 examples in Appendix B showed subjects reapplying procedures by assuming that a novel feature sufficiently resembled used features, and was therefore subject to the same operations. Figure 3 illustrates the 'lines' example which is of Type 4. This shows subjects' comprehension of the metaphor leading to erroneous assumptions about the applicability of known procedures. It demonstrates the generalization of procedures from examples, a type of reasoning on metaphor-based interfaces that has been suggested by among others Polson and Lewis [13] to be an important part of display-based learning. In these examples action is specified on the basis of metaphor-based assignment rules, i.e. the grouping of interface features by mapping assignment rules from the metaphor domain. In the 'Lines' example the subjects have assumed that procedures which apply to 'lines' apply to the arc option also. However, the system does not support the assumption that the set of lines for which the procedures apply includes arc lines. This represents a problem of consistency in design described by Reisner [14]. The inconsistency seems to come from the users' model of a domain concept (i.e. partitioning of drawn items into sub-categories). As Reisner points out, the system should partition the sub-categories in the same way as the user for (this aspect of) consistency to be achieved.

**Feature Specific Procedure Specification.** The Type 1 example in Appendix B shows a feature being identified by subjects as connoting a procedure which was unique to that particular feature. In this example, the 'Cut', 'Copy' and 'Paste' facilities have a feature-specific operational procedure. No other item on the menu operates in the same way. Therefore the procedure has to be inferred from the feature cue. The subjects whose reasoning was recorded reasoned that the procedure would be the same as other cut and paste facilities that they had used on text editing packages. This contrasts with one subject who attempted to select and paste without using copy or paste. The attempted procedure for those subjects is identical with the standard menu operation of selecting an object and an operation from the menu bar. This exemplifies a potential dilemma for novice users reasoning about how to perform action. They may reason from experience of using 'similar' features on the device, but feature cues may, in contradiction, suggest that a different procedure is needed.

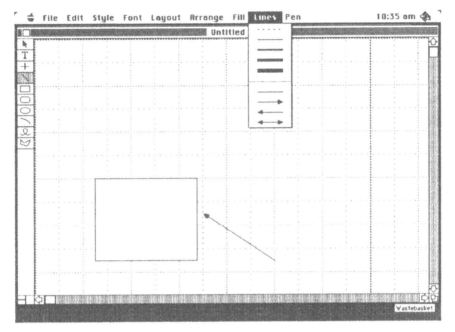

**Figure 3.** The MacDraw 1 interface. The 'Lines' menu shows left and right pointing arrows which, when selected, can automatically be placed on the end of perpendicular lines (third palette option from the top, to the left of the screen) diagonal lines (fourth option from top) but not arc lines (eighth option from top).

## 3.3 Analysis of Users Inferring Feature Utility from Cues

The examples we consider here demonstrate the way in which both feature cues and other interface items are relied upon by users to communicate feature utility. Our argument is that there is a deal of variance in what the user needs from a feature cue. We believe that this is conditioned by the design of the metaphor as a whole, including high-level metaphor concepts, and the way that locations and groups of features are presented.

**Feature Representations as Information Sources.** In Type 3 the example is of a specified and partially executed procedure for creating a composite object (the example being an arrowed line). In this example the subjects search for a feature to instantiate a task action procedure. Subjects who chose incorrectly all suggested that they required an arrow pointing in a certain direction, and that the cue suggested the direction. Figure 3 shows this menu on the Menu on the MacDraw interface. This suggests that the feature was selected on the basis of the cue's resemblance to the goal-state of the subjects' action, namely, an arrow pointing in a specified direction. In this case, an evaluation of usability is likely to cite the cue as a misleading signal to the user. The issue appears to be, straightforwardly, that the feature representation gives an inaccurate signal about its function.

**Feature Representations as Part of a Distributed Information Source.**
The type 2 reasoning examples show how evaluation of cues may, in some cases, be
less simple than in the example in 3.3.1. above. In type 2 examples, the role of
informing the user about the feature is distributed between the feature cue and other
on-screen items. Here two menu options produce similar reponses from subjects
with contrasting results. In both cases the action is unspecified as the menus are
being searched. In the first example 'Send to Back' the subject matches the semantic
description with a task action and goal-state, and retrieves the standard operational
procedure with success. In the case of the 'Reduce to Fit' feature similar reasoning is
employed unsuccessfully. On this occasion the subject makes an erroneous
assumption about the object of the expressed operation. In both examples the
interface leaves it to the user to infer the object (or set of objects) for which the
feature is intended. In the former case the subjects correctly assumed that on-screen
shapes are the referent object of the facility, but in the latter case subjects failed to
recognise the draw space as a whole as the referent object.

The diagnosis of the 'Reduce to Fit' error may be that the cue did not contain
sufficient information. However, it may also be argued that the location of the
feature is sub-optimal (that it misleads the user through being situated amongst
features of a different type). The naming of the menu in which it resides may also be
questioned. If, for example, the menu name had made it clear that operations on the
draw-space were contained within it, it can be argued that the user would not be
moved to scan its options in the first place.

The example above emphasises the dilemma that evaluators have in assessing
usability. In order to be clear about whether a feature adequately plays an information
supplying role the evaluator has two issues to face. One, naturally enough, is
whether it does what it is intended to do (e.g. it speaks the users language, explains
clearly). The second issue is to clarify what the feature representation's role is with
reference to other on-screen information sources. Feature evaluation which ignores
this wider context is unlikely to prove adequate.


# 4   Summary of Findings

What is clear from the examples provided by the studies is the considerable diversity
of ways in which the interface may fulfill its role in prompting user action. For
example, some feature cues contain semantic information about the objects that they
may operate on. In other cases this is provided by menu headers (e.g. Fill) or the
user is left to infer the legality of candidate operations for certain objects. Equally, in
some instances, the visual structuring that the screen image suggests may provide
most of the information a user needs (e.g. palette/draw space). This poses problems
for evaluation methods which refer exclusively to feature level issues, such as
contemporary usability walkthroughs [17]. In DM the role of the feature
representation is conditional on how it relates to, for example, the general metaphor,
a feature-specific metaphor, or a spatial grouping.

Another source of diversity is the knowledge that environmental cues attempt to tap. We have discussed evidence to suggest that users' comprehension of the general metaphor plays a large part in their ability to know what to do in a range of search and drawing tasks. If this is so, evaluation of DM implies evaluation of the metaphorical representation of the domain. Furthermore, this would precede examination of individual functions. Another consideration is that users appear to assume that tried operations may be legal for features which (in their view) are similar to one already used (e.g. arc lines and diagonal lines). It is also possible that specific metaphors for small groups of features may be referenced in feature cues. In other words, the system will induce the user to draw an analogy with a concept outside the general metaphor.

Given these issues considered above, it is hard to measure a DM interface for consistency. A system which makes all tasks similar in operation may be seen as inconsistent due to users' perception of the metaphor. Conversely, a design which rigorously partitions concepts with reference to the metaphor domain may too be dismissed as inconsistent by some users.

## 5. Conclusion

Our findings suggest that evaluation of DM design features require an integrated approach which can capture the diverse nature of feature recognition, and reasoning, leading to the selection of procedures and features to use. Such a method would require ways of accounting for the influence of the user's internalised procedural knowledge, metaphor knowledge and learning from examples. This may well require the combination of two elements. One is the examination of metaphor and task design. The other is examination of how and where information for specifying actions is provided by the interface.

Metaphor requires examination as to whether it provides the correct information about the nature of task performance, given that it seems to have such a strong influence on user expectations. Conformance with the user's notion of what metaphor implies seems crucial. It is likely that a high-level general model of the system is internalised when basic procedures are learned, influencing user expectations about the structure of the system and the range of task that the system will support. Therefore, metaphor has a crucial role in supporting learning by analogy, and providing visual structuring to aid users' navigation. However, there are also issues of feature presentation that are beyond the scope of such analysis (but nevertheless partly dependent on it).

We suggest that the second key element of evaluation is examination of how and where the interface provides necessary prompting. This implies judging meaning within the context of the task and the domain as a whole. The adequacy of a feature cue is dependent upon what it implies in the context of the user's comprehension of the current task and the nature of the device.

It has also been shown that the role of signposting has various components. These include navigational information, feature identification, telling the user the appropriate procedure to use, and the set of objects for which it can be used. Our studies show that these roles may be distributed amongst feature icons, headers, menu names, or left to be implied from the user's prior knowledge. Evaluation of an individual task design therefore implies tracing where on the interface these roles are played.

We believe that whilst a number of approaches already documented in the literature can provide partial understanding of DM, a complete evaluation involves relating diverse elements covered in those approaches. This may perhaps be thought of as integrating a feature-level usability checklist method such as a cognitive walkthrough [17] or Heuristic Evaluation [10], with higher-level evaluation of metaphor [7] or task-structure design [6]. What this also implies is that evaluators should be armed with a good knowledge of the target users' domain and task knowledge, which in itself may be a considerable challenge.

## References

1.      J.M. Carroll, R.L. Mack, W.A. Kellogg: Interface Metaphors and User Interface Design. In: Handbook of Human-Computer Interaction, M. Helander (ed.) Elsevier North Holland, (1988)

2.      J.M. Carroll: Artifact as theory-nexus: hermeneutics meets theory-based design. in: proc. CHI 89, Human Factors in Computer Systems, ACM press, pp 7-14,(1989)

3.      K.A. Ericsson, H.A. Simon: Protocol Analysis, MIT press, (1984)

4.      J. Grudin: The Case Against User Interface Consistency. in: Communications of the ACM vol.32, no.10, (1989)

5.      E.L. Hutchins, J.D. Hollan, D.A. Norman: Direct Manipulation Interfaces. in: User Centred System Design New Perspectives on Human-Computer Interaction D. Norman & S. Draper ed Lawrence Erlbaum Associates, New Jersey, pp 31-62, (1986)

6.      D.E. Kieras, P.A. Polson: An approach to the formal analysis of user complexity. in: International Journal of Man Machine Studies, Vol 22, pp 365-395, (1985)

7.      B. Laurel (Ed.): The Art of Human Computer Interface Design, Addison Wesley, Reading MA.,(1990)

8. J.T. Mayes, S.W. Draper, A.M. MacGregor, K. Oatley: Information Flow in a User Interface: The Effect of Experience and Context on the Recall of MacWrite screens. in: People and Computers IV, D.M. Jones and R. Winder (eds.), Cambridge University Press, pp 275-289, (1988)

9. J. Nielsen: Traditional Dialogue Design Applied to Modern User Interfaces.Communications of the ACM, 33, pp 109 - 118, (1990)

10. J. Nielsen: Finding Usability Problems Through Heuristic Evaluation. in: proc.CHI-92, P Bauersfeld et al (eds.). pp 373-380, (1992)

11. D.A. Norman: Cognitive Engineering. in: User Centred System Design: New Perspectives on Human-Computer Interaction, D Norman & S Draper (eds.) Lawrence Erlbaum Associates, New Jersey, pp 31-62, (1986)

12. S.J. Payne: Interface Problems and Interface Resources. In: Designing Interaction, J.M. Carroll (ed.), Cambridge University Press, (1991)

13. P.G. Polson, C.H. Lewis: Theory based design for easily learned interfaces. In: Human-Computer Interaction 5, 191-220, (1990)

14. P. Reisner: What is inconsistency?. in: proc. Interact 90, Diaper et al (eds.), Elsevier North-Holland, pp 175-181, (1990)

15. M.V. Springett: The Utility of User Action Models For Direct Manipulation Design. in: proc. IFIP TC2/WG2.7 Working Conference, Engineering for Human-Computer Interaction, J Larson and C Unger (eds.), Elsevier North-Holland, pp 205-222, (1992)

16. A.G. Sutcliffe, M.V. Springett: From user's problems to design errors: Linking evaluation to improved design practice. in: Proc. People and Computers vii, A. Monk et al (eds.), Cambridge University Press, pp 117-131, (1992)

17. C. Wharton, J. Bradford R. Jeffries M. Franzke: Applying Cognitive Walkthroughs to More Complex Interfaces: Experiences, Issues, and Recommendations. in: proc. CHI 92, P.Bauersfield et al (eds.), pp 381-388, (1992)

# Appendix A: Subjects responses to the recall questionnaire on MacDraw task procedures

1. You are in MacDraw and the screen is blank. Describe how you would get from this state to having a line with a left-facing arrow on the screen.

This includes the procedures for palette selection, object creation and menu selection. All subjects answered this question perfectly. All had practiced this procedure for task action in the protocol studies seven days earlier. Two subjects pointed out the option of selecting the arrow direction before creating the line, but neither referred to this as the setting of a default.

2. You wish to move an object to a new location on the MacDraw screen. How do you do it?

This involves clicking onto a drawn object and dragging as desired. All subjects had performed this operation seven days earlier. Again, all subjects answered this question without any problem.

3. You wish to reshape a drawn object on the screen. How do you do it?

On this occasion four of the seven subjects were unable to describe this. All four said 'select the object' but were unable to describe the manual procedure of clicking on and dragging the 'handles' on the object. Of these four subjects two had nothing to add. One referred to the 'Reshape' option on the 'Edit' menu. Another referred to 'looking on the menu for a reshape option'.

4. You wish to draw two identical irregular closed 5-sided shapes alongside each other. How do you do this?

This was a task that the subjects had not been asked to perform in the protocol studies. The nearest analagous task was the drawing of a datastore. The quickest method for this is to select a polygon, draw the shape, select 'Duplicate' from the 'Edit' menu, click on the new shape, either moving it manually, or performing a multiple select with the 'lasso' cursor mode for multi-selection and selecting 'Align Objects' from the 'Arrange' menu.

Two subjects only got as far as describing making the shapes from line options on the palette. One of those subjects also claimed erroneously that 'Duplicate' could be used to create the second shape (the cursor mode for multi-selection, or 'Select All' features would need to be used). The other 5 correctly described selecting the polygon option along with the 'Duplicate' menu facility.

# Appendix B: Reasoning types observed from subjects' utterances during task-action

**Type 1**                Declare goal -- search -- recognise cue -- hypothesise -- procedure
(4 examples)

These are examples of subjects employing the procedure for menu search in order to find a feature. On seeing the cue (in these examples the Cut and Paste facilities) the user is retrieving and using knowledge from text editing packages to specify the nature of action. The phrase 'hypothesise procedure' is used because these examples show subjects guessing that the procedure is different from standard menu procedures already used.

**Type 2**                Declare goal -- search -- recognise cue -- retrieve procedure
(8 examples)

In these examples the feature and procedure were unspecified at the point where the search strategy was employed. The subjects, on discovering a cue which matched their goals, then retrieved what they believed to be the appropriate known procedure. Subjects who scanned the menus for features tended to retrieve the standard procedure: select object; drag menu; select option.

**Type 3**                Declare goal -- retrieve procedure -- search/recognise cue
(9 examples)

In these examples the procedure is known and partially executed, but the actual feature requires specification, given that the current goal is different from previous goals. Subjects here described the procedures as known and unproblematic, and specified action by guessing the identity of a feature. For example, the 'Lines' menu offers a range of alternative line thicknesses and arrow options for lines. The correct option must be inferred from the system image. The default convention of placing the arrow either at the start or end of the line, is denoted by either an arrow pointing left or pointing right. This representation caused erroneous choices to be made by some subjects.

**Type 4**        Declare goal -- specify feature -- retrieve and extend known procedure
(19 examples)

The examples here are those of a feature being specified along with a set of operations. In these examples subjects assumed that the operations were legal because they regarded the feature as analogous to one already used. For example, the procedure for drawing arrowed lines was extended from the original example to both perpendicular lines and (erroneously) arc and freehand lines. The figures show that a common form of reasoning is the generalization of procedures to new examples. We believe that there were a somewhat greater number of these than was suggested in verbal reasoning. An analysis of users' non-verbalised behaviour (or when declarative statements were made rather than reasoning) revealed a much greater incidence of used procedures being reapplied to novel features.

# Positive Test Bias in Software Testing Among Professionals: A Review

Laura Marie Leventhal†, Barbee M. Teasley†, Diane S. Rohlman‡ and Keith Instone†

| | |
|---|---|
| †Computer Science Department | ‡Oregon Health Sciences University |
| Bowling Green State University | CROET, L606 |
| Bowling Green, Ohio   43403   USA | 3181 S.W. Sam Jackson Park Road |
| *lastname*@cs.bgsu.edu | Portland, OR 97201-3011 USA |

**Abstract.** Fundamental but virtually unexplored issues in human-computer interaction involve the roles of biases in software engineering tasks. In studies of naturalistic testing tasks, as well as ones which follow common laboratory models in this area, we have found ample evidence that testers have positive test bias. This bias is manifest as a tendency to execute about four times as many positive tests, designed to show that "the program works," as tests which challenge the program. In our prior work, we have found that the expertise of the subjects, the completeness of the software specifications, and the presence/absence of program errors may reduce positive test bias. Skilled computer scientists invent specifications to test in the absence of actual specifications, but still exhibit positive test bias.

## 1    Introduction

Empirical studies of programming and software development have focused on many aspects of software development, such as program comprehension, program design, organizational and group issues, and the effects of notations. However, one area that has received virtually no attention is software testing. This is a surprising and unfortunate omission. Software testing, after all, accounts for up to 50% of the total cost of software development [Myers, 1979], and the costs of software errors are often mind-boggling (e.g., see the regular "Risks to the Public" section of *ACM Software Engineering Notes*.)

At Bowling Green State University, we have an on-going program of research on behavioral issues in software testing. In particular, we have focused on the impact of the behavioral phenomenon called *positive test bias* on software testing. In this paper, we will define positive test bias and review some of our results.

### 1.1  Positive Test Bias

Behavioral biases can be thought of as "rules of thumb" that people employ as they participate in judgement and decision-making tasks. The use of these biases is sometimes inappropriate or debilitating to the task at hand [e.g., Tversky and Kahneman, 1974]. Positive test bias is one sort of behavioral bias that has been identified. Positive test bias is defined as a tendency to test a hypothesis with data which is consistent with the hypothesis (and may confirm the hypothesis), rather than testing with data which is inconsistent with the hypothesis (and may disconfirm the hypothesis) [Klayman and Ha, 1987; Tweney, Doherty and Mynatt, 1981]. Ratios of 4:1 between the numbers of consistent and inconsistent tests are quite common in this area [e.g., Wason, 1968]. Attempts to eliminate positive test bias through manipulations such as instructing subjects to use disconfirmation are typically not successful [e.g., Tweney, Doherty, Worner, Pliske, Mynatt, Gross and Arkkelin,1980; Gorman, Stafford and Gorman, 1987].

Although positive test bias is difficult to eliminate, there are three factors which have sometimes been found to affect it. One factor is expertise level or previous experience of the tester [cf., Kern, Mirels and Hinshaw, 1983]. For example, Rohlman, Mynatt, Mynatt and Leventhal [1992] found that advanced computer science majors were better than both advanced students from other majors and first-year computer science majors at performing various versions of Wason's classic four-card selection task. A second factor is the completeness of the rule to be tested and, consequently, the completeness of the subject's problem representation [e.g., Griggs and Newstead, 1982; Rohlman,1992; Tweney, et al., 1980]. The results of these studies suggest that when the subject's hypothesis is more complete by virtue of a more complete statement of the rule to test, they are more likely to test hypothesis-inconsistent cases. The third factor is the presence of feedback from errors [e.g., Walker and Harper, 1990]. The results of this study suggest that errors do not reduce positive test bias and may exacerbate it.

# 2 Software Testing Concepts

Software testing is "the process of exercising or evaluating a system or system component by manual or automated means to verify that it satisfies specified requirements or to identify differences between expected and actual results" [IEEE, 1983]. The testing process involves establishing test objectives, designing test cases, executing the tests, and validating the outcomes. A wide variety of testing techniques have been proposed. Of these, most can be broadly categorized as either structural or functional in nature [e.g., Omar and Mohammed, 1991]. In structural or "white box" testing, one tests the internal, logical structure of the code and exercises each of the possible paths through the code. In contrast, functional testing is based on an external description of what the software is supposed to do. The goal of functional testing is to discover any discrepancies between the actual behavior of the system and the desired behavior, as described in the external specification. Functional testing is also referred to as "black box" testing. This is because the software is treated as a black box that has specified functions, but unknown and unseen internal logic. While complete software testing requires both structural and functional testing, our focus is on functional testing only.

## 2.1 Functional Testing

To truly compare the behavior of a software system to its external specification, one would need to test an infinite set of inputs. Of course all of this testing is impossible in any practical sense, even for trivially-complex software. As a consequence, alternative approaches to functional testing have been developed. Equivalence partitioning and boundary testing are two related techniques which are widely used in functional testing. In Figure 1, we have diagrammed the steps that one would follow to perform equivalence partitioning and boundary testing for software to handle registration to the East-West HCI conference.

The preliminary step in both equivalence partitioning and boundary testing is to break the system up into functional units that can be tested independently of each other. Examples of functional units might be a single command or operation, or a function that is utilized by other functions in the system. In the registration system example from Figure 1, some functions are "Enter Registration Information," "Mail Confirmation," and "Handle Room Assignments." This step of breaking up the system into functional units is necessary to reduce a highly complex task to manageable units.

The tester next applies the techniques of equivalence partitioning and boundary testing independently to each functional unit that was identified in the first step. In Figure 1, we will discuss equivalence partitioning and boundary testing of the function of "Enter Registration Information."

In order to test "Enter Registration Information," the tester refers to the specifications for the system. We will focus on the specification that describes the postal codes. The tester now selects an input (e.g., postal codes in Figure 1) that is related to the specification. For that input, the tester identifies relevant dimensions, such as the number of characters in the postal code. Note that because the nature of individual specification varies, the process of selecting dimensions is not algorithmic, and its success is dependent on the expertise of the tester.

For each dimension, the tester performs equivalence partitioning. The underlying assumption of equivalence partitioning is that if a program functions correctly for one test case selected from an equivalence class, it will function correctly for any case from the equivalence class [e.g., Pressman, 1992; Beizer, 1990]. ("Function correctly" means that the software will accept and process valid input as specified, and will gracefully handle invalid input.) In order to perform equivalence partitioning, the tester identifies a set of equivalence partitions or classes. That is, for each dimension of the input data identified in the earlier step, a number of valid and invalid ranges or subsets of possible inputs are identified. In Figure 1, for the dimension of the number of characters in the country code, there are three equivalence classes. (e.g., a character string containing too few characters cannot be a valid postal code). The process of identifying equivalence classes is algorithmic, in contrast to the earlier step of identifying relevant dimension.

In the final phase of equivalence partitioning, a single test case is selected from each partition and the tests are executed. In Figure 1, "12" is an example of a test that covers equivalence class 1. In our previous work, we have labelled tests which are selected from equivalence classes which reflect valid data as +$S$ tests($S$ refers to specification). In Figure 1, the specification says that "the postal code for the person's country will consist of 3 to 9 characters." The equivalence class which is consistent with this specification is equivalence class 2, "a number of characters between 3 and 9." A representative +$S$ test is "125252."

In our previous work, we have labelled tests of equivalence classes representing invalid data as -$S$ tests. In Figure 1, equivalence class 1, "less than 3 characters," is inconsistent with the specification that "the postal code for the person's country will consist of 3 to 9 characters." "0123456789" is an example of a -$S$ test.

A set of test cases which exercise all of the equivalence classes for a dimension, both +S and -S, are said to obtain *coverage* of that dimension.

The popularity of boundary testing has grown out of the observation that the boundaries or extremes of continuous or interval input data dimensions are often where errors occur (e.g., entering a 10 character postal code, when 9 is the intended limit). Testing on and near boundaries often detects errors that may go undetected by equivalence partitioning testing. When equivalence partitioning and boundary testing are used together, as they often are, certain test cases may satisfy the demands of both types of testing at the same time, as shown in the lower part of Figure 1. [See

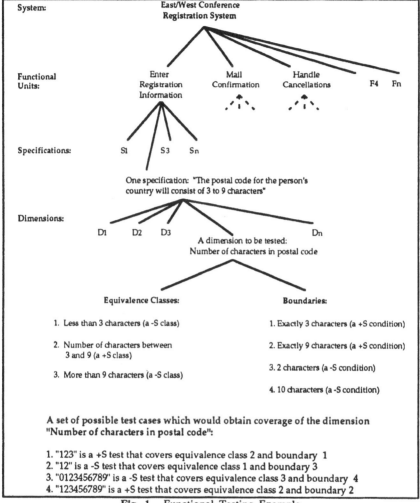

**Fig. 1.** Functional Testing Example

Mynatt, 1990, or Beizer, 1990, for more complete descriptions of the process of functional testing.]

## 2.2 How is functional software testing related to hypothesis testing and positive test bias?

A number of authors have suggested that program verification and debugging involve hypothesis testing [e.g., Pennington and Grabowski, 1990; Katz and Anderson, 1988; Vessey, 1985, 1986]. We agree, and suggest that positive test bias is likely to be manifest in software testing, just as it is in other hypothesis-testing situations. We expected this bias to appear as a failure to test cases which are outside of or inconsistent with the software specification. For example, Zweben, Barton and Stringfellow [1989] found that novice programmers tend to test their programs with data consistent with the way that the program is supposed to work, and do not use inconsistent data. We interpret this result to indicate that testers tend to use valid data in testing their programs. In our work, we have operationally-defined positive test bias to be an overrepresentation in testing of +S tests as compared to -S tests.

Assuming that software testers do exhibit positive test bias, the consequences may be quite detrimental to effective testing. We have already noted that in functional software testing the tester must isolate separate functions, determine the relevant dimensions of the input space and then describe the equivalence partitions for each dimension. There may be hundreds or even thousands of such equivalence classes for a given piece of software. Effective software testing consists of complete coverage of all of the classes, including those represented by +S and -S tests. While +S testing can and does lead to the detection of errors (e.g., the program does not accept valid postal codes), it is essential to test -S instances as well (e.g., does the program crash when a 2-digit postal code is entered?).

## 3  Review of our Work

One facet of our research has been to replicate the classic laboratory tasks that have previously been used to study positive test bias in a form that maps onto software testing. The goal of this research is to identify which features of standard laboratory tasks are generalizable to software testing concepts. We have found that test bias variables such as the subjects' familiarity with the task domain and the completeness of the task specification do influence testing behavior [e.g., Rohlman, Mynatt, Mynatt and Leventhal, 1992; Rohlman, 1992].

A second facet of our research has used experimental studies of subjects actually engaging in testing tasks, and interpreted their behaviors within the framework of positive test bias. We have also used verbal protocol techniques. The goal of the verbal protocol studies is to identify how positive test bias occurs in naturalistic software testing. In the following sections, we will review our previous work involving naturalistic testing tasks [see Teasley, Leventhal, Mynatt and Rohlman, 1993; Mynatt, Mynatt, Rohlman and Leventhal, 1992]. In our review below, we will refer to Studies 1, 2, 3 and 4. Studies 1 and 2 are experimental tasks and Study 3 and 4 are combinations of experiments and verbal protocol studies.

### 3.1  Experiments (Studies 1, 2, 3 and 4)

In our model, a "positive test," or +S test, is operationally-defined as any test case which tests valid input (i.e., is from a valid equivalence class reflecting valid input.) A test from the equivalence class(es) which test invalid data is a -S test. Under this model, a tendency to use more +S tests than -S tests is considered positive test bias. Studies 1, 2, 3 and 4 all used a naturalistic testing task as a means of gathering data. In this task, each subject was given a written specification describing some software that performed a simple task and was asked to test the software to see if it met the specifications. Subjects were allowed to execute as many tests as they wished. Background software collected all of their input (test cases). The test cases were then categorized as +S or -S tests. Analyses were done on both the number of +S and -S tests, and on the percentage of coverage of the possible +S and -S tests (a measure of completeness) obtained by the subject. Our results demonstrate strong evidence of positive test bias. We find typical ratios of +S tests to -S tests of four to one. In addition, the coverage of +S tests is much higher than the coverage of -S tests, with ratios of +S test coverage to -S test coverage of about two to one. These previous results give strong evidence that testers have positive test bias in software testing and are more likely to cover positive equivalence classes than the inconsistent classes.

Previous studies of hypothesis testing have shown that clarifying the problem statement to make hypothesis-inconsistent tests more salient can moderate positive test bias [e.g., Griggs and Newstead, 1982; Tweney, et al., 1980]. Studies 2, 3 and 4 varied the completeness of the software specifications to vary the saliency of the -S tests. In one condition, the specifications were minimal (a few sentences). In a second condition, the specifications were complete, but stated only positive functions (e.g., "this program will accept integers"). In the third condition, the specifications stated both what the program would do and what it would not do. In Studies 3 and 4, only the minimal and complete conditions were used. In Study 2, subjects with the more complete specifications tested more +S and -S cases. However, even with complete specifications, subjects still exhibited positive test bias and executed more +S tests than -S tests.

Although some studies have found that increasing subject expertise tends to reduce biased behavior [Kern, Mirels and Hinshaw, 1983], observational studies of practicing scientists nonetheless show that they have a definite positive test bias [Mitroff, 1974; Mahoney and DeMonbreun, 1978; Tweney, 1985]. Studies 1 and 2 varied level of expertise. While increasing levels of expertise led to increasing use of -S tests, even the most expert subjects exhibited positive test bias and failure to obtain complete coverage.

Finally, a study by Walker and Harper [1990] suggested that error feedback does not reduce bias in a hypothesis-testing task, and may exacerbate it. In Study 2, 3 and 4, an independent variable was the presence or absence of errors. In Study 2, we found that the presence of errors did mitigate positive test bias.

Table 1 summarizes the results of our experiments.

## 3.2 Verbal Protocol Study (Studies 3 and 4)

In Studies 3 and 4, the testers were asked to talk aloud while they were performing the testing task. Analysis of their protocols indicated that subjects primarily tested according to the specifications they were given. That is, the subjects used the specifications as a check-list of equivalence classes to be tested. The protocols also revealed that subjects were often able to generate their own specifications. Thus, even when they had the minimal specifications, they were able to test a number of dimensions. We speculate that these testers used their expertise with the domain (e.g., character counting) to generate an enriched hypothesis when the specifications were incomplete. We noted, however, that subjects with the minimal specifications tended to focus more on testing the processing aspects of the software (e.g., did it give the right answer?) than the data integrity aspects (e.g., did the program crash if a non-digit was entered or if too many values were entered?). Finally, like prior studies, we observed that subjects who found errors during testing were more likely to repeat a test, although there was no significant reduction in positive test bias.

From the Study 3 protocols, it appeared that the testers who were given the Minimal specifications were able to "fill in" missing specifications based on their own knowledge. This tendency was even more evident with the professional testers in Study 4. For example, one tester, who had the Minimal specifications, said "Is there a limit to the size of the list? Specifications do not indicate that. However, if there is, then I would certainly want to test it".

| Study 1 | |
|---|---|
| *Subject Expertise Level* | • beginning computer science students vs. advanced computer science students |
| *Specifications* | • minimal |
| *Presence/Absence of Errors* | • no errors |
| *Results* | • strong evidence of positive test bias among both groups of testers<br>• advanced testers were better testers overall |
| **Study 2** | |
| *Subject Expertise Level* | • non-computer science students vs. beginning computer science students vs. advanced computer science students |
| *Specifications* | • minimal vs. positive-only vs. complete |
| *Presence/Absence of Errors* | • no errors vs. errors |
| *Results* | • strong evidence of positive test bias among all groups of testers<br>• advanced testers had less positive test bias than other groups<br>• complete specification group had less positive test bias than other levels<br>• groups with errors had less positive test bias |
| **Study 3** | |
| *Subject Expertise Level* | • advanced computer science students |
| *Specifications* | • minimal vs. complete |
| *Presence/Absence of Errors* | • no errors vs. errors |
| *Results* | • strong evidence of positive test bias |
| **Study 4** | |
| *Subject Expertise Level* | • professional programmers |
| *Specifications* | • minimal vs. complete |
| *Presence/Absence of Errors* | • no errors vs. errors |
| *Results* | • strong evidence of positive test bias |

Table 1. Summary of Previous Research

## 4 Conclusion

Previous research in hypothesis testing has suggested that testers tend to test with cases that are consistent with the hypothesis. This behavior has been labelled *positive test bias*. In four previous studies, we have demonstrated that positive test bias is at work in functional software testing. Subjects tend to test about four times as many specification-consistent (+S) cases than inconsistent (-S) cases. They also cover the +S equivalence classes about twice as well as they cover the -S classes. The results suggest that bias may be mitigated but not eliminated by increased programmer expertise, more complete specifications and the presence of errors.

**Acknowledgements.** We appreciate the feedback of Winnie Rex, Daryl Stone, Deanna Beall, John Beck, Elsa Emmanuelli, Koulis Peratopoulous, Hugh Garavan, John Farhat, and Erik Brown.

This research was supported by funds from an Ohio Board of Regents Academic Challenge Grant.

# References

Beizer, B. (1990). *Software Testing Techniques,* 2nd ed., New York: Van Nostrand Reinhold.

Griggs, R.A. and Newstead, S.E. (1982) The role of problem structure in a deductive reasoning task. *Journal of Experimental Psychology, Memory & Cognition.* 8. 297-307.

Gorman, M. E., Stafford, A., & Gorman, M. E. (1987). Disconfirmation and dual hypotheses on a more difficult version of Wason's 2-4-6 task. *The Quarterly Journal of Experimental Psychology.* 39A. 1-28.

IEEE (1983). *IEEE Standard Glossary of Software Engineering Terminology.* ANSI Std 729-1983. New York.

Katz, I.R. & Anderson, J.R. (1988) Debugging: An analysis of bug-location strategies. *Human-Computer Interaction.* 3. 351-399.

Kern, L. H., Mirels, H. L. & Hinshaw, V. G. (1983) Scientists' understanding of propositional logic: An experimental investigation. *Social Studies of Science.* 13. 131-146.

Klayman, J. &. Ha, Y.-W. (1987) Confirmation, disconfirmation and information in hypothesis testing. *Psychological Review.* 94. 211-228.

Mahoney, M. J. & DeMonbreun, B. G. (1978) Psychology of the scientist: An analysis of problem-solving bias. *Cognitive Therapy and Research.* 1. 229 - 238.

Mitroff, I. (1974) Norms and counter-norms in a select group of Apollo moon scientists: A case study of the ambivalence of scientists. *American Sociological Review.* 39. 579 - 595.

Myers, G. J. (1979). *The Art of Software Testing.* New York: Wiley.

Mynatt, B. T. (1990). *Software Engineering with Student Project Guidance.* New York: Prentice-Hall.

Mynatt, C.R., Mynatt, B.T., Leventhal, L.M., and Rohlman, D.S. (1992) Software Testing as Hypothesis Testing: A Study of Positive Test Strategy. *2nd International Conference on Thinking.* July 27 - 31, 1992. Plymouth, U.K.

Omar, A. A. & Mohammed, F. A. (1991). A survey of software functional testing methods. *ACM SIGSOFT Software Engineering Notes.* 16. 75-92.

Pennington, N and Grabowski, B. (1990) The tasks of programming. In Hoc, J.-M., T.R.G. Green, R. Samurcay & D.J. Gilmore (Eds.) *Psychology of Programming.* San Diego, CA: Academic Press LTD. 45-62.

Pressman, R. S. (1992). *Software Engineering: A Practitioner's Approach* (3rd ed.). New York: MaGraw-Hill, Inc.

Rohlman, D. S. (1992). The influence of problem representation on hypothesis testing. Unpublished manuscript.

Rohlman, D. S. Mynatt, C. R., Mynatt, B. T., & Leventhal, L. M. (1992, April) The Influence of Expertise on the Four-Card Selection Task in the Domain of Software Testing. Presented at the *Annual Meeting of the Midwestern Psychological Association,* Chicago, IL.

Teasley, B.M., Leventhal,, L.M., Mynatt C.R., & Rohlman, D. S. (1993) Why Software Testing Is Sometimes Ineffective: Two Applied Studies of Positive Test Strategy. Submitted to: *Journal of Applied Psychology*.

Tversky, A. and Kahneman. D. (1974) Judgement under uncertainty: Heuristics and biases. *Science*. 185. 1124-1131.

Tweney, R. D. (1985) Faraday's discovery of induction: A cognitive approach. In D. Gooding, & R. James (Eds.), *Faraday Rediscovered*. London: MacMillan. 159-206.

Tweney, R. D., Doherty, M. E., & Mynatt, C. R. (Eds.) (1981) *On Scientific Thinking*. New York: Columbia University Press.

Tweney, R. D., Doherty, M. E., Worner, W., Pliske, D., Mynatt, C.R., Gross, K., & Arkelin, D. (1980) Strategies of rule discovery in an inference task. *Quarterly Journal of Experimental Psychology*. 32. 109-123.

Vessey, I. (1985) Expertise in debugging computer programs: A process analysis. *International Journal of Man-Machine Studies*. 23. 459-494.

Vessey, I. (1986) Expertise in debugging computer programs: An analysis of the content of verbal protocols. *IEEE Transactions on Systems, Man, and Cybernetics*. 16. 621-637.

Walker, B. J. and Harper, D. R. (1990) Decision-making under system failure conditions. Final report to Air Force Office of Scientific Research, Contract Number F49620-88-C-0053. (Unpublished manuscript).

Wason, P. C. (1968) Reasoning about a rule. *Quarterly Journal of Experimental Psychology*. 23. 273-281.

Zweben, S. H., Stringfellow, C., & Barton, R. (1989) Exploratory studies of the software testing methods used by novice programmers. In *Third Software Engineering Institute Conference on Software Engineering Education*. New York: Springer-Verlag.

# Applying the Wizard of Oz Technique to the Study of Multimodal Systems

Daniel Salber and Joëlle Coutaz

Laboratoire de Génie Informatique, IMAG
B.P. 53 X, 38041 Grenoble Cedex, France
Phone: +33 76 51 44 40, Fax: +33 76 44 66 75
E-mail: salber@imag.fr, coutaz@imag.fr

**Abstract.** The Wizard of Oz (WOz) technique is an experimental evaluation mechanism. It allows the observation of a user operating an apparently fully functioning system whose missing services are supplemented by a hidden wizard. From our analysis of existing WOz systems, we observe that this technique has primarily been used to study natural language interfaces. With recent advances in interactive media, multimodal user interfaces are becoming popular but our current understanding on how to design such systems is still primitive. In the absence of generalizable theories and models, the WOz technique is an appropriate approach to the identification of sound design solutions. We show how the WOz technique can be extended to the analysis of multimodal interfaces and we formulate a set of requirements for a generic multimodal WOz platform. The Neimo system is presented as an illustration of our early experience in the development of such platforms.

## Introduction

Communication between the user and the computer has been shown to be significantly enhanced when different input media are simultaneously available [16]. There is a high potential for systems allowing the use of combined input media, but our knowledge for designing, building, and evaluating such systems is still primitive. Evaluation techniques and user observation provide ways to improve the design of interactive systems. In this paper, we focus on the Wizard of Oz (WOz) experimental evaluation technique. We show how this technique can be extended to the analysis of multimodal interfaces and formulate a set of requirements for multimodal WOz platforms. The Neimo system is presented as an illustration of our early experience in the development of such platforms.

# Evaluation Techniques and Wizard of Oz Experiments

## Evaluation Techniques

Evaluation techniques are twofold. They may be based on predictions from theory or they may rely on experimental data.

Predictive models and techniques do not require any system implementation nor do they need effective users. Examples of such techniques include GOMS [5] and its related models such as CCT [18], theory-based models such as ICS [4], KRI [20], and the "cognitive walkthrough" method [19]. Their main benefit is to allow user interface evaluation at an early stage of the development process. However, such predictions rely on theoretical hypotheses, not on real data. Thus, predictive models and techniques may lack precision or they may be limited in scope when the case study (e.g., multimodal interaction) is not supported by the underlying theory. In addition, the setting and interpretation of such models are sometimes complex and as time consuming as an effective implementation.

At the opposite, experimental techniques deal with real data observed from real users accomplishing real tasks, and operating a physical artifact. Artifacts may be paper scenarios, mock-ups, computer system prototypes, or Wizard of Oz systems. A WOz system allows the observation of a user operating an apparently fully functioning system whose missing services are supplemented by a hidden wizard. The user is not aware of the presence of the wizard and is led to believe that the computer system is fully operational. The wizard observes the user through a dedicated computer system connected to the observed system over a network. When the user invokes a function that is not available in the observed system, the wizard simulates the effect of the function. Through the observation of users' behavior, designers can identify users' needs when accomplishing a particular set of relevant tasks and evaluate the particular interface used to accomplish the tasks.

## Existing Wizard of Oz Systems and Lessons Learned

**Existing WOz Systems.** Most of existing WOz systems have been primarily developed to study the usage of natural languages for retrieval information systems. Telephone information services such as telephone directories, flights or trains information and reservation services, have been an interesting field for experiments [11, 23]. The experimental setup is quite simple: the wizard answers phone calls and pretends callers are talking to an automatic information system. In order to give callers the illusion that they are actually talking to a computer, the wizard's voice is filtered through a distortion system (e.g., a vocoder) that gives the voice a robotic flavour. Questions and answers are tape-recorded for later manual transcription and analysis. Other case studies involve databases or advisory systems interrogation [14, 17, 26] as well as dialogues with expert systems [8, 22]. Most of them aim at collecting vocabulary corpus in order to tune and augment the robustness of spoken or written natural language recognizers. The platform described in [7] is an attempt to support the observation of graphical direct manipulation combined to natural language. A recent paper [21] describes Turvy, an intelligent agent simulated using a WOz, that can be taught using speech and direct manipulation.

Although limited in scope, results from WOz experiments already form an interesting body of knowledge about wizards and evaluation experts.

**Lessons Learned From Wizards.** An interesting result from WOz observations is that wizards' tasks, although apparently simple, are cognitively expensive. The realism of the apparatus requires wizard's actions to be consistent in content, style, and pace. In particular,

- in similar contexts, a given command from the subject must trigger the same behavior from the wizard,
- response time must comply to the subject's expectation: if the wizard is too slow at reacting, the subject may avoid using simulated functions or may believe that the system is overloaded.

In summary, wizards cannot afford improvisation. To achieve an acceptable consistent behavior, wizards must be trained at well defined tasks, and must be assisted by powerful tools. To this end, some WOz systems include limited but useful mechanisms such as a set of predefined replies or menus containing pre-stored parts of answers [6].

In order to alleviate cognitive overload, recent studies suggest a two-wizard configuration where one wizard is specialized in I/O whereas the second one performs task level processing [1]. The I/O wizard acquires user's requests and transmits simulated answers; the task wizard interprets the requests translated by the I/O wizard and generates the answers to be formulated by the I/O wizard. This collaborative task sharing is more likely to guarantee consistency. It doesn't add noticeably to the response time provided that the wizards are appropriately trained. Another experiment using a two-wizard configuration has proven to be successful [10].

**Tools For Analysis.** Another lesson learned from WOz experiments is the need for analysis tools that support efficiently the task of the evaluation experts. Manual analysis of a large body of data requires expertise and is time-consuming. When collected data is recorded electronically, the analysis can be partly automated. For example, in natural language dialogues, the use of pronouns can be identified [6] or, as in the Wizard's Apprentice, the dialogue structure can be analysed [8]. Although the apparatus described in [15] is not a WOz platform, it provides a precise searchable record of user's behavior: events related to graphical menus and buttons are captured and aggregated into higher abstractions, then linked through timestamps to videotape frames. Although this system tracks direct manipulation actions, the salient features of user behavior must be extracted by hand.

In summary, most of existing WOz systems have been developed on a case-per-case basis and support the observation of one modality only. Similarly, automated analysis tools are limited in scope and are rarely integrated into the WOz platform from the start. Although [7] is intended for the combined use of graphics and natural language, the system is limited by technical constraints and supports one wizard only. There has been no attempt to produce a generic, reusable WOz platform that would make possible the observation and analysis of multimodal interaction. With multimodal interaction, new problems arise with specific requirements.

# Requirements for a Multimodal Wizard of Oz

Requirements for multimodal WOz platforms can be defined from the users' perspective (i.e., the wizards and the evaluation experts) as well as from the software point of view. Before discussing these issues, we must introduce the notion of multimodal interaction.

## Multimodal Interaction

Multimodal interaction is characterized by the possibility for the user to exploit multiple communication channels. It requires the system to represent and manipulate information at multiple levels of abstraction including the dynamic maintenance of meaning in the task domain [3, 13].

As discussed in [3, 13], multimodal interaction may be characterized along two dimensions:

• the temporal use of modalities (i.e., communication channels) which can be sequential or concurrent,

• the level of fusion between modalities: modalities may be used in a combined way (e.g., the "put that there" paradigm) or used independently.

The usage of multiple modalities along the fusion and temporal constraints have direct implications on software design as well as on users. The wizard is one such user.

## Requirements From The Wizards' Perspective

From the wizard's perspective, multimodality increases the complexity of the task as well as information bandwidth.

**Task Complexity.** In a traditional WOz system, the wizard supplements a single missing service such as the interpretation of typed natural language. Within an interaction where the subject can use multiple modalities concurrently, the wizard must simulate more complex functions such as the synergistic combination of modalities. Thus, the wizard must have a very efficient way of observing the subject. As shown by early experiments in face-to-face communication, internal video circuits are not accurate enough to track every of the subject's actions [12]. Clearly, the wizard must also have a dedicated computer of his own. The computer is less prone to tracking failure than the human wizard and, as discussed above, it can provide ready for use answers or encapsulate elementary subject actions into higher abstractions such as commands.

**Information Bandwidth.** In a multimodal system, the subject has many ways for providing inputs. The same semantic content may take multiple forms. Thus, the amount of information to be conveyed to the wizard is likely to be much more important than in a traditional system. The required input processing bandwidth may become too high for a single wizard and may result in inconsistent behavior with respect to content, form, and response time. Thus a multiwizard configuration seems a reasonable way to go.

**Multiwizard Configuration.** The difficulty in a multiwizard configuration is to organize the collaboration between the wizards in a way that guarantees consistent behavior.

Ideally, the workload should be equally distributed among the wizards. However, the workload is difficult to estimate a priori since it heavily depends on the subject's behavior. In these conditions, it should be possible for the wizards to dynamically change their respective roles. In addition, we feel the need for a specialized wizard who would act as a supervisor. This superwizard would not accomplish any regular wizard task but would regulate wizards' behavior, monitor the session, and make proper decisions in case of system malfunction.

Task allocation among wizards is currently being investigated. Although we know that it depends on the peculiarities of the experiment, we are working on a set of general features that could help in supporting task distribution. For example, we have found useful to structure a typical wizards' task in three steps: acquisition, interpretation, and formulation.

  • acquisition consists of analyzing the message issued by the subject, and of extracting the relevant information in the problem space,
  • interpretation corresponds to the task level problem solving in the domain,
  • formulation covers the form and emission of an answer to the subject.

This decomposition in three steps suggests the allocation of a combination of steps to different wizards. The I/O wizard and the task wizard discussed above are one such possibility. However, when multiple modalities have to be combined, the fusion process requires an extra acquisition step that complements the acquisition over each communication channel. In this case, it may be wise to define a specialized wizard for performing the fusion of multiple modalities.


## Requirements From The System Perspective

The overall property of a platform for multimodal WOz experiments is performance and flexibility. Flexibility covers configuration and software communication protocol.

**Performance.** As discussed above, the wizard is an important element in response time conformance. However, if the system is slow, the wizard cannot compensate the flaw. Thus the system has to provide the effective foundations for efficiency.

**Configuration Flexibility.** Configuration flexibility covers the variable number of wizards as well as the variety of input and output devices. Multiple wizards, each equipped with a dedicated computer, are recommended when task overload must be shared. In addition, a multimodal WOz system should be flexible enough to accept new interaction devices. The adjunction of a new device should simply result in the development of a new module that would allow the subject to use the new modality and let the wizards track, interpret and simulate its operation. By doing so, devices that are not yet supported by the software under test could be conveniently simulated by a wizard.

**Communication Protocol Flexibility.** In an ordinary WOz system, communication between the subject's computer and the wizard's computer is a major issue. In a multimodal WOz system, this point is even more critical for two reasons. First, such a system may require multiple wizards with multiple workstations possibly exchanging information with each other. Second, a generic multimodal WOz platform requires that the information exchanged over the communication channels may be of any level of abstraction. As an illustration, consider the design of a drawing software where modalities available to the subject are mouse pointing and voice-enabled commands. Designers should be able to perform the following experiments:

 • in the very first step, the tested software would implement mouse gestures only, and voice recognition would be performed by wizards. In this experiment, low level events should be transmitted to the wizards' workstation (e.g., mouse movement in terms of "x,y" coordinates along with the replication of the subject's utterances).
 • in a further development stage, the software would be enhanced with a speech processing system. Events of a higher level of abstraction such as the recognized sentence and the identification of the selected object, should be sent to the wizards' computer.

This example shows the need for a flexible communication protocol, allowing communication between the subject and the wizards systems, as well as communication between the wizards. This protocol should also be flexible enough to allow easy transmission of any level of information, from low-level user events up to high-level information of any kind.

## Requirements for Evaluation Experts: Powerful Analysis Tools

A long-term goal for multimodal WOz systems is to include computerized automatic evaluation tools. This objective, however, still requires theoretical research. In the short run, it is realistic to provide an integrated way to retrieve and manipulate a posteriori data collected during the experiment. With this perspective in view, we propose the following requirements:

 • data should be collected on the same physical support; a support that allows collecting from different media and that offers great flexibility is a computer file. Since we intend to have a fully-computerized WOz system, integration of all history data into computer files is a natural choice.
 • data should be correctly and automatically synchronized to allow real time replay and analysis.
 • automatic processing should be used whenever possible; for example, if speech is recorded in history data, detection of syllables should be performed automatically while analyzing the history data.
 • a powerful filtering mechanism should be available to provide an efficient way to reduce the amount of data to be analyzed, or to allow a direct focus on a particular aspect of the experiment. For example, in the case of the voice-controlled drawing software, one should be able to focus on the choice of

modalities used for drawing new objects; the analysis tool would locate the instants of the session where the user decided to draw a new object and would display the modalities used.

• versatile visualization capabilities could be very useful. For example, to study the use of an electronic pen or a mouse, evaluation experts should be able to analyze the pointer motion in terms of (x, y) coordinates as well as replaying in real time the movements of the pointer.

• detection of multiple repeating patterns of behaviour from the user is a useful evaluation strategy [24]. Since the history data is stored in a computer file, it can be processed electronically and such processing as well as statistical computations on history data should be integrated.

## The Neimo Project: A Multimodal Wizard of Oz Platform

With the requirements exposed above in mind, we designed and developed Neimo, a multimodal Wizard of Oz platform, generic and extensible [2]. We have already performed early tests with Neimo. The purpose of these first experiments is to observe and analyze multimodal interaction with a mouse-based application along with speech recognition and interpretation of facial expressions [25].

### System Configuration

The current configuration for our experiments with the Neimo platform consists in a workstation for the observed user, and a workstation for each wizard. All workstations are Apple Macintosh Quadras. Figure 1 shows an example configuration involving the following modalities: mouse pointing, speech, and facial expression.

**Fig. 1.** An example configuration
for a Neimo experiment

In this example, three wizards collaborate:

• The "mouse wizard" tracks the use of the mouse and cooperates directly with the speech wizard when fusion of a user's speech command and mouse designation is required.

• Speech recognition and interpretation is simulated by a dedicated "speech wizard". The observed user's utterances are digitized and saved in history files, using a sound digitizing board.

• A CCD camera is focused on the user's face and connected to a video acquisition board. The "face wizard" can observe the user's face digitized in real time, interpret the user's expressions, communicate the interpretations to the other wizards to help them in their task, and store the interpretations for later analysis.

## Software Organization

One of our major requirements for a multimodal WOz platform is independence regarding the observed application: we want to be able to plug any client application onto the WOz platform, as long as its source code is available. To fulfill this requirement, Neimo includes a library that allows any client application to use services provided by the WOz platform. These services include:

• sending messages to the wizards, for example to request the simulation of a missing function,

• receiving messages from the wizards, that are taken into account by the client application,

• saving information in history files.

The format of the messages exchanged between the application and the wizards is defined by the client application. More precisely, a set of standard messages has been defined for usual functions required by applications and for usual modalities, but application-specific or modality-specific messages can also be defined; in this case, a specific software component must also be developed for the wizards, to interpret these messages on the wizards' side. This mechanism guarantees the flexibility of the platform, and allows for future evolution.

Therefore, Neimo accepts any application as client, and any specific modality can be integrated into the platform.

**The Communication Services.** The software organization of our multimodal WOz platform is built around a communication kernel (Neimo Com) as shown on figure 2. The studied application and the wizards' applications have access to the communication services via libraries.

Neimo Com is a process that can run on any workstation part of the experiment, or even on a dedicated workstation. All the messages exchanged between the observed user's computer and the wizards or among the wizards themselves are sent through Neimo Com. Thus, Neimo Com is a time base for the whole system: it time-stamps all the messages and also records pertinent information in history files. Neimo Com is in charge of dispatching the messages between the wizards: it distributes to each wizard the messages he is able to process, and collects replies to be transmitted to the observed user as well as operations the wizards want the observed application to perform. Neimo Com also arbitrates possible conflicts, and handles network-related errors and failures.

In short, Neimo Com is the communication control center of the Neimo platform. It supports any number of wizards, and allows them to connect to the system and disconnect from it dynamically, thus allowing the wizards to come into play when needed, even during an experiment.

Neimo provides libraries to allow client access to the communication services. The library on the client application side allows sending and receiving messages, as well as saving information in history files. Since the types of messages are client-defined, they can be of any level of abstraction. On the wizards side, the library provides the following services:

• receiving messages from the observed application. A dynamic subscription mechanism allows the wizards to express interest in certain category of messages. For example, the speech wizard subscribes to the *speech* message type to receive the user's utterances. In addition, the dynamics of the subscription allows wizards to change roles in the course of an experiment.

• sending messages to the observed application. These messages may then be interpreted by the application as operations to perform; this allows remote control of the observed application.

• saving interesting information to history files.

• exchanging messages with other wizards. Up to now, only a "talk"-like exchange tool has been designed, that allows the communication of short typed messages; but we would like to provide the wizards the possibility to exchange audio, and even video messages.

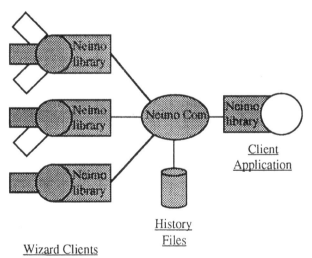

**Figure 2.** The software components of the Neimo platform.
Dimmed areas denote common services and white areas specific components

As a summary, the originality of the Neimo communication framework is three-fold:
• messages from different media are processed in a uniform and integrated way,

• the format of messages is not imposed by the system, but is client-defined. Thus the messages can convey information of any level of abstraction, from low-level events such as mouse clicks up to high-level commands.

• the Neimo Com communication center allows dynamic dispatching of the messages, according to their type and the subscriptions of the connected wizards.

**The Wizards.** Requirements we exposed above concerning the wizards are very strong. To fulfill them, our approach to the design of the wizards' software is to allow as much flexibility as possible. So, we will be able to test many configurations, and we will study a set of rules to configure most efficiently the wizards' operations.

On the wizards' side, Neimo allows for any number of wizards. In our early tests, we assign each wizard the handling of messages corresponding to a given modality. Each wizard has an application that suits his specific needs. Specific modules can be plugged onto a wizard application to provide specific services. Each different kind of message sent by the observed application has a corresponding module in one of the wizards' application. For example, the speech wizard has a speech module that handles the processing of received *speech* messages; it allows the wizard to hear the user's utterances and to perform a set of possible actions in response to a spoken command of the user. A wizard application can accept many plug-in modules; so, a wizard may be able to play many roles, at once or successively during the session. This architecture guarantees a great flexibility for wizard applications.

### After the Session: Analyzing the History Data

As we emphasized above, the analysis of the session after the experiment can be a very long and heavy task. With Neimo, we provide analysis services to help this task.

All data collected during the experiment is stored in history files, and is automatically synchronized. Neimo includes a library that allows exploitation of history files. Since the messages exchanged during a Neimo session, as well as the messages saved in history files, have client-defined content (i.e. defined by the observed application and its specific wizard modules), these history files can only be exploited by client applications that are aware of this content. So, Neimo provides the "history library", which can manipulate history files, and let client applications exploit their content. It allows reading and selective browsing of history files. It also integrates a tool for detecting multiple repeating patterns of behaviour.

### A Few Technicalities

The Neimo system runs on Apple Macintosh Quadra workstations connected through an Ethernet network. It is written in C and C++, and is developed with MacApp, an object-oriented application framework. The communication protocol relies on Apple Events, a powerful high-level inter-application communication protocol introduced by Apple with System 7. The history files use a QuickTime-based format; QuickTime [27] is an extension to Apple's System 7 for manipulation and storage of time-based data from different media.

# Conclusion and Perspectives

We exposed requirements for a multimodal Wizard of Oz platform, and presented Neimo, an attempt to meet these requirements. Two major areas still need further investigation. First, the organization of the wizards' work requires a lot of testing and experiments; we intend to define a set of rules that would help configure the wizards' operations. Second, the tools for the analysis of history files need further development; a long-term goal for this analysis is partial or total automation.

# Acknowledgements

We would like to thank Jean Caelen of the Institut de la Communication Parlée (ICP, Grenoble, France) who provided very valuable help and advice as well as René Amalberti and Claude Valot from CERMA, Jean-Marc Francony and Evert Kuijpers from CRISS, Grenoble, who shared their skills and experiences with us.

# References

1.  R. Amalberti and C. Valot: "Le Magicien d'Oz", CERMA, journée du PRC Rhône-Alpes, 1993.
2.  G. Ambone, B. Noz, D. Salber: "Projet Neimo, Spécifications Externes", internal technical report, équipe IHM, LGI-IMAG, 1992.
3.  S. Balbo, J. Coutaz and D. Salber: "Towards Automatic Evaluation of Multimodal User Interfaces", Workshop on Intelligent User Interfaces '93.
4.  P.J. Barnard, "Cognitive Resources and the Learning of Human-Computer Dialogs", in Interfacing Thought, Cognitive Aspects of Human-Computer Interaction, J.M. Carroll Ed., MIT Press Publ., 1987, pp.112-158
5.  S.K. Card, T.P. Moran and A. Newell: "The Psychology of Human-Computer Interaction", Lawrence Erlbaum Associates, 1983.
6.  N. Dahlbäck and A. Jönsson: "Empirical studies of discourse representations for natural language interfaces", Fourth Conference of the European Chapter of the ACL, proceedings 291-8 1989.
7.  N. Dahlbäck, A. Jönsson and L. Ahrenberg: "Wizard of Oz studies — why and how", Third Conference on Applied Natural Language Processing, Trento, Italy, 31 march—3 April 1992.
8.  D. Diaper: "The Wizard's Apprentice: A Program to Help Analyse Natural Language Dialogues", People and Computers V, proceedings of the 5th Conference of the British Computer Society, 1989.
9.  P. Falzon: "Ergonomie Cognitive du Dialogue", Presses Universitaires Grenobloises, 1989.
10. J.-M. Francony, E. Kuijpers and Y. Polity: "Towards a methodology for Wizard of Oz experiments", Third Conference on Applied Natural Language Processing, Trento, Italy, 31 march—3 April 1992.
11. N. Fraser, N. Gilbert and C. McDermid: "The Value of Simulation Data", Third Conference on Applied Natural Language Processing, Trento, Italy, 31 march—3 April 1992.

12. R.S. Fish, R.E. Kraut, R.W. Root: "Evaluating Video as a Technology for Informal Communication", in the CHI'92 Conference Proceedings, ACM Press Publ., 1992, pp. 37-48

13. A. Gourdol, L. Nigay and D. Salber: "Multimodal Systems: Aspects of Event Fusion and a Taxonomy", to be published in IFIP Conference '92 Proceedings.

14. R. Guindon and K. Schuldberg: "Grammatical and Ungrammatical Structures in User-Adviser Dialogues; Evidence For Sufficiency of Restricted Languages in Natural Language Interfaces to Advisory Systems", proceedings of the 25th Annual Meeting of the Association for Computational Linguistics.

15. M.L. Hammontree, J.J. Hendrickson, B.W. Hensley, "Integrated Data Capture and Analysis Tools for Research and Testing on Graphical User Interfaces", in the CHI'92 Conference Proceedings, ACM Press Publ., 1992, pp. 431-432

16. A.G. Hauptmann: "Speech and Gesture for Graphic Image Manipulation", CHI '89 Proceedings, pp. 241-245.

17. A. Jönsson and N. Dahlbäck: "Talking to A Computer is Not Like Talking To Your Best Friend", Proceedings of the Scandinavian Conference on Artificial Intelligence '88, pp. 53-68.

18. D. Kieras, P.G. Polson: "An Approach to the Formal Analysis of User Complexity", International Journal of Man-Machine Studies, 22, 1985, pp. 365-394

19. C. Lewis, P. Polson, C. Wharton, J. Rieman: "Testing a Walkthrough Methodology for Theory-Based Design of Walk-Up-and-Use Interfaces", CHI '90 Proceedings, pp. 235-241.

20. J. Löwgren and T.Nordqvist: "A Knowledge-Based Tool for User Interface Evaluation and its Integration in a UIMS", Human-Computer Interaction— INTERACT '90, pp. 395-400.

21. D. Maulsby, S. Greenberg, R. Mander: "Prototyping an Intelligent Agent through Wizard of Oz", InterCHI'93 Proceedings, pp. 277-284.

22. Y. Polity, J.-M. Francony, R. Palermiti, P. Falzon, S. Kazma: "Recueil de dialogues homme-machine en langue naturelle écrite", Les Cahiers du CRISS, n° 17, 1990.

23. M. Richards & K. Underwood: "How Should People and Computers Speak to Each Other", Proceedings of Interact '84 — First IFIP Conference on Human-Computer Interaction, pp. 268-273.

24. A. Sochi & D. Hix, "A study of Computer-Supported User interface Evaluation Using Maximal Repeating Pattern Analysis", in Proceedings of the CHI'91 Conference, ACM Press, pp. 301-305, 1991.

25. M. Turk and A. Pentland: "Eigenfaces for recognition", Journal of Cognitive Neuroscience, Vol. 3, No. 1, pp. 71-86, 1991.

26. S. Whittaker and P. Stenton: "User Studies and the Design of Natural Language Systems", Fourth Conference of the European Chapter of the ACL, proceedings 291-8 1989.

27. QuickTime Reference Guide, QuickTime CD, Apple Computer Inc.

# The MSM Framework:
# A Design Space for Multi-Sensori-Motor Systems

Joëlle Coutaz, Laurence Nigay and Daniel Salber

Laboratoire de Génie Informatique, IMAG
B.P. 53 X, 38041 Grenoble Cedex, France
Phone: +33 76 51 44 40, Fax: +33 76 44 66 75
E-mail: coutaz@imag.fr, nigay@imag.fr, salber@imag.fr

**Abstract.** One of the new design goals in Human Computer Interaction is to extend the sensory-motor capabilities of computer systems to better match the natural communication means of human beings. This article proposes a dimension space that should help reasoning about current and future Multi-Sensori-Motor systems (MSM). To do so, we adopt a system centered perspective although we draw upon the "Interacting Cognitive Subsystems" psychological model. Our problem space is comprised of 6 dimensions. The first two dimensions deal with the notion of communication channel: the number and direction of the channels that a particular MSM system supports. The other four dimensions are used to characterize the degree of built-in cognitive sophistication of the system: levels of abstraction, context, fusion/fission, and granularity of concurrency. We illustrate the discussion with examples of multimedia and multimodal systems, both MSM systems but with distinct degrees of built-in cognitive sophistication.

## 1 Introduction

Parallel to the development of the Graphical User Interface technology, natural language processing, computer vision, 3-D sound, and gesture recognition have made significant progress. Artificial and virtual realities are good examples of systems that aim to integrate these diverse interaction techniques. Their goal is to extend the sensory-motor capabilities of computer systems to better match the natural communication means of human beings.

The sensory-motor abilities of systems may be augmented with various degrees of sophistication. This extension may range from the construction of new input/output devices to the definition and management of symbolic representations for the information communicated through such devices. The span of possibilities and the novelty of the endeavour explain the variety of the terms, such as multimedia and multimodal, used to qualify these systems. As demonstrated by our framework, multimedia and multimodal systems are both "multi-sensory-motor" (MSM) systems but with distinct degrees of built-in cognitive sophistication.

This article proposes a framework that should help reasoning about current and future MSM systems. It is a refinement of the dimension space presented in [5, 9, 13]. To do so, we adopt a system centered perspective although we draw upon the

"Interconnecting Cognitive Subsystems" (ICS) psychological model [2]. As shown in Figure 1, our framework is comprised of 6 dimensions:

- The first two dimensions deal with the notion of communication channel: the number and direction of the channels that a particular MSM system supports. Issues related to communication channels and the symmetry with ICS are presented in the next section.

- The other four dimensions are used to characterize the degree of built-in cognitive sophistication of the system: levels of abstraction, context, fusion/fission, and granularity of concurrency. These issues are discussed in detail before we comment on the distinction between multimedia and multimodal interactive systems.

Finally, we illustrate the discussion with examples of multimedia and multimodal systems, both MSM systems but with distinct degrees of built-in cognitive sophistication.

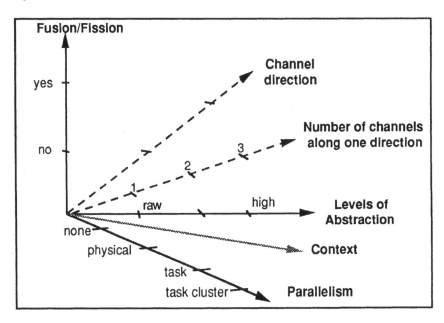

**Fig. 1.** The MSM framework: A 6-D space to characterize multi-sensory-motor interactive systems.

## 2 Communication Channels

A communication channel can be viewed as the temporal, virtual, or physical link that makes the exchange of information possible between communicating entities (e.g., a human being and a computer system). Instead of considering the linkage dimension of communication, we stress the importance of the sources and recipients involved in a communication act. Thus, a communication channel covers a set of sensory (or effector) means through which particular types of information can be received (or transmitted) and processed.

A sensor is a physical device that allows a communicating entity to acquire information from the environment (e.g., another communicating entity). An effector plays the symmetrical role for transmitting information to the environment. Interestingly, sensors and effectors are not insulated randomly. Multiple sensors (effectors) may be grouped together to form a cluster associated to a processing facility.This grouping of physical devices under the hat of a processing unit corresponds to a communication channel. This view of a communication channel matches nicely the ICS psychological model.

In ICS, the human information processing system is subdivided into a set of specialized subsystems. As shown in Figure 2, the sensory subsystems transform sensed data into specific mental codes that represent the structure and content of the incoming data. These representations are then handled by subsystems that are specialized in the processing of higher-level representations: the morphonolexical subsystem for processing the surface structure of language, the object subsystem for processing visuospatial structures, and the propositionnal and implicational subsystems for more abstract and conceptual representations. The output of these higher representational subsystems are directed to the effector subsystems (articulatory and limb).

For example, the retinas capture space-time patterns of photons which are processed by the visual subsystem into a mental form usable by the representational or effector subsystems. The retinas (which are two input physical devices) and the visual subsystem (which is the corresponding processing facility) define a *human communication channel*. As an example from the computer side, the X window server handles both mouse and keyboard input devices. It transforms interrupt signals into a higher level representation, an "X event", that may be of interest to client processes. The keyboard, the mouse, and the X server define a *digital communication channel*.

Figure 2 shows an example of correspondence between digital and human communication channels. In this illustration, hands acting on a touch screen, a keyboard or a mouse may be sensed by the same process P4. They can also be observed, as well as the face and the body, by a camera managed by process P1. Thus, in the particular configuration shown in Figure 2, the human channel limb can be sensed, simultaneously or not, by multiple input devices organized as two digital channels.

Information types conveyed by human and digital communication channels define an abstraction from the physical representations used by I/O devices. This abstraction is the boundary with higher internal representations. It conveys phenomena, not meaning. Meaning is covered by the internal processes, responsible for executing the interpretation and rendering functions.

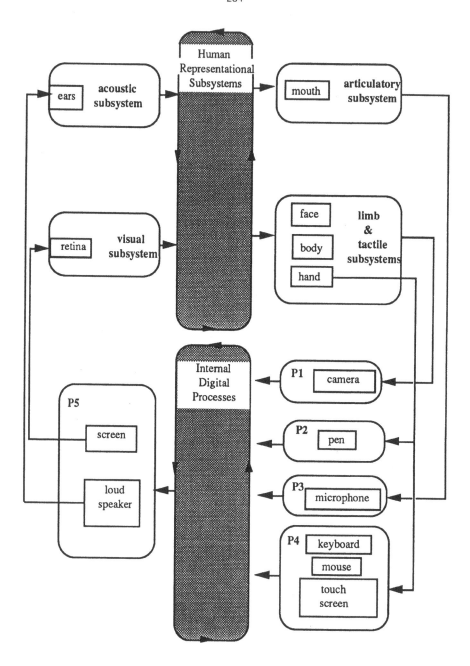

**Fig. 2.** An example of correspondence between digital and human communication mechanisms. Rounded rectangles represent computing facilities. Arrows indicate information flow between the computing facilities. Rectangles denote human and digital effectors or sensors (i.e., physical input and output devices). Dark grey areas correspond to the higher representational computing facilities.

# 3 Interpretation and Rendering

Information acquired by input digital channels is transformed through multiple process activities. This sequence of input transformations forms the interpretation function. In the other direction, internal information (e.g., system state) is transformed to be made perceivable to the user. This sequence of output transformations defines the rendering function. The interpretation and the rendering functions can be both characterized with four intertwined ingredients: level of abstraction, context, fusion/fission, and parallelism. These dimensions are presented in the following paragraphs.

## 3.1 Level of Abstraction

The notion of level of abstraction expresses the degree of transformation that the interpretation and rendering functions perform on information. It also covers the variety of representations that the system supports, ranging from raw data to symbolic forms. The span of representations should be considered on a per-digital channel basis. Thus, for a given digital input channel, the interpretation function can be characterized by its power of "abstracting" raw data into higher representational expressions. The rendering function is characterized by the level of abstraction it starts from to produce perceivable raw information through output digital channels.

Computer vision, speech recognition as well as speech synthesis systems operate along these principles. For example, speech input may be recorded as a signal, or described as a sequence of phonemes, or interpreted as a meaningful parsed sentence. Each representation corresponds to a particular level of abstraction resulting from an interpretation function. For output, the process is similar: data may be produced from symbolic abstract representations or from a lower level of abstraction without any computational knowledge about meaning. For example, a vocal message may be synthesized from an abstract representation of meaning, from a pre-stored text (i.e., text-to-speech) or may simply be replayed from a previous recording.

## 3.2 Context

The capacity of a system to abstract along a channel may vary dynamically with respect to "contextual variables". Contextual variables are like cognitive filters. They form a set of internal state parameters used by the representational processes to control the interpretation/rendering function. For example, in vi, when in command mode, typed text is transformed into a high level abstraction whereas the same text entered in input mode is recorded as is without any transformation. Contextual variables constrain the configuration of digital processes used at some point in time to process information. We observe an analogy with the cognitive resources configuration claimed in ICS.

In Figure 1, we have not provided salient values for the "context" dimension. We have however identified one discriminatory feature shared for input by current MSM systems: commands versus task domain data. We have observed that current MSM systems support high level interpretation in the context of commands but very little for task domain related data. The "vi" example mentioned above is one of many illustrations. Although the contextual variable "command/task domain data" may be of interest to characterize current systems, its scope is rather narrow. More work needs to be done to identify additional contextual variables that would be shared by most systems.

### 3.3 Fusion and Fission

Fusion refers to the combination of several chunks of information to form new chunks. Fission refers to the decomposition phenomenon. Fusion and fission are part of the abstracting and materialization phenomena.

**The Interpretation Function and Fusion.** Considering fusion for the interpretation function:
- at the lowest level, information chunks may (or may not) originate from distinct digital input channels;
- at higher levels, information chunks may (or may not) come from distinct contexts.

For example, the sequence of events "mouse-down, mouse-up" that occurs in the palette of a graphics editor are two information chunks that originate from the same input channel and from the same context (i.e., the palette). They are combined within the context of the palette to form a higher information chunk (i.e., the selection of a geometric class). The drawing area constitutes another context. Events that occur in the drawing area are interpreted as the effective parameters of the geometric function. They are combined with the selected geometric class to complete the function call in the task-domain. Thus, in this example, fusion occurs between information chunks originating from the same digital channel but, as the interpretation proceeds at higher levels of abstraction, it also involves different contexts.

The "put that there" paradigm as in Cubricon [12] and ICP-Plan [6] offers an example of fusion between chunks originating from distinct input digital channels. In this example, fusion is required to solve the coreferences expressed through distinct channels.

**The Interpretation Function and Fission.** It may be the case that information coming from a single input channel or from a single context need to be decomposed in order to be understood at a higher level of abstraction.

For example, consider the utterance "show me the red circle in a new window". This sentence, received through a single digital channel, references two domains of discourse: that of the graphics task (i.e., "the red circle") and that of the user interface (i.e., "a new window"). In order to satisfy the request, the system has to decompose the sentence into two high level functions: "create a window" and "draw a red circle" in the newly created window.

**The Rendering Function and Fusion.** The rendering function can perform fusion at multiple levels of abstraction. One of them, which takes place at the highest level of abstraction (i.e., the domain adaptor) has been discussed in [8]. At the lowest level, it appears as multiple information chunks rendered through a single output channel.

For example, the picture of a town may be combined to a graphical representation of the population growth. The notions of town and population which are handled by two different contexts within the internal processes of the system, are combined at the lowest level and presented through a single output digital channel.

**The Rendering Function and Fission.** Rendering may also incorporate fission at multiple levels of abstraction. The highest level has been discussed in [8]. At the lowest level, fission occurs when an information chunk gives birth to multiple representations whether it be through a single or multiple digital output channels.

For example, the notion of wall in our mobile robot system [3] may be represented as a line or as a form on the screen. These distinct representations of the same concept use only one digital output channel. Alternatively, the spoken message "watch this wall!" along with a blinking red line on the screen uses two distinct output channels to denote the same wall.

### 3.4    Parallelism

Representation and usage of time is a complex issue. In our discussion, we are concerned with the role of time within the interpretation and rendering functions. How does time relate to levels of abstraction and contexts? How does it interfere with fusion and fission? Parallelism at the user interface may appear at multiple grains: at the physical level, at the task and task cluster levels.

**Parallelism at the Physical Level.** For input, the physical level corresponds to the user actions that can be sensed by input digital channels as an information chunk (e.g., an event). For example, a mouse click, a spoken utterance are information chunks. For output, the physical level denotes output primitives, that is the information chunks that can be produced by output digital channels in one burst. For example, a spoken message or the reverse video of an icon.

For input, parallelism at the physical level allows the user to trigger multiple input devices simultaneously. If these devices are organized along distinct channels, then the user solicits multiple input digital channels in parallel. Similarly, physical parallelism for output may take the form of simultaneous outputs through distinct digital channels or may occur through a single channel. The fission example "watch this wall" associated with "the blinking red line", requires parallelism at the physical level using multiple digital output channels.

**Parallelism at the Task Level.** From the system's perspective, a task (i.e, an elementary task) cannot be decomposed further but in terms of physical actions. For input, an elementary task is usually called a command, that is, the smallest fusion/fission of physical user's actions that changes the system state. For output, an elementary task is the set of output physical primitives used to express a system state change.

True parallelism at the command level allows the user to issue multiple commands simultaneously. It necessarily relies on the availability of parallelism at the physical level. Pseudo-parallelism at the command level as in Matis [13], allows the user to build several commands in an interleaved way as in multithread dialogues. Then, parallelism at the physical level is not required.

Figure 3 illustrates all possible relationships between parallelism at the physical level, and fusion and fission, to form commands within the interpretation function. In 3-a, multiple simultaneous inputs from channel 1 must be dispatched into two higher contexts (e.g., agents) to build two distinct commands in parallel. For example, in MMM, two users may manipulate two physical mouses simultaneously to respectively modify the size and color of a shared rectangle [4]. In configuration 3-b, simultaneous actions on distinct input channels must be combined to build a single command (as in the "put that there" paradigm). In 3-c, physical actions follow two independent paths. For example, the user may say "close top window" while moving a file icon in the trash. In this case, two independent commands must be built in parallel.

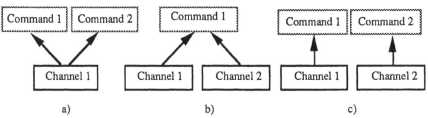

**Fig. 3.** Relationships between parallelism at the physical level, fusion and fission, and commands.

The diversity of the relationships shown in Figure 3 is a good indicator of the difficulty to implement the interpretation function. In particular, which criteria should be considered to trigger fusion and which strategy should be adopted? Early experiences with Matis [13] and ICP-Plan [6] show that temporal and structural proximities are valid criteria for fusion. Temporal proximity expresses parallelism between physical actions. (Due to the technological limitations of current speech recognition systems, mouse clicks are detected long before sentences are recognized, although expressed by the user at "the same time".) Structural relationships expresses syntactic links between inputs. Thus, two inputs linked by temporal and structural properties are good candidates for fusion.

The strategy could be "eager" as opposed to "lazy". Eager fusion makes attempts to combine inputs as soon as criteria are met at the lowest levels of abstraction. Lazy fusion postpones fusion to the highest levels. The advantage of eager fusion is the ability to generate early feedback. Its drawback is the necessity to be able to perform backtracking. This is particularly true when interleaving or parallelism is supported at the command level.

A similar analysis should be done for output elementary tasks. So far, we have not experienced enough exemplars to generate a sound discussion on this issue. However, we can relate two interesting examples. The first one is usage of time to synchronize information chunks over digital output channels. QuickTime is a good illustration of this capacity. The second example is interleaving between inputs and outputs at the task level. For example, as the system moves an object, the user may dynamically change the speed or the color of the object. We observe a temporal overlap between input and output at the task level. In this example, the duration of the system's outputs covers the duration of a sequence of user's commands and can be dynamically affected by these commands. In the other way round, rubber banding or reverse video of candidate recipients in the Macintosh finder are examples of duration of user's inputs covered by system's outputs.

**Parallelism at the Task Cluster Level**. From the system's perspective, a task is a cluster of tasks that structures the interaction space. For example, in our mobile robot system, the command space is organized into three subspaces: one for providing the robot with cartographic details, the second to specify missions to be accomplished, the third one to observe and control the robot during mission execution. For input, parallelism at the task level expresses how much parallelism (actually pseudo-parallelism) is supported by the system between clusters of commands. Note that parallelism at the cluster level does not necessarily imply parallelism at the command level.

For output, a similar organization in terms of clusters of parallelism may be observed. We have not studied this perspective yet.

# 4 Multimedia and Multimodal Interactive Systems

Both multimedia and multimodal systems are characterized by communicating information either through multiple input digital channels or through multiple output digital channels, or both. The multiplicity of communication channels along one direction (whether it be input or output) provides the basis for multimedia-lity and multimodality.

The distinction between multimedia-lity and multimodality lies in the degree of built-in cognitive sophistication of the system along the axis "level of abstraction". Multimodality is characterized by the capacity of the system to interpret raw inputs up to high levels of abstraction (e.g., that of the task domain) or to render information starting from high level representations. Although multimedia-lity includes interpretation and rendering, it is not capable of handling the highest task-domain level representations.

As examples of multimedia systems, electronic mails from Xerox PARC, NeXT and MicroSoft allow messages to include text, graphics as well as voice annotations. FreeStyle from Wang, allows the user to insert gestural annotations which can be replayed at will. Note that voice and gesture annotations are recorded but not processed to discover meaning. Authoring systems such as Guide, HyperCard and Authorware allow for the rapid prototyping of multimedia applications. Hypermedia systems are becoming common practice [7].

On the multimodal side, Xspeak [15] extends the usual mouse-keyboard facilities with voice recognition. Vocal input expressions are automatically translated into the formalism used by X window. Xspeak has no fusion capability between multiple input channels. The user can choose one and only one channel among the mouse-keyboard and speech to formulate a command. Concurrency is supported by the underlying platform, X window/Unix, at the physical level only. Similarly, Glove-Talk [11] is able to translate gesture acquired with a data glove into speech (synthesis). Eye trackers are also used to acquire eye movements and interpret them as commands. Although spectacular, these systems do not support fusion between input channels.

On the other hand, ICP-Draw [16] and Talk and Draw [14] are graphics editors that support the "put that there" paradigm. In Talk and Draw however, fusion is speech driven: deictic mouse events must happen after the utterance of the sentence. Talk and Draw performs fusion in a sequential way. CUBRICON [12] supports fusion and parallelism at the physical level. This system accepts coordinated simultaneous natural language and pointing via a mouse device. The user can input natural language via the speech device and/or the keyboard. Speech recognition is handled by a Dragon System VoiceScribe which supports discrete speech only. Although non continuous speech is unnatural to the user, it greatly simplifies the problem of fusion.

More generally, an MSM system may be both multimedia and multimodal. For example, an hypermedia system would illustrate task-domain concepts using images and sound replayed from a CD-ROM, and it would be controlled by the user in a multimodal way using both speech and mouse to navigate through the hyper space. Note that current multimedia systems are all able to handle the highest task-domain level representations but they do so for commands only and through a unique channel. Thus any multimedia system is at least monomodal in order to recognize input commands.

## 5  Summary

The analysis of the behavior of MSM interactive systems should be considered along the following dimensions:
  • the nature of input and output physical devices and their grouping as digital input and output communication channels,
  • the granularity of parallelism supported by the system along the input and output channels (i.e., physical actions, task level, task cluster),
  • for each channel and context, and for combinations of input or output channels, the capacity of the system to support abstraction/materialization through the fusion and fission mechanisms.

As discussed in [13], this framework can be used to classify current and future MSM systems. Although system centered, it draws upon psychology and HCI with the notions of communication channel, concurrency at the user interface, and levels of abstraction. By doing so, it identifies salient parameters for protocol studies as in Wizard of Oz experiments [1]. In addition, it makes explicit issues, such as fission and fusion, that are relevant to the design of software architecture models and building tools. The MSM framework identifies properties of systems behavior that are currently being captured within a theory of interactors [10].

## Acknowledgements

This work has been supported by project ESPRIT BR 7040 AMODEUS2 and by PRC Communication Homme-Machine.

# References

1. S. Balbo, J. Coutaz, D. Salber: Towards Automatic Evaluation of Multimodal User Interfaces; International Workshop on Intelligent User Interfaces, Orlando, USA, Jan., 1993.
2. P. Barnard, "Cognitive Resources and the Learning of Computer Dialogs", in Interfacing Thought, Cognitive aspects of Human Computer Interaction, J.M. Carroll Ed., MIT Press Publ., pp. 112-158.
3. L. Bass, J. Coutaz: Developing Software for the User Interface; Addison Wesley, 1991.
4. E. Bier, S. Freeman, K. Pier, "MMM: The Multi-Device Multi-User Multi-Editor", in CHI'92 Proceedings, 1992, pp. 645-646.
5. M.L. Bourguet, J. Caelen: Interfaces Homme-Machine Multimodales : gestion des événements et représentation des informations; ERGO-IA'92 Proceedings, pp. 124-134, 1992.
6. M.L. Bourguet: Conception et réalisation d'une interface de dialogue personne-machine multimodales; Thèse de docteur de l'INPG, mars 1992.
7. J. Conklin, "Hypertext, an Introduction and Survey", IEEE Computer, 20(9), September, 1987, 17-41.
8. J. Coutaz, S. Balbo: Applications: A Dimension Space for User Interface Management Systems. In Proc. CHI'91, ACM Publ., May, 1991, pp. 27-32.
9. Multimedia and Multimodal User Interfaces: A Taxonomy for Software Engineering Research Issues, East-West HCI'92, St Petersburg, August, 1992., August, 1992.
10. D. Duke, M. Harrison: Abstract Models for Interaction Objects; ESPRIT BR 7040 Amodeus Project document, System Modelling/WP1, Nov. 1992.
11. S.S. Fels, "Building Adaptative Interfaces with Neural Networks: the Glove-Talk Pilot Study", University of Toronto, Technical Report, CRG-TR-90-1, February, 1990.
12. J. Neal, C. Thielman, K. Bettinger, J. Byoun, "Multi-modal References in Human-Computer Dialogue", Proceedings of AAAI-88, 1988, pp. 819-823.
13. L. Nigay, J. Coutaz: A design space for multimodal interfaces: concurrent processing and data fusion, Interchi'93, Amsterdam, May, 1993.
14. M. W. Salisbury, J. H. Hendrickson, T. L. Lammers, C. Fu, S. A. Moody, "Talk and Draw: Bundling Speech and Graphics", IEEE Computer, 23(8), August, 1990, 59-65.
15. C. Schmandt, M. S. Ackerman, D. Hndus, "Augmenting a Window System with Speech Input", IEEE Computer, 23(8), August, 1990, 50-58.
16. J. Wretö, J. Caelen, "ICP-DRAW, rapport final du projet ESPRIT MULTIWORKS no 2105.

# Radiological Reporting Based on Voice Recognition

G. Antoniol, R. Fiutem, R. Flor and G. Lazzari

IRST, Pantè di Povo, I-38050 Trento, Italy

**Abstract.** Speech recognition has proved to be a natural interaction modality and an effective technology for medical reporting, in particular in the speciality of radiology. High-volume text creation requirement and the complex structure of these texts make voice technologies useful. By employing speech, professionals in the field can generate reports and do so at a speed that approaches traditional dictation methods.

However, the integration of speech recognition in a user interface creates new problems: speech recognizers may introduce errors and moreover they should be adaptable to spoken language variations.

This paper describes a radiological reporting system and the related motivations for the use of the speech modality. A preliminary evaluation of the system has shown that, on average, although text recalling functions and keyword shortcuts are available, more than two thirds of a radiological report are generated by means of dictation.

## 1    Introduction

Recent progress in Automatic Speech Recognition (ASR) and software technology makes it possible to use speech as a new interaction modality. Given the actual performance of ASR systems, speech interaction modality is gaining popularity for medical reporting, in particular in the specialism of radiology [5, 7]. The main reasons are the need of producing a high volume of texts and their complex structure.

The use of voice allows the physician to look at the X-ray photograph while he or she are dictating at a speed that approaches traditional dictation methods. Having a secretary dedicated to each physician to type the reports is in many cases too expensive.

Prototypes [5, 7] for dictating radiological reports have already been developed; for the Italian language, a joint project with the Italian Health Ministry was started by IBM at the end of 1990 to assess the feasibility of speech recognition for medical reporting [5].

However, the integration of speech recognition in a user interface creates new problems due to the fact that ASR systems may introduce errors and should be adaptable to spoken language variations (both acoustically and linguistically), in order to exhibit acceptable performance.

Methodologies and tools have been recently developed [8, 12, 11, 6] for the use of speech modality. As stated in [9] little work has been done on user interface evaluation mainly involving guidelines, indications and specifications.

This paper describes a radiological reporting application, the Automatic Reporting by Speech (A.Re.S) system. Motivations for using speech modality are analyzed and the evaluation results of an A.Re.S prototype are presented. Besides recognition rate, comparisons on the use of speech input with respect to mouse and keyboard input have been performed within the report generation task. Subtasks for which this modality is most adequate have been identified.

In Section 2, the radiological report generation task is analyzed. Section 3 gives a description of the functionalities of the A.Re.S system prototype and briefly illustrates its architecture. Section 4 outlines some considerations about the use of automatic speech recognition in the A.Re.S. system. In Section 5 the on-site experiment is described, while in Section 6 the output data of the A.Re.S prototype test are analyzed and discussed with reference to report production times, recognition accuracy, adaptability and user interaction modalities. Finally some conclusions and related future work are presented.

## 2    Radiological Report Generation Task

The radiological report is the typed document that describes and summarizes the physician's observations about an X-ray photograph. Among other things, it deals with examination conditions, clinical signs, anatomical and/or other relevant pathological clues. It mostly consists of certain routine sentences and texts plus other non *standard* elements related to the pathology; therefore, besides free dictation, useful for unpredictable text insertion, it is important to provide the user with the interaction modalities allowing shortcuts dependent on the inherent report structure. By its examination, a report generation can be seen as a mixture of dictation, selection of predefined texts, and editing. Therefore, three sub-tasks have been identified:

- standard sentences and text generation,
- variable text generation,
- keyword generation.

Within the variable text generation subtask, two activities can be identified, closely related to the nature of ASR correction of recognition errors and insertion of words unknown to the system.

Although the chosen input modalities ( keyboard, mouse, voice) can be shared among all the sub-tasks, each of them has its own *natural* interaction method. Thus standard sentences and texts are selected by keyboard and mouse, while for variable text generation, direct editing or voice entry are preferable. The keyword generation sub-task allows the direct insertion of symbols, corresponding to words (such as punctuation marks and digits), accomplished whilst the voice input channel is activated: keyboard is its natural input modality. This feature speeds up the average reporting time. In fact, recognition of words that can be entered by pressing a single key requires more time.

The use of mouse and keyboard has been selected for the error correction task, in order to reduce user's frustration due to possible recognition errors during corrections.

# 3 The A.Re.S. Project

The A.Re.S project, developed at IRST in collaboration with the Radiological Department of S.Chiara Hospital, Trento - resulted in the implementation of a prototype for real time dictation of reports related to chest examinations imposing a small pause between words. As the system is speaker-dependent, a short training procedure for adapting the recognizer to the radiologist's voice is needed. The lexicon used by the recognizer is medium-sized (2500 - 5000 words) and it is integrated with a statistical language model based on *bigram probabilities* [10, 4]; run-time modification and user adaptation of the lexicon and language model (LM) are possible, through the insertion of new words and new bigrams.

When the system is turned on, it remains ready in a pause state, providing an empty report form.

Variable text insertion by voice is made possible, by an input event causing a move to a dictation state. Once a word is uttered, the ASR system proposes a stack of possible candidates, ordered by likelyhood, to the user. If the user continues with the next word, it is assumed that the word at the top of the stack was correct. This word is moved to the report form. Otherwise the user can select the right word from the stack using the mouse or function keys. The correction mechanism allows also the user to insert new words in the lexicon and new bigrams in the LM.

Standard sentences and text generation is available by menu selection. Function keys or keywords for the generation of negative reports [1] are available. Other keys allow the user to insert punctuation marks and digits during dictation. Finally, the user can directly edit the report, if desired.

Once the report is complete, it can be printed and stored in a database.

In order to perform in real time, the system has been divided into three communicating subsystems, called *managers*: an Interface Manager, a Voice Signal Manager and a Recognizer Manager (Figure 1).

Each manager is implemented as a separate process and handles its own knowledge domain, i.e. man-machine interaction, digital signal processing and automatic speech recognition.

The Voice Signal Manager communicates with a Digital Signal Processing (DSP) board that performs real time voice signal processing; the Recognizer Manager, based on discrete Hidden Markov Models (HMM), decodes the acoustical description extracted from the observed signal by the Voice Signal Manager in the word sequence with the highest probability [2].

Finally, the Interface Manager controls the interaction with the user and coordinates the activity of the other two managers; the overall system behaviour is based on the interaction of the managers.

---

[1] A negative report is a report in which no pathologies are found.

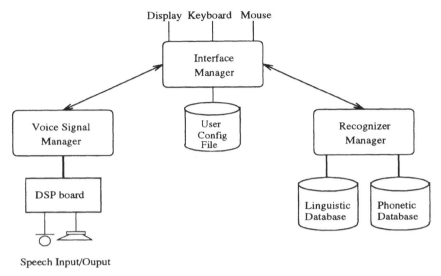

Display  Keyboard  Mouse

**Fig. 1.** Overall system architecture.

# 4 Implications of Speech Recognition Use in the A.Re.S. System

Due to limitations of the present technology, the integration of speech recognition in a user interface should provide the user with effective means to correct errors, by using other input channels (mouse, keyboard and function keys). During correction, as well as in other system states, the voice channel can be deactivated in order to avoid repetition of errors.

With a lexicon size ranging from 2000 to 5000 words and a LM perplexity (see [3] for a definition of perplexity) of about 160 and a size for the correction stack between 4 and 8 items, almost always the right word appeared in the stack even if not in the first position. Moreover, the use of a stack with 10 or more items can result in a search time longer than the time required for typing in a missed word. To introduce a word not belonging to the stack and to implement the linguistic structure adaptation, it is useful to provide an incremental word search procedure, where the set of lexicon words beginning with an already typed substring, ordered by likelyhood, is presented to the user.

Sometimes yawns, coughs or even breaths can be recognized and inserted in the text as words. This problem cannot be avoided constraining a user to emit no other sound than words during dictation because the user may feel uncomfortable with the voice channel. By adding specialized noise models and carefully tuning the signal processing algorithms, the introduction of these non-linguistic events can be minimized. In any case an *undo* function, is provided for erasing the last word in the already produced text.

From the implementation perspective, the integration of an ASR system with an editor of report forms requires a complex representation and handling of the editor's text. Consistency should be maintained between the editor's text and the status of the ASR subsystem. This implies complex communication protocols between these two modules and makes it convenient to conceive the editor text not simply as a stream of bytes, but as a collection of objects, each describing a word.

## 5 On-site Test Description

Experiments made in the actual application environment and with a non-trained user can give results quite different from those obtained in a controlled environment. Therefore, after a prototype system of A.Re.S has been developed and tested in laboratory, an on-site test has been organized, to evaluate its performance as objectively as possible.

The experiments were performed by a physician who has been involved in the A.Re.S. project since the beginning as the application domain expert. On the other hand, as he had never used the system before, he could be classified as a non-trained user.

The prototype has been installed in the S.Chiara hospital for a period of three months during which test sessions took place twice a week. With the exception of a first training session, all the remaining ones have been carried out without any assistance by the technical staff or other personnel.

The report's time-to-ready [2] obtained with the new system has been compared with the emergency reporting and the usual (in medical sense) reporting methods.

In the usual reporting generation method, reports are recorded by physicians on tape cassette decks and are subsequently transcribed by secretaries. The complete time-to-ready of a report usually results in more than one day, because there is no dedicated personnel for this task.

The emergency reporting method requires secretaries typing reports with a customized word processor under physician's dictation. This method is the fastest although the most expensive one, since it requires full time dedicated personnel for report transcription; in the present organization of S.Chiara hospital, it is limited to emergencies only.

An experienced nurse chose the reports to be used in the experiments. They were routine examples, but also pathologically interesting, thus avoiding the physician only typing the keywords necessary to generate negative reports. All the reports concerned chest examinations, because this set constitutes the majority [1] of the total requests and is therefore a good candidate for automation.

The working area (see Fig. 2) was organized in a pre-existing room, already used for reporting, and was comprised of:

- a workstation equipped with a graphic display and a printer
- a head-set high quality microphone;
- a diaphanoscope to the left of the workstation, to visualize X-ray photographs.

---

[2] By time-to-ready we mean the time interval between the start of the report preparation by the physician and its delivery.

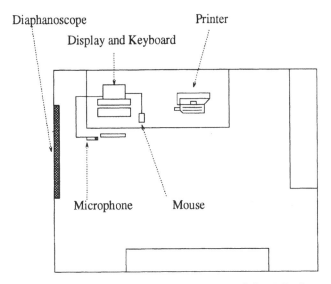

**Fig. 2.** Working area organization for the on-site test of the A.Re.S prototype.

This disposition allowed dictation without looking at the workstation display or at the keyboard. In fact, a short sound informed the user that the system was ready to process a new input word. Actually, after some sessions, the physician chose to disable such "ready sound", and preferred to look alternatively to the diaphanoscope to examine X-ray photograph and at the display, to dictate a new sentence and control the correctness of the system output.

Data has been collected by tracing the system activity in *log files*. At the beginning of a session a log file is created for each of the manager modules defined in Section 3. At the end, these files contain the sequence of the actions performed by the module during the session, together with the interactions performed with other modules and, in the case of the Interface Manager, the user's actions. The Interface Manager log file is the main source of information about report generation times, interface functionalities and the use of the different input channels. The Recognizer Manager's log file provides the data related to ASR system accuracy and linguistic adaptation.

## 6 Experimental Results

In the following, besides the quantitative data of the experiment and the time-to-ready, the ASR system performance is reported, together with the language adaptation measurements. Finally, the incidence of each subtask within the report generation task is presented and discussed.

### 6.1 Report Structure and Production Time

Table 1 shows general information about the user sessions and the report structure (sentences per report, words per report). The second column concerns reports produced by the A.Re.S. prototype; the third concerns emergency reporting, while the fourth provides data about usual reporting.

On a total number of 49 meaningful sessions with A.Re.S (aborted sessions are excluded), 357 reports have been produced.

|  | A.Re.S | Emergency | Usual |
|---|---|---|---|
| SESSIONS | 49 | - | - |
| REPORTS | 357 | 2000 | 18000 |
| SENTENCES/REPORT | 6.59 | 4 | 6.45 |
| WORDS/REPORT | 29.21 | 28 | 27.72 |
| MEAN TIME-TO-READY | 5' 35" | 2' | $> 1 day$ |

**Table 1.** Session and report information.

The average report length, measured in words per report, is more or less the same in all the three reporting methods.

In the last row of Table 1, the mean report time-to-ready is shown. This time comprises dictation, X-ray photograph examination and reviewing time.

Comparing the mean A.Re.S report time-to-ready with the one for the emergency reporting method, it can be observed that A.Re.S time is longer. Although isolated word dictation is not as fast as continuous speech dictation, the major time increase is due to ASR system error checking and correction and the final text review. However, the report delivery is dramatically shortened with respect to the usual reporting method, in which the lack of secretaries dedicated to transcription activity is a bottleneck that slows down report delivery.

## 6.2 ASR Recognition Rate

To maintain recognition rate as high as possible, ASR has been made speaker dependent. Speaker adaptation customizes the baseline system to new users, requiring a training session of about half an hour that creates a user's phonetic database.

A.Re.S allows a user to adapt the microphone gain so that background noise, breaths and so on are automatically reduced during dictation. By reducing spurious words, two results are obtained: the increase in the recognition rate, but, most of all, the increase of the user's confidence in the system.

When the first release of A.Re.S was installed, it was discovered that the overall recognition performanced dropped from 90-95 % to around 50 %. Working on the voice input channel, adopting a high-quality head-set microphone with good directivity, we were able to increase the recognition performance. Figure 3 shows a bar graph of the recognition rate distribution within the report set (see

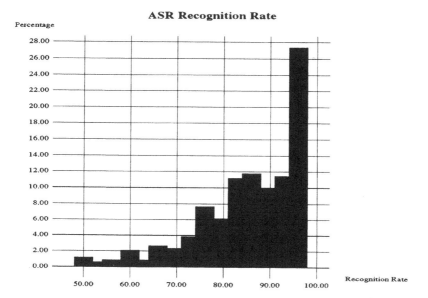

**Fig. 3.** ASR recognition rate.

Table 1). At present the recognition rate is over 90 % in about 50% of reports. However, sometimes the recognition results are still poor and even drop below 40 %. Though it doesn't seem a critical point in the global A.Re.S functionality, future work will investigate the reason why this happens and how to further increase ASR sub-system performance.

## 6.3 ASR Language Adaptation

The most important form of user adaptation of the system is the update of the linguistic structures, i.e. the lexicon and LM. By means of correction, the user can add new words to the lexicon and new bigrams to the LM, that results in a user customization of the linguistic structures.

Table 2 provides statistics about the insertion of new words in the lexicon and new bigrams in the language model, that is the adaptation of the system to the user linguistic structures. The original lexicon and LM have been created through the statistical analysis of thousands of samples in the radiological report domain [1] collected at S. Chiara Hospital. Even though our test user's previous reporting is included in this data base, nevertheless unseen words and new bigrams have been added to the the system.

However insertion of new words has been decreasing with the physician adaptation to the system. Interestingly, about 20 of the 117 updates are due to items created by concatenating two Italian words separated by an apostrophe, for example:

| | INIT. SIZE | FINAL SIZE | INCREASE |
|---|---|---|---|
| WORDS N. | 2293 | 2410 | 5% |
| BIGRAMS N. | 24932 | 25754 | 3% |

**Table 2.** Lexicon and LM upgrade.

*"l ' eta"'* $\implies$ *"l'eta"' (the age)*

or

*"l ' esame "* $\implies$ *"l'esame" (the test).*

These two examples show that two words separated by the apostrophe become a single word in the lexicon, containing the apostrophe. Since in the Italian language the apostrophe is not pronounced, this user concatenation operation corresponds to the use of a discrete word ASR system as a continuous speech ASR system. As a result of this, the speed of recognition obviously increases, without affecting the recognition rate.

### 6.4 Report Generation Subtasks Analysis

The physician's report generation activity, divided in the different subtasks outlined in Section 2, is summarized in Table 3, where each subtask is associated with its interaction modalities.

It can be observed that the variable text generation subtask takes most of the physician's time within report drafting. This can mean either that a report consists, for a great part, of unpredictable text, or that the physician chooses voice as the most natural way of interaction, sometimes inserting via voice what could be inserted through standard sentence selection.

From the analysis of all reports, the incidence of digits and punctuation marks is about 20 %; comparing this value with the percentage for the Keyword Insertion subtask, it can be observed that most of these symbols have been typed, thus confirming the usefulness of keyboard insertion for this subtask.

Table 4 reports the percentage of ASR correction and new word insertion activities, within the Variable Text Generation subtask. The amount of correction activity that results is rather remarkable, but we must consider that some of the corrections are due to the bigram nature of the LM that enforces some ASR choices over others. Anyway it still remains very important to have simple and efficient mechanisms for ASR system correction.

Some interesting considerations can be made by analyzing the use of the predefined sentences insertion function.

Table 5 shows that the number of predefined sentences inserted (reported in the second row) is about 20 % of the total number of sentences of all reports

| SUBTASK | CHANNEL | PERCENTAGE |
|---|---|---|
| Variable Text Generation | Voice | 68 |
| Standard Text Generation | Mouse/Keyboard | 17 |
| Keyword Insertion | Keyboard | 15 |

**Table 3.** Comparison of the different report generation subtasks.

| SUBTASK | CHANNEL | PERCENTAGE |
|---|---|---|
| ASR Correction | Mouse/Keyboard | 20 |
| New Word Insertion | Mouse/Keyboard | 2.4 |

**Table 4.** Amount of correction and new word insertion activities within variable text generation subtask.

considered (first row). Moreover, only in about 10 % of the cases have two or more consecutive predefined sentences been inserted; this data again confirms the fact that a radiological report cannot be seen as a structured document consisting of predefined blocks; moreover, if a predefined sentence is inserted, it is rarely modified by the user (about 5 % of the cases, as the fourth row of the table shows).

This means that all input modalities supplied by the system are equally important and their use becomes more or less convenient depending on the situation. In fact, the use of a system based only on predefined sentences insertion could be quite frustrating and unnatural for the user, as he would be constantly taken up in menu switching or list selection for retrieving the right piece of text.

| | |
|---|---|
| TOTAL SENTENCES | 2352 |
| PREDEFINED SENTENCES | 437 |
| TWO CONSECUTIVE | 48 |
| EDITED | 26 |

**Table 5.** Use of predefined sentences.

# 7  Conclusions

The integration of speech recognition in user interfaces is feasible and, for certain kind of applications, voice represents the natural interaction modality. This is the case for the task presented in this paper, the radiological report generation, for which the A.Re.S prototype system has been implemented.

The analysis of the data collected during the on-site evaluation of A.Re.S show that, on average, more than two thirds of a radiological report are generated by means of dictation. Nevertheless, the availability of standard text recalling functions and keyword shortcuts is useful in shortening report generation and increasing user satisfaction.

Besides ASR subsystem performance enhancement, future work will be devoted to interface the A.Re.S system with digital X-ray machines, in order to enable display and processing of X-ray images. A sound recording feature will also be added to the system as a memo facility that will allow a user to associate vocal notes to documents.

# References

1. G. Antoniol, F. Brugnara, F. Dalla Palma, G. Lazzari, and E. Moser A.RE.S.: An interface for automatic reporting by speech. In Proceedings of the European Conference on Speech Communication and Technology, Genova, Italy, 1991.
2. L. R. Bahl, F. Jelinek, and R. L. Mercer. A maximum likelihood approach to continuous speech recognition. IEEE Transactions on Pattern Analysis and Machine Intelligence, PAMI-5(2):179–190, 1983.
3. L. R. Bahl, F. Jelinek, and R. L. Mercer. A Maximum Likelihood Approach to Continuous Speech Recognition. IEEE Transactions on Pattern Analysis and Machine Intelligence, 5(2):179–190, March 1983.
4. J. K. Baker. Trainable Grammars for Speech Recognition. In Proceedings of the Spring Conference of the Acoustical Society of America, 1979.
5. H. Cerf-Danon, S. DeGennaro, M. Ferretti, J.Gonzalez, and E. Keppel. Tangora - a large vocabulary speech recognition system for five languages. In Proceedings of the European Conference on Speech Communication and Technology, pages 215–218, Genova, Italy, September 1991.
6. M. Grice and B. Barry.  Esprit project 2589 (sam) multi-lingual speech input/output assessment, methodology and standardisation, 1985. Doc. SAM-UC-149.
7. R. Joseph. Large vocabulary voice-to-text systems for medical reporting. Speech Technology, 4(4):49–51, 1989.
8. L. F. Lamel, R. H. Kassel, and S. Seneff. Speech Database Development: Design and Analysis of the Acoustic-Phonetic Corpus. In Proceedings of the DARPA Speech Recognition Workshop, 1986.
9. J.A. Larson. Interactive software: tools for building interactive user interfaces. Prentice-Hall, Englewood Cliffs, NJ, 1992.
10. H. Ney and U. Essen. On Smoothing Techniques for Bigram-Based Natural Language Modelling. In Proceedings of the IEEE International Conference on Acoustics, Speech and Signal Processing, pages 825–828, Toronto, Canada, 1991.

11. David S. Pallett. Performance assessment of automatic speech recognizers, 1985. Journal of Research of the National Bureau of Standards.

12. A. I. Rudnicky and M. H. Sakamoto. Transcription Conventions and Evaluation Techniques for Spoken Language System Research. Technical Report 9204-11, School of Computer Science, CMU, Pittsburgh, PA, 1989.

# Task Interference with a Discrete Word Recognizer

Caryn Hubbard and James H Bradford

Department of Computer Science, Brock University,
St. Catharines, Ontario, Canada L2S 3A1

**Abstract.** Speaker dependent, discrete word recognition is the simplest and most successful form of automatic speech recognition. In the near future, it is likely that this technique will be the basis for a variety of commercial speech interfaces. However, discrete word recognition requires users to insert relatively long pauses between each word of an utterance. This paper describes an experiment that was performed to determine whether this unusual way of speaking will interfere with the performance of complex tasks.

## 1 Introduction

Speech recognition technology has reached a point were it may soon be incorporated into many kinds of user interface. At present, the most robust and readily available speech recognizers are those based on discrete word recognition. Such recognizers match individual words against pre-recorded speech templates and as a result, cannot discriminate the words spoken in continuous speech. Thus a user must speak with a distinct pause between each word. Clearly this is an unnatural way for users to speak. The user of an interface based on discrete word recognition must devote attention to maintaining the cadence of discontinuous speech. As a consequence, the user must attend to two distinct tasks: the speaking task, and the system operation task. Will the speaking task interfere with the operation task and thus degrade user performance? Our paper describes an experiment which suggests that such interference not only occurs but may be quite significant. This may have important implications for applications which already place a heavy cognitive load on the user. Applications such as cockpit interfaces, weapon controls, teleoperation systems, and other performance-critical real-time systems may be unsuitable for this kind of speech interface.

There have been a number of recent papers which have listed potential applications for speech recognition systems [1, 9, 10]. The recommendations tend to favour complex environments such as airplane cockpits, the "CanadaArm" aboard the Space Shuttle, and a variety of mechanisms designed to assist the disabled. In addition, several authors have made the point that current speech recognition technology does not come close to achieving the competency of the average human listener. It is frequently pointed out that the most reliable variant of the various speech technologies handles only discontinuous speech [4, 6, 7, 8].

Thus current wisdom would argue in favour of discontinuous speech recognition as a basis for interfaces to complex systems. Such a perspective is understandable since practical speech recognition technology is a recent enough development that the human factors of using it in an interface are only now being studied. For example, Casali et al. [2] have examined the effects of recognition accuracy and vocabulary size of a speech recognition system on overall task performance and user acceptance. An important aspect of Casali's work is the examination of the task interference that may occur with interfaces that use speech as well as other interaction modalities. Most dual task interference research has focussed on speech that is articulated in a "natural" continuous style [1, 2, 6, 7, 8, 9]. However, since the first practical speech interfaces will probably be based on discontinuous recognition, work needs to be done on the interference effects for this speaking style. This is particularly true since the envisioned applications are primarily associated with complex environments where the user is already under a heavy cognitive and perceptual load.

## 2 The Experiment

In preparing our experimental design we gave considerable thought to the choice of a suitable system task. Since speech interfaces have been proposed for a number of systems in which the user's hands and eyes are kept busy, we looked for a challenging hand/eye task. In addition, the task we chose would have to be easy to explain to those subjects with no prior system experience. We also wanted a task that was common enough so that we could find at least a few subjects who could be considered experts. As a final criteria we sought a task in which user performance would be easy to measure.

We eventually chose the video game, Super Mario Bros by Nintendo™ as the task that came closest to satisfying all of our criteria. This video game requires a player to navigate through a simulated environment while solving various problems encountered during the trip. The game is played under a time constraint and the game hardware automatically computes a score based on the speed and efficiency with which the player solves the problems present in the game environment. The game can be extremely challenging and we believe it qualifies as a "complex environment" such as those proposed for speech-based interfaces.

Our subjects were 54 first year psychology students (30 females and 24 males) with an average age of 20.12 years. All subjects were native English speaking and had no detectable speech impediments. Subjects were required to have some experience with video games and self-reported their experience level with the video game (we used a 5 point scale ranging from novice to expert).

The experiment was conducted under 3 separate conditions: silent (playing the game silently), continuous (playing the game while articulating in "normal" continuous speech), and discontinuous (playing the game while articulating in discontinuous speech). The subjects were divided so that the 3 conditions were performed in each of 6 possible orders with an equal number of subjects performing in each order. A three minute break was allotted between the performance of each condition. The 3 conditions were explained to the subjects, and an instruction manual was provided to each subject. In addition, subjects were given a 5 minute practice session with the video game.

For the conditions which involved either continuous or discontinuous speech the subjects were required to articulate short phrases describing their current game activity[1]. The utterances consisted of the following: "punch from below", "jump on top of", "shoot with fireballs", and "escape enemy" (each utterance corresponds to some game activity). The possible articulation errors were: not articulating the correct phrase or not articulating when appropriate. Subjects were informed of articulation errors by an acoustic signal, and then corrected to prevent future errors. The number of articulation errors in the game was recorded along with the final game score. The discontinuous condition allowed the possibility of a third kind of articulation error.

Specifically, subjects were required to pause for at least 1 second between words. An inadequate pause was considered to be an articulation error for discontinuous speech.

## 3 Results

The main finding of our experiment was that discontinuous speech degrades task performance. Not only were the game scores lower in the discontinuous condition but the number of articulation errors was higher as well. By analyzing the subjects' mean scores for all 3 conditions and it was found that there was no significant effect between the silent and continuous conditions.

A repeated measures analysis of variance was performed for the total score across the three conditions and a significant interaction was found $F (2, 106) = 15.680$, $p < .001$. A repeated measures analysis for level reached across the three conditions also produced a significant interaction, $F (2, 106) = 5.834$, $p < .01$. The mean score and mean level reached in each condition is shown in table 1. A main effect for total score was found between the silent and discontinuous conditions $F (1,53) = 21.296$, $p < .001$, and between the continuous and discontinuous conditions $F (1, 53) = 18.761$, $p < .001$, although there was no significant effect between the silent and continuous conditions[2]. This suggests that articulation per se does not degrade task performance. The implication is that the observed task interference arose solely from the effort involved in producing discontinuous speech.

| Condition | Total Score | | Final Level Reached | |
|---|---|---|---|---|
| | $M$ | $SD$ | $M$ | $SD$ |
| silent | 57004.630 | 56942.906 | 3.722 | 2.884 |
| continuous | 50723.148 | 48893.307 | 3.481 | 2.546 |
| discontinuous | 32122.222 | 34014.186 | 2.852 | 2.227 |

Table 1  The Means (S.D.) of the Total Score and Final Level Reached for Each Condition

Our experiment also indicated that the impact of expertise varied in each of the 3 conditions. In the silent condition the difference in scores between novices and experts were much greater than in the discontinuous condition (the continuous case was intermediate but closer to the silent case).

A repeated measures analysis of variance was performed on experience level and the total score for each condition. A significant interaction was found, $F (1, 52) = 89.524$, $p < .001$, indicating that experience has an effect across conditions. The mean experience level was 2.241 ($SD= 1.098$, $N=54$). Experience was found to affect the variance in scores between the silent and discontinuous conditions, $F (1, 52) = 23.826$, $p < .001$; between the silent and continuous conditions, $F (1,52) =6.685$, $p < .05$; and between the continuous and discontinuous conditions, $F (1, 52) = 8.997$, $p < .01$. These results indicate that experience has an effect on performance, but affects each condition differently.

A linear regression was performed on experience and each of the conditions, to determine the relationships. Experience was shown to positively correlate with performance in, the silent condition, $r = .631$ ($p < .001$); the continuous condition, $r = .517$ ($p < .001$); and in the discontinuous condition $r = .459$ ($p < .001$). A regression was also performed for the mean of performance score across conditions with experience level and a positive correlation was found $r = .633$ ($p < .001$). The results indicate that experience has a positive correlation with each condition. However, this relationship is strongest in the silent condition, has less of an effect in the continuous condition, and has the weakest effect in the discontinuous condition. An increase of one unit of experience level coincided with a larger increase in total score in the silent condition compared to the continuous and discontinuous conditions.

Thus the relative importance of prior expertise with respect to the game task was minimized under the discontinuous condition. This suggests that training a skill to automaticity may not protect a user from significant performance degradation if the user is required to produce discontinuous speech.

Previous studies [3, 5] have examined the role of phonetic difficulty in the dual task paradigm. These studies have concluded that an increase in articulatory control demands an increase in the level of attention, which in turn leads to interference in the performance of a concurrent task. The same process can be used to explain the interference effects of discontinuous speech on the performance of a complex task. Specifically, the articulatory control necessary in discontinuous speech requires an increase in attention which subsequently interferes with the concurrent performance of a complex task.

## 4 Conclusions

The effect of discontinuous speech on the user of complex systems is cause for concern. Speech is an entirely new modality for user interaction and the implications for user performance have only just begun to be explored. One of the motivations for using speech in an interface is that the new modality promises to relieve some of the cognitive and perceptual load from the user of very complex systems. For example, in the cockpit of an airplane the user's visual system is already used to the point of information overload to gain input from traditional displays. The user's hands are often busy operating a variety of controls. Thus the possibility of interacting verbally with at least some of an airplane's systems holds the promise of easing the user's burden. The promise may indeed be realized as the technology of speech recognition improves. However current technology places constraints on the verbal utterances of users that are different enough from normal speech to be distracting. Our preliminary results suggest that this distraction may impair the performance of the users of complex systems.

More work is needed on the human factors of speech interaction with computers. For example, our experiment focussed on subjects who had no prior experience with discontinuous speech. It is possible that speaking discontinuously can be trained to automaticity. Even then, there is no guarantee that task interference will be eliminated. However, longitudinal studies are clearly required. In addition, it seems plausible that the nature of the spoken dialogue will influence the degree of interference. Spoken commands may complement hand/eye tasks or they might relate to some other task that must be accomplished in the same time frame as the hand/eye tasks. It is not clear which situation would produce the least amount of interference.

The paper begins the work of examining the human factors of discontinuous speech recognition. As the strengths and weaknesses of the new speech recognition technology are identified, this new kind of user interaction will take its rightful place in the family of techniques available to the user interface designer.

## Notes

1. This was of particular interest to us because one of the authors (James Bradford) is developing an interface for teleoperation systems in which the operator verbally describes what he or she is doing while operating the system. Thus speech and action are redundant and provide the basis for a much more error resistant interface.

2. In addition, a between groups analysis of variance was performed on both the total score and level reached to determine order effects. There was no significant interaction between the groups or within the conditions.

**Acknowledgements.** This research was supported in part by the Natural Sciences and Engineering Research Council of Canada grant OGPIN007.

## References

1. W.D. Byblow: Effects of redundancy in the comparison of speech and pictorial displays in the cockpit environment. Applied Ergonomics 21 (2), 121-128 (1990)

2. S.P. Casali,, B.H. Williges, R.D. Dryden: Effects of recognition accuracy and vocabulary size of a speech recognition system on task performance and user acceptance. Human Factors 32 (2), 183-196 (1990)

3. R.E. Hicks: Interhemispheric response competition between vocal and unimanual performance in normal adult human males. Journal of Comparative and Physiological Psychology 89, 50-60 (1975)

4. D. Jones, K. Hapeshi, C. Frankish: Design guidelines for speech recognition interfaces. Applied Ergonomics 20 (1), 47-52 (1989)

5. A.G. Kahmi,, J.J. Masterson: The reliability of the time-sharing paradigm. Brain and Language 29, 324-341 (1986)

6. K. Lee, A.G. Hauptmann, A.I. Rudnicky: The spoken word. Byte 1, 225-232 (1990)

7. R.G. Leiser: Improving natural language and speech interfaces by the use of metalinguistic phenomena. Applied Ergonomics 20 (3), 168-173 (1989)

8. J. Makhoul, F. Jelnik, L. Rabiner, C. Weinstein, V. Zue: Spoken language systems. Annual Review of Computer Science 4, 481-501

9.  J.M. Noyes, R. Haigh, A.F. Starr: Automatic speech recognition for disabled people. Applied Ergonomics 20 (4), 293-298 (1989)

10. M.R. Taylor: DVI and its role in future avionic systems. Research Report: Smiths Industries Aerospace and Defence Systems, UK (1990)

# Model of Utterance and Its Use
# in Cooperative Response Generation

Koichi YAMADA*, Riichiro MIZOGUCHI**, Naoki HARADA*,
Akira NUKUZUMA*, Keiichi ISHIMARU*, Hiroshi FURUKAWA*

\* Laboratory for International Fuzzy Engineering Research
Siber Hegner Building 3FL, 89-1 Yamashita-cho,
Naka-ku, Yokohama-shi 231, JAPAN

\*\* The Institute of Scientific and Industrial Research, Osaka University
8-1, Mihogaoka, Ibaragi, Osaka 567, JAPAN

**Abstract:** A cooperative response model is proposed for interactive intelligent systems that recognizes user intentions and makes cooperative responses. Though many models developed so far have shown that they can achieve some form of cooperative responses, the coverage of each model is limited. In this paper, we propose a model which covers various types of cooperative responses. The paper starts with a classification of cooperative responses and discusses the relation between intentions and responses. Based on the discussion, a user utterance model is introduced and an intention recognition mechanism is developed employing domain-independent rules and knowledge about the normal usage of the topic object. The recognized intentions are then used to generate appropriate cooperative responses.

## 1 Introduction

A major problem in the area of user-computer interaction is the lack of natural communication. Person-machine dialogues do not have the "cooperative" feel that person-person dialogues do. The essential difference between these two types of communication is in how responses are generated.

Since the early 1980s, many models [1-6] for cooperative responses have been developed. In the field of databases, a common idea is to rewrite the original query so that the answers to the rewritten queries would be cooperative responses [2,5,6]. Kaplan [2] showed that indication of the smallest failing subquery can be a cooperative response when the original query is failed. He also considered to generalize a query by removing the failing part in order to generate answers related to the original query. Motro [5] also considered a user interface which informs the user of the failing subquery and shows subqueries to the user that provide related information. Cohen et al. [4] proposed a framework of cooperative expert systems, which adds various reasons (including alternative plans) to the answer according to the user's goals and background. The generation of the reasons and inference of goals are, however, conducted in the expert system. In the area of speech act theory, Allen & Perrault [1] proposed a model that achieves a few helpful responses by inferring the speaker's potential obstacles (goals impossible to achieve without the respondent's help).

While so many approaches have been proposed so far, the coverage of each model is not wide enough. There are few studies that deal with various types of cooperative responses. The objective of our research is to develop a more complete response model which integrates various cooperative responses done by human beings.

We start by classifying cooperative responses and showing the role user's intentions play in generating them. We then introduce a user utterance model and develop an intention recognition mechanism, employing both domain-independent rules and knowledge about the normal usage of the topic object. Finally, we show how the recognized intentions are used to generate all the cooperative responses classified.

## 2 Cooperative Responses

We assume that a cooperative response consists of one direct and one or more indirect responses. A direct response is one that responds to the direct intention (literal meaning) of a question, and an indirect response is one that responds to an indirect intention[1] or to a precondition of an intention. Then, we identified 13 types of responses classified into four major groups (Table 1). Before going into the details of cooperative response generation mechanism, we describe each response type in turn.

### 2.1 Precondition-related Responses (PRR)

These are responses to a precondition of an intention. Preconditions are the conditions that need to hold for the intention to be satisfied.

Table 1. Indirect Responses

1) Precondition-related responses (PRR)
• Correcting precondition (CRP)
• Notifying precondition (NTP)
• Confirming precondition (CNP)
• Showing alternative (SHA)
2) Information-related responses (IRR)
• Adding desired information (ADI)
• Adding relational information (ARI)
• Adding alternative information (AAI)
• Adding indirect information (AII)
3) Reason-related responses (RRR)
• Reasons for disappointment (RDS)
• Reasons for unusual answer (RUN)
• Reasons for usual answer (RUS)
4) Responses by question (RBQ)
• Questions to cooperate (QCP)
• Questions to identify intentions (QII)

---

[1] For now, this means non-direct intention. Later, we will give a more precise definition for intentions.

Correcting Precondition (CRP) response is that which corrects the questioner's misunderstanding of a precondition such as:

Q1: From where does the bus for the Yokohama Museum (YM) leave?
A11: There is no bus for the YM.
A12: Over there, but the YM is not open today.

A11 is a response that has been studied mainly in the field of databases [2,6]. Preconditions are derived from noun phrases in the query and checked to see if the database supports them or not. However, A12 cannot be generated in that way. The respondent must infer the higher-level intention that the questioner wants to enjoy fine arts at the YM, and know that it is impossible unless the YM is open.

There is also the case where the respondent indicates a precondition of an intention (NTP), rather than correcting it, though this has not been discussed in the previous works.

Q2: Can I park here?
A2: Yes, but you must buy a parking ticket.

Which type of response we use may depend on the linguistic custom, but NTP tends to be used when the subject of the precondition is the questioner,
otherwise CRP is used. In the case where the respondent does not know if a precondition is satisfied or not, he/she might respond by a question to confirm whether the questioner has a parking ticket or not (CNP).

When a precondition does not hold, the intention cannot be achieved. In this case, a cooperative respondent might give an alternative plan which still satisfies a higher-level intention (SHA).

Q3: When is the next flight for New York?
A3: The next flight is completely booked,
      but there's still room on one that leaves at 8:04. [7]

## 2.2 Information-related Responses (IRR)

These are responses that add information to the direct response. Depending on what kind information is added, there are four types of IRRs.

Adding Desired Information (ADI) and Adding Relational Information (ARI) are indirect responses giving information which the questioner might want and giving information related to the question, respectively.

Q4: Does the flight leave in the morning?
A4: Yes, it leaves at 8:00 a.m. from gate 5.

In the above example, 8:00 a.m. is the desired information (ADI) and Gate 5 is relational (ARI). If the respondent does not know the desired information, he may give some indirect information (AII) such as "I don't know, but it arrives at Tokyo in the early afternoon."

Besides these responses studied in the previous works [1,2,6], we introduce a little different response (AAI) added to the "no" answer to a question about the existence or possession of something.

Q5: Is there a curtain in the living room?
A5: No, but there is a blind instead.

In the above, the respondent infers what the questioner wants to do with a curtain, then informs of the existence of an alternative which satisfies the intention. The respondent would not give an answer like "No, but there is one in the bedroom" in this case, because the intention of the questioner is *to cover the window of THE LIVING ROOM with something.* If the question were about a TV set, however, it would be appropriate to respond that there is one in the bedroom.

## 2.3 Reason-related Responses (RRR)

There are cases where we state a reason after the direct response. Some of CRPs such as A11 are interpreted as reasons why queries are failed. Besides such cases, we have classified reasons into three groups: Reasons for Disappointment (RDS), Reasons for Unusual Answer (RUN), and Reasons for Usual Answer (RUS).

RDS is observed when the respondent cannot meet the questioner's expectation, which is an intention with an action whose subject is the respondent.

Q6: Will you go back with me ?
A6: No, I will drop by at a book store.

RUN occurs when the direct response is unusual or is different from the standard one. The next is a typical example of RUN.

Q7: Has flight 208 been canceled?
A71: Yes, the fog is too thick.

Sometimes, a reason is added even if the flight has not been canceled (RUS). This is because usualness depends on the situation.

A72: No, though it is foggy.

## 2.4 Responses by Question (RBQ)

Besides CNP, there are cases where the respondent answers with a question. One is Question to Cooperate (QCP), which is a question asking for the information needed to respond to the questioner's request.

Q8: Do you have a blind on this floor?
A8: Yes. Which color do you want?

The other is Question to Identify Intentions (QII), which is done when intentions are not recognized.

Q9: Do you have a spoon with you? (in a train)
A9: No. What do you want to do with it?

## 3 Utterance model

We assume that each *speech act* by a user has a primary goal (*primary intention*), which can be organized as a goal hierarchy as shown in Fig. 1. The goals in the hierarchy are expressed as *actions* which the speaker wants to do. When a speech act is observed, a terminal of the goal hierarchy could be its *direct intention*. The parent of the direct intention is an *indirect intention*.

The actions are divided into two groups: *know-actions* expressed in "know" predicates and *do-actions* expressing other kinds of actions. The lowest goal with a do-action between the primary and the direct intentions is called *purpose*, and subgoals of the purpose with a know-action are called *relational intentions*. For example, when the direct intention is "to know if train-1 leaves at 8:00 or not", the indirect intention might be "to know when train-1 leaves" and the purpose might be "to get on train-1". A relational intention might then be "to know which gate train-1 leaves from". Of course, there are cases where the purpose coincides with the direct or the indirect intention.

All goals between the direct and the primary intentions are the user's intentions at different levels. However, we deal with only a few of the intentions mentioned above. Recognizing intentions in the model means building the lower part of the hierarchy corresponding to the user's speech act, that is, inferring the purpose, indirect, and relational intentions from the direct intention.

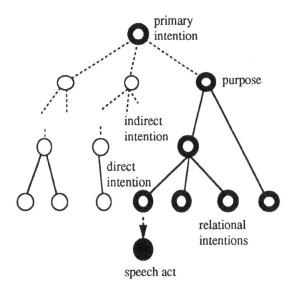

**Fig. 1.** User utterance model

# 4 Intention Recognition

## 4.1 Intention Inference Rules

The goal hierarchy is built by interpreting intention inference rules, which are domain-independent in the sense that they have unspecified actions, such as "do-something" or "know-something", instead of concrete actions in their antecedents and consequents.

These rules are divided into two groups: know-rules and do-rules (Fig. 2). Know-rules are used to infer the indirect intention with a know-action in the backward manner. Do-rules are used in both the forward and the backward manner to infer the purpose and relational intentions, respectively.

Inference itself is done by simple pattern matching. If the direct intention is given as

know(subj:user, if:is(subj:size(apartment-1),comp:big)),
/# know if the size of apartment-1 is big #/

and rule K1 is applied to it in the backward manner, we can get the indirect intention:

know(subj:user, that:is(subj:size(apartment-1),comp:?)).
/# know what the size of apartment-1 is #/

Then, if we apply rule D2 to the indirect one in the backward manner, the next purpose with an unspecified action is obtained:

do(subj:user,?P:apartment-1).
/# do something about apartment-1 #/

Finally, if we apply D2 in the forward manner, we can obtain the following relational intentions:

know(subj:user, that:is(subj:z(apartment-1),comp:?)),
/# know what other attributes of A-1 are #/

K1: know(subj:x,that:is(subj:y,comp:?))
-> know(subj:x,if:is(subj:y,comp:z)
K2: know(subj:x,that:is(subj:y(?|c),comp:w))
-> know(subj:x,if:is(subj:y(z|c),comp:w))
  (a) examples of know-rules

D1: do(subj:x,?P:(y|c)(is(subj:z(y),comp:w)))
-> know(subj:x,that:is(subj:z(?|c),comp:w))
D2: do(subj:x,?P:y)
-> know(subj:x,that:is(subj:z(y),comp:?))
  (b) examples of do-rules

Fig. 2. Examples of Intention inference rules

where, variable z is not specified, but can be assigned an arbitrary attribute, such as rental-fee or distance-from-station.

## 4.2 Identification of purpose

In the previous section, the purpose of the user's utterance was not identified. To determine the concrete action, we use knowledge about the normal-use of the topic object[2], which is (and must be, as described later) the value of parameter "?P:" in the unidentified purpose. In the example above, the topic is apartment-1 and its normal-use is "to rent it". We can then identify the purpose as rent(subj:user, obj:apartment-1).

There are objects, however, which have different uses in different situations. To cope with these cases, we need additional knowledge for the normal-use shown in Fig. 3. The figure shows that curtains are regarded as daily-necessaries or goods. In the former case, its normal-use is to cover a window, and the situation in which it is used is home-life. In the latter case, the normal-use is to buy it, which occurs when the situation is shopping.

The issue then is how to identify the situation. To do this, we employ the following two kinds of information: 1) previous topics and 2) place information (from the question or from where the speech act happens). If "home-life" or "shopping" exists in the previous topics, the situation must be home-life or shopping, respectively. When neither of them is found, the system uses place information and knowledge of "normal-place" to express the place where it is normally used. For example, let's consider Q5 and the next question:

Q10: Is there a curtain in the store?

From the place information in the questions and the knowledge of normal-place, we can determine that Q5 and Q10 are uttered in the situation of home-life and shopping, respectively.

Finally, "normal-area" is knowledge which restricts the area in which the normal-place is located. This is used when a cooperative response is generated.

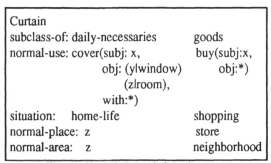

Fig. 3. Knowledge of Curtain

---

[2] In this model, topics are managed by a Topic Packet Network [8].

### 4.3 Conflict Resolution

So far, we have discussed the inference mechanism without considering conflict resolution, choosing a rule from several applicable rules.

First, we will discuss inference of intentions expressed by a know-action. In this case, we do not have to resolve any conflict of rules, because it does not make a response less cooperative to give more information than needed. When you are asked if there is a restaurant on this block, your response can include the direct answer, the specific place, the name, and the type of the restaurant, like "Yes, there is an Italian restaurant named Antonio's on the corner".

In the case where we need to infer the purpose in the backward manner by do-rules, we use the current topic to choose a rule. As described before, parameter "?P:" of a do-action in the do-rules must have the topic object as its value. This restriction eliminates some rules from the candidates that have been selected from all rules by pattern matching. If there still remain multiple rules, we choose one by using the priorities assigned to them.

## 5 Response Generation

### 5.1 Precondition-Related Responses

In order to make a Precondition-related response, the system must derive preconditions from intentions. We do this by using knowledge about actions expressing intentions. In Q1, suppose that the purpose is obtained as follows from the normal-use of a museum:

enjoy(subj:user,obj:(x|fine-arts), where:YM,area:YM).
/# enjoy fine arts at YM #/

The preconditions of the purpose are obtained from the knowledge of actions in Fig. 4:

1) possess(subj:user,obj:fee(YM)),
2) possess(subj:user,obj:qualification(YM)),
3) is(subj:YM,comp:open),

where fee and qualification of YM are obtained from the object, the-Yokohama-Museum.

The derived preconditions are checked in the database to see if they are satisfied or not. If there is an unsatisfied one, CRP or NTP is generated.

NTP is chosen when the value of parameter "sub:" is the user, otherwise CRP is chosen. NTP and CRP are generated by adding "must" and "not" to the precondition, respectively.

must(possess(subj:user, obj:qualification(YM)))
/# user must possess qualifications for YM #/

not(is(subj:YM,comp:open))
/# YM is not open #/

```
enjoy(subj:(xlperson),obj:y,where:(zlhall))
    preconditions:
        possess(subj:x,obj:fee(z))
            default=satisfied, priority=3
        enter(subj:x,obj:z)
            priority=1


enter(subj:(xlperson)obj:(ylhall))
    preconditions:
        possess(subj:x,obj:qualification(y))
            default=ask, priority=1
        is(subj:y,comp:open)
            default=satisfied, priority=2


go-to(subj:(xlperson),obj:(ylplace))
    decomposition:
        take(subj:x,
            obj:(zlconveyance)
            (bound-for(subj:z,obj:y))
```

**Fig. 4.** Knowledge of actions

When there is no data which determines if the precondition is satisfied or not, the default action is used. When the action is ask or notify, a CNP or NTP response is given, respectively. If it is satisfied, no PRR response is given.

When a precondition of the purpose is not satisfied so that it cannot be achieved, the system tries to give a SHA response. To do so, the higher-level intention of the purpose must be inferred and another purpose found which satisfies the upper one. We do this using the rules in Fig. 5.

DD1 and DD2 rules are saying that a person who wants to do something wants to do its decomposed or preconditional actions. From these rules and knowledge about actions, the system can infer that a person whose purpose is to take a flight somewhere actually wants to go to that place, and that a person who asks about a membership in a club actually wants to join that club.

Suppose that for the next purpose, one of its preconditions is not satisfied.

take(subj:user, obj:plane-1 (bound-for (subj:plane-1, obj:New-York)))
/# take plane-1 bound for New York #/

By using rule DD1 and knowledge about go-to action in Fig. 4 in the backward manner, the upper-level intention is inferred as

go-to(subj:user,obj:New-York).
/# go to New York #/

Then, by applying the same rule and knowledge in the forward manner, the following action is derived:

```
DD1: do(subj:(x|person))
      -> do-decomposition(subj:x)
DD2: do(subj:(x|person))
      -> do-precondition(subj:x)
```

**Fig. 5.** do-do rules

take(subj:user, obj:(x|conveyance) (bound-for(subj:x,obj:NY)).
/# take a conveyance bound for New York #/

Finally, if the system finds an instance of conveyance which matches "x" in the database, it can show it as an alternative (such as the answer A3).

## 5.2 Information-Related Responses

Among the four types of Information-Related Responses, ADI and ARI are easily realized by finding an answer to the know-action of the inferred intention. ADI is a response to an indirect intention with a know-action, and ARI is a response to a relational intention.

In case of AII, however, the system must have some domain knowledge to infer the necessary information from other information. When the system does not know the necessary information, but knows something else which has some relation to it, it can add the related information as AII to the direct answer "I don't know".

As for AAI, we can see how to realize it by the Q10 example. Suppose that the purpose of question Q10 is obtained as follows using the knowledge in Fig. 3:

buy(subj:user,obj:(x|curtain), where:(y|store), area:the-neighborhood).
/# buy a curtain at a store in the neighborhood #/

Notice that the value of the parameter "where:" is uninstantiated. This means that the user does not care which store it is, if it is in the neighborhood. So, if the direct answer to the question is no, the system can check other stores in the neighborhood and add an AAI giving another store that has curtains.

In the case of Q5, the situation is "home-life" and the purpose is obtained as follows:

cover(subj:user, obj:(x|window)(LR), with:(z|curtain), where:LR, area:LR).
/# cover a window in LR with a curtain #/

Notice that the value of parameter "where:" is instantiated, unlike Q10 here. Therefore, even if there is a curtain in the bedroom, the system does not say that "There is one in the bedroom". Rather, the system tries to find an object which has the same normal-use as curtain in a home-life situation, and if it finds blind instead of curtain, it says "No, but there is a blind in the living room".

## 5.3 Other Responses

RRRs and RBQs are responses which need considerable domain knowledge, besides the knowledge needed for intention recognition.

An RDS response is achieved when the purpose of the user has an action which the system should, but cannot do. In order to obtain the reason, the system must have the domain knowledge that gives what the obstacle is. One of the easiest cases is when the system does not have the capability to do it. Another is the case of missing data in the database.

RUN can be implemented by regarding the usual answer as the default. A RUN response is triggered when the direct answer is different from the default. The reason is obtained from the antecedent of the domain rule which determined the unusual answer. On the contrary, RUS is generated when the rule failed because the certainty factor of a datum is slightly smaller than the threshold needed to fire it.

QCP occurs when the system must solve a problem to answer the user's question or to meet the user's expectation. The knowledge needed is therefore domain-dependent. Finally, QII occurs when the system fails to recognize the intentions. However, caution is needed at implementation to avoid the system becoming too meddlesome.

## 6 Conclusions

A cooperative response model for interactive intelligent systems was proposed. This model includes a user utterance model used to define different kinds of intentions. Intentions are recognized by building a part of the hierarchy using intention inference rules, which are domain-independent in the sense that they have unspecified actions in their antecedents and consequents. The concrete actions are identified by referring to normal-use knowledge regarding the topic object. When there are different uses in different situations, additional object knowledge is used to identify the situation.

Ways to generate cooperative responses were then shown. These are composed of direct and indirect responses, which are generated using knowledge about actions and objects together with some domain knowledge.

The examples presented demonstrate that the proposed model enables various types of cooperative responses, some of which had not been dealt with in previous models.

## References

1. J.F. Allen, C.R. Perrault: Analyzing Intention in Utterances, *Artificial Intelligence* **15**, 143-178 (1980).
2. S.J. Kaplan: Cooperative Responses from a Portable Natural Language Query System, *Artificial Intelligence* **19**, 165-187 (1982)
3. D.J. Litman, J.F. Allen: A Plan Recognition Model for Subdialogues in Conversations, *Cognitive Science* **11**, 163-200 (1987)
4. R. Cohen, et al.: Providing Responses Specific To A User's Goals And Background, *Int. J. Expert Systems* **2**(2), 135-162 (1989)
5. A. Motro: FLEX: A Tolerant and Cooperative User Interface to Databases, *IEEE Trans. Knowledge and Data Engineering*, **2**(2), 231-246 (1990)
6. T. Gaasterland, et al.: An Overview of Cooperative Answering, *J. Intelligent Information Systems* **1**, 123-157 (1992)
7. E. Rich: Users are individuals: individualizing user models, *Int. J. Man-Machine Studies* **18**, 199-214 (1983)

8. Y.Yamashita, et al.: MASCOTS II: A Dialog Manager in General Interface for Speech Input and Output, *Trans. on Information and Systems*, Vol.E76-D, No.1, 74-83 (1993)

# Special Computer Interfaces for the Visually Handicapped: F.O.B.[1] The Manufacturer

Arthur I. Karshmer & Richard L. Oliver

Computer Science Department
Computing Research Laboratory
New Mexico State University
Las Cruces, NM 88003 USA

*karshmer@nmsu.edu*
*rroliver@nmsu.edu*

**Abstract.** Many techniques have been suggested, and some even brought to market, to allow the visually handicapped person to more easily interact with modern computing equipment. Most of the work to date has focused on providing special purpose hardware and software to accomplish this task. In the current work, we describe an approach that would allow all computer manufacturers to ship systems based on today's popular graphical user interfaces (GUIs) that will also serve the needs of the visually handicapped user. By building the user interface into the GUI normally supplied by the manufacturer, the cost of such interfaces should go down, while the availability should go up.

## 1    Introduction

The need to lend support to visually handicapped computer users has been acknowledged for some time. Many systems have been designed and developed over the years and a few have even made it to market. In somewhat typical projects [25, 26, 10, 11] the philosophical approach taken was to redesign the computing environment to suit the visually handicapped user. These systems involved the synthesis of technologies uniquely suited to the visually handicapped to provide a more *comfortable* interface without much concern for the bandwidth of the interface, and it was suited only for use by the visually impaired. Recent thought has lead us to believe that this was a philosophically incorrect approach. Our current approach is to use a variety of highly organized sounds to enhance already existing visually based interfaces so they will provide a compatible and reasonably high bandwidth communication channel for sighted and non-sighted users on the same hardware/software platform. Thus, our new approach should lead to more economical products for the visually impaired, facilitate interactions between sighted and non-sighted users and may enhance the satisfaction and performance of sighted users.

Recent developments in computer interfaces have made it possible to present ever increasing amounts of information to the user in a visually meaningful form. Window and graphical display systems make it possible to display in many windows, and in many forms, large amounts of information. Nearly all of this information is visually presented;

---

1. F.O.B. is a commonly used abbreviation in English. It is short for Free-on-Board which implies that it is shipped directly from the manufacturer.

only a small fraction is presented via auditory channels. With the rapid advances in, and availability of technology, sound enhanced user interfaces are becoming increasing possible and attractive. Research in many areas has produced results that can be directly applied to the problems of sound enhanced interface design.

Research into computer generated **virtual worlds** [4] has produced the notion of an "audio window" in which a spatial sound presentation system positions sound sources associated with a three-dimensional audio space. "Flitters" are used to emphasize or mute particular audio windows based upon their current activity. Sound generation uses audio signal processing to exploit the psycho-acoustic properties of human hearing. The generalization of display systems for three-dimensional acoustic information has been examined in [23, 24], thus providing a reasonable expectation that non-individualized sound based interfaces can be constructed.

In the area of speaking interfaces, the XSpeak system [19, 20] demonstrates that spoken commands can be used to aid in the navigation through a set of windows. Speech input proved to be neither faster nor slower than navigation with the mouse. Playback of digitally recorded speech for fixed text has long been possible; however, high quality text-to-speech synthesis for arbitrary text is also now possible [18].

Considerable research has been done to identify non-speech sounds for use in sound enhanced interfaces. One proposal is to use a system of naturally occurring sounds or 'everyday sounds' to represent actions within the interface [8]. In another interesting work, a musical sound was used to represent the peaks and valleys in the infrared spectrum of a chemical compound [17]. It has also been demonstrated that a rich set of musical variables (rhythm, pitch, timbre, register, dynamics) can be used to establish families of the audio equivalent to *icons* [1]. An excellent introduction to this area of research is given in [3].

While researchers have used sound to enhance learning and usability of computer interfaces, the choice of which sounds (pitches) to use has often been made without the benefit of solid empirical data. The frequent implication is that an individual who is not musically trained might not be able to make use of real musical information presented by the interface. There is however, a growing body of research which indicates that even untrained listeners can consistently identify sounds in a given tonal context. Studies have shown positive results in "well-fittedness," indicating the presence of perceivable qualities in sounds from an established context [12, 2].

Further, parallels have been shown between speech and sound cognition [5, 13], with results pointing to the possibility of developing a functional hierarchy of sounds to be attached to an interface/menuing system. The important finding here is that a listener's understanding of a particular aural event depends heavily on how that event relates to any prior events, and this in turn affects potential future events as well.

The implication for our work is that many of these theories have not yet been fully explored and tested empirically. We are developing hierarchical sets of context related sounds and attach them to related features in an interface. By measuring learning and response times for non-sighted users, we expect to show that the appropriate use of such sounds can help visually impaired users learn a system faster and use it both faster and more efficiently than with more conventional systems. The major departure here is that we are embedding our enhancements into already existing visual interfaces. The net result of the work will be to extend a common computing environment to a number of groups of users: each having different needs. The interface tools will present no obstacle

---

2. The term *earcon* has been suggested to be the auditory equivalent to the now commonplace icon [10].

to sighted users, and indeed may prove to be beneficial to them as well. Our approach should make the delivery of *special* services to *special* users transparent and therefore encourage major manufacturers to move in this necessary direction. In a world of different interfaces for different people, the result was predictable - if the special user group did not represent a significant number of potential sales, the probability of offering such products was dramatically reduced. Hence, special needs have often gone unmet by commercial developers.

# 2  Project Description

The goal of our research effort is to test several new concepts in computer interface design for the visually handicapped, and then to integrate these concepts into a commercial product. For a variety of reasons, we have selected OpenWindows as our implementation environment. After testing, we will integrate two packages into OpenWindows. The final product will have exactly the same appearance to the normal user, but will supply a sound based interface to the non-sighted user.

## 2.1  A Sound Navigator

The use of menus in user interfaces has become commonplace and research results pertaining to them have been reported in the literature [15, 16]. From Macs to PCs running Windows, the menu has become the preferred mode of item selection. Unfortunately for the non-sighted user, the menu presents more problems than solutions. In this portion of our research we plan to create a menu environment that behaves exactly as expected by a sighted user, but adds musical tones to aid the non-sighted user in her navigation through the various levels. Figure 1 shows a simple test environment that we have developed and will test to determine the viability of tonally based menu searching. As the user moves the mouse across the top level of menu selections, different notes are sounded as she moves into the area of a new menu item (all tones at a given level are notes from a given family of tones). At any time, the user can request (via a mouse push) a chord which describes the current level. Once an item is selected and the appropriate mouse button is pushed, the user is taken down to the next level and again supplied with a chord that describes that level. Naturally, at any time, the user is free to move up one or more levels.

In addition to the use of musical notes, the menu navigator allows the user to turn on/off synthesized speech output at any time. In this mode, the sound navigator will supply spoken output, which in Figure 1 would be the word *animals*. We see this feature to be mainly a training tool to acclimate the user to the given menu system.

One goal of our experiments will be to assess how much faster users can navigate through tonal sequences compared to synthesized verbal labels. The primary focus here is in improving peak performance for menu-based systems that are used frequently by the visually handicapped. This amounts to enhancing the identity-matching process for aural speech [16] to levels commensurate with those for visual search. It is hoped that sighted users may also benefit from tonal cues to a menu structure, particularly when depth exceeds three levels.

In an extension to this concept we also plan on allowing the user to *pin* different levels of the menu to the virtual screen, which in this case would be represented by a multidimensional sound space. Once *pinned* the menu can be found through a mouse push that will identify all *pinned* items in the sound space by their base chords. The user will then be free to move about the sound space[3] with the mouse to randomly select a *pinned* menu.

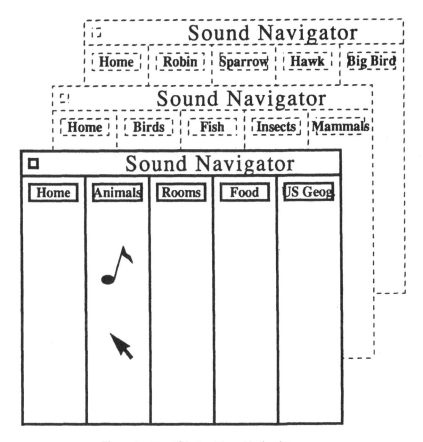

Figure 1. - Tonal/Verbal Menu Navigation

## 2.2    A Tonal Desktop

As a result of earlier work [25, 26] a system called SoundStation was developed at New Mexico State University. The culmination of these efforts was a specially modified programming environment which is shown in Figure 2 which delivered verbal and Braille output. In essence the product was a synthesis of existing technologies that included a knowledge network intended to help the visually handicapped programmer navigate through the complex task of program editing. Special *earmarks* were added to the source code both by the programmer and a modified version of the **emacs** editor. The earmarks enabled the programmer to get verbal aid in the process of editing C language programs. The system was able to describe many aspect of the program being edited including such features as: the name of the current function, the variables local to the function, the parameters being passed to the function, what functions it in turn called (one level only),

---

3. Given mouse technology, we are restricting our current concept of a sound space to two dimensions. This could be easily enhanced with the addition of the appropriate pointing device.

etc. Advanced search and replace functions were offered with verbal output. In general, the system offered a friendly environment for the visually handicapped programmer. The system was accessible through standard command line statements and its benefits were not available until the user was *in* the editor.

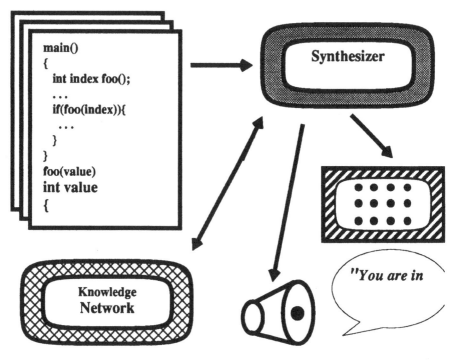

Figure 2. - Editing with Earcons in SoundStation I

Our previous experience again demonstrated that the special purpose approach we had chosen was not the best solution to the problem. While it does offer advantages, it was predicated on being part of a special user interface, not one that could be readily shared with sighted users, and further the bandwidth of the output devices was quite limited. In the **tonal desktop** part of our work, we intend to improve on our previous work and integrate it into a broader and more general environment that will be of value to sighted users as well.[4]

Figure 3 shows a typical OpenWindows desktop which includes an editing session as well as several other application icons. As the user moves the mouse about the screen, she is given tonal cues that tell the location of, or her proximity to the various icons and windows. Certain mouse key pushes allow the user to obtain more information about the current environment, or *home in* on the nearest object. Again, we have chosen to enhance

---

4. All of the features we are including in our interface can be easily turned off or on and can therefore be avoided by any user, leaving the standard OpenWindows interface intact.

an existing product to accommodate a different user group rather than create an environment suited solely to a special group.

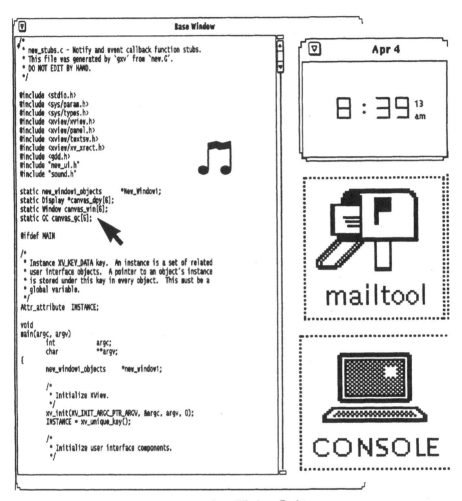

**Figure 3. - An OpenWindows Desktop**

The edit window displayed has many of the features included in the modified emacs of our previous system, with the exception of Braille output. Additionally, the user is given tonal feedback as she moves the mouse about the edit window. Different tones are used to indicate: new line, new statement, new function definition, level of indentation, etc. The tonal information should prove to be a valuable and higher speed method of navigating through program text. Naturally, at any time, the user may ask for verbal output.

When the mouse is moved outside of the edit window, more tonal information is provided describing the total work environment. As many sighted user tend to stack windows and other objects on the screen, we intend to use multidimensional sound to our advantages. With the press of a mouse key, the user will be able to identify all icons and windows and their spatial relationship to each other. Again, this feature should be of interest to the sighted user as well.

# 3 Development and Test Environment

Our initial efforts have been carried out independent of any specific computing environment. As we are a large Sun *shop*, we are embedding our interface into the OpenWindows product marketed by Sun Microsystems. It is a reasonably rich window/icon based environment and should prove an interesting testbed for our ideas. In the empirical testing portion of our work, we intend to use a variety of subjects. First, we have a large test population composed of university students. Second, we have made an agreement with the New Mexico School for the Visually Impaired in Alamagordo (approximately 100 kilometers away) to test our system using their students.

# 4 Summary

The needs of the visually handicapped segment of our society in the area of access to the fruits of the information revolution have not been adequately met. For a variety of reasons, special products developed in this area have not gained general acceptance, partially due to their prohibitive price which is a function of market size. Further, while major hardware/software suppliers have shown interest in the problem, no generally available and inexpensive systems have been produced. The major systems suppliers have viewed this area of research and development as potentially high risk and low profit. The result of all the above is that the visually impaired computer user is at a distinct disadvantage in our electronic society.

The approach we have taken combines known and available technologies, several new and promising concepts, and a sound development and testing environment which is being integrated into a standard window/icon based user interface. The result will be a product that can be shipped with every system sold, adding little cost and providing a useful, novel and higher bandwidth interface for visually impaired users. We also expect that our testing will demonstrate that the new interface will prove useful to sighted users as well.

# 5 References

1.  Blattner, M.M., et al., "Earcons and Icons: Their structure and common design principles," *Human-Computer Interaction*, volume 4, number 1, 1989, pp.: 11-44

2.  Butler, D. "Describing the Perception of Tonality in Music," *Music Perception*, Spring 1989, 6(3), 219-241.

3.  Buxton, W., "Introduction to this special issue on nonspeech audio," *Human-Computer Interaction*, volume 4, number 1, 1989, pp.:1-9.

4.  Cohen, M. and Ludwig, L. F.,"Multidimensional audio window management," *Int. J. Man-Machine Studies*, 1991, 34, pp. 319-336.

5.  Dowling, W. J, and Harwood, D.L. *Music Cognition*, Academic Press, Inc., Orlando, 1986.

6.  Edwards, A. D. N. "The Design of Auditory Interfaces for Visually Disabled Users," *Human Factors in Computing Systems (Proceedings of CHI 88)*, ACM SIG-CHI, 89-94.Edwards, A.D.N., "Soundtrack: an auditory interface for blind users," *Human-Computer Interaction*, volume 4, number 1, 1989, pp.: 45-66.

7.  Ganesan, K and Ganti, M., "A multimedia front-ent for an expert network management system," *IEEE J. Sel. Areas Commun. (USA)* volume 6, number 5, June 1989, pp.:788-91.

8.	Gaver, W.W., "The SonixFinder: an interface that uses auditory icons," *Human-Computer Interaction*, column 4, number 1, 1989, pp.: 67-94.

9.	Kapauan, A. A., et al, "Wideband packet access for workstations: integrated voice/data/image services for the UNIX PC, " GLOBECOM '86: IEEE Global Telecommunications Conference, Communications Broadening Technology Horizons Conference Record, volume 3, 1-4 December 1986, Houston, Texas, pp.: 1439-4.

10.	Karshmer, A.I., Davis, R.D. and Myler, H., "The Architecture of An Inexpensive and Portable Talking-Tactile Terminal to Aid the Visually Handicapped," *Computer Standards and Interfaces*, Vol. No. 5, 1987, North Holland Publishing, pp. 135-151.

11.	Karshmer, A.I., Davis, R.D. and Myler, H., "An Inexpensive Talking Tactile Terminal for the Visually Handicapped," *The Journal of Medical Systems*, Vol. 10, No. 3, 1986.

12.	Krumhansl, C., & Kessler, E. "Tracing the dynamic changes in perceived tonal organization in a spatial representation of musical keys," *Psychological Review*, 1982, 334-368.

13.	Lerdahl, F. and Jackendoff, R.," A Generative Theory of Tonal Music," *The MIT Press*, Cambridge, Massachussets, 1983.

14.	Ludwig, L. F., Pincever, N., and Cohen, M., "Extending the Notion of a Window System to Audio," *IEEE Computer*, August 1990, pp. 66-72.

15.	Paap, K. and Roske-Hofstrand, R., "The Optional Number of Menu Options per Panel," *Human Factors*, 1986,28(4), 377-385

16.	Paap, K. and Roske-Hofstrand, R., " The Design of Menus," *Handbook of Human-Computer Interaction*, M. Helander, ed. Elsevior Science Publishers B. V. (North Holland), 1988

17.	Peterson, I., "The Sound of Data," *Science News*, Volume 127, June 1, 1985, pp.: 348-50.

18.	Sagisaka, Yoshinori, "Speech Synthesis from Text," *IEEE Communications Magazine*, January 1990, pp. 35-41.

19.	Schmandt, C., Ackerman, M. S., Hindus, D., "Augmenting a Window System with Speech Input\," *IEEE Computer*, August 1990, pp. 50-56.

20.	Schmandt, C., McKenna, M.A., "An audio and telephone server for multi-media workstations," *Proceedings of the 2nd IEEE Conference on Computer Workstations*, 7-10 March 1988, Santa Clara, California, pp.: 150-9.

21.	Suzuki,T., et al., "CSES: an approach to integrating graphic, music and voice information into a user-friendly interface," *MIV-89 Proceedings of the International Workshop on Industrial Applications of Machine Intelligence and Vision (Seiken Symposium)*,10-12 April 1989, Tokyo, Japan, pp.: 349-54.

22.	Ting, T.C., et al, "A multi-sensory and multi-media laboratory for human-computer interaction," *1984 IEEE Computer Society Workshop on Visual Languages*, 6-8 December 1984, Hiroshima, Japan, pp.:149-56.

23.	Wenzel, E. M., Wightman, F. L., and Foster, H. S., "A Virtual Display System for Conveying Three-Dimensional Acoustic Information," *Proceedings of the Human Factors Society 32nd Annual Meeting*, 1988, pp. 86-90.

24.	Wenzel, E. M., Wightman, F. L., and Kistler, D. J.,"Localization with non-individualized virtual acoustic display cues," *CACM*, March 1991, pp. 351-359.

25. York, B.W. and Karshmer, A.I., "Tools to Support Blind Programmers," to appear in *Visual Programming Environments*, edited by E.P. Glinert, IEEE Computer Society Press (1991).

26. York, B.W. and Karshmer, A.I., "An Overview of $T^3$ - PBE," *SIGCAPH Newsletter*, ACM Press, Number 41, January, 1989.

# INTELTEXT: Producing Coherent Linear Texts While Navigating in Large Non-Hierarchical Hypertexts

Martin Subbotin and Dmitry Subbotin

State Scientific Technical Center
of Hypertext Information Technologies,
52/16 Zemlyanoj Wal, Moscow 109240, Russia
Fax: 7 (095) 200-3937
Phone: 7 (095) 297-7004, 952-0175
E-mail: HINTECH@CS.MSU.SU

**Abstract.** Inteltext is a new software technology able to automatically construct a unified text from separate text items. The main advantage of Inteltext is its ability to support those whose main work is thinking and exposing thoughts in textual form. Inteltext is capable of drawing out text items from a large heap of information and representing them in a logical and ordered form. This ordered selection should complement and confirm the assigned topic. The paper describes the underlying approach which has been developed in Russia since the 70s and the software product implementing it.

## 1   Introduction

IntelText is intended for accessing and arranging information which has no rigid structure. The approach used in it is based on a set of heuristic rules of navigation in a hypertext network.

IntelText is able to construct automatically a unified text from separate text items - nodes. Text items can be thoughts, facts, statements, assertions in a brainstorming process, etc. IntelText constructs the resulting text, picking the relevant nodes and arranging them in an order which carefully unfolds the given theme. This method is based on links which are established between the nodes.

IntelText is not just a hypertext tool, but rather an agent oriented on automatic getting of relatively complete intellectual result. Unlike AI systems, its aim is not to get a derivative knowledge, but to arrange and organize the existing information elements according to their content. The resulting text can have various names: analytical report, appreciation of a situation, survey and so on. However, for the user it looks to be meaningful, coherent and logical.

The software project began in March 1990 conducted by the authors. Since January 1992 its first commercial variants appeared under the names Sempro (Hypertext Semantics Processor) and BAHYS (Basic Hypertext System). They have got a number of users in Russia, mostly in research institutions and government bodies. In Spring 1993 a new product of this line has been issued, named IntelText.

The technology implemented in IntelText was presented at the international conferences in Moscow [4], St.-Petersburg [5], Prague (Czechoslovakia) [6] and Phoenix (USA) [7]. A number of publications describing it exists in Russian and US editions [1, 2, 3, 8].

## 2 Treatment of Hypertext

The treatment of hypertext realized in IntelText is based on the following conception.

*HYPERTEXT NODE* is a separate text item, carrying one thought or fact or assertion, i.e. a monosemantic unit.

*KEYWORD* can be assigned to the node to define its content. The main usage of keywords is for automatic linkage process, where the system selects node-candidates for linkage based on similar sets of keywords. Thus, the keywords are not used as hot spots for navigation and even do not need to be present in the text of a node. Essentially, they are external descriptors of the content of a node.

*HYPERTEXT LINK* is established between two nodes based on their semantic closeness. We assume that the semantic closeness takes place when a pair of nodes can be connected by some linking expression like "for this purpose", "in consequence of", "for example", "basing on this", "as a result of" etc. In order to avoid the arbitrary, one-sided approach, the link must be established in all cases where it could be established; that is, when some direct semantic relation between two nodes takes place.

Links are bi-directional. They have no weights or other characteristics, because the coherence of a text does not depend on the particular kind of relations connecting its sentences. They go from a node to a node rather than from a word to a node. Links can be established either manually or automatically, based on common keywords. IntelText has a fully automatic linkage mode as well as semi-automatic mode (where it suggests pairs of candidates for linkage to the user for confirmation).

As a result, the emerging net turns out to be very dense and poorly structured for browsing. However the navigation by semantic links in such net proves to be very efficient.

*HYPERTEXT NAVIGATION* in IntelText has two modes: manual and automatic. The latter constitutes the core of the technology. The automatic (algorithmic) navigation is based on the correspondence between topological and semantical connectedness of nodes in a hypertext net. The algorithms provide for composing of well-ordered sequences of text items. They are based on theoretical and empirical research conducted by the first author since early 70-s concerning patterns of semantic interconnection in coherent texts.

While navigating in the net, the possibility exists at each step to choose the next node upon a criteria of high degree of its topological connectedness with the nodes previously included in the navigation route. The resulting navigation route forms a coherent text elaborating the semantic content of the initial node(s).

A conventional example of semantic navigation is shown on the figure.

# INTELTEXT: Navigation through
# hypertext net using topological criteria

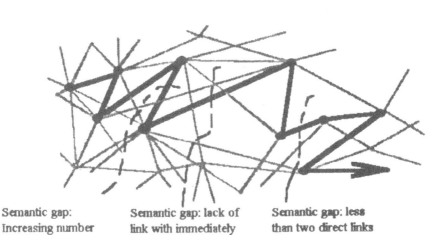

Semantic gap: Increasing number of links of the node.

Semantic gap: lack of link with immediately preceding node.

Semantic gap: less than two direct links with preceding nodes.

Three semantic gaps are shown on the figure with dashed lines crossing the edges of the network.

# 3 Versions of the Intelligent Text Processing

The first way to use IntelText is: *Construction of logically-ordered selections of textual information.*
Characteristics of source information:
- large volume.
Required speed of processing:
- high.
Required quality of constructed text:
- sufficient for perception or use as an instant working material.
Method:
- automatic extraction of keywords from texts or usage of preliminary built indexes;
- automatic linking of nodes.

*Example:*
Construction of text, confirming or complementing a judgement by retrieving appropriate facts from a hyperbase containing messages of information agencies during the Gulf war. The theme was set as the following expert opinion: SOME SIGNS SHOW THAT THE LAND OFFENSIVE OPERATION WILL BE HELD IN THE NEAREST FUTURE.

Groups of special destination of multinational forces have begun preparations for offense. They are installing mines at the communications on the territory of Iraq and Kuwait. [1]

Mr. Powell at the press-conference in Washington has claimed that the superiority in air forces at Iraq is reached, though Iraqi military aviation still constitutes a threat to multinational forces. He also said that the blows at the communication lines, warehouses of ammunition, food and arsenals of Iraq has begun and will grow. [2]

At 3.00 the CNN company has broadcasted a message that marine guards attacked Iraqi troops in Kuwait. At the moment the 1st division performs artillery shooting. [2]

The units of 4th and 5th divisions and also ships of 2nd and 3rd amphibian groups began work off the landing operation near the beach of Saudi Arabia in process of maneuvers named "Sea soldier-4". [1]

82nd US air-landing division took battle array at the Saudi-Kuwait frontier in relation to possible attack to positions of the Iraqi troops in Kuwait. As the headquarters of the multinational forces consider, the simultaneous attack from the sea and land at the Iraqi forces in Kuwait can lessen the losses of the allied troops during the breach of the defensive boundaries of the enemy. [3]

By January 24 multi-national forces have liberated the Kuwaiti island Karu. In the battle two minesweepers and one patrol cutter of Iraqi forces were drowned. [2]

1. TV Dubai
2. CNN
3. Reuters

Another example is: *Compiling of coherent texts.*
Characteristics of source information:
- medium volume;
- preliminary filtering of relevant information has been carried out.
Required speed of processing:
- medium.
Required quality of constructed text:
- as of a prototype or a first version of a survey, report, etc.
Method:
- manual or interactive extraction of keywords;
- interactive linking.

*Example:*
Construction of reasoning on a given topic by assembling opinions and ideas of the participants of the so-called BYTE Summit - 1990 where "63 of the World's Most Influential People in Personal Computing Predict the Future, Analyze the Present". The theme was set with the keyword: BETWEEN PROGRAMMING AND NATURAL LANGUAGE.

It's kind of halfway between programming and natural language. You're going to train your computer, both by giving it instructions and having it watch you, but it will just feel more natural. Ten years from now, people are going to say, "Oh, yeah, training your computer - that's so intuitive". And of course it won't be, but it will be taken for granted. [1]

The concept of the program generator that lets people tailor programs is going to be important. We have to be looking for the higher-level, tailored, specialized application. [2]

Lots of packages will go into the hands of end users, and they will take the design of the system, and play with the interface, and change it the way they want it, and then they just generate the system that they need. [3]

It would be systems for design of integrated work settings, something with user customizability, group customizability. People are beginning to use computers much more that way. [4]

There are new opportunities in figuring out new ways of interacting with the user. The really great applications invent new metaphors in each application domain. That is going to be really exciting. [5]

We'll see tools that will permit the average user to customize applications. [6]

1. Esther Dyson, p. 335
2. Chuck Peddle, p. 338
3. Carma McClure, p. 338
4. Terry Winograd, p. 246
5. Bill Joy, p. 248
6. John Markoff, p. 338

The third version is: *Authored construction of text basing on available sketches, notes, formulations.*

Characteristics of source information:
- small or medium volume (can be grasped by the user).

Required speed of processing:
- less essential then quality.

Required quality of constructed text:
- very high requirements to the logical order and coherence of the text.

Method:
- manual linking of nodes.

*Example:*

Construction of text discussing a certain aspect of hypertext from a hyperbase about hypertext technology. The theme was set with first two statements.

Hypertext, or nonlinear text, consists of separate text fragments which are called "nodes".

Possibility to move from one node to another is called link. Any two linked nodes are called "adjacent" nodes.

Each node has a prescribed set of links (adjacent nodes).

Since every node may have many links (adjacent nodes), the so called "hypertext network" emerges. A hypertext networks may be very large and of high complexity.

Following links, it is possible to traverse a hypertext network in various directions and by different routes.

Exploration of a hypertext network content by following the network's links is called "navigation".

While in process of navigation, user has access to information content of nodes that are adjacent to the current node, and according to this information he/she bases his/her route through the network.

In complex networks, where each node has many links (adjacent nodes), node/link selection for the next navigational step becomes associated for user with large effort and concentration.

Many researchers point out, that in large hypertext networks it is easy for user to become disoriented or to get lost.

A necessity arises to have something like a compass for hypertext navigation.

Compass-like rules have to be contrived to direct navigation from each current node in accordance with user's subject matter (the topic he/she is interested in).

Navigation can be based on a set of rules. With the rules, navigation may be carried out either in pure automatic mode or in interactive mode that provides semi-automatic link-filtering to escape non-effective routes.

Soviet researchers indicate that navigational rules may be based on structural, in graph theory sense, characteristics of hypertext network.

IntelText, a hypertext system developed in Russia, uses mechanism of structural navigation both in automatic and
interactive modes.

## 4 Experience in the Design and Implementation

### 4.1. Data model

While building the data model the focus was on efficiency. The algorithms presuppose that at each step of navigation the amount of nodes involved in consideration grows significantly. Also, due to the lack of a predefined structure of the hypertext net, it is impossible to foresee the order of the node rendering or to build-in this order into the data model. Therefore, for a large hypertext net very quick access to any node is necessary. We chose for representing the net a DBMS with a network rather than a relational model - db_Vista from Raima Corp., providing quick direct access to any record independently of the size of the base.

### 4.2. Main working modes

Automatic construction of texts. The user sets the theme by selecting keywords or by just pointing to a particular node or a pair of linked nodes in the catalog. The system automatically compiles nodes into a constructed text. The user can control some features of the constructed text (corresponding to variations of the algorithms), or can participate in choosing the next node in those branching points where a few nodes have equal characteristics. IntelText can also show 'semantic gaps' in the constructed text.

Manual navigation. The user can transfer from one node to another by the links, searching for some information or just reading the base under some angle. He also can remember the navigation route and modify it as a whole, changing positions of nodes in it, adding new nodes, etc. Then he can convert it into linear form - the constructed text.

Combined mode. Automatically constructed text is decompiled into a path - the sequence of nodes forming it. The path can be processed and modified in manual navigation mode and then the satisfying variant can be converted back to linear form - the constructed text.

Conventional means of text editing, search by attributes, input/output are supported.

## 4.3. Limitations

The current version of IntelText works under MS-DOS or Windows on the IBM PC or compatible computer with 640K RAM.

The maximum number of hypertext nodes in one information base is 65536. The maximum length of the text of one node is 32 Kbytes.

Each node can possess a number of user-defined attributes: keywords - defining its content; labels - defining its subject domain; references - defining its bibliographical origin or referring to graphical images (illustrations). The number of attributes of each kind for a node is not limited.

## 5 Application Experience

The main areas of experienced application of IntelText are:
- authoring work with text;
- binding documentation consisting of a large amount of interrelated fragments lacking rigid structure and clear sequence;
- automatic arrangement of information elements (possibly filtered from a network) in a sequence promoting better perception by the user;
- analysis of systems of ideas, concepts, arguments in order to reveal discrepancies and gaps in it.

A possible application area is also education and training:
- creation of dynamic electronic books for automatic compiling of information on a theme set by the reader;
- creation of an electronic textbook with pre-built paths and the possibility for independent study.

# 6   Further Development

One direction is connected with *linguistics*. Processing of large dynamic hypertexts assumes completely automatic modes of linking that in turn assumes that the keywords are assigned to nodes automatically. Thus, very sensitive linguistic means for automatic extraction of keywords from texts should be added to IntelText.

Another problem deals with *interfaces*. Developing interfaces between IntelText and widely-used text-processors, databases and networks for importing source information and exporting the constructed texts.

A possible trend of development is also in *groupware*. A network version of IntelText with means for collaborative work including the exchange of ideas, viewing discrepancies and construction of summaries would be very useful.

# References

1. M.M.Subbotin. Computer applications and the construction of chains of reasoning. Automatic Documentation & Mathematical Linguistics, 1986, v.20, N 6, USA.

2. M.M.Subbotin. A new information technology: generation and processing of hypertexts. Automatic Documentation & Mathematical Linquistics, 1988, v.22, N 3, USA.

3. R.S.Gilyarevskii and M.M.Subbotin. Evaluating the prospects for new information technologies (a study of hypertext technology). Scientific and Technical Information Processing, 1988, v.15, N 6, ISSN 0147-6882, USA.

4. M.M.Subbotin. Hypertext systems with algorithmic navigation. Proceedings of the International Colloquium "New Information Technology". Moscow, USSR, October 8-10, 1991.

5. A.S.Lakayev, M.M.Subbotin, D.M.Subbotin. Hypertext Structural Analysis. Proceedings of the 2nd East-West International Conference on Human-Computer Interaction (EWHCI'92). St.-Petersburg, Russia, August 4-8, 1992.

6. Sempro - Active Hypertext. In: Rel-EAST. The East-West High-Tech Business Report. N 3, 1992. A Publication of EDventure Holdings Inc., 375 Park Avenue, New York, NY 10152.

7. Hypersoft - Active Hypertext. In: Release 1.0. A Monthly Report by Esther Dyson. N 2, 1993. A Publication of EDventure Holdings Inc., 375 Park Avenue, New York, NY 10152.

8. Gilyarevskii R.S., Subbotin M.M. Soviet experience in hypertext: automatic compiling of coherent texts. - Journal of the American Society for Information Science, N 4, 1993.

# The Challenge of Effectively Integrating Graphics into Hypertext

Keith Instone, Erik Brown, Laura Leventhal and Barbee Teasley

Computer Science Department, Bowling Green State University
Bowling Green, Ohio 43403   USA   instone@hydra.bgsu.edu

**Abstract.** It is important that designers of hypertext do not assume that the way information is presented in traditional media such as paper books will necessarily be effective in hypertext. Several studies have shown that graphics presented with text on a screen are not necessarily used effectively, or even used at all. In our study, we explored three ways of presenting textual and graphical information about geographical locations and objects. In all cases, the user had to point with a mouse to a item name in order to see text, and the text appeared near the mouse cursor. In one presentation style, no graphic was present. In a second style, a graphic was present, but the text appeared as a caption. In the hypertext style, the user pointed to item names on the graphic. The results showed that the hypertext style resulted in about 20% better learning of both spatial information (which was illustrated by the graphic) and of information not illustrated by the graphic.

## 1   Introduction

An important challenge to the designers of hypertext systems is effectively integrating information from a variety of media, including text, graphics, sound, and animation. Integrating several media can lead to interesting, useful and innovative hypertext documents (see [6] for examples). However, as with any software, poor design can mean annoying, ineffective or even useless hypertext.

Two commonly integrated media in hypertext are graphics and text. Others have suggested that graphics can serve several functions when integrated into text, such as embellishment or clarification of points in the text, or providing an overview or summary of text [7, 8]. However, in recent studies of hypertext and on-line systems with integrated text and graphics, it has become clear that simply placing textual and graphical information on the same screen or card does not guarantee that the information will be used successfully, or even used at all. A challenge to the hypertext designer is to effectively integrate graphics into hypertext. Design guidelines are needed to assist in this process. It is important, as well, that these guidelines be grounded in empirical work and, eventually, be theory based. This paper presents our work on identifying factors which influence the effectiveness of various styles of graphics on learning from hypertext. This work suggests design guidelines, and begins efforts toward combining theories of comprehension with hypertext design theory.

We have previously described a comparative study of question-answering performance using either a hypertext encyclopedia or an equivalent paper encyclopedia

[5, 2, 4]. While the users were quite successful in some tasks with the hypertext encyclopedia, they were not particularly effective in using the integrated graphical information. In a later study [3], we compared two versions of the same hypertext encyclopedia. One version (the same one used in the earlier studies) included overlapping windows and several alternative ways to accomplish the same task. The other version used tiled windows and had simplified tools. While the graphical/textual information was identical in both cases, subjects were better at using graphics in the simpler version (and were also much better at using other tools, performing better than paper book users in many instances). The authors could offer no definitive explanation of this unexpected result, beyond the observation that improving the interface generally improved users' ability to comprehend the text and graphics. This possibly results from reducing the cognitive load required to use the tools themselves.

A series of studies in which subjects extracted information from diagrams that were integrated with text have been done [8]. The researchers looked at the subjects' willingness to study the diagrams and the amount of information that subjects gained from the diagrams. They found that when subjects had free access to diagrams, they spent relatively little time studying the diagrams and generally made minimal use of the information in the diagrams, despite variations in the diagrams and in instructions. However, when subjects were forced to look at diagrams when they came up unexpectedly, their performance improved.

Others have investigated the impact that pictures, presented with text in a computerized presentation, had on the resolution of anaphora[1] [1]. Subjects read texts that contained short descriptions of single objects. Four or five parts of the objects were described in the text. In the descriptions, antecedents described the name and location of the part. The anaphor repeated the spatial location of the part described in the antecedent, and also elaborated on its function. One-third of the texts had no accompanying picture, one-third of the texts had an accompanying picture that was always present, and one-third of the texts had a picture that either disappeared or appeared late. These authors found that the presence of pictures did generally help, but they did not improve comprehension of texts requiring far anaphor resolution. These findings suggest that subjects did not use the information in the picture effectively.

The goal of the present study was to identify those factors which influence the effectiveness of graphics that are integrated into hypertext. Prior research, such as the studies mentioned above, shows that readers may not benefit fully from graphics that are simply present on the same screen as textual information. We hypothesized that characteristics of the interface would influence the effectiveness of integrated graphics. In this study, users were asked to learn information about geographical locations, parts of objects, and various incidents presented with or without an accompanying graphic. In all cases, the user was forced to perform a pointing action with a mouse in order to see the textual information, and in all cases, the text appeared next to the cursor. (This is in contrast to the situation described in [8], where in most cases the user had to perform a special action to see the graphics, while the text was always present.) Where the text appeared relative to the graphic was varied, however. It appeared either below the graphic, or right next to the part of the graphic that the text related to. The users were then tested on their memory for the information they had

---

[1]An anaphor is a word or phrase that is interpreted in relation to previous elements in a discourse. A good example of an anaphor is a pronoun. The process of anaphor resolution is sensitive to the distance between the anaphor and the antecedent.

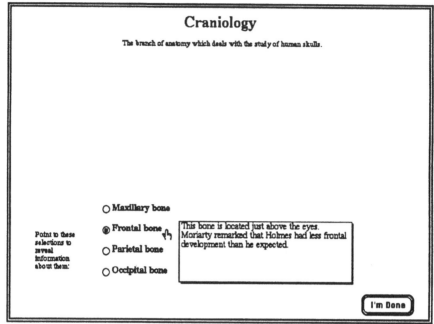

**Fig. 1.** Interaction style #1: Text only

seen. We hypothesized that the subjects would learn the best when the text appeared next to graphic. We also expected that having the text below the graphic would be no more effective than no graphic at all.

## 2  Method and Procedures

### 2.1  Materials

The materials consisted of a hypertext stack (implemented in HyperCard 2.1) containing a series of topic cards. Each topic was related to incidents from the Sherlock Holmes stories by Sir Arthur Conan Doyle, and contained information about geographic entities or devices of interest to Sherlock Holmes. Some sample topics are: the reproductive system of spaghnum sporophyte, Ireland, a gasogene, and Australia. For each topic, there were four or five items. Each item consisted of one piece of spatial information and one fact related to a Sherlock Holmes story or about the object. For example, for the topic of Switzerland, one item was Davos Platz. The spatial information about Davos Platz was "A town of eastern Switzerland, pop. 8,089." The fact was "The consumptive Englishwoman was said to have come from here." (See Figure 2.)

The topics were presented in three interaction styles: *text-only, caption* and *hypertext*. In the text-only interaction style, there were no pictures or maps. Four or five item names were listed at the bottom of the card. When users moved the cursor over the item name, text information about that item popped up to the right of the name. The text appeared in the same location on the screen for each item. The text-

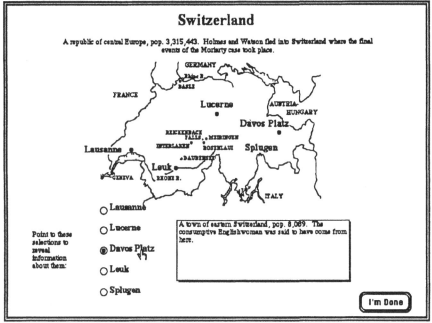

**Fig. 2.** Interaction style #2: Caption

only style is shown in Figure 1, where the user has selected "Frontal bone" and the text has appeared.

The caption interaction style was similar to the text-only, except that a graphic (map or picture) appeared above the list of items. As in the text-only style, the text appeared to the right of the list of items. Each item name also appeared in the graphic as a bold word, to make it stand out from the rest of the picture (Figure 2).

In the hypertext interaction style, users pointed directly at the item on the graphic to reveal the text information. As shown in Figure 3, the information appeared near the location of the item on the graphic.

Each subject saw twelve topic cards. The three interaction styles were randomly distributed across the cards, with the limitation that each subject saw four cards in each interaction style. The order of the topics was also randomly generated. Each topic was presented about an equal number of times in each of the three conditions across all of the subjects.

Following the presentation of each topic, subjects saw a card which directed them to work on a word search task (on paper) for 30 seconds. The word search served as distractor task, so that the subjects could not answer the questions based on short term memory. At the end of 30 seconds, subjects were presented a series of eight multiple choice questions. Four of the questions concerned the fact information from the topic and four concerned the spatial information from the topic. All questions were the same, regardless of interaction style. A sample spatial question is: "Which of the following is located above the eyes?" One of the fact questions was: "From where was the cardboard box mailed?"

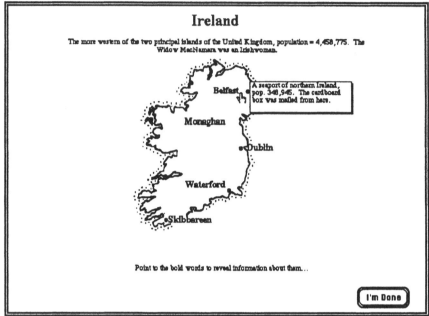

**Fig. 3.** Interaction style #3: Hypertext

## 2.2 Experimental Design

The experiment used a within-subjects design. There were two independent variables: interaction style (text only, caption or hypertext) and type of question (spatial or fact). The dependent measures were the number of questions correct on the multiple-choice quiz and the time spent on the topic card.

## 2.3 Subjects

The subjects were eighteen students from introductory computer science programming classes. They all had previous experience using a mouse for pointing in their introductory programming class. All students indicated that they were not extremely familiar with the stories of Sherlock Holmes.

## 2.4 Procedure

The subjects were first given training by being presented with a sample topic and demonstration of the three interaction styles. In these examples, instructions appeared on the screen along with the text or graphics. The instructions explained where to point and what button to press when they were finished, for each interaction style. Next, a sample topic was presented in one of the three interaction styles (randomly chosen), with no instructions present on the card. This initial topic was the same for all users, and served as a practice trial.

Subjects then performed the primary task, which consisted of 12 trials. Each trial consisted of presentation of the topic card (which the subject was allowed to study as long as she or he wished), followed by 30 seconds of word searching, followed by the eight multiple choice questions. They were allowed to spend as long as they wished in answering the questions.

# 3 Results

For each topic, there were a total of four spatial information questions and four factual information questions. Subjects received a one for each correct answer and a zero for each incorrect answer. There were four topics presented in each of the three interaction styles. Thus, the maximum score for each type of question (spatial or fact) for each of the three interaction styles was 16. The mean number correct (out of 16) for each condition is shown in Table 1.

Preliminary analyses indicated that there were no order effects across trials. Thus, subsequent analyses did not include trials as a factor. Using a repeated measures ANOVA, the main effects of question type and interaction type were significant ($F(1,34) = 14.4$, $p < .05$ and $F(2,34) = 5.7$, $p < .05$, respectively). As shown in Table 1, the mean total questions correct was higher for the fact questions (mean = 11.4) than for the spatial questions (mean = 9.7). This suggests that the spatial information was more difficult to learn overall than the factual information, in spite of the fact that for two-thirds of these questions, the graphic was present and might have been expected to serve as an aid to learning the material. The factual information, on the other hand, would not be particularly enhanced by the graphic (e.g., the fact that "the consumptive Englishwoman was said to have come from here" is not actually illustrated or demonstrated by the graphic). Overall, the total correct for the questions presented in hypertext style were higher than either of the other two styles (mean = 11.9 versus 10.0 for Caption and 9.7 for Text Only). This suggests that the hypertext style is the most effective way to present either factual or spatial information.

To explore whether the presence of a graphic was useful, two sets of pairwise t-tests were performed. One set was done on the spatial data, and another set on the fact data. Comparisons of the spatial question data indicated that there was no significant difference between the text-only and caption conditions. This indicates that the presence of the graphic did *not* enhance learning of spatial information when the textual material was presented as a caption. In addition, scores on spatial questions for the hypertext interaction style were significantly higher than the caption style (paired t, two-tailed = 3.0, DF = 17 $p < .05$). This shows that the critical factor which enhanced the learning of the spatial material was the placement of the text next to the graphic, and not solely the presence of the graphic.

A second set of pairwise t-tests was done on the fact questions. The results parallel those found for the spatial questions. For the fact questions, text-only and caption were again not significantly different from each other, suggesting that the simple presence of a graphic did not enhance learning. On the other hand, the comparison of the caption scores to the hypertext scores was significant ($t = 2.8$, DF = 17, $p < .05$), indicating that the hypertext style, and not just the presence of the graphic, was responsible for the improved learning.

The time spent studying each topic card was also analyzed. The mean times were 76.3 seconds, 91.0 seconds and 80.6 seconds, respectively, for text only, caption and hypertext. This difference was not significant.

| N=18 | TYPE OF INTERACTION | | | |
|------|-----------|---------|-----------|---------|
| TYPE OF QUESTION | Text-Only | Caption | Hypertext | Overall |
| Spatial | 8.6 (SD 3.4) | 9.1 (SD 3.3) | 11.4 (SD 2.4) | 9.7 (SD 3.3) |
| Fact | 10.8 (SD 3.5) | 10.9 (SD 3.5) | 12.3 (SD 3.1) | 11.4 (SD 3.4) |
| Overall | 9.7 (SD 3.7) | 10.0 (SD 3.5) | 11.9 (SD 2.8) | |

**Table 1.** Mean scores (and standard deviations) on the multiple choice questions as a function of the type of question (spatial vs. fact) and interaction style.

# 4 Conclusions

One of the exciting prospects of hypertext is that it can be a more efficient and effective way of presenting information and of learning than through the use of more traditional media. Our earlier studies showed that hypertext can surpass paper books in information retrieval tasks. In this study, we looked at the power of hypertext for enhancing learning from material supplemented with graphics. Prior studies have found that graphical information is not always used effectively when presented in either paper or electronic media. We were particularly struck by the finding that learning was best when users were forced to look at the graphics [8]. We speculated that hypertext offers a natural way of "forcing" the user to look at graphics. In what we call the "hypertext style of interaction", the user must actively select the portion of the graphic of interest in order to reveal the textual information, which then appears adjacent to the graphic. This turns the user from a passive reader of text who has the option of looking at a graphic (the style typical of paper media), to an active user, who must look at and process the graphic to at least some extent in order to reveal the text. Our study showed that this style of presentation enhanced learning by 20%. Interestingly, we also found that learning of factual information (which was *not* illustrated by the graphic) was improved just as much as spatial information (which was illustrated by the graphic).

Additional work needs to be done to isolate the factors that lead to the enhanced learning. For example, is it the kinesthetic feedback from moving the mouse which improves learning, or the fact that the text is beside the important element in the graphic? In addition, work is needed to further explore the range of information types for which the hypertext style is effective. For example, it seems likely that the hypertext interaction style might also be more effective than paper media for teaching definitions, contrasts and comparisons. Consider a student who needs to learn the names of and differences among various styles of dresses from the late 1800's. The user might explore diagrams or pictures of various dresses. As they move the cursor over the diagrams, textual information appears which points out the characteristics of each style.

Although further studies are needed to broaden and clarify the design issues relevant to incorporating graphics into hypertext, the present study suggests that designers of hypertext may wish to consider the following guidelines when the goal of the hypertext is to teach the user information:

- Reverse the usual order of saliency of text and graphics. That is, make the graphic what the users see first, and have them perform an action to see the associated text.

- Present the information relevant to the graphic as much as possible next to that part of the graphic that it relates to.

- Even if some information is not illustrated by the graphic, associate it in a meaningful way with the other text that is illustrated by the graphic. Place both types of text near the graphic.

## References

1. Glenberg, A. M. and Kruley, P. Pictures and anaphora: Evidence for independent processes, *Memory & Cognition*, 1992, 20 (5), 461-471.

2. Instone, K., Leventhal, L. M., Teasley, B. M., Farhat, J. and Rohlman, D. S. *What do I want?* and *How do I get there?*: Performance and navigation in information retrieval tasks with hypertext documents, *Proceedings of the East–West International Conference on Human-Computer Interaction* (St. Petersburg, Russia, August 4-8, 1992), 85-95.

3. Instone, K., Teasley, B., and Leventhal, L. M. Empirically-based re-design of a hypertext encyclopedia, *INTERCHI '93 Proceedings*, 1993, 500-506.

4. Leventhal, L. M., Teasley, B. M., Instone, K., Rohlman, D. S. and Farhat, J. (1993) Sleuthing in HyperHolmes: Using hypertext vs. a book to answer questions, *Behaviour and Information Technology*, 12, 1993.

5. Mynatt, B. T., Leventhal, L. M., Instone, K., Farhat, J. and Rohlman, D. S. Hypertext or book: Which is better for answering questions?, *CHI '92 Proceedings*, 1992, 19-25.

6. Nielsen, J. *Hypertext and Hypermedia*. New York: Academic Press, 1990.

7. Waddill, P. J. and McDaniel, M. A. Pictorial enhancement of text memory: Limitations imposed by picture type and comprehension skill. *Memory & Cognition*, 20 (5), 1992, 472-482.

8. Wright, P., Hull, A. and Black, D. Integrating diagrams and text. *The Technical Writing Teacher*, 17 (3), 1990, 244-254.

# Coherent Navigation in Hypertext Environments: The SMIsC Conception

## Valery M. Chelnokov and Victoria L. Zephyrova

MosCHI, State Scientific and Technical Center
for Hypertext Information Technologies, Moscow, Russia
STC-GINTECH,
109240, Zemlyanoy Val, 52/16
Phone: 7 (095) 297-7004, 287-2968

**Abstract.** The key usability problem in hypertext and hypermedia is the Navigation Problem. This problem can be divided into the problem of disorientation and the problem of cognitive overhead. We believe that one systematic approach to the Navigation Problem consists in developing mechanisms to assist users to navigate coherently; that is, to blaze trails which imitate semantically coherent discourses in hypertext/hypermedia networks. The main purpose of such a mechanism is the maintenance of the macrocontrol over local transitions among nodes of information during a navigational (interactive) session. This macrocontrol should provide the trail's global (thematic) coherence.

Based on the works of such well-known psycholinguists as van Dijk, Kintsch and Levelt, we demonstrate that a good portion of the macrocontrol maintenance can be implemented on a computer. We describe the portion as content-independent navigational strategies, which are formulated in terms of only the network's node-link structure, and are expressible in the form of machine instructions. The strategies mechanism we have developed aids users to move in the network, maintaining the trail's global coherence in relation to a chosen theme. This trail imitates a so-called canonically-ordered discourse based on the network's nodes. With this mechanism, the macrocontrol is shared among the computer and the user and this makes the user's burden significantly less. We use the term 'System of Meaning Integrities structural Creation', or SMIsC, to denote our hypertext system with such shared macrocontrol.

## 1. An Introduction to the Coherent Navigation Problem

### 1.1. General Problems with Navigation

It belongs to the basics of hypertext that the freedom is provided for users to move through the database, to browse in it, or navigate at will, making a journey of discovery. Here we have the most distinguishing feature of hypertext [1].

However, this freedom has its cost: it becomes necessary for users to make additional cognitive efforts of a rather unusual kind.

According to the accepted terminology, the difficulties are created by the problem of disorientation ("getting lost in hyperspace") and the problem of cognitive overhead (overload) [2]. The disorientation problem consists in the tendency to lose one's sense of location and direction within a complex, nonlinear information structure - the tendency which the fact that the structure is buried invisibly in a computer database can only contribute to. The problem of cognitive overhead (in reading) results from that users, while an interactive session, must constantly deal with more than one links available to continue the process. Hypertext readers must not only attend to the textual content of a current node but also have to decide which node to visit next and therefore have to make choices which, in case of linear text, have been already made for them by the text's author.

These problems jointly form what may be called the Navigation Problem (NP). Here "navigation" means users' information-seeking activity based on travelling through a database hypertext network with a meaningful directing this movement in regard to a current position within the network. Such navigational access to the database content predominates in hypertext and hypermedia systems. This makes the NP being a key usability problem in the area. The related fundamental questions were among those to which the Hypertext'91 conference was devoted [3]:

> Are hypertexts intrinsically confusing, disorienting, and distracting? Is hypertext disorientation a danger which skilled writers can avoid, or which technological tools can ameliorate? Or is the Navigational Problem a myth, an artifact of early efforts, a misunderstanding? These questions lie at the center both of current hypertext research and of current technical writing practice; the answers will profoundly influence the design of human machine interface.

Most technological solutions helping to ease the NP constitute graphical browsers (displaying hypertext network node-link structures), query/search mechanisms and backtracking facilities. Also tools were developed by Carolyn Foss to visualize the network's fragment, a user has examined in a current interactive session, in the form of a "history" trail or tree. The purpose of all the solutions consists mainly in creation spatial context helping users to answer the question "where can I go from here?" or temporal context helping to answer "how did I get to here?" [4].

## 1.2. Coherence Networks

Our work is devoted to the problems of what we call "coherent navigation". We mean (semantic) coherence of the user's trail considering its maintenance in a session as a way not to get "lost in hyperspace". In this connection, one may refer to Carolyn Foss's observation that "forming a coherent understanding or abstraction of what you have viewed is important for effective browsing" (cited in [1]).

Some reservations must be made here concerning hypertext nodes and links.

It's a tradition of hypertext that nodes represent single ideas and links semantic interdependencies among these ideas [2]. We'll imply that nodes are paragraphs (episodes). A paragraph is considered as a group of related sentences that develop an idea; this idea dominates over other ideas of the paragraph and is called its main idea (it's commonly found at the beginning of the paragraph as underlying its initial thematic sentence).

As to the links, for our purposes, they must be node-to-node. These links are anchored to their nodes as wholes rather than to points within them. It's considered that a link represents a semantic relation between two main ideas of the link's two nodes.

We'll deal with networks of this kind only. We call them *coherence networks* for they consist of nodes containing internally coherent wholes and of links representing local coherence relations.

It's worth noting that such network can contain multimedia nodes, too: since in hypermedia systems nodes of information are also connected by meaningful links, a general coherence network can be considered in which nodes are coherent entities of any nature.

## 1.3. Macrocontrol

The task of coherent navigation implies that the sought-for trail should imitate a coherent discourse. And this is mainly the task of global coherence maintenance, because local coherence is provided by links themselves. The situation is exactly one discourse theorists address [5]:

> Without such a global coherence there would be no overall control upon the local connections and continuations. Sentences might be connected appropriately according to the given local coherence criteria, but their sequence would simply go astray without some constraint on what it should be about globally.

It's said that locally coherent transitions need *macrocontrol* in the form of so-called "macrostructure". The last is a theoretical reconstruction of the intuitive notion "topic" or "theme" and is what provides the overall unity, or global coherence, or meaning integrity to a discourse [6].

There are innumerable examples illustrating the situation of "going astray" or lacking of macrocontrol in the presence of microcontrol, maintaining simply connectedness ("This morning I had a toothache. I went to the dentist. The dentist has a big car. The car was bought in New York. New York has had serious financial troubles." [5]). As Patricia Ann Carlson notes [7], "even one who begins in a goal-directed mode, may start out reading (an encyclopedia) about Admiral Chester Nimitz and end up perusing the history of ballet".

The hypertext macrocontrol means the power to direct one's movement so as not to follow links which are locally meaningful but globally distracting. In other words, being careful of the trail's global coherence turns out a kind of knowing where to go next (or at least where not to go).

Of course, there are cases in which macrocontrol can be considered as unnecessary and unjustifiably laborious. Such may be browsing depending on serendipity or searching for an answer to a particular question.

But, equally, other cases can easily be pointed out in which the trail's incoherence seems to be unnatural. The examples are browsing hypertext on a specific topic, learning by hypertext exploration or preparing a paper's draft from hypertext nodes.

Actually, the cognitive significance of coherent navigation may be considered from a rather general viewpoint, if one takes into account the aspects of hypertext which mimic the associative quality of the human memory. The memory, Carlson recalls [7], is frequently modeled in terms of patterns of associations interlinking information items. She observes that unlike flat database access, search in the human memory often addresses "Gestalts" - associative configurations being perceived as wholes distinct from the sum of their parts. To complete the analogy, hypertext users should engage in searching for reach collections of nodes and links representing semantic wholes. And such a collection is perceivable only through the process of coherent navigation owing to "the discoursiveness of the human mind, which is able to conceive the unity of the object only in successiveness", as Hans-Georg Gadamer put it [8, p. 428].

The problem is how to assist users to move coherently and how to retain, at the same time, some of the hypertext freedom at an acceptable cognitive cost - that is, how to ease the coherent NP , or cNP, for short.

Graphical browsers, for example, are, on their own, uninformative from the viewpoint of the coherence task and need at least some filtering technique to reduce the amount of extraneous information being passed on the user.

Speaking generally, the most significant source of difficulties is hidden in the non-hierarchical form of most hypertext networks and their large numbers of nodes and links. However, these form and size aren't ones to be abandoned, for hypertext excels at the collection of large amounts of relatively unstructured information and this is a very important advantage from cognitive and merely practical viewpoints [2]. At the same time, hierarchical information structures have a clear navigational advantage due to the global context they create: traversing a hierarchy in a depth-first fashion often gives a meaningful linearization [9, p. 185]. In this connection, the idea is useful to impose temporary hierarchical structures on hypertext networks - for example, by "picking up" a node, as it were a knot of a fishing net, and making other nodes "falling about" the selected (thematic) node "in a cascade" [1].

## 1.4. Our Approach

We'd like to demonstrate that one gains a benefit in combating the cNP if one has recourse to psycholinguistic models of discourse comprehension and production [6, 10-13].

These models represent the semantic content of a discourse through a propositional network that consists of nodes corresponding to propositions ( or their sentential expressions, clauses) and of local coherence links. Comprehension and production are described as the networks construction and linearization, respectively. These processes are modeled as being controlled by the "strategies", effective working hypotheses, expressing procedurally what's required theoretically (formally, they can be represented as if-then productions) [6, p. 11]. The key advantage proceeds from that a part of (or an approximation to) these strategies can be expressed in terms of the network's node-link structure only, that is, independently of the nodes' content.

We suggest to share the operational macrocontrol over the trail blazing among the system and the user (probably, placing its most part onto the former) in such a way that, at each step of the trail, the system does its "structural" work first and then the user may enter the play.

Since each coherent trail is a discoursive presentation of a meaning integrity (more completely expressed by the subgraph on the trail's nodes), we use the term 'System of Meaning Integrities structural Creation', or SMIsC, to denote a system that supports coherent networks and provides users with an assistance based on such sharing.

# 2. Modeling Discourse Comprehension and Production

Though what SMIsC macrocontrol has directly to deal with is trail generation, i.e., discourse production, its main grounds lie in the domain of comprehension.

The basic model of discourse comprehension decomposes it into the following major component processes [6, 11]:
- the initial parsing of the text into semantic units, propositions, underlying the text clauses;
- the arrangement of these units into a propositional network, or coherence graph, or microstructure;
- the derivation of macro- or global propositions from the initial micro- or local propositions and from the comprehender's world knowledge;
- the establishing the text's macro- or global structure as an hierarchy of macrounits.

## 2.1. Semantic Units - Propositions

*Semantic units* (propositions), in intensional terms, express the individual meaning of the text's clauses; extensionally, such unit corresponds to a certain fact in some possible world. A proposition is analyzed in terms of a predicate referring to a relation or property and of one or more arguments referring to persons, things, or circumstances. Propositional truth or falsity is considered as connected not so much with the meaning aspect of a discourse but rather with the pragmatic one [6, p. 116]. A person seeking understanding may leave open the truth of what's said and consider, rather, the latter "not as true, but merely as meaningful, so that the possibility of its truth remains unsettled" [8, p. 338].

## 2.2. Propositional Networks and Coherence Graphs

During the second component process, *local coherence* links are recognized among the units as wholes.

Two units form a link if there exists a temporal or cause-effect relationship among the denoted facts (a conditional link) or if one of the clauses has a semantic function with respect to another, such as comparison, contrasting, example, information-adding, explanation or definition, generalization or specification (a functional link). The explicit indicators of links are connective words or markers, sentence connectors and other expressions. The two link types may overlap to some extent [6].

A more formal method exists allowing to link units in a purely mechanical way (for this reason, it's often used in experimental studies): two units form a link if one of them contains an argument having the same referent as an argument of the other. Although such coreference isn't a sufficient and sometimes not even necessary condition for the existence of a true link, it gives a good first approximation to link recognition [6, 10]. The method is used in SMIsC to form links with new incoming nodes (arguments are specified as "keywords").

A propositional network is abstractly represented as a graph with nodes labeled *1, 2, ..., N* and unlabeled, non-oriented links. We call it *coherence graph*, yet more traditional use of this term implies purely coreference links [10, 11]. In this graph, the numerical label of a node is the respective unit's number in the "physical" sequence induced by the sentence ordering in the discourse.

## 2.3. Modeling Connectedness Control

Comprehension goes on line with reading or hearing [6, p. 6]. Local coherence connectedness is controlled by the comprehender's mind. The principal moment is that this control is severely restricted by the comprehender's short-term memory (STM), the place where links are established: in each cycle of the model, at most $s$ of the already processed units can be retained in the STM's buffer ($s = 4$, for example [10]).

Clearly, the appropriate selection of the $s$ nodes becomes of great importance. They must be "unfinished reference points" and ones which the new incoming nodes are linked with (refer to). Otherwise, resource-consuming operations will be required to search for interlinking units among other previous units in the long-term memory (LTM) or to generate entirely new, "bridging", units - if the LTM search fails, showing a semantic gap. These operations interrupt the normal flow of the comprehension and can even block it. When there is no need for them, comprehension goes almost automatically [10].

In the model [10, 11], the selection rule is used, as the most plausible, such that the favorites are the nodes that are important, in a certain sense, and are recent.

The importance measure is introduced as follows. In the initial processing cycle a node $a$ is specified as the "most important" or "central" reference point. In principle, a must be a thematic unit with high semantic relevance to the entire text. Then the importance of the other nodes is measured in a way equivalent to the following: the closer a node is in the coherence graph to $a$, the more important it is. Indeed, according to experimental studies, the coherence graph distance defined as the number of links in the shortest path indicates the "psychological distance" among semantic units [14].

Thus a hierarchy of node levels emerges in which a level is formed by the nodes being one and the same number of links distant from $a$. The emerged structure, $G(a)$, is exactly one that's implied by the fishing net metaphor from the previous section. An expanding fragment of $G(a)$ is maintained in the LTM and on this fragment the selection rule operates. For our purposes it's sufficient to consider this rule in a simplified form.

The 'leading edge' sequence of nodes is defined. Its first member is $a$ (Level zero); then the ith member is picked as the most recent node of the Level $i$ provided it's more recent than the previous member. The portion retained in the STM is formed by the first $s$ members, or by the full sequence, if its length doesn't exceed $s$.

## 2.4. Canonically-ordered Discourses

We introduce an infinite class of graphs that are recognized as connected by any processor based on this leading edge rule.

Take a connected hierarchical $G(a)$ and traverse it from $a$ through the depth-first procedure choosing each time a downward link that leads to yet unvisited node with the least number and storing "unfinished choice points" on a stack. The traversal imposes an additional, 'depth-first', order $I(a)$ on the nodes of $G(a)$ and specifies a hierarchical rooted tree $T(a)$, consisting of all nodes of $G(a)$ and of those its links which lead to a new node when traversed [15].

Let's call a discourse *depth-first ordered* if its $I(1)$ coincides with its "physical" sequence.

(A) Suppose a depth-first ordered discourse is given that has $s+1$ or less levels. Then it's recognized as connected by any processor based on the leading edge rule.

The statement is true because each input node in a processing cycle finds its parent (by the tree) either among the nodes retained in the STM or in the previous input node. FIG. 1 gives an example of the $T(1)$ of a depth-first ordered discourse.

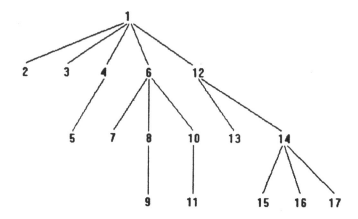

*FIGURE 1. The tree of a depth-first ordered discourse having four levels and N=17 semantic units (propositions)*

Let $x$ be a node in $T(a)$. Then the *height* of $x$ is defined as the number of levels minus 1 in the subtree with the root $x$.

Take a depth-first ordered discourse, such that in its $T(1)$ the recency ordering of each parent's children is, at the same time, their height ordering: the more the height of a child, the more the child's recency (its numerical label). Then the discourse is called *canonically-ordered*. The tree on FIG. 1 is canonically-ordered.

Take a canonically-ordered discourse with more than $s+1$ levels. Suppose that all its units of the height $s$ or more are marked in a way (the precise way of marking doesn't matter now, but a natural one would be one induced by these units' initial thematic position in the paragraphs). Then the following modification of the leading edge rule is proposed: if the input chunk of a processing cycle contains one or more marked units, then the most recent of them is taken as the head of the leading edge.

(B) Suppose a canonically-ordered discourse is given. Suppose if there are nodes of the height $s$ or more in its tree, then all these nodes are marked. Then the discourse is recognized as connected by any processor based on the modified leading edge rule.

The statement is true under the following assumption: a comprehender perceives each marked unit as being connected with the unit *1*. If this is the case, then the statement's truth is derived from that, in the "physical" sequence of such discourse, every unmarked unit has one or more marked units before it and the most recent of them is an ancestor of the unit (by the tree) and is the root of a depth-first ordered subtree having all its nodes, except the root, unmarked and arranged into *s* or less levels. The assumption's validity can be provided by the macroprocesses onto which the focus of attention is now shifted.

## 2.5. Modeling Macroprocesses

In the standard case, once a text fragment such as a paragraph, has been read, a relatively small set of the *macrounits* is formed and the sequence of units of the fragment is substituted by a hierarchy of the set's elements. The theory says and experiments confirm that such hierarchical *macrostructures* are formed when reading or hearing independently of whether they are stated explicitly in the text or not and whether subjects are asked to do so or not [6, pp. 226, 232]. But comprehension becomes impeded if the macrostructure proves inconsistent with the explicitly stated structure, that is, one signaled by the text's features, such as a system of section headings and thematic sentences in paragraphs. A harmony is achieved when coherence graph hierarchy is perceived as hierarchy of macrounits.

Such harmony isn't necessarily the case. What's generally stated is that, during comprehension, special derivation processes reduce the set of sententially expressed (local) units into a set of macro-, or global, or thematic units, being propositions again. Or one may say that local units are semantically mapped upon more general, more abstract macrounits, performing a condensation of information [5, 6].

The macrounit formation is modeled through the macrorules called 'deletion', 'generalization' and 'construction' [6, p. 190]. Of these three, limit ourselves to the second:

*generalization*: given a sequence of propositions, replace it by a (dominant) proposition that is, entailed by each of the propositions of the sequence.

(Entailment is a semantic relation among propositions, say *P1* and *P2*, such that *P1* is entailed by *P2* if there is no conceivable state of affairs making *P2* true and *P1* false - e.g., "being a machine" is entailed by "being a computer".)

Hierarchical macrostructures emerge because macrounits can be derived in a recursive way: given a sequence of macrounits, the macrorules can be reapplied. Through this derivation or mapping process, higher and higher levels of generalization or abstraction are formed until a hierarchical thematic structure is arrived with the most global theme at the top [5, 6].

If a discourse hasn't such macrohierarchy, then no global coherence, no meaning integrity can be attributed to the discourse whereas, by Gadamer, "only what really constitutes a unity of meaning is intelligible" [8, p. 261].

Macrounits of the same level of generality have themselves to form a coherent discourse (macrotext) [6, p. 210]. There must be local (macro)links of specification, contrast, etc. and a macrostructure. A harmony is achieved if macrounits are local units and if macrolinks are local coherence links: in this case, the macrostructure of a macrotext is formed by the higher levels of the original text's macrostructure.

Moreover, the macrotext of a given level of generality gives one of the possible *summaries* of the discourse. Depending on a macrolevel, there can be a long summary, a shorter summary, and a still shorter summary [6, pp. 203, 208]. If all macrounits belong to the set of local units, then all summaries are contained in the text.

Modeling a Macrostructure upon a Microstructure. Though macrounits aren't necessarily shown in the surface structure of the text, their direct indication is commonly practiced to facilitate comprehension (or because of production processes in the mind of a text author). The intended macrounits underlie so-called thematic expressions in episodes (paragraphs). Often such expression is found at the beginning of (macro)episode. Following this tendency up to the extreme, we suppose that:

(C) All macrounits of all macrolevels are directly present in the text in the form of clauses. Moreover, in each (macro)episode, the initial position is occupied with a unit, such that it dominates (according to the generalization macrorule) over the rest units and thus is the topmost macrounit of the episode. This last is equivalent to the existence of the respective general-to-specific links of local coherence.

A formal macrohierarchy satisfying this condition is shown on FIG. 2. The depicted structure is one of Fig. 6.1 from [6] with the only exception that the last doesn't contain Ps at M-levels. From this hierarchy, an unique tree of local coherence links (of the general-to-particular kind) can be drawn, and this is the tree of FIG. 1, that is, the macrostructure underlies the canonically-ordered discourse defined by that tree. And vice versa, if the tree's links on FIG. 1 are general-to-particular links of local coherence - and thus parents dominate over children - then the respective canonically-ordered discourse is underlied by the shown macrostructure.

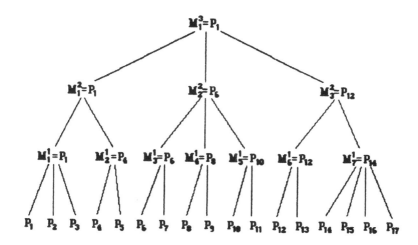

*FIGURE 2. The macrohierarchy of a canonically-ordered discourse satisfying (C). The macrounits are M-labeled nodes. The P nodes form the "physical" sequence of local units (propositions) and a coherence graph, having the depth-first spanning tree shown on FIG. 1.*

In general, we have the following statement true:
Given a discourse, the statements **(D1)** and **(D2)** are equivalent to each other:

**(D1)** The discourse has an integral macrostructure and the macrounits satisfy **(C)**.

**(D2)** The discourse is canonically-ordered and each of the local units, except the topmost unit $I$, is dominated by its parent unit through a general-to-particular link of local coherence.

Note, that if a globally coherent, canonically-ordered discourse is given, and **(C)** is satisfied, then all summaries are defined by the discourse's tree: the summary of the order $l$ is the subsequence of units of the height $l$ or more.

**Modeling Node Macrostatus through Distances and Centrality.** Since a direct application of the macrorule remains beyond the SMIsC scope, we use some indirect - namely, structural - evidences of domination.

First, when local units function as macrounits, it's reasonable to consider that macrolevels are formed consistently with unit levels formed on the basis of cognitive-psychological relevance (measured by "psychological distance") to the topmost global thematic unit [14]. This condition is satisfied by the construction of the tree.

Second, take into account that semantic units denote facts of some possible world and discourses interlink these facts into propositional networks [6]. Given a discourse, one may assume that some larger propositional network can exist within which the discourse's network is embedded, such that its links not entering the coherence graph can be considered as local coherence links of other possible discourses. Such network (graph) may be called the *supernetwork (supergraph)* of the discourse's network (coherence graph).

Such supernetwork can be thought of as a representation of (a region of) the possible world of a discourse. Something like thus networked facts is probably represented in the human LTM memory. And, clearly, such "world" can be represented through a vast coherence network stored in a hypertext database.

In any propositional (super)network, nodes can be distinguished one from other by their propositions or, simply, by their numeration. In other words, one way to differentiate nodes is to assign them different labels by considerations having no direct relation to the structure formed by links.

However, there exists another way to distinguish among the nodes - namely, by using their structural characteristics which are independent of any label assignment and called, in graph theory, 'node invariants'. By means of a node invariant, it's possible to determine whether two nodes are "dissimilar" by their structural positions.

By definition [16], two nodes $u$ and $v$ of a graph are said to be 'similar', or 'symmetrical', to each other, if there exists an automorphism of the graph translating $u$ into $v$. The characteristic property of a node invariant is that this function (defined on the nodes of a graph) assumes one and the same value on any two nodes, if these nodes are similar. If a node invariant assumes different values, then the respective nodes are certainly dissimilar (however, if it assumes one and the same value, then the respective nodes aren't necessarily similar).

Among node invariants, such exist that the values, they assume at the nodes of a graph, impose a certain ranking on these nodes, allowing to separate them into those forming the core of the graph's structure and those forming its periphery. Such invariants are called *node centralities* [17]. We offer to interpret them as measures of the unit generality, to adopt the ranking as the basis for semantic domination assignment and hence to consider the structural core and the structural periphery of a network as its semantic core and its semantic periphery, correspondingly.

The simplest form of node centrality is given by node degrees: the larger the degree, $d$, of a node (the number of its links), the more "central" the node. If $d(x)>d(y)$ for some interlinked $x$ and $y$, then the unit $x$ semantically dominates the unit $y$ - the former is "more general", the latter is "more particular". This measure is appropriate if it's adopted that the degree of a node measures the "aspectness" of the respective unit.

Another form of node centrality is based on the sum, $r(x)$, of the distances between a given node $x$ and all other nodes of the network. The less the $r$ of a node, the more "central" the node. The semantic significance of this measure follows from the correlation between the "psychological distance" among semantic units and their distance in the coherence graph: if $r(x)<r(y)$, then the average "psychological relevance" of $x$ to other units is higher than the same of $y$.

At last, one more function, $e(x)$, can be used being defined as the maximal distance between a given node $x$ and other nodes. The less the $e$ of a node, the more "central" the node. The "psychological distance" argumentation is applicable again.

There exists a purely formal reason to deal mainly with large (super)networks. When using a node invariant in order to differentiate nodes, it's naturally to prefer the situations when few nodes have equal (tied) values of the invariant. Various invariants can differ one from other in their discriminating power, but the "field of competition" for them is always limited to the set of dissimilar nodes. Structurally similar (symmetrical) nodes, if they exist, form unavoidable source of ties. For this reason, the networks should be favored where such nodes don't exist. And the theorem is true stating that the proportion of graphs having no similar nodes (that is, of asymmetrical graphs) tends to one when the number of nodes tends to the infinity [18]. More qualitative considerations are connected with the evolution of a given coherence (super)network. If such network is small, then its any node invariant's ranking is extremely sensitive to adding new nodes and links and therefore has to be considered as lacking any "objective significance".

Thus we adopt the following convention:

**(E)** Given two interlinked units $x$ and $y$ of a discourse, it's considered that $x$ dominates $y$, if $x$ is closer to the topmost unit than $y$ and $x$ is more central than $y$ by a node centrality defined on the supernetwork.

By this convention, in a canonically-ordered discourse, each of the local units is dominated by its parent unit, if each of these units is less central than its parent.

## 2.6. In Harmony with Levelt's Linearization Strategies

Now, consistently with **(A)**, **(B)** and **(D)**, we direct SMIsC to the task of generation of discursive trails, being canonically-ordered and centrality-guided. The tendency to create canonically-ordered trails is also in agreement with general properties of linearization strategies in *discourse production*, as they were formulated by Willem J. M. Levelt [12, 13].

Levelt considers linearization as a mapping a given information structure (having no intrinsic linear order) on a sequence of clauses, such that it allows a comprehender to reconstruct the structure, at least within certain limits [13]. Linearization is characterized by very general, content-independent properties that "are partly speculative but in large part also based on empirical research" [12].

Empirical studies dealt with the most easily observable domain of spatial networks, such as city maps, apartment layouts, electric circuits, etc. But, because of the extremely general nature of the revealed properties, dealing with connectedness and economy of human STM only, it's supposed that these properties aren't limited to this particular domain, but apply more generally to other types of discourse as well. On this basis, linearization problem is attributed to the field of thought, or of dialectic, rather than of rhetoric [12]. This explains why linearization can also be observed in other, non-linguistic human behavior, e.g. in walking through museum, in playing music or chess [13].

For the case of hierarchical tree structures, the following strategies were confirmed experimentally [12, 13]:

L1) a structure is traversed in a depth-first fashion;

L2) everything else being equal, a shorter branch is preferred to a longer branch in describing from a choice point (minimization of the duration of STM load of unfinished choice points);

L3) let the "complexity" of a branch be the number of potential choice points in the branch; then, everything else being equal, a "simpler" branch is preferred to a more "complex" branch in describing from a choice point (minimization of the size of STM load, i.e., the size of stack).

Clearly, the L1-L2 combination results in a canonically-ordered tree. This type of trees becomes a fundamental determinant of both comprehension and production (one may remember that the leading edge rule is a product of STM limitations only, that all above examination of comprehension was content-independent and that it's possible to consider the meaningful form of not only a discourse, but also, e.g., a melody [8, p. 197]).

As to L3, the combination of this strategy with L1 and L2 leads to a prevalence of hierarchical right-branching structures in discourses. Levelt observes that a similar prevalence is also typical for syntactic structures where it emerges, by Yngve's depth hypothesis [19], as a result of STM's limited span: we are able to memorize at a glance and repeat back correctly about seven random digits, about seven nonsense words, about seven items (the "magical number seven plus or minus two").

## 3. The SMIsC Macrocontrol

### 3.1. Initial Thematic Nodes and Prestructures

On the basis of examination carried out in the previous section, we formulate the strategies that enable the system to control coherent navigation. They need the following preface.

It's implied that the database hypertext network is a sufficiently large coherence network. By definition, such network can be interpreted as a propositional (super)network.

Building a trail begins always with indication an initial *thematic node*, specifying the trail's global theme. This indication can be made by the user with the help of a keyword index and/or a node-centrality ranking provided by SMIsC. The maximal number of nodes, which a coherent trail can include, can be very sensitive to the centrality of this initial node.

When a thematic node is chosen, SMIsC temporarily deforms the network graph in the way implied by the fishing net metaphor: the system "picks up" the thematic node and makes other nodes "falling about" this node "in a cascade". A hierarchy of node levels (but not a tree yet) emerges where a level is formed by the nodes being one and the same number of links distant from the thematic node. Lower levels can be suppressed by the macrocontrol system and according to the user's instructions. This hierarchy is called *prestructure*.

## 3.2. The Strategies

The specified thematic node is the first current node. Subsequently, being in a current node, SMIsC applies a kind of machine expertise in order to reduce the set of possible next nodes to a (sub)set *NEXT* of probable coherent continuations of the trail. The situation is possible when the system finds the set *NEXT* empty; such event terminates the session of coherent navigation from the given thematic node. Otherwise, *NEXT* is displayed before the user. The following strategies of choosing the nodes for *NEXT* constitute the core of the SMIsC's macrocontrol subsystem (the strategies are applied in the order presented).

Observe the depth-first character of travelling across the database network:

**S1:** If the current node has yet unvisited children in the prestructure, choose each of them to form the set *NEXT*.

Observe the convention **(E)**:

**S2:** If the set *NEXT* is nonempty and if the current node has the centrality $c$, then remove from the set each node of the centrality $c$ or more.

Build a canonically-ordered tree:

**S3:** If the set *NEXT* contains more than one node and if the current node has no visited children, then: (a) for each node from *NEXT*, find the number $H$, the upper estimate of the height of yet unvisited node (see commentaries below); (b) find the number $H1$, the minimum of $Hs$; and (c) remove from the set each node with $H>H1$.

**S4:** If the set *NEXT* is nonempty and if the current node has one or more visited children and if the most recently visited child has the height $h$, then remove from the set each node with $H<h$.

Build a right-branching tree:

**S5:** If the set *NEXT* contains more than one node, then: (a) for each node from *NEXT*, find the number $B$, the upper estimate of the complexity of a branch hanging onto yet unvisited node (see commentaries below); (b) find the number $B1$, the minimum of $Bs$; and (c) remove from the set each node with $B>B1$.

Tend to be locally coherent with other non-dominant units of the (macro)episode:

**S6:** If the set *NEXT* contains more than one node and if the current node has a nonempty set $Q$ of visited children, then favor in the set *NEXT* every node that, having a specified $H$, has links with $Q$ nodes, having $h \leq H$.

Stack "unfinished choice points" and backtrack to them:

**S7:** If the set *NEXT* is empty then if *STACK* of "unfinished choice points" is nonempty then pop out the node being the last "unfinished choice point", make this node the current again and then apply **S1**; otherwise (if *STACK* is empty), terminate the trail and the session.

**S8:** If, after application **S1-S6**, the set *NEXT* is nonempty and if the user chooses one of its members as the next node of the trail, then: (a) reduce the valency of the current node by 1 (see commentaries below); (b) if the valency remains nonzero, store this node on *STACK* as an "unfinished choice point"; and (c) take the node chosen by the user as the new current node and apply **S1**.

**S9:** If, after application **S1-S6**, the set *NEXT* is nonempty and if the user refuses to choose one of its members as the next node of the trail, then (a) reduce the valency of the current node to zero and remove this node from *STACK*; (b) if *STACK* remains nonempty, then pop out the node being the last "unfinished choice point", make this node the current again and then apply **S1**; (c) otherwise, if *STACK* is empty, terminate the trail and the session.

## Commentaries

1. The valency of a node is equal to the number of yet unvisited nodes belonging to the node's children by the prestructure. When visiting one of these children for the first time (either from this node or from another), the valency of the node is reduced by 1.

2. The upper estimate $H$ of the height of yet unvisited node $x$ is equal to the maximal number of links in a downward chain of yet unvisited nodes that leads from $x$ to a terminal node.

3. The upper estimate $B$ of the complexity of a branch hanging onto yet unvisited node $x$ is equal to the maximal number of nodes of valency more than 1 in a downward chain of yet unvisited nodes that leads from $x$ to a terminal node.

### 3.3. Output of a session: trail, semantic outline, and summaries

At the end of a session, a sequence of textual nodes is formed imitating a semantically coherent, canonically-ordered discourse. Together with the sequence, a hierarchical tree is given of which the sequence is a depth-first traversal (the tree consists of the links actually chosen when traversing). The tree defines an *outline* that organizes information in a logicosemantic fashion, going from general to specific, or from most important to least important (in the context of the sequence's overall theme). The sequence can be arranged into "parts", "chapters", "sections", "subsections" and "paragraphs", heading by the nodes of a sufficiently large height.

A coherent sequence, having a given initial thematic node, may be obtained or continued and completed by the system in an *automatic* mode, on the basis of random choosing in *NEXT*.

At last, if a sequence is completed, then, instead of it, one of the shorter *summaries*, or "skip-trails", may be read, printed out and saved. Each of them can be generated by the system in automatic mode - as a subsequence of nodes of the height exceeding a certain threshold.

A prototype of SMIsC runs on IBM PC AT.

# References

1. R. McALEESE: Navigation and browsing in hypertext. In: R. McAleese, ed. *Hypertext: theory into practice.* Norwood, NJ: Ablex, 1989, 6-44.
2. J. CONKLIN: Hypertext: an introduction and survey. *IEEE Computer*, 20(9), 1987, 17-41.
3. HYPERTEXT'91 ADVANCE PROGRAM.
4. K. UTTING, N. YANKELOVICH: Context and orientation in hypermedia networks. *ACM Transactions on Information Systems*, 7(1), 1989, 58-84.
5. T.A. van DIJK: Semantic discourse analysis. In: T.A. van Dijk, ed., *Handbook of discourse analysis*, Vol. 2. London: Academic Press, 1985, 103-136.
6. T.A. van DIJK, W. KINTSCH: *Strategies of discourse comprehension.* New York: Academic Press, 1983.
7. P.A. CARLSON: Hypertext and new tools for knowledge workers. In: J. Gornostaev, H. Lantsberg and S. Zinoviev, eds. *Proceedings of the International Colloquium "New Information Technologies" (Moscow, USSR, October 8-10, 1991).* Moscow: ICSTI, 1991, 106-122.
8. H.-G. GADAMER: *Truth and method* (translated and edited by G. Barden and J.Cumming). New York: Seabury Press, 1975.
9. R. RADA: *Hypertext: from text to expertext.* London: McGraw-Hill Book Co., 1991.
10. W. KINTSCH, T.A. van DIJK: Toward a model of text comprehension and production. *Psychological Review*, 85(5), 1978, 363-394.
11. J.R. MILLER, W. KINTSCH: Readability and recall of short prose passages: a theoretical analysis. *Journal of Experimental Psychology: Human Learning and Memory*, 6(4), 1980, 335-354.
12. W.J.M. LEVELT: The speaker's linearization problem. *Philosophical Transactions of the Royal Society of London*, B-295(1077), 1981, 305-314.
13. W.J.M. LEVELT: Linearization in describing spatial networks. In: S. Peters and E. Saarinen, eds. *Processes, beliefs, and questions.* Dordrecht: D.Reidel, 1982, 199-220.
14. G.H. BOWER, R.K. CIRILO: Cognitive psychology and text processing. In: T.A. van Dijk, ed., *Handbook of discourse analysis*, Vol. 1. London: Academic Press, 1985, 71-105.
15. R. TARJAN: Depth-first search and linear graph algorithms. *SIAM Journal on Computing*, 1(2), 1972, 146-160.

16. F. HARARY: *Graph theory.* Reading, Mass.: Addison-Wesley, 1969.
17. G. SABIDUSSI: The centrality index of a graph. *Psychometrica,* 31(4), 1966, 581-603.
18. F. HARARY, E.M. PALMER: *Graphical enumeration.* New York: Academic Press, 1973.
19. V.H. YNGVE: The depth hypothesis. In: R. Jakobson, ed., *Structure of language and its mathematical aspect.* Proceedings of the Symposia in Applied Mathematics, XII. Providence, R.I.: American Mathematical Society, 1961, 130-138.

# Generating Self-Adaptive Human-Computer Interfaces.

Aline BERTHOME-MONTOY
Boursière de Doctorat CEA/Industrie

LISI
Université Claude Bernard Lyon I - Bat 710
43 Bd du 11 Novembre 1918
F-69622 Villeurbanne cedex
e-mail : montoy@lisisun.univ-lyon1.fr

**Abstract.** Self-adaptive interfaces can be considered at different levels : adaptation to the user's habits and experience, adaptation to the user's task, adaptation to the user's knowledge. In this paper, we explain what we mean by adapting to the user's experience and task, how we detect the need of such adaptations and how we realize them, and why we have been led to consider automatic generation of interfaces. We expose then what we aim to do about adaptation to the user's knowledge.

## 1 Introduction.

Self-adaptivity may cover a great variety of modifications of an interface. In this paper, we will distinguish three levels of adaptations. The first level concerns the relations between the user and the computer tool. Two types of adaptations are considered here : automating commands a user realizes systematically at the beginning of a session to create his own working environment, and adapting the dialog, simplifying texts of questions and becoming less directive , when the user becomes experienced. This level is the *adaptation to the user's habits and experience*. The second level is the *adaptation to the user's task.* It aims at speeding up the user's work, according to what he does more frequently. This adaptation uses two means : adaptation of default values and creation of specific commands for sequences of actions frequently used. The third level is the *adaptation to the user's knowledge.* This level concerns essentially explanations and intelligent help. When a user asks a question or help, it is interesting to adapt the answer to his knowledge on the domain of application, in order to give him answers he can understand, but not to give him too many details.

Examining the first two levels, we can notice two things. First, adaptation to the user's experience supposes to create several versions of the same interface for each functionality, each version corresponding to a different level. But we know that the time spent in designing an interface is yet more than half the time to realize the whole software. Second, adaptation to the user's task supposes to modify the interface when adding a personal command. But in this case, we cannot ask the user to modify by himself the interface. These remarks led us to consider automatic generation of interfaces.

## 2   Context of our Work.

For our purpose, we are using the Gosseyn Machine (MG) [5], a knowledge based system founded on an actors language which provides us with an inference engine and a spying mechanism to record each user's action. In fact, we record the user's actions in two different ways, used for different purposes : one records, for each command, the number of uses and given answers and is useful to study the user's experience and the default values; the other one contains the chronology of actions, it is recorded in files at the end of the session and is useful to detect the user's habits and the frequently used sequences of commands. We will call these records functional history (FH) and chronological history (CH).

We said that MG is founded on an actors language, i.e. an object language in which objects communicate only by sending messages. It respects the model "everything is an actor". So the user himself is considered as an actor of the language, and each click on a command 'com' is seen as a message the actor 'user' sends to the actor 'com'. By intercepting these messages, the system will have a complete history of each intervention of the user.

FH is formed of temporary actors, one for each command used during the session. When the user clicks on a command, the corresponding actor is created if it does not exist, and the following informations are recorded :

> _ number of uses
> _place in the history
> _parameters given
> _presence of mistakes
> _interruptions of the command (by the "stop" key)
> _requests for help.

CH is the record of exchanged messages, in chronological order.  For each message, it contains (the value for a user intervention shown inside parentheses):

> _its level (1 for the selection of a command, which initiates a sub-dialog)
> _its sender (the user)
> _its receiver (the selected command)
> _its selector (click)
> _the answer returned, eventually (parameters asked in return to the user)
> _sub-messages (messages of the sub-dialog initiated)
> _the cpu time.
> _the wall-times of beginning and end (in seconds)

**Example.** Using MG, a user wants to create an object. He selects in the menu the functionality *create-an-object*. He is asked successively :

> *Select the class to be instantiated*
> > attribute
> *Give the name of the new object*
> > is-the-son-of
> *Do you want to place this object on the screen?*
> > no
> (*Click on the place where you want to display it.* is not asked because of the previous answer)

This will be recorded in the CH in the following form :

*(1 aline create-an-object clic (details of the interaction) (attribute is-the-son-of nil)
190000 2944546566 2944546598*

   *(2 create-an-object aline give-me-an-object (details) attribute 50000 2944546566
2944546584)*

   *(2 create-an-object aline answer-me (details) is-the-son-of 40000 2944546584
2944546596)*

   *(2 create-an-object aline answer-me-by-yes-or-no (details) nil 30000 2944546596
2944546598)*

*)*

Only level 1 will be useful for our purpose. Messages of level 2 or more are used for other purposes, by other researchers.

In FH, the object representing *create-an-object* will be added some values :

   *t187*

*my-command : create-an-object*

*number-of-uses : 5*

*places-in-history : (28 19 12 7 2)*

*frequence-of-normal-uses : (2 help 1 error)*

*given-answers : ((attribute is-the-son-of nil) (attribute colour nil) (objects-of-this-
application cars t (150 70 aa.wnd)) (attribute place nil) (nil place nil))*

The values of frequence-of-normal-uses means that the user made a mistake during the first use of this command (*nil* can not be instantiated), then he made a normal use, during the 3rd use he asked for help, and the last 2 uses were normal.

Everything that will be detected concerning one of the levels of self-adaptivity will be recorded in the user's profile. This profile will be used at the beginning of each session to restore the user's personal interface, and will be updated at the end of each session by new elements detected during this session. It contains the actions to execute automatically at the beginning of the session, the user's level of experience for each action, the useful default values and macro-commands. In the future, it will also contain the knowledge the user has about the domain of application.

## 3  The User's Habits and Experience.

### 3.1  Objectives.

Each user has his own preferences concerning the working environment : for instance, one will resize a given window, another one will close it, a third one will position a variable. We want the interface to execute automatically these commands to give the user the interface he likes, adapting itself to his habits. Concerning his experience, the problem is to simplify the questions and be less directive. In a first time, parameters will be asked one after the other and the text of questions will be rather detailed to explain to the user what parameters he has to give. In a second time, this text will be shortened, and in a third time the user will be shown a list of parameters he can enter in any order. This evolution has to be done independently for each functionality, since a given user does not have the same experience on every actions of the system. For more details about what we expect from the interface, see [7].

## 3.2 Detection of the User's Habits and Experience.

In order to determine the user's habits, we use the chronological history, and consider only the beginning of each session. By comparing these sessions, the system will detect that the first commands are always the same (even if in a different order) with the same action and the same object concerned (e.g. resizing always the same window) and then will record these commands in the user's profile to execute them automatically when the user initiates a session. For details (e.g. the final size of the window), the system will take the mean value of those given by the user.

In order to determine the user's experience, things are rather simple. When he has used five times an action without errors, help nor stop, the system considers that he can access to the upper level. When he asks for help, he is first informed that the new presentation asks the same parameters as the previous one, and if he does not understand, he is demoted to the lower level. If there is an error or a stop once, the system considers it to be just a mistake. But if it is repeated the effect is the same as for a help.

## 4 The User's Task.

We have noticed two adaptations to the user's task : creation of specific macro-commands, and adaptation of the default values to the most frequently used by a given user. This is a little more complex than the previous level of adaptation.

In order to determine the useful default values, the system will use the FH. We have seen that it contains for each functionality the given answers, in chronological order. The system will examine the last ones (for the moment, it looks at the ten most recent answers, but this number can be modified after experiments). We cannot do this research on the whole history, because if a user gives 1000 times the answer $a$, and then gives always the answer $b$, it must be detected before he has given 1000 times the answer $b$ ! Then if more than half of the last answers are the same (for a given parameter) and are different from the present default value, this value is changed.

The problem of determining sequences of actions is rather difficult for different reasons. First, the elements of a sequence are not necessarily consecutive : there may be noise, i.e. actions which are not part of the sequence, between its elements. Second, there may be permutations in a given sequence. Third there may be different manners to realize a same goal. Fourth, we want to detect coherent sequences : it is not sufficient to have the same actions, there must be the same relations between elements (i.e. it is not the same to open window $a$ and resize another window $b$ as to open window $c$ and resize the same window $c$ : the first is not a sequence, the second is). To solve this problem, we have chosen to separate actions according to the objects concerned. Then, having the history of each object, we search for similar sequences in these histories, and eventually, we reconstruct sequences concerning several objects, using pairs of "hinge" commands concerning several objects (for more details, see [6]). This method solves the problem of coherent sequences and the greatest part of the problem of permutations. For the different manners to reach the same goal, we assume that a given user uses most of the time the same way to do it.

**Example.** The separation of actions according to concerned objects leads the system to detect that the following sequences concerning windows aa and bb are similar :

| | |
|---|---|
| *7 open window aa* | *15 open window bb* |
| *13 display object rr in aa* | *18 display object tt in bb* |
| *14 resize aa* | *21 resize bb* |

Histories of objects rr and tt will show that the following sequences are similar :

| | |
|---|---|
| *10 modify object rr* | *12 modify object tt* |
| *13 display object rr in aa* | *18 display object tt in bb* |
| *17 print attributes of rr* | *19 print attributes of tt* |

The hinge pair of commands (*display object rr in aa, display object tt in bb*), present in both of the pairs of similar sequences, and the positions in the history, allow to reconstitute the pair of similar sequences (containing permutations) :

| | |
|---|---|
| *7 open window aa* | *12 modify object tt* |
| *10 modify object rr* | *15 open window bb* |
| *13 display object rr in aa* | *18 display object tt in bb* |
| *14 resize aa* | *19 print attributes of tt* |
| *17 print attributes of rr* | *21 resize bb* |

## 5  Model and Generation of Interfaces.

### 5.1  The Model.

Self adaptivity implies some constraints on the model of interface : first it implies to have the interface independent of the application (it is a general recommendation for interfaces design), but it implies also that the interface is easily modifiable (default values, presentation of sub-dialogs corresponding to a command, adding new functionalities and then modifying menus, ...). We have said that we work in an actors environment, so we have naturally examined the possibility of multi-agents interfaces. They seem very well adapted for self-adaptive interfaces, since the elements to be modified are represented by values of attributes and can thus easily be modified. Moreover, this model presents a great modularity, so an agent can be modified or added without affecting the whole interface. This is essential for self-adaptive interfaces.

We have explained in §1 why we have been led to consider automatic generation of interfaces. This implies constraints too, since the designer of the system will have to specify the application, and these specifications must be compatible with the model of interfaces. A rather natural way to specify an application seems to be the specification of functionalities. The designer will specify the actions that will be available for the user, giving indications about the composition of actions (it will be more or less inspired by the decomposition of the user's task into subtasks that should have been done during the ergonomic analysis of the software).

We have said that the interface will adapt itself to the user's experience for each functionality, that it will have to add some functionality to adapt to the user's task, and that we think natural to describe an application by the possible actions. This explains why we have chosen a model of interfaces based on the functionality. Each functionality will be formed of three parts : application, control of the dialog and presentation. These functionalities will form a tree thanks to the composition of functionalities. The root of this tree will be the session. Each instance of the class *functionality* will have the form shown in figure 1 (this schema is simplified) :

The concerned objects that we see in the application part will be described as instances of the class *object* . Each instance of this class will also be formed of three parts : abstraction, presentation and control. Here, the control maintains the coherence between the presentation and the abstraction. The presentation of an object will not be generated automatically. We think it is impossible, since the representation on the screen must be compatible with the object of the real world when it exists, or with the mental representation the user has of this object. So, the designer will have to specify the presentation of objects. These objects can be decomposed into several parts that each have a representation, the global object will then be represented by the juxtaposition of elementary representations. An object can also have several representations according to its state.

**fonct**

| **a-fonct** | **c-fonct** | **p-fonct** |
|---|---|---|
| functions called | correspondence | objects of presentation |
| parameters | parameters/objects of | |
| composition of functionalities | presentation/level of experience | |
| concerned objects | default values | |
| pre- and post-conditions | text of questions | |
| | dialog control | |

**Fig. 1.** The three parts of an instance of functionality

## 5.2 The Generation of Interfaces.

We have chosen not to use existing tools (an overview of these tools is presented in [3]) to generate our interfaces, for several reasons. First, we do not know any tool that generates several presentations for a functionality. But above all, we need to use tools of low enough level, in order to be able to access all necessary informations in the dialog to construct the histories used to detect useful adaptations, and to know enough details of the interface to be able to adapt it to the user.

**Specifications of the Application.** We have used ideas essentially from [4] and [8]. The specifications of the applications are directly adapted from [4]. Figure 2 shows the class of objects used to specify the application.

In comparison with Foley's model, pre- and post-conditions that were classes of objects are just values of attributes with a special syntax (to be specified) here. But the main difference resides in the attributes *composed-of* and *status-of-components* . In [4], all actions are at the same level, and then the specifications reflect only the logic of functioning of the software. The attribute *composed-of* allows the designer to specify a hierarchy in the functionalities, that reflects the decomposition into tasks and subtasks. The attributes *status-of-components* allows to specify whether some actions are mandatory, must be realized in a given order, must be realized prior to any other action, or things like that. These two attributes reflect the logic of use of the software. In order to reflect this logic, the designer will also have the possibility to introduce in the hierarchy some nodes of a different type : *workspace* [8]. A workspace will group functionalities which form a whole, which manipulate a defined set of concepts. Workspaces aim at guiding the user in the software, separating distinct groups of actions which have goals of different types. In the interface, the effect of this notion will consist in affecting a different window to each workspace.

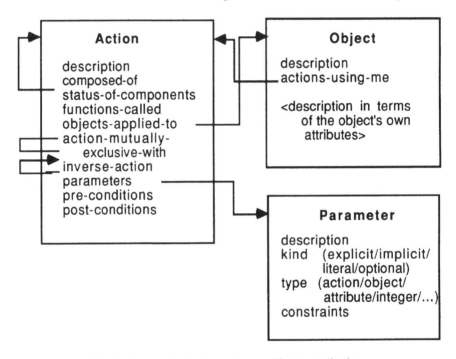

**Fig. 2.** classes of objects used to specify the application.

**The Generation.** The generation itself has not a great originality, except the restructuration of the tree of actions in order to have well-balanced menus with a reasonable number of actions, and the generation of three different presentations (corresponding to the levels of experience) for each action.

The stages of the generation are :
_ the restructuration of the tree, based on similarities between the types of parameters, the objects concerned, the names, or the post-conditions (i.e. affectations of values to attributes of objects),
_ the compilation of constraints on parameters and pre- and post-conditions into a form directly usable by the interface, and compilation of status of components into pre- and post-conditions,
_ the generation of presentations and control : the first one is based on the correspondence between types of parameters and objects of interaction, the second consists in selecting elements of a skeleton of control, according to the presence or absence of elements such as explicit parameters, pre- and post-conditions, some status of components not translatable into pre-conditions, etc,

_ the interactive modification of the interface, if the designer is not satisfied or on requests of users.

To sum up, the main originalities of this generator are the hierarchy of actions using the composition of actions, that reflects the logic of use of the software, the generation of several presentations for each functionality allowing an independent adaptation to the user's level of experience for each action, and the other aspects of self-adaptivity provided by this tool.

## 6 Implementation and Perspectives.

At present, the detection of elements to adapt is implemented : detection of the user's experience, of the useful default values, of the frequently used sequences, and of the user's habits. The generation of interfaces is currently being implemented. In order to limit the number of messages exchanged between actors, the three parts of each functionality do not constitute three distinct objects, but the attributes of these parts are joined together in a unique object. The generator will be tested on the example of VIFLEX, a software that calculates vibrations of transmission shafts. The detection of adaptations to make (i.e. the user's profile) have been tested on the interface of the Gosseyn Machine, which does not really respect the model of interfaces presented, but allows us to build the two histories we need.

In the future, we would like to study the adaptation of explanations and of answers to questions, to the user's knowledge. This implies to provide a mechanism of explanation and to detect the user's knowledge. So we will need to have knowledge at our disposal. This knowledge base should contain informations about the domain of application, eventually about the mathematical tools used by the software, and about the relations between the commands and the knowledge (what concepts are concerned by each command). We will probably use technics of intelligent tutoring systems (to adapt the explanations) and of machine learning (to determine what the user knows). It would be interesting too to detect during the session when the user is in difficulty, in order to suggest to him what to do next. This implies to be able to detect his goals, and to be able to generate plans of actions.

## 7 Conclusion.

In this paper, we have shown that we have realized self-adaptivity for the first two levels presented in the introduction : we can detect the user's habits and experience for each command, using the two histories built during the session, and we can detect useful default values or macro-commands, using these same histories, without using any particular knowledge. Let us notice that whereas the histories are built during the session, the study of the informations they contain is realized after the session, when the user quits the application. We have seen that self-adaptivity implies to have several presentations for each functionality, to be able to add some commands and to modify the interface. That is why we have considered the problem of generation of interfaces. Nothing is done yet concerning the third level of self-adaptivity, i.e. the adaptation to the user's knowledge, which implies to have knowledge about the domain application.

**References**

1. BENNETT, W.E., BOIES, S.J., GOULD, J.D., GREENE, S.L. & WIECHA, C.F., "Transformations on a Dialog Tree : Rule-Based Mapping of Content to Style", Proceedings ACM SIGGRAPH Symposium on User Interface Software and Technology, Williamsburg, November 1989.

2. COUTAZ, J., "Interface Homme-Ordinateur : Conception et Réalisation", Dunod Publ., 1990.

3. EL MRABET, H., "Outils de Génération d'Interfaces : Etat de l'Art et Classification", Technical report, INRIA Rocquencourt, France, February 1991.

4. FOLEY, J., KIM, W.C., KOVACEVIC, S. & MURRAY, K., "The User Interface Design Environment", Technical Report n°GWU-IIST-88-4, Department of Electrical Engineering and Compter Science, George Washington University, January 1988.

5. FOUET, J.M., Technical Report, Contract 90/CNES/3760, June 1991.

6. MONTOY, A., "Auto-amélioration de l'interface homme-machine de la Machine Gosseyn", DEA report, Lyon I, June 1991.

7. MONTOY, A., "Determination du niveau de compétence de l'utilisateur pour les interfaces auto-adaptatives", ErgoIA'92, Biarritz, France, 7-9 May 1992.

8. NORMAND, V., "Le Modèle SIROCO : de la Spécification Conceptuelle des Interfaces Utilisateur à leur Réalisation.", Thèse de Doctorat, Université Joseph Fourier Grenoble I, April 17, 1992.

9. PETOUD, I. & PIGNEUR, Y., "An Automatic and Visual Approach for User Interface Design", IFIP WG2.7, Engineering for Human Computer Interaction, Napa Valley, August 1989.

10. ROGER, B., "Un Système de Dialogue Intelligent avec un Interlocuteur à la Découverte du Monde Simulé par un Logiciel Quelconque", Thèse de Doctorat, Paris VI, June 25, 1987.

11. SCAPIN, D.L., "Guide Ergonomique de Conception des Interfaces Homme-Machine", Technical Report, Unité de Recherche INRIA-Rocquencourt, October 1986.

# The Practical Use of Macro Recording: A Case Study

Allen Cypher

Advanced Technology Group
Apple Computer, Inc.
Cupertino, CA 95014

**Abstract.** Macro recording is a practical technique for automating repetitive tasks on computers. The user records a series of actions, and then the computer can re-execute those actions. This paper discusses a variety of macros that were used to assist in a real-life task of editing a book manuscript. The capabilities of current tools are presented, followed by a discussion of how the limitations of these tools restrict current end users, and how some of these limitations can be overcome.

**Keywords:** macro recording, automation, end user programming, demonstrational interfaces, programming by demonstration.

## 1 Introduction

Most of the users of personal computers today do not know how to program. They use computers in their daily work to write letters, to keep track of finances, and to design illustrations. They have no interest in computers *per se* — they just want to accomplish their tasks, and the computer is the best available tool.

Although computers are powerful tools and excel at performing repetitive tasks very quickly, it is nonetheless true that users must often perform repetitive tasks themselves, since there is no easy way for them to instruct the computer to perform the repetition.

Macro recorders can potentially solve much of this problem, since they offer a means to automate tasks without requiring the user to program. The user turns on the macro recorder program, performs a sequence of actions on the computer (such as typing text, selecting menu commands, and clicking on objects with a mouse), and the macro recorder records these actions. Later, when the user wants to perform that sequence of actions again, he or she simply gives a single command, and the macro program automatically executes the entire sequence.

In this paper, I will discuss a variety of repetitive tasks that I encountered while editing a manuscript for a book. This will hopefully convince the reader of the prevalence of computer activities that are appropriate for automation. I will show how some of these tasks could be effectively automated with a macro recorder. I also want to document some of the idiosyncratic problems that arise in real-life situations that can derail simple recorders. I will discuss why some of the tasks were difficult to automate, and why some could not be automated. Finally, I will discuss how some of these difficulties can be overcome.

## 2 The Case Study

I recently edited a book which consisted of 30 chapters, prepared by different authors. The chapters were all prepared on Macintosh computers using Microsoft Word. I had supplied the authors with "paragraph styles", which automatically formatted most of the text correctly. Nonetheless, there were a variety of stylistic issues which were not covered by the styles, and so I had to edit all of the chapters to ensure consistency.

Here is a brief description of some of the repetitive activities that I had to perform:

**1. Link chapters.** Each chapter is a separate document. In order to number the pages correctly, it is necessary to "link" the chapters in order. I needed to open each chapter in turn, select the "Next File..." command, and then click on the name of the next chapter in the list of files that appeared.

**2. Add headers.** The top of every even page in the book should contain a header showing the page number and the name of the author of that chapter. The top of every odd page shows the page number and a short form of the title of the chapter. To help with this task, I prepared a table as an Excel spreadsheet which listed the author and short title of each chapter. I needed to open each chapter in turn, select the even header, copy and paste the author from the spreadsheet, select the odd header, and then copy and paste the title from the spreadsheet.

**3. Verify sections.** I wanted to make sure that the first page of each chapter was formatted as a separate section. I needed to open each chapter in turn, go to the second page of the chapter and verify that "S2" (which stands for "Section 2") was displayed at the bottom of the window.

**4. Create table of contents.** As part of the process of creating the table of contents, I needed to open each chapter in turn and copy and paste the chapter number, the title, the author, and the number of the first page.

**5. Verify spacing before headings.** Each chapter had major headings to mark the main sections of the chapter. I wanted to be sure that the authors had inserted two blank lines before each heading. However, if the heading occurs at the top of the page, there should be no preceding blank lines. I needed to open each chapter in turn, search for each heading, and verify that the preceding blank lines were correct.

**6. Format captions.** I wanted the caption for every figure to begin with the word "Figure" capitalized, a space, the number of the figure, a period, and a space. The text of the caption was to continue on the same line. Some authors used colons instead of periods, some did not capitalize the word "Figure", and some started the text on the next line. I needed to open each chapter in turn, search for each figure caption, and put it into the correct format.

**7. Capitalize headings.** Each of the words in a heading was supposed to be capitalized. However, the words "a", "an", "and", "or", and "the" were to be left in lowercase, unless they were the first word in the heading. I needed to open each chapter in turn, search for each heading, and verify that it was capitalized properly.

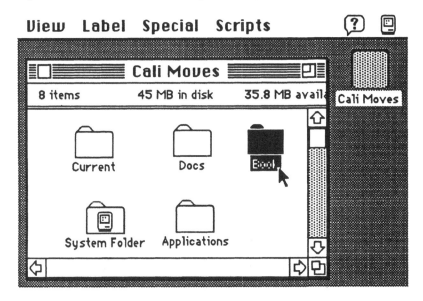

**Fig. 1.** Clicking twice to open the "Book" folder.

**8. Change "programming by example" to "programming by demonstration.** The authors of the book agreed that we should consistently use the term "programming by demonstration" to describe our field, rather than the older term "programming by example". I needed to open each chapter, search for every occurrence of "programming by example", and replace it with "programming by demonstration".

## 3 Automation Through Recording

Ideally, the user should be able automate any of the above tasks by turning on the recorder and performing one iteration of the task. The user would then give a command to "Complete the task", and the macro would repeat the sequence automatically until the task was completed. We will now investigate the extent to which macro recorders can successfully capture and repeat user actions, the various ways in which reality falls short of the ideal, and what can be done to improve the situation.

A natural way to perform the first iteration of the "Link chapters" task, would be to:

1) Click twice on the "Book" folder to open it (see Figure 1).

2) Click twice on the file Chapter 1. This displays Chapter 1 using the Word program.

3) Select the Document menu item. This brings up a dialog box.

4) Click on the "File Series..." button in the dialog. This brings up another dialog.

5) Click on the "Next File" button in the dialog. This brings up the "Open File" dialog, which contains a scrolling list of file names.

6) Click twice on Chapter 2 in the list. (see Figure 2).

7) To close the dialogs, click on the buttons "Open", "OK", and "OK".

8) Click in the Close box to quit working on Chapter 1.

I would want to repeat steps 2-8 for Chapter 2, Chapter 3, and so on, until I reached the last chapter.

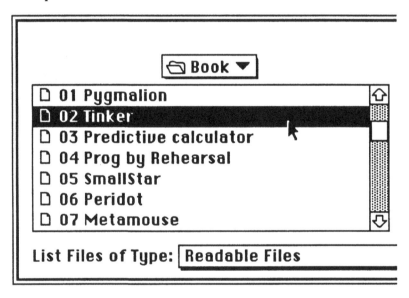

**Fig. 2.** Selecting Chapter 2 from a list.

## 4 Problems with Recording

If I were to simply record the above sequence of commands, and then have the macro recorder execute the sequence repeatedly, there would be a variety of problems that would cause the macro to not complete the task as desired.

**a) Low-level events.** Macro recorders often only have access to low-level descriptions of events. For instance, when I double-click on the "Book" folder in step 1, this action gets recorded as "Click twice at location (192, 48)". When I replay this macro, the "Book" folder may be at a different location on the screen, so the macro will not work correctly.

The macro recorder that I was using — QuicKeys — offers one approach to the problem of low-level events: it allows the user to replace certain low-level events with higher-level ones. For instance, I can replace the command "Click twice at location (192, 48)" with the command "Open 'Book'". This high-level command does not depend on the location of the "Book" folder, and so it will work reliably.

One good feature of macros is that the user can watch how they replay the actions, and it may become obvious why a certain step is failing. For instance, the user could observe the macro clicking on the screen at the location where the "Book" folder used to be, and thereby understand why it was not working correctly.

**b) Timing.** When a macro is executed, it performs its actions very quickly. Often, it performs too quickly: Steps 3 - 7 above involve selecting menu items and clicking on buttons in dialogs, and very often these commands are executed before the menu item or dialog box has appeared on the screen. As a result, an incorrect item may be clicked or the macro may abort. Timing is one of the main reasons that even simple tasks are often not properly automated by recordings.

Macro designers have provided a variety of features to help overcome this problem. Some systems allow the macro to be played back at a slower speed, to insert pauses between steps in the macro, or to explicitly specify that the macro is to pause until a certain menu item or button has appeared. In the example above, I inserted pauses before each click on a button, and the macro performed correctly.

**c) Generalization.** When a user performs an action while recording a macro, it may not be clear what the user intends to do at that step in general. That is, it is difficult to infer the user's intent by just observing a single example of that intent. The macro recorder has no idea what generalization of that action is intended. In step 2 above, when I click on Chapter 1, my intent is to open the *next chapter* in the book. For the first iteration, this happens to be Chapter 1, but for the next iteration, it will be Chapter 2. Similarly, when I select Chapter 2 in step 6, I am selecting the chapter after the current one. For the next iteration, I will want to select Chapter 3 at this step.

One possible solution to the abstraction problem is for the user to perform the activity in a manner which will work appropriately when it is executed later. In our example, step 2 can be performed instead by pressing the "down arrow" key and then selecting the "Open" menu item. This achieves the same effect of opening Chapter 1, but in future executions, it will have the desired effect of opening the *next* chapter. Step 6 can also be replaced by "down arrow" and "Open".

I was able to automate the "Link chapters" task by modifying my recorded macro to overcome the problems of low-level events, timing, and generalization. The "Verify sections" task presented a different problem which could not be fully overcome.

**d) Data access.** To perform the "Verify sections" task, I needed to verify that the bottom of the window contained the text "S2", which stands for "Section 2" (See Figure 3). Although this information is readily available to the human computer user, it is inaccessible to a macro recorder, since there is no way to select this data.

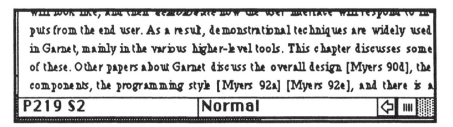

puts from the end user. As a result, demonstrational techniques are widely used in Garnet, mainly in the various higher-level tools. This chapter discusses some of these. Other papers about Garnet discuss the overall design [Myers 90d], the components, the programming style [Myers 92a] [Myers 92e], and there is a

P219 S2          Normal

**Fig. 3.** Verifying that there are two sections in a document.

The data access problem is a major barrier to automating tasks on a computer. Richard Potter presents a good discussion of this problem in [Potter 93]. He also offers a solution: a program that can search for bitmaps on the screen. Anything that the user can see on the screen can potentially be accessed in this way. "Verify sections" could be fully automated by this approach, since the macro could search for "S2" in the bottom part of the window.

I ended up partially automating this task: I used a macro to automatically close the current chapter, open the next chapter in turn, and go to the second page. I then visually inspected the section number myself, and then executed the macro again. This sort of "task-sharing" is a very useful strategy. The computer does the simple, repetitive tasks automatically, and the user performs those parts of the task that are easy for a person, but that would be difficult or impossible to program.

**e) Exceptions.** The "PBE -> PBD" task is seemingly very simple, since Word (and indeed most word processors) has a global replace command. However, the actual task had an exception: occasionally the phrase "programming by example" appeared in a sentence whose verb was "demonstrate". Since it would sound awkward to say, for instance, that "this program demonstrates that programming by demonstration is effective ...", I wanted to change such sentences to "this program shows that programming by demonstration is effective ...".

Most macro recorders have very weak facilities for handling exceptional cases. Tempo allows the user to compare a copied item to a string, and QuicKeys can test whether a certain button or menu item exists or is enabled. Nonetheless, it is clumsy and tedious to add such tests to a recorded macro.

In the case of "PBE -> PBD", I chose to perform the global replace one step at a time and visually inspect the sentence containing the phrase. This meant inspecting numerous Finds in each of 30 chapters.

**f) Complex patterns.** The final problem for recording is that repetitive tasks may contain complex patterns, which are simply too difficult, or even impossible, to express to a simple recorder. The "Capitalize headings" task included several steps which were too difficult to automate. First of all, it is hard to capitalize each word in a sentence. You can capitalize a single word, by selecting the first character in the word and setting its Style to "Uppercase", but it is difficult to tell a macro recorder to iterate over all of the words in the current sentence. Secondly, I wanted to leave the words "a", "an", "and", "or", and "the" in lowercase, and it was too difficult to express this exception. I therefore chose to perform this entire task by hand, using only the Find command to locate Headings.

The "complex pattern" problem comprises a wide range of problems, including flow of control (i.e. branches and iteration) and comparisons. Solutions to these problems generally lie outside the realm of macro recorders: "Programming by demonstration" systems are required for these capabilities, since they can make use of domain knowledge, multiple examples, and inferencing to augment recorded programs.

One notable exception is that iteration can sometimes be easily introduced into a macro by use of a "relative" command. For instance, I used the "down arrow" key to select the next file in the "Link chapters" task, since this makes a selection *relative* to the current selection.

## 5 Summary

While macro recorders can effectively automate many repetitive user activities, they encounter problems with low-level events, timing, generalization, data access, exceptions, and complex patterns. In certain cases, these problems can be overcome by replacing low-level recorded events with high-level events, introducing pauses, performing the task differently, searching for screen bitmaps, and introducing explicit decision steps. While these techniques enable sophisticated users to modify recordings so that they will work properly, this does little to help the normal end user. Not until programming by demonstration becomes successful will end users be able to easily automate their repetitive activities. Until then, many problems with macro recording can be handled by having the user and the macro cooperate in performing the task: the macro performs the simple, repetitive steps, and the user performs the steps that require intelligence.

## References

[Potter 93] Potter, Richard: Just-in-Time Programming. In: A. Cypher (ed.): Watch What I Do: Programming by Demonstration. Cambridge, MA: MIT Press 1993, p. 518.

# HyperLecture: A Self-organizing Lecture Presentation and Revision System

Damian Conway

Victorian Centre for Image Processing and Graphics,
Department of Computer Science, Monash University
Clayton, Victoria 3168, Australia

**Abstract.** This paper presents an overview of HyperLecture, a hypertextual, gesturally-controlled lecture presentation system originally designed for teaching introductory computer programming. HyperLecture provides genuinely user-friendly mechanisms with which a presenter can quickly produce linear and non-linear presentations, hard-copy hand-outs, audio and textual annotations, complete self-driving interactive tutorials and graphical programming code simulations.

## 1 Introduction

### 1.1 Deficiencies in current lecture presentation techniques

Technological advancement has largely bypassed the average lecture theatre [1]. Standard lecture presentation techniques still use Renaissance-level technology: the blackboard and chalk, or their modern equivalents: the whiteboard or overhead projector. The same is largely true of the methods students use to record lecture material (ie: pen and paper).

This need not be the case. Since the early 1970s educators have been heralding the rise of Computer Mediated Presentation (CMP) [2]. Yet it is only in the last few years that notebook computers have become sufficiently powerful, reliable, easy to use, portable and affordable to make possible the many sophisticated and effective means of conveying information promised by CMP.

Traditional methods of lecture presentation, such as writing on a blackboard or projecting a series of transparencies, impose significant limitations on the presenter [3]. For example, the lecturer must cope the mechanics of presenting the material (either writing or managing a set of overhead projector transparencies). Even for the well-practised, this cognitive overhead may impair a presentation and distract the presenter from his or her chain of thought.

A common solution to this problem is to prepare a set of 35mm slides, which are loaded into a projection carousel and stepped through at the press of a button. This greatly simplifies the task of presenting, but effectively reduces the presentation to a fixed linear sequence (although simple hierarchical presentations may still be achieved by simulating an ordered traversal of the presentation structure).

Such presentations are also usually costly, time-consuming and complicated to produce and correct (see [4] for example), involving graphical design and layout, image capture and film processing. In addition, the presentation sequence becomes set in celluloid, and the presentation must be redesigned and often recreated if a new sequence is required.

The mechanics of lecture presentation can also be tedious and distracting for the audience [5]. Prepared materials are almost inevitably static in nature and rely on the presenter's skills to animate them, either physically or verbally. Where multiple media are used in presenting materials, the transition between these media is frequently distracting and often poorly coordinated [6].

Problems also arise when, as a result of a question or other interjection, a presenter is required to deviate from the intended presentation sequence, and therefore forced to shuffle through transparencies or over prepared slides, hunting for a display related to the new topic.

## 1.2. HyperLecture

HyperLecture is an Apple HyperCard stack designed to greatly facilitate the design, creation and presentation of linear and non-linear lecture materials (see Section 2) and to enable the reuse of the those materials in later study or revision by the audience (see Section 3).

Features of the HyperLecture stack include:

- A simple and extensible gestural command interface,
- Optional automatic cross-referencing of materials into a hypertext,
- Multiple navigation modes,
- On-screen monitoring of elapsed time of presentation,
- The capacity to quickly produce coordinated lecture handouts and summaries,
- A simple plain-text input format,
- The capacity to annotate materials textually and verbally for later student revision,
- The capacity to quickly design and implement self-driving audio-visual tutorials using the lecture material,
- Audio assistance for visually impaired users,
- An auxiliary stack which facilitates the presentation and explanation of programming code examples.

HyperLecture was originally designed to facilitate the presentation of course materials in an introductory programming lecture series, but has been readily adapted to the presentation of other types of lectures.

Typically, a prepared HyperLecture stack is loaded onto a Macintosh PowerBook and is presented (using screen mirroring facilities of the PowerBook) via an LCD projection panel on a standard overhead projector. Alternatively, the PowerBook may be plugged directly into a large screen display device.

Each card of the HyperLecture stack is used to store and display a single topic within the lecture and the presenter navigates through the stack in a linear, hierarchical or ad hoc manner, depending on the purpose of the presentation, the nature of the material, and/or the response of the audience. The standard topic cards are laid out so as to automatically format the lecture into a clear and readable presentation. Topics may be presented in point or paragraph format, but the automatic layout encourages a series of points (three to eight per topic) up to a maximum of approximately thirty to forty words.

## 2. HyperLecture as a presentation tool

### 2.1. Gestural interface

In order to simplify operation of the presentation interface and to maintain an uncluttered appearance, individual topic cards contain no buttons or other control selectors. Instead, all of the features of HyperLecture are activated using simple mouse-mediated gestures (similar to those described in another context in [7]). A total of eleven standard gestures are recognized by HyperLecture, each mnemonically related to the action it initiates. Figure 2 describes the gestures and their mnemonics. The specific effects of the context-sensitive undo gesture (called "Scrub") are also outlined.

Gestures are performed by holding down the mouse button and dragging the mouse in the appropriate direction(s). If the mouse button is not down, the motion has no effect and the cursor merely acts as a pointer. When the mouse button is down, the system repeatedly samples the mouse position, building up a series of points representing an approximation to the path. This approximation is then interpreted by identifying straight lines segments within the path.

Each path segment is followed until there is a change of sign in either the $\Delta x$ or $\Delta y$ of each subsequent pair of points. Such a change indicates a vertex in the path. Once these vertices are located, the edges connecting them are computed. Edges which are shorter than a user-defined threshold (by default, 50 pixels) are discarded, effectively smoothing the original path. The remaining edges are categorized into one of the four cardinal or four semi-cardinal directions (see Figure 1).

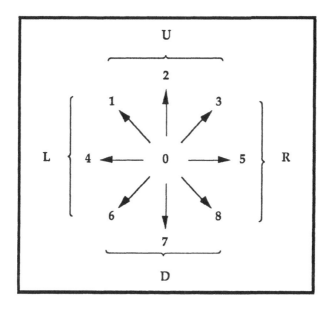

**Fig. 1.** Chain-codes for gesture interpretation

This categorization produces a chain-code signature for the gesture, which is then interpreted to determine the action to be taken. Figure 2 lists the chain-code signatures of the supported operations. Note that gesture signatures may either be specified as precise directional motions (using the numerical codes) or as more general directional sequences (using the letter codes).

After a gesture has been interpreted, the appearance of the cursor is momentarily altered to reflect the selected interpretation, thereby providing immediate feedback to the user. The set of meaningful gestures has been chosen so as to minimize the possibility of misinterpretation, and ambiguous gestures (indicated by an unrecognized chain-code signature) are handled by momentarily setting the cursor to a question mark to indicate uncertainty. An ambiguous gesture is otherwise ignored.

Running on a 68030 processor, gestural interpretation is reliably accomplished in less than 0.7 seconds and therefore does not noticeably affect the real-time response of the system.

As the chain-code interpretation is table driven, it is quite straightforward to extend the range of gestures HyperLecture can interpret. To this end, a gestural macro definition facility has been incorporated. Macros can be used both to create new gestures and to redefine or extend existing ones.

| Gesture | Mnemonic | Signature | Action | On "scrub"... |
|---------|----------|-----------|--------|---------------|
| Up-Right (↗) | Like an outgoing arrow | 3 | Show hot-text marking outlinks | Hide hot-text |
| Down-Left (↙) | Like an incoming arrow (and opposite of Up-Right) | 6 | List (and optionally select from) inward links | Return to source topic (if a jump occurred) |
| Line (↓) | Like drawing the letter "I" | 7 | List (and optionally select from) the index of topics | Return to source topic (if a jump occurred) |
| Right (→) | Like the forwards arrow | 5 | Go to next topic in linear sequence (can also use the →\| key) | Go back to previous topic in sequence |
| Left (←) | Like the backwards arrow | 4 | Go to previous topic in linear sequence (can also use the \|← key) | Go back to next topic in sequence |
| Caret (∧) | Like a printer's insertion mark | 3-8 | Initiate textual annotation system | Delete last text annotation |
| Vee (∨) | Like the letter V (for "voice") | 8-3 | Initiate voice annotation system | Delete last voice annotation |
| Tee (T) | Like the letter T (for "tutor") | 5-7 | Initiate tutoring system | Deactivate tutoring system |
| Esse (S) | Like the letter S (for "speak") | L-R-L | Switch on audio assistance | Switch off audio assistance |
| Em (∿) | Like the letter M (for "macro") | U-D-U-D | Initiate gesture macro definition system | Delete the preceding macro definition |
| Scrub (⇌) | Like rubbing out a mistake | 5-4 | Undo the most recent action or remove an annotation | Undo the previous undo (ie: "redo") |

**Fig. 2.** Gestural interface commands

Macro definition is initiated using the "Em" gesture. The user is then presented with a card into which they may type the signature of their new gesture and the actions to be associated with it. The gesture signature may also be specified by example, simply by performing it over the card. Once the new gesture is confirmed, it becomes immediately available throughout the HyperLecture.

Input directives (see Figure 3) can also be used to embed gestural macros in a HyperLecture input document. In this case the signature must be specified textually as the first such directive in a sequence. Subsequent (contiguous) directives specify the actions to be associated with the new gesture.

## 2.2 Automated hypertext generation

An innovative aspect of the HyperLecture system is the use of self-correlating hypertext. When a lecture is constructed from its plain-text input (see Section 2.4 below), the individual words of its component topics may be optionally cross-referenced to create "hot-text" links. These links may be selected by mouse-click, in order to jump immediately to another topic. In addition an index of inward links (similar to those described in [8]) is automatically created, allowing the presenter to navigate directly to any topic with a hot link leading to the current one.

Content-free words (such a "the", "and", "therefore", etc.) are culled from the cross-referencing procedure, in order to prevent a potentially $O(n^2)$ explosion of topic linkages and hence, of the time required for cross-referencing.

Cross-referencing is achieved by comparing words in the text of each topic for case-insensitive inexact matching with all other topic names. This inexact matching succeeds if the candidate word either contains, or is contained by, another topic name. For example, the word "Presentation" would match a topic name "Present" (which it contains) or a topic name "Presentation Techniques" (which contains it.)

If a word matches more than one topic name, HyperLecture provide three alternative link resolution mechanisms. By default, the first match after the current card is used (as it represents the "closest" topic not yet seen in a linear presentation). However, when initiating the loading process, the user may select an option which causes HyperLecture to list all alternative links, either for once-off arbitration as the text is being loaded, or for selection each time the hot-text is actually clicked.

If no potential topic link leading from a particular candidate word is found, the matching process is repeated. This time however, the text of each other topic card is searched to find complete matches for the candidate. That is, if the topic "Public Speaking" contained the candidate word "presentation", a hyperlink would be constructed from the candidate word to that topic.

If more than one topic presents such a potential link, the one with the most instances of the candidate word is selected (on the problematical assumption that the frequency of the candidate word is proportional to the significance of the word in the context of a topic.) Where two or more topics contain the candidate word an equal number of times, the link is resolved using one of the three methods mentioned above.

## 2.3 Code Player

The original purpose for which HyperLecture was designed was the teaching of introductory computer programming. It was therefore important to provide a simple but flexible mechanism for demonstrating small example programs.

An auxiliary stack, called CodePlayer, provides facilities with which fragments of code in the imperative paradigm can be displayed, executed and "tinkered with". CodePlayer provides a visual representation of variables and function parameters (as boxes containing values) and may be used to demonstrate principles such as type, scope, input/output, stream-based and random access file handling, repetition and selection control structures, records, arrays and other data structures, function and procedure calls, passing by value or reference, function return, aliasing of variables, pointers and dynamic memory allocation.

Code examples must be manually translated into the internal language of the code simulator (an extension of HyperTalk.) This allows CodePlayer to present code fragments written in many different imperative languages. The translated code is partially compiled to determine function calls, variable names, typing and scope information, but most other aspects of a code fragment can be interactively adjusted during the demonstration to cater to a "what-if" style of teaching.

## 2.4. Plain-text input format

Presentation material can be added to and removed from a HyperLecture stack in a straightforward and consistent manner, greatly simplifying revision and extension of existing presentations. The use of a text-based input format also simplifies the conversion of existing presentation materials to HyperLectures.

HyperLecture takes as its input a plain-text file consisting of a series of topics and individual points within each topic. Presentation structure is encoded using a simple formatting scheme: topic headings are left justified whilst topic points are indented either by a bullet ("•") or by white space.

It is quite possible to develop complete presentations using only these three constructs. However, the system also recognizes a number of embedded directives (each of which is specified by a keyword preceded by a backslash) which provide more sophisticated presentation and formatting options.

| Embedded directive | Effect |
|---|---|
| \boxed *<text>* | Put the specified text in a movable box. |
| \courier *<text>* | Change the font of the current line to courier (useful for highlighting code fragments.) |
| \syntax *<text>* | The text is a syntax description (to be set in bold courier). The first such directive encountered in each topic inserts the heading **Syntax**. |
| \pause | Causes HyperLecture to display the text of the topic up to the \pause and then wait for a "next topic" command ("Left" gesture or $\boxed{\rightarrow}$ keystroke) to continue listing the current topic. |
| \example *<name>* | The name of a piece of embedded code. This directive causes HyperLecture to automatically create a link to the appropriate CodePlayer stack. |
| \code *<text>* | The text of a line of embedded code suitable for use in the CodePlayer stack. Such embedded code can be loaded into a CodePlayer stack directly from the same input file, ensuring consistency between the stacks. |
| \tutorial *(level)* *<action>* | Indicates an action to be performed on the current card at a certain level of tutorial assistance (see Section 3.2 below) when tutorial mode is activated. |
| \gesture *<chain-code>* | Specify a signature for embedded gesture definition. |
| \action *<instruction>* | Specify a HyperTalk instruction associated with the current gesture macro definition. |
| \series *<name>* | Specifies the name of the lecture series to which this HyperLecture belongs. This information (together with that supplied by the remaining directives listed below) is assembled into a title card which is automatically displayed at startup. |
| \title *<name>* | Specifies the title of this lecture. |
| \number *<integer>* | Specifies the number of this lecture (within a series of related lectures.) |
| \lecturer *<name>* | Specifies who is giving the lecture. |
| \affiliation *<institution>* | Specifies the lecturer's origin. |
| \contact *<address>* | Specifies an address for the lecturer. |
| \duration *<minutes>* | Specifies how long the lecture is supposed to run. |

**Fig. 3.** Embedded directives

There are three groups of directives. The first four specify simple text formatting variations. The next five permit the lecture designer to embed code sequences (to be demonstrated with CodePlayer), self-driving tutorials (see Section 3.2) and gesture macros. The remaining seven directives are used to document important facts concerning the lecture.

## 2.5  Automated timing of lectures

The embedded directive \duration allows the user to specify the intended duration of the presentation. Once a presentation is commenced (by moving past the automatically generated title card), HyperLecture keeps track of the elapsed time and the amount of the material already covered.

These two quantities are displayed as moving bars across the bottom of the screen. The upper bar represents the percentage of the material already seen and the lower bar, the percentage of available time elapsed. This comparison gives a clear but unobtrusive indication of the success or otherwise of the presentation pacing, as well as an indication of the remaining time (see Figure 4). In addition to these indicators, as the presentation nears its conclusion (defined as the last 10% of the talk or the last five minutes, whichever is shorter) the background of the bar begins to flash a warning.

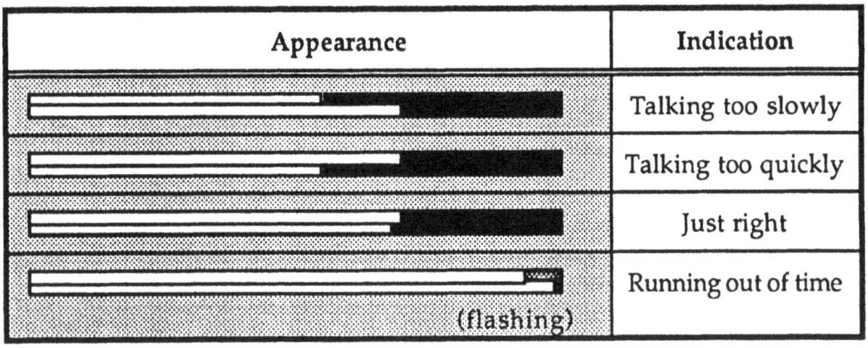

| Appearance | Indication |
|---|---|
|  | Talking too slowly |
|  | Talking too quickly |
|  | Just right |
| (flashing) | Running out of time |

Fig. 4. Pacing indicator

# 3  HyperLecture as a study and revision tool

### 3.1  Hand-out generator

A second purpose in the design of HyperLecture was to create a presentation system which would also be useful to an audience for revision of material. For example, it is often desirable to circulate the text of a presentation beforehand (as a framework for note-taking) or afterwards (as a summary).

HyperLecture allows the user to automatically generate either a condensed reproduction of the actual topic cards (2 topics to an A4 page) or a more tightly formatted summary document. The ease and speed with which such hard-copy materials may be generated greatly simplifies the task of providing up-to-date and comprehensive lecture notes.

## 3.2   Tutorial-mode

With the increasing availability of portable computers, it will eventually become feasible to distribute revision materials in an electronic form, either directly over a network or indirectly, via removable media. This greatly extends the potential for providing sophisticated tutorial assistance (so called "intelligent documents").

HyperLecture provides the lecture designer with the capacity to embed tutorial materials into each topic of the presentation, so that later revision by the audience can be automatically guided or otherwise assisted.

Tutorial mode is entered (as indicated in Figure 2) by performing the "Tee" gesture on any topic. Once entered, the tutorial system is capable of delivering a prerecorded written or spoken commentary on the material in the topic, synchronized with appropriate navigation. This commentary may be hierarchical and may be set up to respond to the student's indicated level of understanding.

Tutorial material is embedded into the plain-text source document using the \tutorial directive. Tutorial specifications consist of sequences of HyperTalk commands which are used to drive the system without user intervention. Each tutorial directive may optionally be followed by a numerical depth value (the default is 1), indicating the hierarchical position of the information (see Figure 5 for example).

The tutorial instructions are treated as guarded statements, where the guard condition is that the specified tutorial depth value of the action is greater than or equal to the current value of the global HyperTalk variable tutorialLevel (which is initially set to 1).

All standard HyperTalk commands and features may be used to construct the tutorial, but to facilitate designing such tutorials, a small set of special functions are also provided within HyperLecture stack (see Figure 6.) Using these functions a presenter can quickly script a tutorial presentation incorporating textual and verbal commentary, text highlighting and automated pointer motion.

The tutorial controller also incorporates a simple test of the escape key. If it is pressed, tutorialLevel is immediately set to 0. Whenever a guarded statement detects a such a zero value, it immediately aborts the entire tutorial. Naturally, this effect can also be achieved by explicitly setting tutorialLevel to zero in response to some user input (as in line four of Figure 5, for example).

```
\tutorial(1)        VoiceNote         -- will give a welcome message

\tutorial(1)        answer "Instructions?" with Yes or No or Abort

\tutorial(1)        if it is Yes then put 2 into tutorialLevel

\tutorial(1)        if it is Abort then put 0 into tutorialLevel
                                      -- will abort at once

\tutorial(1)        answer "Read or show text?" with Read or Show or
                    Both

\tutorial(1)        put false into ShowTextNotes

\tutorial(1)        put false into ReadTextNotes

\tutorial(1)        if it is Read or Both then put true into
                    ReadTextNotes

\tutorial(1)        if it is Show or Both then put true into
                    ShowTextNotes

  \tutorial(2)      TextNote  "The tutorial system is designed to
                    assist you to understand the materials pre-
                    sented  on each topic. It will....etc."

  \tutorial(2)      VoiceNote         -- announce the instructions

\tutorial(1)        VoiceNote         -- explain the first point

\tutorial(1)        HighlightPoint(1)

\tutorial(1)        VoiceNote         -- explain the second point

\tutorial(1)        HighlightPoint(2)
```

**Fig. 5.** A sample tutorial specification

| Function | Purpose |
|---|---|
| TextNote *<text>* | Displays and/or reads a text annotation and waits until it is (manually) closed and/or completely spoken before proceeding. The global variables **ReadTextNotes** and **ShowTextNotes** control which form(s) of presentation are used. |
| VoiceNote | Asynchronously plays a recorded verbal annotation. The first time this function is called from a particular tutorial it prompts the user to record the required annotation |
| MoveCursorTo *<x,y>* [smoothly] | Repositions the cursor instantaneously, or as if it were being dragged (if "smoothly" is specified.) |
| HighlightPoint *<N>* | Causes the Nth point of the current topic to be highlighted (if N=0, the topic title is highlighted.) |

**Fig. 6.** Tutorial functions

## 3.3. Annotation

As well as formal tutorial additions to the presentation, it is possible for the user (either the presenter or the audience member) to make ad hoc textual or verbal annotations to the text of the presentation. The ability to make such additions to the standard presentation text opens the intriguing possibility that annotation of copies of a HyperLecture, running on portable computers belonging to audience members, might totally replace the standard pen and paper techniques of lecture note-taking.

Annotation is initiated using one of the two annotation gestures listed in Figure 2. A textual annotation is created using the "Caret" gesture. The text of the annotation is stored in a relocatable and resizable text window created for the purpose. When the annotation is closed, its location is marked by a small iconic button (as depicted in Figure 7.) Clicking on this button reveals the annotation, which may then be inspected, updated and dismissed.

**Fig. 7.** A TextNote marker

HyperLecture also provides an operational mode specially designed to assist the visually impaired. This mode is activated using the "Esse" gesture. When the mode is activated, textual annotations are read aloud as well as being displayed, whenever a marker button is clicked. "Speech" mode also causes annotation buttons (both textual and verbal) to verbally announce to the user when the mouse is placed over them.

The effect of activating the annotation reading mode is to permanently set the global variable `ReadTextNotes` to true. Hence all textual annotations (including those in tutorials) are spoken, regardless of user-initiated changes in the value of `ReadTextNotes`.

Live sound annotations may also be created, using the "Vee" gesture. The annotation is recorded when it is first created and is then stored in the resource fork of the HyperLecture stack. Sound recordings are marked by another iconic button, shown in Figure 8. Clicking on such a marker causes the recording to be replayed. Once created, verbal records cannot be edited.

**Fig. 8.** A VoiceNote marker

Both types of annotation marker can be easily relocated within a particular topic by clicking on and dragging them (note that this does not cause the annotation to be activated.) Annotations can be removed by performing the

"Scrub" gesture directly above them. A confirmation of the deletion request is always required in order to avoid accidental erasure.

## 4. Extensions and work in progress

The most obvious extension to the existing system is to incorporate the use of graphics and animation into the range of presentation media. HyperCard provides extension commands to handle both of these types of information and work on integrating these capabilities (without significantly increasing the complexity of the interface) is currently underway.

A second area of continuing development is in extending the CodePlayer stack to enable it to simulate code fragments in non-imperative languages. The most promising lines of research are in the presentation of the object-oriented and functional paradigms. By comparison the visualization of program execution under the logic (declarative) and constraint-based paradigms offers more significant design challenges.

Another improvement would be an improved cross-referencing mechanism which could identify significant partial matches (such as "Presentation" and "Presenting"). This would probably involve enhancing the matching mechanism to compute a threshholded textual edit-distance between words.

## 5  Conclusion

HyperLecture provides a usable and versatile method of designing, presenting, documenting, revising and distributing augmented presentation materials. The use of a computer based display system frees the lecturer from much of the mechanics of presentation, whilst the incorporation of hypertext techniques preserves the capacity to respond quickly and flexibly to audience needs and interests and permits presentation structures of arbitrary topology to be developed.

The gestural interface mechanism employed provides a wide range of functionality without interfering with the appearance of the presentation and may be easily customized to the taste of the individual presenter.

HyperLecture supports a range of options for distributing lecture materials, from hard-copy reproduction to fully automated and integrated tutorials. The system also provides facilities to assist the visually impaired.

HyperLecture in currently in use in the Department of Computer Science at Monash University. In a survey of 300 First Year students who were taught using the system, over 50% reported that CMP was significant beneficial to their learning and over 90% reported some benefit. Approximately 80% of the students indicated that computer-mediated presentation improved their understanding of lecture material and a similar percentage showed a clear preference for computer-mediated presentation [9].

# Acknowledgements

I would particularly like to thank Frederic Rinaldi, Nigel Perry and P. Mercer, whose superb public domain XCMDS are the foundations on which this project was built. Special thanks to Professors Cliff Bellamy and Les Goldschlager whose personal interest in the HyperLecture concept, and whose generous special funding of the work have made the project possible.

# References

1. P. Dressel, P. Marcus: Enriching Learning through Technology. In: On Teaching and Learning in College, Jossey-Bass, San Francisco, 1982, pp. 66-84.

2. R.E. Levien, C. Mosmann: Instructional Uses of Computers. In: The Emerging Technology, McGraw-Hill, New York, 1972, pp. 51-81.

3. J.G. Penner: Interest And Attention In The Classroom. In: Why Many College Teachers Cannot Lecture, Charles C. Thomas Books, Springfield IL., 1984, pp. 114-133.

4. M. Smith (pseudonym): Preparing a Presentation. In: SIGCHI Bulletin, vol. 21, no. 4, April 1990, pp. 62-64.

5. D. Sharpe, M.J. Willshire: Human Factors In Teaching. In: SIGCHI Bulletin, vol. 20, no. 3, January 1989, pp. 58-62.

6. T.R. Guskey: Time Use and Student Involvement. In: Improving Student Learning In College Classrooms, Charles C. Thomas Books, Springfield IL., 1988, pp. 83-102.

7. G. Kurtenbach, B. Buxton: GEdit: A Test Bed For Editing By Contiguous Gestures. In: SIGCHI Bulletin, vol. 23, no. 2, April 1991, pp. 22-26.

8. K. Instone, L.M. Leventhal, B.M. Teasley, J. Farhat, D.S. Rohlman: What Do I Want? And How Do I Get There?: Performance And Navigation In Information Retrieval Tasks With Hypertext Documents. In: Proc. EWCHI'92, ICSTI, Moscow, 1992, pp.85-94.

9. D. Conway: Improving Educational Outcomes With Computer-Mediated Presentation. Submitted to the 1993 Computers in Education Conference, Taiwan, Republic of China, December 1993.

# Towards an Adaptive Hypermedia Component for an Intelligent Learning Environment

Peter Brusilovsky, Leonid Pesin and Mikhail Zyryanov

International Centre for Scientific and Technical Information,
Kuusinen str. 21b, Moscow 125252, Russia
E-mail: plb@plb.icsti.su
and
Department of Applied Mathematics and Cybernetics,
Moscow State University, Moscow, Russia

**Abstract.** This paper discusses the problem of integration of hypermedia and Intelligent Learning Environments (ILEs) technologies and the problem of creating an adaptive hypermedia component for ILEs. Our experience of creating an adaptive on-line help facilities for ITEM/IP system is described. This experience forms a background for our hypermedia work and provides some good ideas for it. We also present our approach to integration of a hypermedia component into internal structure of ILE and illustrate it with two examples of adaptive hypermedia components for the most recent versions of our ILEs ISIS-Tutor and ITEM/PG. Finally, we summarize main features of this approach, provide some references to related works, and consider some issues of adaptive hypermedia in general.

## 1 Introduction

An intelligent learning environment is a relatively new kind of intelligent educational system which combines the features of traditional Intelligent Tutoring Systems (ITS) and learning environments. Some years ago many developers of educational systems considered ITS and learning environments as different and even contradictory ways of using computers in education. The recent success of well-known ILEs Smithtown [20], Sherlock [16], and Quest [23] showed that these approaches are not contradictory but rather complementary. ITSs are able to control learning adaptively on various levels, but generally do not provide tools to support free exploration. In comparison, learning environments and microworlds support exploratory learning, but they lack the control of an intelligent tutor. Without such control the student often works inefficiently and never discovers some important features of the subject.

The same situation happens now with ITSs and educational hypermedia systems. They are most often considered as two different approaches to using computers in education, while these approaches are really complementary. Recent research has demonstrated that hypermedia can provide the basis for an exploratory learning system but that by itself such a system is insufficient, needing to be supplemented by more directed guidance [13]. This guidance is often an important ingredient of effective learning from hypermedia, and it can be provided by an intelligent tutoring component. In comparison, hypermedia approach can add a new dimension to traditional ITS/ILE by providing a tool for student driven acquisition of domain knowledge.

We think that in many domains it is possible to achieve a good results by developing an educational computer system which integrates the capabilities of an intelligent tutor, a learning environment, and a hypermedia system. The problem is, however, to find an appropriate paradigm or basis for such integration. Our position is that an integrated system should be not just a sum but a real integration of its components. First, one component should be able to use the capabilities of another component as well as exchange or share data with it. Second, the results of students' work with any of the components during the session should be taken into account by other components to adapt their performance to the knowledge level and personal features of the particular student.

For a number of years we have been investigating the problem of creating an intelligent learning environment in the domain of teaching programming. We have designed and tested the Intelligent Tutor, Environment and Manual for Introductory Programming (ITEM/IP). ITEM/IP [4] integrates an ITS for programming, a programming environment, and adaptive on-line help facilities on the basis of the structural domain model and the overlay student model.

The results of students' work are reflected in the student model and used by other system components to adapt themselves to the knowledge level of the particular student. We have specially investigated the use of student models for adaptive curriculum sequencing by the tutoring component of ILE [3], and for developing an adaptive interface for the environment components of ILE [5].

More recently we have tried to apply our approach to some other domains. We have developed ILEs for mathematics [8], information retrieval [18], and geography [7]. First versions of these ILEs contained an intelligent tutor and a learning environment integrated together on the basis of the domain and student models, but did not contain hypermedia components. It was not an extension of our initial approach, but rather a validation of its applicability to another domains.

Now we are trying to extend our approach by integrating hypermedia technology into our existing ILEs. The problem here is not just to design a hypermedia component for one of the existing ILEs, but to find ways to integrate this component into a particular ILE. It means that the hypermedia component has to use the student model both to adapt its performance to the given student, as well as to update the student model to reflect the results of the student's work with the component.

This paper discusses the problem of integration of hypermedia and ILE technologies and the problem of creating an adaptive hypermedia component for ILEs. First, we present our experience of creating an adaptive on-line help facility for ITEM/IP system. This experience forms a background for our hypermedia work and provides some good ideas for it. Then we present our approach to the integration of a hypermedia component into the structure of ILE and illustrate it with two examples of adaptive hypermedia components for the most recent versions of our ILEs: ISIS-Tutor and ITEM/PG. Finally, we summarize the main features of the suggested approach, provide some references to related works, and discuss some problems of adaptive hypermedia in general.

## 2 Adaptive access to teaching material in ITEM/IP: Lessons learned

ITEM/IP stands for Intelligent Tutor, Environment and Manual for Introductory Programming. ITEM/IP is an intelligent learning environment for teaching and learning introductory programming by the mini-language approach [2]. In the mini-language approach beginners learn what programming is, while learning how to use a simple mini-language to control a robot which acts in a microworld environment. ITEM/IP [4] was designed in 1985 to support an introductory programming course based upon the educational mini-language Turingal for first-year students at Moscow State University.

The student can use ITEM/IP in the following modes:

1. *Novice Programming Environment*. To work with Turingal programs the student can make use of a complete set of tools for program design and debugging. One of the functions of the environment is to display visualizations of the student's programs. With the help of the environment, the student can observe various programs "at work", experiment with them, and gradually learn from experience, observations and mistakes.

2. *Instruction*. At any moment of work the student can ask the teaching component to generate the next teaching operation: a new concept or construct, an example construct, a test, an example for

problem solving, or a programming problem to solve. The teaching component analyses the domain knowledge and the student model and offers the student both the optimal teaching operation and a list of all relevant (i.e. ready to be applied) teaching operations. The student who is not satisfied with the optimal operation suggested by the system can choose any relevant teaching operation using adaptive hierarchical menus.

3. *Repetition and On-Line Manual.* At any moment of work the student has menu-based access to all previous teaching material: presentation of any previously learned concept, demonstration of all learned examples, and analysis of any explained or solved problem. This mode offers access to the learned material of the course as reference, thus supporting on-line help and example-based programming.

ITEM/IP provides both instruction and reference access to the teaching material. Generally, these two modes of access require different presentation and structuring of the material, so many good books on programming languages consist of two independent parts: the tutorial and the reference manual. In the ITEM/IP project, we have tried to make an integrated tutorial and manual by providing adaptive presentation of the same teaching material on the base of domain and student models.

The domain model in ITEM/IP is a net with nodes corresponding to programming concepts and mini-language constructs (i.e. domain knowledge elements) and with links reflecting several kinds of relations between nodes. The overlay student model reflects by a set of integer counters the extent to which the student has mastered the concept or the construct. The student model is always kept up to date and supports adaptive work of all modules.

All the teaching material is stored in the base of teaching operations in a form of frames. There are three kinds of frames: concept/construct frames, example frames and problem frames. The presentation module uses these frames in both instruction and repetition modes to generate the five kinds of teaching operations mentioned above. Since the presentation of teaching material is adapted to the current level of student knowledge, a repeated explanation is usually more concise and complete than the original one.

For example, presentation of a concept or a construct consist of some textual information about it followed by a presentation of the relations which link the presented element with other domain knowledge elements. The textual information which is stored for the given concept or construct can be divided into a sequence of text fragments. Each fragment has a condition which addresses the knowledge level of the given and related constructs. While producing a description of the concept, the presentation module presents only the fragments whose condition is true. The more the concept or construct is learned, the more concise its presented description. The information about the relations of the given construct is not stored as text, but is generated using simple templates. To avoid confusion, only the relations with already-known nodes are presented.

The method of adaptive presentation used in ITEM/IP provides a smooth transition from learning to on-line help access and supports adaptive student-driven access to teaching material. This method was tested in a real classroom. We were quite satisfied with the adaptive presentation itself, but we were not satisfied with using hierarchical menus as the only access to teaching material in instruction and repetition modes. The idea of student-driven access to teaching material was to support exploratory learning and student-driven acquisition of conceptual knowledge. However, the mechanism used for it in ITEM/IP appears to be too complicated for novice programmers.

For example, when learning or repeating a description of a construct, the student was provided with the references to all previously learned related concepts and constructs. However, to refresh knowledge about it, the student needed to re-enter the repetition mode from the top and access the related information by a three-level menu. An even bigger problem was that the menus for the instruction and repetition modes provided two different views of the domain knowledge, making understanding of the domain knowledge structure much more difficult for the students.

To overcome these problems, we decided to redesign the high level architecture of the system and to apply hypermedia technology to support unified access to all of the teaching material. Our goal was to develop an adaptive educational hypermedia, using our general student model based approach to adaptation in ILEs, in a way that was similar to the way we used it to create the adaptive presentation. The rest of this paper reports on our approach and recent experience in creating adaptive hypermedia components for intelligent learning environments. We briefly describe two systems - ISIS-Tutor and ITEM/PG - which employ adaptive hypermedia, and discuss our work in the context of related works.

## 3  Towards an adaptive educational hypermedia

The first important step in integrating the hypermedia network into an intelligent learning environment is to take the domain model network of an ILE as a basis for the hypermedia network. More exactly, we suggest that the hypermedia network be designed precisely as a visualized (and externalized) domain network. Each node of the domain network should be represented by a node of the hyperspace, while the links between domain network nodes constitute main paths between hyperspace nodes. Thus the structure of the overall hyperspace resembles the pedagogic structure of the domain knowledge. Each domain network node will have a hypermedia 'page' as an external representation, and a frame as an internal representation. We suggest also that these hypermedia pages be constructed from the corresponding frames by a special program rather than being stored directly in presentation format. This saves page design time and provides space for adaptation.

We used the above approach in our recent work on adaptive hypermedia components for ILEs. The following two subsections report on how the domain and student models were used in ISIS Tutor and ITEM/PG to generate the 'adaptive pages' for hypermedia nodes.

## 3.1 The adaptive hypermedia manual in ISIS Tutor

ISIS-Tutor [18] is an ILE to support learning of the print formatting language of a well-known information retrieval system: CDS/ISIS. This system is supplied by UNESCO and used widely in ICSTI and other information centres in the world. The print formatting language is the key to many CDS/ISIS operations, and mastering this language is important for effective use of the system.

The architecture of ISIS-Tutor resembles the architecture of ITEM/IP in most details. It contains an environment for experimenting with the language and a tutoring component which deals with three kinds of teaching operations: concept presentations, examples and problems. However, the domain model - which is a network of 69 concepts and constructs - is twice as complex as the one in ITEM/IP. The overall 'space' of teaching material is larger as well.

ISIS-Tutor applies the same ideas of student model based adaptation as ITEM/IP, but adds some important improvements. When presenting a concept or construct, ITEM/IP and ISIS-Tutor provide an adaptive list of related concepts and examples. To reduce the student's cognitive load, ITEM/IP puts only learned related concepts in the list, and only those examples which do not use unknown constructs. ISIS-Tutor lists both learned and ready-to-be-learned concepts (a concept is ready to be learned if all of the preceding concepts are known to the student). To distinguish old and new concepts, two different colours are used. Another new feature of ISIS-Tutor is hypermedia-like access to related concepts and examples. The student can select any related concept or example from the generated list to move to a related page of teaching material. The selected concept or example is presented adaptively to the student, who can then read information about the concept or experiment with an example and then use its links to navigate to other related concepts or examples.

Thus ISIS-Tutor provides a hypermedia-like way to investigate the teaching material. Navigating along the links to related concepts and examples, students can repeat learned pieces of knowledge as well as learn new material. To support navigation and learning, all links to new material are visibly marked. ISIS-Tutor unifies the instruction and repetition modes of ITEM/IP and provides a unified adaptive view of the structured teaching material. Note that ISIS-Tutor and ITEM/IP both use two similar menu-based entries into the teaching material (for new and repeating material), but in ISIS-Tutor, these menus are a secondary way of access, a kind of index.

## 3.2 The adaptive hypermedia component of ITEM/PG

ITEM/PG [7] is an ILE for 13-14 year old students taking a course in the physical geography of oceans and continents. The pedagogical goal of the work with ITEM/PG is to learn the relationships between the different natural components of an island, located somewhere in the northern part of the Atlantic Ocean. The island is characterized by several components, such as position, origin, climate etc. Each component has several possible values. For example, the options for the origin of the island are continental, volcanic, roof or atoll. The values of the components are related to each other. For example, the climate depends on the position of the island. A more detailed description of the domain and a pedagogical basis for the overall project can be found in [6].

The main components of ITEM/PG are the domain model, the student model, the tutor, the learning environment and the hypermedia network. The student can work in exploratory mode, browsing the hyperspace or experimenting with the environment. At any given moment the student can apply to the tutor for the next "optimal" teaching operation, and can then follow the tutor's suggestion or give up.

According to our general approach, the hypermedia network is just the visualized domain network. There are three main kinds of hyper-nodes: component, value and rule. Each kind of hyper-node has a special screen representation which is not stored in screen format, but generated from the corresponding frame by a special program. For example, the program for the "value" kind of node generates a window which contains the name of the value, the description, the icon and the hyper-links to the component node and related rule nodes.

The student model is used by the hypermedia component to adapt the screen representation of hyper-nodes to the current knowledge level of the given student. Applying the student model, the hypermedia component distinguishes four states for hyper-nodes: not ready to be learned, ready to be learned, known and well known. Thus, at any moment, the hyperspace is divided implicitly into several "zones". In particular, the ready to be learned nodes form a "zone of proximal development" [22] or a "knowledge front" [12].

Our idea is that different zones have different meanings for the student, and marking these zones visually should help the student in hyperspace navigation just as bookmarks help the student with textbooks. To mark the zones, the hypermedia component marks the hyper-links of each node in four different ways. For example, the links to the nodes which are not ready to be learned are dimmed, so as not to distract the student. The links to ready to be learned nodes are colored green, inviting the student to visit them.

Another important feature of ITEM/PG is the bilateral linking of the student model and the hypermedia component. The links are used in one direction when the hypermedia component accesses the student model to adapt itself. The links are used in the other direction when student visits to a particular node of the hypermedia component cause a change in the value of how well learned that node is in the overlay student model. Thus ITEM/PG provides a good example of how the hypermedia component can be integrated into the structure of an ILE.

## 4  Discussion

We have presented three systems which demonstrate some steps towards an integration of adaptive hypermedia and ILEs. Using our experience, we can now formulate the main features of our approach to developing an adaptive hypermedia component for ILE.

- The hypermedia network is designed as the visualized and externalized domain network.
- An external representation of a knowledge element (a page), is generated or assembled from its internal representation (a frame).
- The content of the hypermedia page is adapted to the student knowledge reflected in the student model.
- The links from any node to related nodes are marked visually, reflecting the current "educational state" of the related nodes for the given student.
- Student interaction with the hypermedia component is reflected in the student model and can be used by other components of ILE.

All these techniques are important for creating a truly integrated hypermedia for ILE. Each of the listed items provides a good area for research. Here we provide some references to existing works in these areas. The idea about creating the hypermedia network from domain network is quite popular and has been discussed in [14, 15]. Generation of adaptive concept explanation is another popular field of research [17, 21]. An application of these ideas to hypermedia was reported recently in [11]. Adaptive "history-based" navigation tools were discussed in [10].

Some problems, however, are not well studied and need additional investigation. For example, we use different methods to deal with links from the given node to not ready to be learned nodes: these links are hidden in ITEM/IP and ISIS-Tutor and dimmed in ITEM/PG. We can't say now which way is better. By hiding these links completely we can reasonably limit the cognitive load of the student, which is quite important for novices. However, hiding any links looks unnatural for hypermedia. It can form an incorrect mental model of the domain knowledge. Such adaptation is also more intrusive than just dimming these links. To investigate this problem, we plan to compare hiding vs. dimming in an experiment.

Another important problem is the relevance of adaptation. A system can use very elaborate strategies to provide the student with the "best" teaching operation or "optimal" help detail. The problem is whether the student agrees with the choice. The student could prefer another next operation or more (less) detailed help. To deal with this problem, we feel that the adaptation should not be intrusive, and that the student should be provided with control over adaptation. In our future work we plan to provide the student with the possibility to customize the level of adaptation. We plan to make the student model visible to the student and let the student change some part of it. We have not heard of any existing ITS or ILE with a student-accessible model. However, some ITS's [1] use a student-entered part of the student model for the purpose of adaptation. We consider techniques for creating visible and accessible student models to be the general line for the future development of ITS's [9, 19].

# References

1. A. Barr, M. Beard, R.C. Atkinson: The computer as tutorial laboratory: the Stanford BIP project. International Journal on the Man-Machine Studies 8, 567-596 (19 75)

2. P.L. Brusilovsky: Turingal - the language for teaching the principles of programming. In: EUROLOGO 91. Proc. Third European Logo Conference, Parma. Italy, 27-30 August 1991, A.S.I., Parma, pp. 423-432

3. P.L. Brusilovsky: A framework for intelligent knowledge sequencing and task sequencing. In: C. Frasson, G. Gauthier and G.I. McCalla (eds.): Intelligent Tutoring Systems. Proceedings of the Second International Conference, ITS'92. Berlin: Springer-Verlag 1992, pp. 499-506

4. P.L. Brusilovsky: Intelligent Tutor, Environment and Manual for Introductory Programming. Educational and Training Technology International 29, 26-34 (1992)

5. P.L. Brusilovsky: Student as user: Towards an adaptive interface for an intelligent learning environment. Paper accepted to AIED'93 World Conference.

6. P.L. Brusilovsky, T.B. Gorskaya-Belova: The Environment for Physical Geography Teaching. Computers and Education 18, 85-88 (1992)

7. P. Brusilovsky, M. Zyryanov: Intelligent learning environment for geography: towards an integration of emerging educational technologies. In: N.Hammond and A.Trapp (eds.): CAL into the Mainstream. CAL 93 Conference Handbook 1993, pp.47-48

8. V.G. Brusilovsky, P.L. Brusilovsky: The student model in a teaching system for mathematical differentiation. Design and application of PC software in the education process. In: Proc. of the 5-th All-Union Workshop. Moscow: 1989, pp. 23-24 (In Russian)

9. A.T. Corbett, J.R. Anderson: Student modeling and mastery learning in a computer-based programming tutor. In: C. Frasson, G. Gauthier, G.I. McCalla (eds.): Intelligent Tutoring Systems. Proceedings of the Second International Conference, ITS'92. Berlin: Springer-Verlag 1992

10. B. de La Passardiere, A. Dufresne: Adaptive navigational tools for educational hypermedia. In: I. Tomek (ed.): Computer Assisted Learning. Proceedings of the 4th International Conference, ICCAL'92. Berlin: Springer-Verlag 1992, pp. 555-567

11. F. De Rosis, N. De Carolis, S. Pizzutilo: User tailored hypermedia explanations. In: INTERCHI'93 Adjunct Proceedings, Amsterdam, 24-29 April, 1993, pp. 169-170

12. I.P. Goldstein: The Genetic graph: a representation for the evolution of procedural knowledge. International Journal on the Man-Machine Studies 11, 51-77 (1979)

13. N. Hammond: Hypermedia and learning: Who guides whom?. In: H. Maurer (ed.): Computer Assisted Learning. Proceedings of the 2-nd International Conference, ICCAL'89. Berlin: Springer-Verlag 1989, pp. 167-181

14. R.J. Hendley, C.D. Whittington, N. Jurascheck: Hypermedia generation from domain representations. Computers and Education 20, 127-132 (1993)

15. M.R. Kibby: Intelligent hypermedia for learning. In: R.M. Bottino, P. Forcheri, M.T. Molfino (eds.): Knowledge Based Environments for Teaching and Learning. Proceedings of the Sixth International PEG Conference. Genova: 1991, pp. 3-12

16. S.P. Lajoie, A. Lesgold: Apprenticeship training in the workplace: computer-coached practice environment as a new form of apprenticeship. Machine Mediated Learning 3, 7-28 (1990)

17. C.L. Paris: Tailoring object description to a user's level of expertise. Computational Linguistics 14, 64-78 (1988)

18. L.A. Pesin, P.L. Brusilovsky: Adaptive task sequencing in ISIS-Tutor. In: Abstracts of East-West Conference on Emerging Computer Technologies in Education, Moscow, 6-9 April 1992, p. 176

19. J. Self: Bypassing the intractable problem of student modelling. In: C. Frasson (Ed.): ITS'88. Proc. of the Intelligent Tutoring Systems conference. Univ. of Montreal. Montreal 1988

20. V.J. Shute, R. Glaser: A large-scale evaluation of an intelligent discovery world: Smithtown. Interactive Learning Environments 1, 51-77 (1990)

21. D.H. Sleeman: UMFE: a user modeling front end system. International Journal on the Man-Machine Studies 23, 71-88 (1985)

22. L.S. Vygotsky: Mind in society. Cambridge: Harvard University Press 1978

23. B.Y. White, J.R. Frederiksen: Causal model progressions as a foundation for intelligent learning environments. Artificial Intelligence 42, 99-157 (1990)

# An Intelligent Interface for Computer Assisted Language Learning

Eve Wilson

Computing Laboratory, University of Kent at Canterbury
Canterbury, Kent, CT2 7NF, England

**Abstract.** This paper begins by contrasting teacher directed computer assisted language learning with the student directed approaches of recent hypertext learning programmes. It concludes that what is needed is an approach where the level and order of the exercises can be tailored to the needs and requirements of individual students. To do this requires:

1. a means of constructing an original user profile and of updating this in the light of student performance in the tutorial exercises, and
2. a means of generating exercises of an appropriate level from text databases.

The paper next looks at how texts may be automatically assigned a readability grade based on Gunning's Fog Index or Information Density, and how this can be used to generate exercises of varying levels of difficulty. The paper emphasises the importance of giving students feedback to win their co-operation in devising and adhering to a tuition programme. It concludes by discussing the work still to be done.

## 1 Two Traditional Interfaces for Computer Assisted Learning

### 1.1 Computer Aided Instruction

The earliest Computer Aided Instruction (CAI) packages relied on exercises that were compiled and ordered by the teacher. The students were expected to complete them in the prescribed order and this left little room for student choice and initiative. Although the teacher, or compiler of the package, may have provided several different routes through the material, dependent upon the answers students gave to certain questions at selected points, the student had, in the main, to complete every exercise satisfactorily before he could progress to the next. There were never enough routes to cater for the individual inclinations and abilities of the learners. Students who knew the material well frequently resented being compelled to respond to what they perceived as trivial, repetitive questions; weaker students were often bewildered and repelled by their inability to proceed because the computer had rejected their answers but failed to provide adequate explanations of the error and how to correct it so that they could continue. Student confusion was undoubtedly exacerbated by the computer's inadequate handling of natural language. In exercises where the students were allowed to respond freely with their own words and phrases, answers that were factually correct were often judged wrong because the student had paraphrased the answer held by the computer, used a synonym instead of the computer preferred terms, or mis-spelled the expected word. While such inflexibility might demoralise the less confident students, among their more resilient peers it merely brought computer aided instruction derision and scorn.

In an attempt to remedy this deficiency, teachers often abandoned entirely exercises in which the student had to derive the answer independently using reasoning or memory. Instead they resorted wholly to selection exercises. All selection exercises, however skillfully they are disguised, are, in essence, multiple choice questions with all the pedagogical shortcomings of that genre:

1. students have only to recognise the answer, not construct or recall it independently
2. multiple choice demands plausible distractors. These may be difficult for the instructor to devise and, if they are truly plausible, confuse the student confronted by them [4]
3. no variety in task can lead to student boredom.

## 1.2   Learning Through Hypertext

Hypertext learning systems were meant to free the student from all the constraints of traditional CAI. The basic premise of hypertext systems is that students should be liberated from overt direction by the instructor. Within the body of hypertext material they are free to browse at will. By strategically placed highlights and links to additional explanations or extraneous material, competent hypertext authors might endeavour covertly to tempt students to cover the requisite material in the preferred order, but ultimately, the responsibility for learning resides with the students. They decide to follow a link, to expand a passage, to seek further education, complete an exercise, re-do a section inadequately understood or skip completely a topic that they find difficult or boring. Browsing is learning by serendipity and, while a beguiling concept, has not yet been shown to be an efficient or even an adequate philosophy of learning. In traditional non-computerised self-directed and self-paced study schemes, while highly motivated mature learners have been found to progress more rapidly than in instructor directed schemes [2], the weaker, less experienced students achieve less than they might have done with more rigorous guidance [3]. This suggests that if hypertext systems are to be used seriously for imparting knowledge, ways must be sought to provide more guidance to the student on an appropriate path through the material, ideally a path tailored to each individual student. It is also desirable to monitor the student's use of the system, and to motivate the student by providing feedback on progress under this regime. This can only be done effectively if we can construct a learner profile which matches the student's current expected performance and changes as the student's skills evolve.

# 2 Constructing Learner Profiles

## 2.1 Linguistic Skills

A list can be made of required linguistic skills. These have been roughly classified in [7] as follows:

1. Lexical and syntactical skills

   (a) Primarily lexical skills
       Singulars and Plurals, especially irregular ones, e.g. man, child, sheep, radius.
       Comparison of adjectives and adverbs, e.g. good, better, best.
       Word families and the formation of words to correspond with different parts of speech,
       e.g.: operate, operation, operator, operating.
       Differentiating pairs of words that are often confused, e.g.: imply, infer.
       Finding antonyms and synonyms.
       Choosing the right preposition.

   (b) Primarily syntactical skills
       Verb forms, e.g.: subject-verb agreement, tenses, auxiliary and modal verbs, participles, particles.
       Pronouns, e.g. agreement with referent, case.
       Articles.
       Positioning of adjectives and adverbs.
       Voice: active/passive.
       Subordinate clauses.

2. Comprehension and discourse skills
   Use of conjunctions.
   Other linking frameworks that give cohesion to discourse.
   Specific reading techniques, e.g.:
   scanning to locate specific information,
   surveying to get the gist of a passage,
   reading for in-depth understanding.

Obviously the skills in these categories are not distinct; they overlap and impinge upon one another, as do the methods for imparting them. An initial user profile can be devised by listing the skills in order of expected difficulty for each language and using a function of position in list and average attainment of that linguistic group in the TOEFL test to derive a likely proficiency for each skill. A typical initial profile of lexical and syntactic skills in increasing order of proficiency is shown in Fig.1.

Hence, a student whose overall TOEFL score was 30 might have achieved this score from the part scores in lexical and syntactic skills shown in Fig.2. Figure

**Fig. 1.** Lexical and syntactic skills for Chinese student in order of increasing proficiency

| Lexical skills | Syntactic skills |
| --- | --- |
| Word families | Verb forms |
| Singulars/Plurals | Articles |
| Comparison | Passive |
| Word differentiation | Pronouns |
| | Subordinate clauses |
| | Word order |

2 also shows proficiency in each, given as a percentage of the total marks which might have been gained in that skill.

**Fig. 2.** Table of linguistic skills proficiency for Chinese student

| Skills:<br>Lexical | Part score<br>in TOEFL | Proficiency<br>in Skill | Skills:<br>Syntactic | Part score<br>in TOEFL | Proficiency<br>in Skill |
| --- | --- | --- | --- | --- | --- |
| | | | Verb forms | 1.67 | 16.7 |
| Word families | 1.67 | 16.7 | Articles | 3.33 | 33.3 |
| Singular/Plural | 3.33 | 33.3 | Passive | 5.00 | 50.0 |
| Comparison | 5.00 | 50.0 | Pronouns | 6.67 | 66.7 |
| Word | | | Subordinate | | |
| differentiation | 6.67 | 66.7 | clause | 8.33 | 83.3 |
| | | | Word Order | 8.33 | 83.3 |

This can be used as an initial profile for the student. This profile will be modified as the student completes more questions and exercises in the system.

Because it had started with proficiency profiles from TOEFL tests, the original scheme was merely to automate translation of TOEFL or TOEFL-type tests into hypertext [5] and to follow this up with tuition and exercises at the appropriate level until the student had achieved a satisfactory TOEFL score. A table of scores against purpose is shown in Fig.3.

Simple multiple choice type questions are converted automatically into hypertext provided that the teacher/question-setter provides an ASCII file with the following contents:

<skill tested> <test sentences> <random list of answer with distractors>

**Fig. 3.** Table of required TOEFL scores against purpose

| A Guide for Admissions Requirements | | | | |
| --- | --- | --- | --- | --- |
| Admissions Policy | Graduate Humanities | Graduate Sciences | Undergraduate | Technical School or 2-year college |
| Acceptable | 550 - 600 | 500 - 600 | 500 - 600 | 450 - 600 |
| Acceptable with supplementary language training and reduced course load | 500 - 550 | 450 - 500 | 400 - 500 | 400 - 450 |
| Further English training required | Below 500 | Below 450 | Below 400 | Below 400 |

Figure 4 shows a file of questions. Figure 5 shows how this looks to the student after automatic conversions into the Guide hypertext system. At the end of a test session students were given an overall score and a detailed score of performance in each skill. Students were then advised what skill to practise.

There were two main problems with the scheme:

1. the format of the exercise was monotonous
2. teachers still had to devise an endless supply of carefully graded questions.

A variety of disguises for multiple choice questions have been described in [6]. The remainder of this paper will discuss a technique for automatically generating exercises at an appropriate level from general purpose databases.

## 3  The Automatic Generation of Exercises

### 3.1  Readability

The objective of an intelligent tutoring system is that it should be able to produce on demand exercises corresponding with the student's ability. One of the more obvious ways of achieving this is to evaluate the reading complexity of the texts on which the exercises are to be based and then to use a text of an appropriate level of difficulty. There are many ways of determining the readability of a text. Two of the easiest to implement automatically are: Gunning's Fog Index and Information density.

**Fig. 4.** Question file

<verb>
1. An employment survey revealed today that demand
for high level executives — increased this year.
have
be
has   t
were
<conjunction>
2. Lawmakers are considering banning both
beer — wine commercials from television.
also
than
or
and   t
<verb>
3. Every fall geese — over the house located on
the bay.
fly   t
flies
have
flown
<pronoun>
4. Of the many opinions expressed to the council
members by the various citizens groups present,
— was the only opinion that mattered.
their
their one
theirs t
they
<preposition>
5. The rosetta stone has provided scientists — a
link to ancient civilisation.
of
to
by
with   t

1. Gunning's Fog Index

   Gunning's Fog Index uses a function of sentence length and number of poly-
   syllabic words per 100 words of text to give a measure of reading complexity.
   For any sample of text (which must be longer than 100 words), compute

   (a) A: the average sentence length
   (b) B: the number of words per 100 words which have three or more syllables.
   (c) The fog index is then $(A + B) * 0.4$

2. Information density

   The information density measure is particularly useful for scientific and tech-

**Fig. 5.** Hypertext exercise

```
┌─────────────────────────────────────────────────────────────┐
│ Quit   Down/Up          Help                                 │
├─────────────────────────────────────────────────────────────┤
│                                                               │
│   1. An employment survey revealed today that demand          │
│      for high level executives — increased this year.         │
│      have tried                                               │
│      be                                                       │
│      has      SELECTED / Click here to undo                   │
│      were                                                     │
│                                                               │
│   2. Lawmakers are considering banning both                   │
│      beer — wine commercials from television.                 │
│      also                                                     │
│      than                                                     │
│      or                                                       │
│      and      SELECTED  Click here to undo                    │
│                                                               │
│   3. Every fall geese — over the house located on             │
│      the bay.                                                 │
│      fly                                                      │
│      flies    SELECTED  Click here to undo                    │
│      have                                                     │
│      flown                                                   │
│                                                               │
│   4. Of the many opinions expressed to the council            │
│      members by the various citizens groups present,          │
│      — was the only opinion that mattered.                    │
│      their                                                    │
│      their one                                               │
│      theirs  SELECTED  Click here to undo                     │
│      they                                                    │
│                                                               │
│   5. The rosetta stone has provided scientists — a            │
│      link to ancient civilisation.                            │
│      of tried                                                 │
│      to tried                                                │
│      by                                                      │
│      with    SELECTED  Click here to undo                     │
│                                                               │
└─────────────────────────────────────────────────────────────┘
```

nical texts. The structure of a sentence is carried by common function words that most people understand even if they cannot yet use them very well: articles, prepositions, conjunctions, and common verbs. Most of the information content of the sentence lies in nouns and adjectives used in the sentence. The higher the proportion of nouns and adjectives in any text the greater the information content of the passage and the more difficult therefore to understand. Hence, information density can be represented by the proportion of nouns and adjectives in the text.

## 3.2 Ranges of Readability Coefficients

The coefficient for information density shows a tendency to cluster around the 50 per cent mark. While Gunning's Fog Index also clusters a little, for short samples of text the spread is greater. Figure 6 shows a table of Fog indexes and information density coefficients for some samples of literary texts. (For a fuller description of how these results were computed, see [1]

**Fig. 6.** Table of Fog Indices and Information Densities

| Author | Fog Index | Information Density |
|--------|-----------|---------------------|
| Chandler | 10.39 | 52.35 |
| Greene | 10.72 | 45.31 |
| Huxley | 6.77 | 50.81 |
| Lewis | 5.77 | 42.31 |
| Maughan | 9.64 | 42.57 |
| Murdoch | 17.63 | 42.86 |
| Runyan | 29.04 | 49.84 |
| Snow | 17.26 | 47.66 |
| Waugh | 11.79 | 48.70 |
| Wells | 19.76 | 40.00 |
| Woolf | 15.23 | 51.46 |
| Wyndham | 11.31 | 46.00 |

To appreciate how the readability grade affects the level of difficulty of the exercise consider Figs. 7, 8 and 9. These figures show a simple exercise on the use of definite and indefinite articles using text samples with Fog Indices of approximately 5, 10 and 15. Exercise difficulty increases with Fog index.

## 3.3 Readability Grade and Exercise Level

The first step in the process of generating the exercises is to choose a sample of text with the appropriate readability grade which exhibits the lexical or syntactical skill to be improved. As the system builds up a database which correlates user profile coefficient against score for a range of readability grades it should be possible to increase the sensitivity in matching exercise to ability so that the student is given neither an exercise which is so difficult that he feels overwhelmed by it, nor one that is so easy he feels his time has been wasted. Initially however we aim for three levels of difficulty: easy, moderate, advanced with corresponding Gunning's Fog Indices of approximately 5, 10, 15.

**Fig. 7.** Articles exercise from a text sample with Fog Index 5.77

Complete the following passage using:

**the   a   an   null**

Jane extended — hesitant and unconvincing hand to touch — animal's back, but Mr. Bultitude was sulking, and without — glance at Jane continued his slow walk along — passage to — point about — ten yards away, where he quite suddenly sat down. Everyone on — floor below must have known that Mr. Bultitude had sat down. "Is it really safe to have — creature like that loose about — house?" said Jane. "Mrs. Studdock," said Ivy Maggs with — solemnity, "if — director wanted to have — tiger about — house it would be safe. There isn't — creature in — place that would go for another or for us once he's had his little talk with them. Just — same as he does with us. You'll see." "If you would put — tea in my room . . ." said Jane rather coldly, and went towards — bathroom.

**Fig. 8.** Articles exercise from a text sample with Fog Index 10.72

Complete the following passage using:

**the   a   an   null**

Ida went to — window and looked out, and again she saw only — Brighton she knew: she hadn't seen anything different even — day Fred died: — two girls in — beach pyjamas arm-in-arm, — buses going by to Rottingdean, — man selling — papers, — woman with — shopping basket, — boy in — shabby suit , — excursion steamer edging off from — pier, which lay long, luminous and transparent, like — shrimp in — sunlight.

**Fig. 9.** Articles exercise from a text sample with Fog Index 15.23

Complete the following passage using:

**the   a   an   null**

It depended, so she came to think, when invited into his room for — private conference, upon — systematic revision of — card-index, upon — issue of — certain new lemoncoloured leaflets, in which — facts were marshalled once more in — very striking way, and upon — large scale map of England dotted with — little pins tufted with — differently coloured plumes of — hair according to their geographical position. Each district, under — new system, had its flag, its bottle of ink, its sheaf of documents tabulated and filed for reference in — drawer, so that by looking under m or s, as — case might be, you had all — facts with respect to — suffrage organisations of — county at your fingers' ends. This would require — great deal of — work, of course.

## 3.4 Finding an Appropriate Text

Skills can be roughly categorised as lexical skills or syntactical skills. These are not discrete and in places overlap. A distinguishing feature in methods of selection is that exercises which test vocabulary must look explicitly for that vocabulary: exercises which test more general grammatical skills can be found by seeking general syntactic components or structures regardless of information content. For example, an exercise on the use of pairs or words that are frequently confused, such as *imply* and *infer* can only be generated by searching for passages containing those words. More general grammatical skills can be tested on any database simply by looking for a specific structural pattern within a sentence. Sometimes this may be as simple as looking for occurrences of the definite and indefinite article. On other occasions the pattern could be more complex and involve recognition of passive verb forms or sentences that contain subordinate conjunctions. This kind of exercise can only be generated automatically if a syntactically tagged database is available. This may be provided by using a parser locally on selected data or by using a publicly available database which is already tagged. Both methods have been tried in the course of the project and the latter is proving more satisfactory.

## 3.5 Student Feedback and Profile Update

At the end of every session students are given general feedback on their performance during the session: see Fig.10; and feedback on their achievement in each skill: see figure 11.

Fig. 10. General Feedback

| Score |  |
| --- | --- |
| The questioned answered wrongly were: 3, 11, 12, 16, 25, 34, 42, 51, 53, 60. | |
| Final score on this exercise: | |
| Number of questions | 60 |
| Number of questions attempted | 60 |
| Nunber of correct answers | 50 |

The skills achievement record can be combined with the expected performance record to give a new expected performance record. The computer suggests that the student should undertake further tuition/practice in the skills where mastery is weakest. Students may accept or reject this advice but whatever they decide to do, they will be given further help or exercises at a level appropriate to their proficiency.

**Fig. 11.** Itemised Feedback

| Quit Save | Explain | | |
|---|---|---|---|
| Analysis of score | | | |
| Skill | Attempted | Correct | Percentage |
| Verbs | 10 | 6 | 60 |
| Pronouns | 10 | 10 | 100 |
| Articles | 10 | 8 | 80 |
| Word order | 10 | 10 | 100 |
| Voice | 10 | 9 | 90 |
| Conjunctions | 10 | 9 | 90 |

# 4 Conclusion

The aim of this project is to develop an intelligent interface that assesses a student's ability and generates, on demand, exercises corresponding with that ability from standard text databases. If texts of appropriate readability coefficient were selected randomly, the exercises would be infinitely variable, and there would be no danger of the student becoming bored or 'learning' the right answer to a specific question by repetition rather then acquiring the ability to deduce it from general principles. Ideally, there would be no need for human intervention; exercises generated from texts that are syntactically and semantically sound could be assessed by comparing students' answers with the original text and a grade returned to the student without teacher supervision. However, many databases contain text as it has been written by fallible authors. It is unlikely to be perfect English – some of it may not even be 'good' English: some scientific and technical writing is needlessly verbose, and difficult to understand because the author has relied too heavily on passive voice and nominalisations simply to avoid using the first person; fiction is always stylistically suspect especially if it contains dialogue or if it is written in the first person. Even syntactically correct text is not without problems: for example, in exercises on verbs using randomly selected sentences, it is sometimes difficult for students to infer the tense of the original sentence; in exercises on pronouns, students must know what the referent is before they answer and in text samples selected randomly it is difficult to ensure that the referent is always included. In addition, even in some seemingly simple exercises, there may be more than one correct answer: for example, whether or not to use an article is sometimes a matter of taste, not precept. Although we are still considering criteria for defining text suitable for various exercises more strictly it is possible that a human intelligence may be the only true judge of what is a fair and intelligible exercise and what is not. What is not in any doubt is the potential of a tagged text database as a source for language learning programmes. To be able to search large texts automatically to find sentences with specific lexical and syntactical features promises a richness and cohesion of material that would be inconceivable in a manual system where each example sentence has to be laboriously devised by the teacher. The ability to convert these sentences into re-usable hypertext exercises that can be assessed and graded automatically is another marked saving on effort and improvement in efficiency. If approved questions have to be saved in graded banks rather than generated from scratch on demand the project will still have been more than worthwhile.

## Acknowledgment

I would like to thank Mr. R. C. Saunders for advice on the draft version of this manuscript.

## Bibliography

## References

1. Howe, T., *The development of a computerised system to aid the assessment of the readability and cohesion of text*, Project Report, University of Kent at Canterbury, (1989)
2. Kearsley, G. P., & Hillelsohn, M. J., "Human factors considerations for computer-based training", *Journal of Computer-based Instruction*, 8(4), pp. 74-84, (1982)
3. Romiszowski, A. J., *Designing instructional systems*, Kogan Page, London, (1981)
4. Skinner, B. F., "Teaching machines", *Scientific American*, (November 1961), pp. 3-13.
5. Tsutsumi, M., *Implementation of hypertoefl*, Project Report, University of Kent, (1990)
6. Wilson, E., Lindley, I., and Pullen, S., "CALLGUIDE: using programmable hypertext as a shell for CALL programs" in *Proceedings of the Fourth International Conference on Computers and Learning*, Acadia, (June 1992)
7. Wilson, E., "The language learner and the computer: modes of interaction", ACH/ALLC Joint International Conference, Washington, DC, (1993)

# A System to Model, Assist and Control the Human Observation of Microscopic Specimen

## A. Derder and C. Garbay

Equipe Reconnaissance des Formes et Microscopie Quantitative
Lab. TIM3 / IMAG - Université Joseph Fourier
CERMO BP 53X - 38041 Grenoble Cédex - France
Tél : 33 76 51 48 13 - Fax : 33 76 51 49 48 -
Email : derder@imag.fr / garbay@imag.fr

**Abstract.** This paper describes current research on computerized assistance to cytological specimen exploration. The purpose is not to design a new diagnosis expert system, but rather to design a system able to cooperate with the human expert in the execution of specimen exploration task. New man machine assistance models are necessary to this end, which imply not only knowledge-based but also behaviour-based modelling. An information manager is described, allowing access to information supplied by this model. An error monitoring is also presented. Its goal is to control all tasks and activities involved in the cytological specimen exploration.

## 1 Introduction

The examination of microscopic specimens is a tedious task, performed routinely for diagnosis and prognosis purposes by trained personal. The HOME system [1] has been designed to assist routine screening and reviewing tasks : it provides in particular a set of tools supporting computerized marking, relocation and analysis of cells. It is based on a PC connected to a microscope equipped with a camera and offering built-in video text and graphic mixing with the optical image. This system is currently developed in our laboratory in the framework of the IMPACT European Project (AIM initiative). Our purpose is to design a system able to supervise the work performed under the HOME apparatus, thus providing higher level assistance to human activity.

Such objectives imply an original view on man machine assistance. Up to now in fact, the aim of classical approach in Artificial Intelligence has been to build automated systems able to replace human in the performing of various tasks (diagnosis for example). Expert systems have been designed to this end, handling knowledge about the domain under study and the task to be performed [2]. Such approach has been used to design KIDS (Knowledge-based Image Diagnosis System) [3], a multi-agent system devoted to cytological image interpretation ; such system uses a distributed approach to model medical reasoning in cytology. Our purpose is different, since it is to design a system able to cooperate with a human agent in the execution of a complex task ; to achieve this, it appears necessary to develop not only knowledge-based but also behaviour-based modelling, that is a technology able to model and control human behaviour in front of a task.

We first of all present the problem at hand, then discuss our approach to man machine assistance and human behaviour modelling. System architecture and functionalities are finally presented and discussed before concluding.

## 2 Presentation of the Problem

The microscopic investigation of specimen in cytology is divided in two phases : a screening phase performed by cytotechnicians and a reviewing phase performed by cytopathologists. The aim of the first phase is to select and mark a few fields of interest, to be reviewed for diagnosis purposes by a trained cytopathologist. These two phases are complementary and the quality of diagnosis widely depends on the quality of screening. The aim of this phase is to provide a first diagnosis hypothesis, together with a set of marks facilitating the reviewing of fields of interest. It implies the handling of a variety of information, including patient clinical records, sample type and staining quality, previously selected fields and current diagnosis hypothesis ; it further implies a rigorous approach to specimen exploration. Such work may only be conducted after several years of formal and practical training.

## 3 Assistance Type

Advances in computer science and artificial intelligence (AI) are providing powerful new computational tools that greatly expand the potential to support cognitive activities in complex problem-solving worlds : monitoring, plan generation and adaptation, fault management, problem formulation. The outcome of these new computational tools is to offer man-machine assistance, to reduce cognitive load and to understand how the tasks have been executed by the computer. Figure 1 presents two types of assistance : Expert System and Cooperative System.

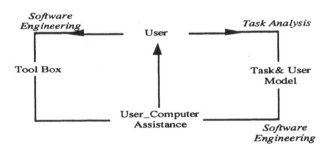

**Fig. 1.** Two types of Man-Machine Assistance : Expert System and CooperativeSystem.

Many of the initial expert systems were called expert machine or consultant systems, these systems possessed minimal capabilities for supporting cooperative interaction with human. The interaction was based on the conventional expert system question and answer dialogue and the machine's explanations of its solutions were limited [4]. For example, in medicine, the expert system asks the user to select a symptom from a list. Expert system also asks the user to make observations about the patient's behaviour and to take measurements from internal test points. When sufficient evidence is accumulated, the expert system draws a conclusion and reports it together with a confidence value computed for that hypothesis. The user has the option of either accepting the hypothesis as the solution and then terminating the diagnosis, or rejecting the hypothesis (in which case the expert system continues for another candidate solution).

However, it has been rapidly recognized that more meaningful interaction between human and intelligent machine is required [5], especially for applications involving supervisory control of dynamic processes.

As a result of this constatation, as well as advances in interface technology and the development of Artificial Intelligence techniques, intelligent systems or more precisely "intelligent interaction" has been developed with more sophisticated man-machine interfaces including graphical displays, windowing abilities, and more extensive explanations capabilities [6]. These intelligent systems must not only be designed to provide support to the routine and familiar tasks of the human operator [7]. These systems must also be more adaptive in the sense that they have knowledge about the user competence and behaviour, the tasks that he performs, and knowledge about how to interact. It is well recognized in fact that modelling the user, predicting his intentions, and behaving in an adaptive manner are important features to build really cooperative man-machine interfaces [8].

## 4 Cognitive Modelling

The purpose of this paragraph is to examine the task model and the human model [9] that are needed not only to model and control work performed under HOME by cytotechnicians and cytopathologists, but also to endow user adapted assistance capacities. If we consider a classical approach, like in expert system KIDS, a Task Model merely takes into account the input and output data that are necessary for its execution. A system based on such Task Model only offers restricted assistance to the user. Such model in fact is a computer model : it defines how to automatize the execution of a task, giving the user only control on output data.

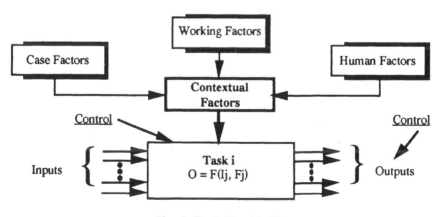

Fig. 2. Black Box Model.

A simple task model that would simply consider the transformation of input into output data is not sufficient to approach the modelling of task implied during screening and reviewing work. These tasks in fact display a cognitive nature, that is they are submitted to a variety of contextual factors that may influence the way the input data is viewed and processed by the human. A new task model is thus proposed (figure 2), so-called "*Black Box Model*", which takes into account not only the input and output to a task, but also considers three *Contextual Factors* : Case Factors (diagnosis hypothesis, slide quality, ...), Working Factors (time spent per event, individual background, ...) and Human Factors (daily workload, ...).

This model implies to reconsider the kind of assistance offered to the user for the execution of complex tasks : it points out the limitation of task automatization, since a distinction has to be made between the performing of low level - potentially automatized - activities, and higher level control routines necessary to adapt the low level activities regarding context (figure 3).

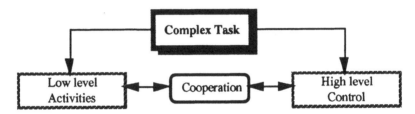

**Fig. 3.** Definition of Complex Task

The possibility of accessing contextual information is thus essential to control correctly the execution of low level tasks : a first step would be to design a system able to capture this information, and make it accessible to the user. We call it "information manager". The user would then use this information, from time to time, to control the validity of its own activities. A second step would be to design a system able to check this information, in real time, and alarm the user in case a discrepancy is found with "normal" behaviour. We call it "error monitoring". A final and long term goal would be to design a system able to supply more explanations about a human error detected during the HOME session.

The system presented in this paper is designed according to the first and second steps (figure 4) : as regards the first step, the information manager is able to capture and supply information on human behaviour at the microscope. The HOME system is used for that purpose : it provides assistance to the execution of basic and simple tasks, such as marking a cell, or counting and designating objects. Information on the way a task is performed (specimen exploration strategy for example), the type of events that have been encountered or the time spent on a given field may thus be obtained. A kind of "task and human model" may then be elaborated by the so-called Watch Dog system : its role is to offer navigation tools through information manager system, to easily access contextual information, and alarming tools, for on-line control of human activity consistency.

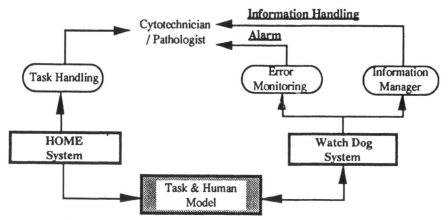

**Fig. 4 :** Assistance Model for the Screening / Reviewing Tasks

Before introducing the second step, we have to give a brief definition of the term "diagnosis" [10]. Diagnosis is the process of detecting failures affecting a system. Two conditions must be met to provide a reliable diagnosis : first, the existence of the object to be observed and its accessibility ; second, the existence of a reference model that permits to control the correctness of the object. The specificity of our work lies in the fact that the object to be controlled is represented by a triplet involving three different factors :

(Case factors, Working factors, Human factors)

According to this model, the "object" to be controlled may be approached under to points of view :

- a static point of view, describing the input and output to the task (case factors in general), as well as the conditions and performances of its execution (time spent, or tiredness, for example) ;

- a dynamic point of view, describing the way the task is approached (sequence of actions to reach the final goal).

The Black Box model task must therefore include two kinds of "variables", static and dynamic, to model, assist and control the cytotechnicians and cytopathologists activities. A dynamic modelling of human behaviour is needed to this end. Modelling the human operator as a finite state automaton is then proposed (figure 5), where each state in the model corresponds to the accomplishment of a given action : case examination, screening (positioning at the upper-left of the slide), low level observation (x10 magnification), high level observation (x20, x30 or x40 magnifications), low level marking (select a cell with x10 objective), high level marking (select a cell with x40 objective for example), case completion (examination of the case is terminated), screening completion (screening task is completed). Such model permits to check whether given behaviour, modelled as a sequence of states, is consistent or not. A variety of variables may furthermore be attached to each state in order to be controlled. This set of variables allow us to reason in terms of time (time spent on slide for example), approach (specimen exploration strategy for example), or number and distribution of the handled elements (numbers and types of marks).

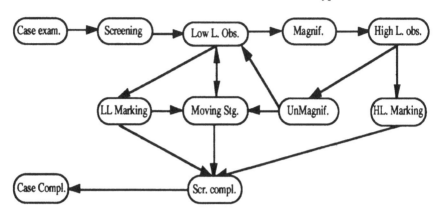

**Fig. 5.** Modelling the human as a finite state automaton. It permits to error monitoring to acquire non perceptual description of the human activity.

## 5 System Design

The system architecture is displayed in figure 6. The Watch Dog system (information manager and error monitoring) is implemented in C++ and runs under UNIX on a SONY workstation. Graphical programming is performed under Motif/X11 environment. Communication in delayed time is currently implemented with the HOME system by means of structured files. Real time *communication* will be realized in a near future.

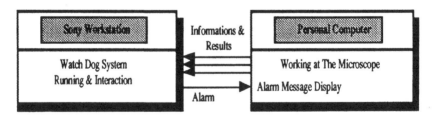

**Fig. 6.** Watch Dog system architecture.

One of the main goals in the design of the information manager is to reduce the cognitive load of the human operator. The information manager is not only used to supply information needed by the operator to continue the execution of the current task, but also to serve self validation purposes by assisting the exploration of current or working models. Three contextual factors (Case factors, Working factors and Human factors) are managed by the system, in the form of three object-based hierarchies. A Hypercard metaphor is used as a mean to facilitate navigation. The Information Manager is accessed through a Base card (figure 7). As may be seen, the Base card gives access to one of the Case, Task or Human card models, more precisely to the root card attached to the corresponding hierarchies.

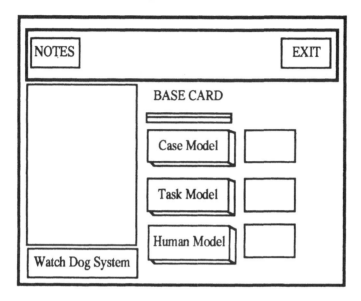

**Fig. 7.** Information Manager Module, the Base card.

Three card hierarchies are implemented, called namely Case, Task and Human hierarchies. A "Slide" card is shown in figure 8 : this card belongs to the Case hierarchy, and gives information about the slide quality and diagnosis. A button allows to access the event summary : this card may be presented according to one of the three presentation style, statistical (statistics about event type frequency for example), textual (short comment), or graphical (visualization of the events location and type). Various means are supplied to navigate among information : other slides may be accessed in a sequential way (previous and next buttons), or through associative retrieval (search button) ; the root of the case hierarchy, as well as the base card may be accessed at any time ; corresponding information in the task and human hierarchies may also be obtained (slide exploration strategy, or global observation time, for example). On the left, the "Notes" button allows to attache notes to a given card to explain the aim and functioning of a given card.

The error monitoring is currently under development ; it is designed as a multi-agent system and implemented in C++. There is a one to one correspondence between the agents and the states presented in figure 4. Two classes of agents are introduced : expert systems agents are responsible for controlling "static" variables, while syntactical parsers analyzers are responsible for controlling "dynamic" variables. Each one represents a sub-class of the generic class "agent". Expert-like agents are composed of a set of attributes (knowledge base), a set of rules (rule base), and a proprietary inference engine. Parser-like agents are composed of a set of terminal and non-terminal nodes and a set of transition rules. The capacity of an agent to detect an alarm depends on its own competence (provided production and transition rules) and on the attribute values describing the activity under control. These agents are triggered by the system supervisor upon reception of external events (perception of a state modification). The error monitoring is displayed in figure 9.

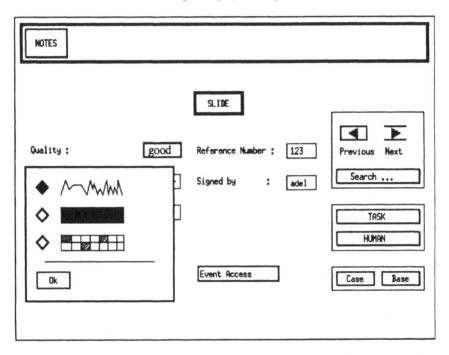

**Fig. 8.** The Information Manager system ; a view of the Slide card (Case hierarchy).

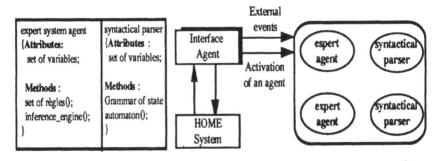

**Fig. 9.** Error monitoring system architecture : each agent is implemented in C++ and performs as either an expert system or a syntactical parser. It is activated by the supervisor upon reception of external events.

# 6 Conclusion

We have described current research on computerized assistance to cytological specimen exploration. The purpose is to design a system able to cooperate with the human expert in the execution of specimen exploration task. A new man machine assistance model has been proposed to this end, which imply not only knowledge-based but also behaviour-based modelling. A "watch dog" system is described, coupled with a task model involving three contextual factors : case factors, working factors and human factors. Such approach is currently extended for quality control purposes. It will also be applied in a near future to the design of an intelligent tutoring system for cytopathology.

# References

1. G. Brugal, R. Dye, B. Krief, J.M. Chassery, H. Tanke and J.H. Tucker : HOME : Highly Optimized Microscope Environment. Cytometry, Vol. 13, pp. 109:116 (1992).
2. Bartels & al. : Expert Systems in Histopathology, Anal. Quant. Cytol. 11(1):1-7 (1989)
3. Ovalle, A. & Garbay, C. : KIDS, a Distributed Expert System for Biomedical Image Interpretation. 12th International Conference on IPMI, pp. 419-433. Colchester et Hawkes (Eds), Springer-Verlag (1991)
4. D. D. Woods, L. Johannesen and S. S. Potter : Human Interaction with Intelligent System : An Overview and Bibliography. SIGART Bulletin, Vol. 2, No 5, pp. 39-50 (1987)
5. E. M. Roth, K. B. Bennett and D.D. Woods : Human Interaction with "Intelligent" Machine. Internationaml Man-Machine Studies, pp. 479-525 (1987)
6. E. Hudlicka, K Corber, R. Schudy, and S. Baron : Flight crew aiding for recovery from subsystem failures. Technical Repport NASA Contractor Repport 181905, Bolt, Beranek and New-man (1990)
7. M. Gonzalez and S. Faure : Des Conditions d'utilisation d'un système d'aide à la decision médicale, Psychologie Cognitive Modèles et Methodes, P.U.G., 1988
8. W. B. Rousse : Adaptive aiding for human/computer control. Human Factors, 30:431-443 (1988)
9. Chandrasekaran, B. : Towards a functional architecture for intelligence based on generic information processing tasks. Proc. 10th IJCAI, pp. 1183-1192 (1987)
10. O. Raoult : Diagnostic de pannes des systemes complexes.Thèse de Docteur de l'I.N.P.G. (France) (1989)

# The "Document-Driven Activity" Approach to Modelling and Designing Office Automation Systems

Alexander Chernin

LANIT Inc., Project manager,
Ph.D. (Economic Cybernetics)
Dobroslobodskaya 5, 107066 Moscow, Russia
Phone (095) 261 42 34, fax (095) 261 57 81,
e-mail GENS@MEKOM.MSK.SU

**Abstract.** A "document-driven activity" approach to office automation (OA) system design is proposed. According to the approach, each action with documents is activated by changes in documents states. The use of Petri nets for modelling and prototyping of OA systems is also suggested. The approach allows a system analyst to incorporate the main features of the office technology and to ensure the correctness of OA system structure and algorithms.

## 1    Office Automation Systems with Manual Control

Office automation (OA) is a quickly expanding application of modern information technologies, and software market abounds with OA systems. However, let us have a glance at user work in the automated office and compare it with duties of technological process operator.

An employee in the automated office continuously analyzes dozens of documents. While making a decision, he is guided by his knowledge, experience, intuition and instructions. In order to implement his decisions, he composes or changes documents, transfers them to other employees and checks execution.

To accomplish his mission, the employee should use various software tools. He resorts to the database management system, the text management system and e-mail to obtain the necessary documents. Afterwards he utilises an expert system or decision support system, and then uses a document management system to compose or change documents. Finally he transmits the documents over e-mail and checks the execution with the project management system.

Therefore, each employee must remember which actions with which documents he should perform in the given state of affairs, and then resort to appropriate information subsystems and documents. However automated specific operations with documents are, the whole OA system operation requires a great deal of manual control. Therefore the total office performance depends greatly upon discipline and responsibility of personnel.

And now let us look at a technological process operator. He continuously monitors thousands of technological parameters. While making a decision, he should follow many operational instructions. In order to implement the decision, the operator controls dozens of interrelated actuators.

To fulfil his tasks, the operator need not scan thousands of dials, skip through volumes of documentation and switch on or off dozens of control keys. A modern process automation system monitors sensors, analyzes changes in process parameters using expert systems, displays summary information to the operator, recommends the sequence of actions and checks it for fulfilment. Moreover, system can start necessary actions without any operator interference. It is really an automated system!

"Groupware" is being proclaimed a solution to OA system user problems. "Groupware" denotes software products designed for communication and interaction between users of integrated office automation system, as well as for provision of unified access to other software products [1, 2]. Among groupware products one can list, for example, NewWave Office (Hewlett-Packard), Cooperation (NCR), Together (Coordination Technology). These products represent the office as a set of "desks". Each user can keep several desks according to his functions. The user "picks" incoming correspondence documents from the desk, processes them and then places the outgoing documents onto the desks of other users. The system notifies users when new documents appear and checks the document processing schedule [3, 4].

However, analysts censure groupware products for absence of an integrated concept based on office technology modelling [5]. Therefore we shall discuss the key features of office paperwork.

## 2 Office Technology from the Information Processing Standpoint

From the information processing standpoint, office activities involve creation, transformation and exchange of data implemented in documents (we shall denote as "document" any material form of data existence). Whatever the specific document form and content (order, instruction, invoice, way-bill, contract etc.), any document has some common features affecting the office activities.

Each document may exist in various states. A contract may be composed, signed, partially or fully executed. An instruction may be composed, published, received by executives. A delivery order may be composed, forwarded to a supplier, paid, shipped, delivered to a warehouse and so on.

The document states are changed by "actors" - office employees or components of OA system. As a rule, each actor is multifunctional, since it executes various actions with documents of different types. The actor chooses the appropriate actions for a specific document according to the type of document to be processed, other states, actions of other actors.

Each action is activated by changes in document state ("document-driven activity"). One would think that office employee performs many actions at his own will. For example, nobody "activates" a manager to compose and sign a contract. Nevertheless, the contract was composed after preliminary discussion and correspondence, that is, after some changes in document states. The signing of the contract in its turn activates the composition of orders, schedules and other documents.

Since each document state change is both the result of some action and the cause of other actions, one can denote by "information flows" the sequences of interrelated actions with documents that are necessary to fulfil various office functions. Almost any document belongs to several information flows causing intersection of flows.

A document is transferred along the information flow according to both routine and informal procedures. On the one hand, office activities are rather strictly regulated by standard business practice. For example, secretarial work, activities of accounting office or warehouse are almost fully determined by routine rules and procedures. On the other hand, many employees, primarily decision-makers, are guided by rather informal considerations. Hence incomplete determinacy of information flows arises.

Finally, the continuous control of information flow is needed to ensure proper office performance ("monitoring of information flow"). The purpose of the monitoring is to provide the correct sequence and timeliness of actions with documents.

## 3    From Manual Control to "Document-Driven Activity"

"Document-driven activity" is the most important feature; nevertheless, it is often neglected in OA system design. Documents are treated by most OA systems as an inert "raw material" moved from one actor to another according to their initiative. OA system design focuses on specific operations with documents at the expense of the interrelation of the actions. Put differently, such systems automate the link "from action to document change" and do not automate the link "from document change to action".

This results in inconsistency of information flow, which in turn leads to OA system design as a set of "islands of automation" that can hardly interact. As indicated earlier, control of information flow is performed almost exclusively by office employees.

The "document-driven activity" approach causes a system analyst to focus on the conditions holding when actions are activated, and to define these conditions explicitly. It allows for automated control of information flow whereby changes in documents states allow the system either to start the appropriate operations or to inform office personnel that such operations are necessary.

It is evident that the system should continuously track document states in order to respond in a timely way to their changes. Thence the monitoring of information flows becomes not an optional, but rather a necessary and intrinsic feature of the office automation system.

Can the monitoring be implemented technically? If the office system is based upon a local network and "client-server" software, the system can monitor documents stored in the electronic form on network servers. The problem becomes more challenging when documents in paper form are taken into consideration, especially incoming paper. There are two possible solutions.

A radical solution is to use image processing system as an integral part of an OA system. All incoming documents pass through scanning and optical character recognition, and are stored as text or image files. The text files can be additionally processed (e.g. indexed) by a document management system [6, 7, 8].

A half-way decision is to manually form an electronic "alter ego" for each incoming document. The "alter ego" should reflect the essential document attributes and allow tracking further changes in document state.

The "document-driven activity" approach enables implementing of active monitoring of information flows. Active monitoring not only checks the correctness and timeliness of actions, but also moves documents from one actor to another according to the logic of processing. Expert systems can be used for active monitoring to take into account the incomplete determinacy of information flows. When expert help is needed, procedures can be activated by changes in document states.

## 4    The Features Required of Office Technology Model

According to various sources [5, 9, 10], an office technology model should:
- be tied to the nature of office activity;
- present an integrated view of the office and span across various office domains;
- incorporate knowledge engineering techniques;
- provide appropriate facilities for its validation;
- be user-friendly.

We would like to add some new requirements as well. An office technology model should:
- allow for adequate implementation of the "document-driven activity" approach;
- reflect multifunctionality of actors;
- provide facilities for description of intersections and incomplete determinacy of information flows;
- provide means for implementation and analysis of quantitative characteristics of office systems;
- enable not only the description and analysis of office technology, but also the design of the office automation system.

Let us consider some of these requirements in more detail, since they affect the choice of mathematical apparatus necessary to model and automate office technology.

## 5 Some Means to Model Multifunctionality of Actors

As discussed above, actors are generally multifunctional. Since actors are key elements of office technology, the adequate representation of multifunctionality is an important task.

Let us denote by "agents" the model elements representing actors. Then the problem can be put thus: How does one project the set of actors into the set of agents in such a way as to achieve the optimum balance between the descriptive power of the model and the facilities to design and analyze it?

"One-to-one" projection can be used so that each actor has an associated agent, representing an employee or an OA subsystem. In this case the number of agents will be small, but almost all agents will be multifunctional. When an agent starts to process a document, it should choose appropriate actions based on the document's attributes. Furthermore, the document itself can contain description of specific operations which permits the use of the object-oriented paradigm to model office technology [11].

In our opinion, the object-oriented approach is not fully applicable to office technology modelling. Object-oriented models describe actions as combination of attributes of both agents and documents, and therefore is difficult to analyze the document processing logic. This approach, however, facilitates the transformation of model descriptions to OA system prototypes using object-oriented programming techniques.

We believe that the office technology model should be described using a "one-to-many" relationship between actors and agents so that each agent represents one action with one type of document. The number of agents can be rather large. Nonetheless, the logic of document processing is explicitly defined by the model structure. Moreover, when agents represent actions instead of actors, model becomes virtually invariant to those changes in organizational structure of office that do not affect its functions.

We shall not dwell on the problem of determining a set of "elementary" operations that can be combined to describe real actions with documents [10, 11]. Suffice it to say that the "elementary" operations can be defined in such a way that each operation consists in changing states of one or more documents.

## 6 Using Models to Analyze and Optimize Office Performance

Modelling of office technology, as well as of any other system, can produce both direct and indirect effect. The direct effect consists in improving office performance; the indirect effect manifests itself as an increase in net profit of company. How can modelling of office technology affect net profit?

We propose to analyze the following characteristics of office technology:
- the time required to accomplish actions that form an information flow;
- the probability of successful accomplishment of information flow;
- the validity of documents used in the information flow;
- the costs of information flow execution.

Let us consider how these characteristics affect the net profit when customer order is processed. The less time required for processing, the more is turnover, the higher the customer satisfaction and the better the company image. Low probability of order fulfilment increases the lost profit and deteriorates company image. Invalid documents lead to wrong or ineffective decisions resulting in lost profit. Finally, costs of information flow processing are part of the total operating costs.

Therefore the office technology model should provide the means to define and analyze these office technology characteristics.

To sum up, the main characteristics of the office model are as follows:
- office actors can be described by agents representing separate operations;
- each operation is activated by changes in document states;
- each operation results in changes of document states;
- some changes in document states can initiate several operations that are executed simultaneously;
- activating conditions for some operations are defined using stochastic or fuzzy parameters.

It is our opinion that the most appropriate mathematical apparatus providing for these characteristics is Petri nets.

## 7 Petri Nets for Office Modelling Based on "Document-Driven Activity" Approach

When a Petri net is used to model office technology, tokens represent documents, places represent document states, and transitions represent agents.

The basic concept of Petri nets (a transition fires when tokens are present on its input places) entirely corresponds to "document-driven activity" concept of office technology. The implementation of parallelism is also intrinsic to Petri net models. Stochastic variants of Petri nets can be used to allocate probabilistic parameters in the model. The descriptive power of Petri nets can be further increased by adding timing parameters.

The modelling of fuzzy logic and expert systems actions is difficult whatever the mathematical apparatus. Nevertheless, some authors propose to use Petri nets for these purpose as well [12, 13].

Therefore, the modelling of office technology using Petri net models permits the system analyst to define bilateral relations between operations and document states as well as to describe intersections and incomplete determinacy of information flows. The model can be studied using analytical and simulation techniques to detect static and dynamic deadlocks, unused states and operations and to obtain timing and probabilistic characteristics of office technology.

The Petri net model can also be used in OA system prototype development. The model description can be transformed by the appropriate CASE software into the description of OA system structure and algorithms.

Further still, the highly illustrative character of Petri net models is beneficial for use in human-computer interaction for presenting OA system to office personnel. Places can be displayed as "desks" and transitions as "demons" that either serve desks on their own or inform users.

We believe that the "document-driven activity" approach to office technology modelling allows the system analyst to incorporate the main features of the technology and to ensure the correctness of OA system structure and algorithms, and that it results in higher OA system effectiveness.

## Bibliography

1. S. Reddy: Automatic Office. - LAN Magazine, 1991, v.6, no 7, p.75-82.
2. J.F. Nunamaker: Automating the flow: Groupware goes to work. - Corporate Computing, 1992, v.1, no 4, p.187-190.
3. D. Ferris: Blending with the workforce. - Computer Weekly, 1992, July 9, p.38-39.
4. P. Jacobs: The tailor-made office. - HP Professional, 1991, v.5, no 10, p.54-60.
5. C.S. Amaravadi, O.R.L. Sheng, J.F. George et al. AEI: A knowledge-based approach to integrated office systems. - Journal of Management Information Systems, 1992, v.9, no 1, p.133-163.
6. A.E. Chernin: Documents management systems. - PC World Russia, 1992, no 6, p.84-92.
7. A.E. Chernin: From hypertext to hypermedia. - Russian Dr. Dobb's Journal, 1992, no 2, p.13-17.
8. S. Wallace: Image archiving. - Corporate Computing, 1991, v.1, no 2, p.74-99.
9. S. Cook, G. Birch, A. Murphy et al. Modelling groupware in the electronic office. - International Journal of Man-Machine Studies, 1991, v.34, no 3, p.369-393.
10. P. Loucopoulos, V. Karakostas: Modelling and validating office information systems: An object and logic oriented approach. - Software Engineering Journal, 1989, v.4, no 2, p.87-94.
11. P. Azalov, F. Zlatarova: An object relational approach to document processing. - Database Technology, 1990, v.3, no 2-4, p.81-85.
12. Y.E. Papelis, T.L. Casavant: Specification and analysis of parallel/distributed software and systems by Petri nets with transition enabling functions. - IEEE Transactions on Software Engineering, 1992, v.18, no 3, p.252-261.
13. D.M. Perdu, A.H. Levis: A Petri net model for evaluation of expert systems in organizations. - Automatica, 1991, v.27, no 2, p.225-237.

# Author Index

# Lecture Notes in Computer Science

For information about Vols. 1–675
please contact your bookseller or Springer-Verlag